CHRISTIAN PERSPECTIVES ON FAITH DEVELOPMENT

a reader

CHRISTIAN PERSPECTIVES ON FAITH DEVELOPMENT

a reader

edited by

Jeff Astley
Director
North of England Institute for Christian Education,
Durham, England

and

Leslie J. Francis
D.J. James Professor of Pastoral Theology
and Mansel Jones Fellow, Trinity College, Carmarthen,
and St David's University College, Lampeter, Wales

Gracewing.

LEOMINSTER, ENGLAND

WILLIAM B. EERDMANS PUBLISHING COMPANY
GRAND RAPIDS, MICHIGAN

First published 1992 jointly by
Gracewing Fowler Wright Books
Southern Avenue
Leominster
Herefordshire HR6 8DE
and Wm, B, Eerdmans Publishing Co.,
255 Jefferson Ave. SE,
Grand Rapids, MI 49505.

Gracewing Books are distributed

In Australia by
Charles Paine Pty
8 Ferris Street
North Parramatta
NSW 2151 Australia

Typeset by Action Typesetting Limited, Gloucester
Printed and bound by Dotesios Ltd, Trowbridge, Wiltshire

Gracewing ISBN 085244 220 3
Eerdmans ISBN 0 8028 0578 7

Contents

Preface

Jeff Astley and Leslie J. Francis

In faith development theory, Professor James W. Fowler has offered the Christian churches a powerful incentive to reconceptualise aspects of their ministry and mission. The theory has immediate relevance to many aspects of practical theology, Christian education, pastoral counselling, public worship and family life. In consequence, a growing number of people worldwide, both inside and outside the churches, have expressed an eagerness to know more about the origins, possibilities and limitations of faith development theory, as well as about the relevance and usefulness of its practical applications.

Faith development theory is still comparatively new, and, like all good innovations, it is beginning to attract a body of informed evaluation, criticism and debate, as well as a secure following among those who are setting the theory to work in specific situations and contexts. A major problem facing those who wish to evaluate this developing body of knowledge, or to contribute further to the field through their own original studies, concerns the inaccessibility of much of the literature. This state of affairs is inevitable in any developing inter-disciplinary discussion.

The aim of the present reader, therefore, is to bring together for the first time, in one volume, English language material on faith development theory, originally printed in journals concerned with religious education, moral education, ministry, counselling, pastoral care, empirical theology, research in religion, and psychology, and published in America, Australia or Europe. Inevitably, the major difficulty experienced by the editors has not been that of finding good quality material to include, but the much harder problem of deciding what to omit. One of our guiding principles has been to select those foundation studies which may prove most difficult for readers to obtain elsewhere. In particular, our choice among Professor Fowler's own work has deliberately set out to make available journal articles which complement the more readily available perspectives presented in his major books, *Stages of Faith* (1981), *Becoming Adult, Becoming Christian* (1984), *Faith Development and Pastoral Care* (1987) and *Weaving the New Creation* (1991).

The task of editing this reader has been appropriately located within the North of England Institute for Christian Education in Durham, and the Centre for Theology and Education at Trinity College in Carmarthen. Both institutions are church foundations, concerned to undertake research in and promote the development of Christian education and practical theology.

We are grateful to the many authors and publishers who have permitted their work to be re-presented in this reader, and especially to Professor James Fowler for encouraging the venture and for preparing an original contribution which stands as the foreword. We also wish to record our thanks to those who have helped in the process of collating resources, compiling material, proof reading, and seeking permissions, especially Karen DeNicola in Atlanta, Anne Rees in Carmarthen, Diane Drayson in London and Dorothy Greenwell in Durham.

Jeff Astley
Leslie J. Francis
April 1992

Foreword

James W. Fowler

The editors of *Christian Perspectives on Faith Development* have performed a valuable service. They have assembled a selection of writings, spanning nearly twenty years, that document the evolution of faith development theory and research, and the variety of critical perspectives they have generated. Unlike other collections, this one does not arise out of a symposium or conference and its commissioned papers. Instead, it gathers into one volume a wide variety of writings, some of them difficult to find, which show the range of uses to which this theory has been put. I want to begin by expressing my appreciation to Drs Astley and Francis for their initiative and for the balanced introduction and arrangement of the articles they have selected. It is exactly two decades since I began researching, teaching and writing about faith development. As an introductory contribution to this collection, perhaps it will be of interest to consider some of the impact of this research and theory, and to indicate my sense of why it has found significant resonance and interest in many different parts of the world. In an introduction to the 1991 German translation of *Stages of Faith*, I wrote the following:

> Since its publication a decade ago [this book] has gone through twenty printings in North America. It appeared in an Australian edition and has been translated into Korean and Portuguese. Incisive interpretations of it have been produced by Danish, Swedish, Indonesian, and British scholars. In the United States it has become a textbook in Catholic, Mainline and Evangelical Protestant, and Jewish colleges and seminaries. It is widely used in hospital based courses in clinical pastoral education. The approach to research and theory it sets forth has given rise to research projects and writing on each of the continents and to an extensive bibliography of secondary and related work. Précis of the theory appear in numerous textbooks in developmental psychology, and three volumes of collected critical essays on faith and religious development or faith and moral development have been published.

What accounts for the durable and widening circle of responses faith development theory and research have evoked? What features of its content and approach have attracted such a diverse range of interests? The following are some of the explanations that occur to the primary researcher and theorist after two decades of living with this evolving work and with the questions, criticisms and responses it has evoked.

First, the focus on faith as a generic, universal, and dynamically unfolding phenomenon has the effect of enabling persons, both religious and secular, to name and affirm the role of valuing and the composing of meaning in their lives. The effort to operationalize the dynamics of faith and to investigate them through empirical research has helped to legitimate this field as an arena for social scientific research. In an era when many are alienated from religious traditions, a time in which many are proud to be without religious affiliations, it seems to have been both a challenge and a stimulation to encounter the claim that they are, nonetheless, involved in the dynamics of faith. The multiple dimensions of faith identified by the theory have proved provocative across religious lines and in conversations with secular persons and groups. Section five of the present volume, with pieces by Mischey, Parks, Furushima, and Kwilecki, presents useful examinations of empirical research in faith development. Section six offers two paths beyond present faith development research. Persons interested in the question of the construct validity of faith development theory should consult John Snarey's article, 'Faith development, moral development, and nontheistic Judaism: a construct validity study,' in W. M. Kurtines and J. L. Gewirtz (eds), *Handbook of Moral Behavior and Development: vol. 2, research*, Hillsdale, NJ, Earlbaum, 1991.

Second, the theory's combining of faith as a constructing of and committing to meanings with one of the chief metaphors of our time, namely development, apparently has given it a deep resonance for the experience of contemporary persons. As one critic said in a 1983 symposium, 'If Fowler's theory had not come along when it did we would have had to have invented it.' The theory of faith development has provided a language and benchmarks for understanding experiences of growth and transformation that wide groups of persons apparently recognize in themselves and others. The theory has helped many make explicit and accountable patterns of awareness and knowing that they already tacitly held.

Third, the use of faith development ideas and texts for courses in contexts of professional education is due, in part, to the theory's building upon integrated accounts of the developmental theories of Erik Erikson, Jean Piaget, and Lawrence Kohlberg. Although critics such as David Heywood, Romney Moseley, and Mary Ford-Grabowsky, in this collection, have questioned the theory's reliance upon the constructive developmental tradition, it has both made possible an operationalization of the concept of faith for empirical research, and has provided the means for discerning and describing in formal terms the operations of faith knowing and valuing.

Fourth, faith development theory has provided a comparative and critical hermeneutical theory for studying the reception of traditions. It offers formal critieria for evaluating the appropriation of religious traditions by persons and groups. In a time and setting where the popular dogma of the relativism of all beliefs, values and ethical opinions receives little effective challenge, the assertion that there are more and less truthful and adequate ways to draw upon and defend traditions is both challenging and controversial. Furushima's cross-cultural study is a welcome effort to test the applicability of these stages in relation to another religious culture.

Fifth, educators – primarily religious educators from various traditions – have sought to mine the insights yielded by the theory to increase teachers' awareness of the varieties of operations of knowing and valuing their students employ. From pre-schoolers to adults the faith stages provide a framework for evaluating and rethinking curricular designs and educational approaches. As did Piaget's and Kohlberg's theories, faith development thinking leads teachers to a new quality of listening and attending to their students' ways of making meaning. It also increases awareness of the constructive role of the person's own imagination, appropriation of symbol and myth, and incorporation of personal experiences in faith. In this volume the articles by Nelson, Webster, Smith and Parks address this thrust of the theory.

Sixth, pastoral and secular counsellors have found in the faith development interview and approach a useful tool to use in diagnosis and treatment. Religion and faith are implicated deeply in many of the disorders of the self that growingly dominate among the numbers of persons seeking counselling help. At the same time, many of the resources of courage, hope, and love that empower healing and growth are grounded in the communities and heritages of religion and faith. In a discipline now overcoming traditions of hostility or neglect toward matters of faith this approach seems to provide methods and language for including them. Section seven of this book, with chapters by Droege, Ivy, Schurter and Shulik, represents this arena of application for faith development theory.

Seventh, the theory of faith stages has established a normative thesis about the shape of human maturity and fulfillment. It makes a claim that is frequently experienced as paradoxical, if not self contradictory. On the one hand, it affirms that each stage of faith has integrity, coherence and dignity. Persons of later stages are not intrinsically of more worth or value than persons of earlier stages; religiously, the stages are not about 'salvation.' On the other hand, the theory clearly argues that, other things being equal, it is desirable for persons to continue the process of development, engaging in the often protracted struggles that lead to stage transition and the construction of new and more complex patterns of meaning making. Jeff Astley's introduction handles this paradoxical claim in an effective way. The claim that there is a normative endpoint defining the *tendenz* of growth in faith universally is an essentially contested aspect of the theory. At the same time, this effort to portray the goal of human transformation in faith constitutes one of its most intriguing features to its audiences.

Finally, faith development theory evokes personal involvement on the part of those who encounter it. With the existential questions it focuses and the studies of persons in the motions and emotions of faith which it draws upon, the theory, in its various presentations, seems to activate and engage those who hear or read it to retrieve their own memories, convictions, and core intuitions. In addition to setting forth a path that traces and defines the course of development in faith, the theory provides what one commentator called a 'scaffolding for remembering', a framework for exploring and reclaiming experiences and relations from the eras of one's past that have served both to form and to deform one's fundamental orientation to self, others, the world and the transcendent. After two and one-half hours of demanding interview and probing, about ninety percent of our respondents say, 'Thank you for the experience of this interview. I *never* have an opportunity to talk about these things!' Apparently those who work with the theory have found in the space it creates a place where their lives and the meanings they make of them can be examined.

In closing this foreword, there are two important issues I would like to address for readers of this volume. The first issue deals with questions of the gender inclusiveness of faith development theory. The second issue deals with theological criticisms arising from this theory's discussion of faith.

First, I address the issues concerned with gender and faith development theory. Since the ground-breaking work of such writers as Jean Baker Miller and Nancy Chodorow in the late seventies, and intensifying with the challenges to Lawrence Kohlberg's work from Carol Gilligan and others in the early eighties, there have been growing questions regarding possible gender biases in faith development research and theory. Real clarity on these issues has been elusive. As attention to the tables in Appendix B of *Stages of Faith* will show, the sample of interviews on which that book is based included among its 359 subjects a virtually equal number of females and males. The research teams and seminar participants who conducted interviews and contributed to the establishing and refining of the stage theory in the period from 1972–79 included as many women as men. Moreover, some of the primary research assistants were also students and researchers with not only Kohlberg, but also with Gilligan during formative years for her thesis.

Our own efforts to pin down gender bias or the non-inclusiveness of women's experience have been vague and inconclusive. Not until the publication of *Women's Ways of Knowing*, written by a team of four researchers (Belenky, Goldberger, Clinchy and Tarule) have we begun to get a clear sense of how our data and theory might be fruitfully re-examined in this regard. Though Belenky and her co-authors do not claim to have offered a stage theory of women's development, the styles of knowing they describe parallel in some signficant ways the developmental stages of William Perry, Lawrence Kohlberg, and our own. Roughly corresponding to our synthetic-conventional stage, they describe a style of knowing they call 'subjective' knowing. Approximating our individuative-reflective stage they describe a style of 'procedural' knowing. Key for our interests is their distinction between two different ways of developing procedural knowing. On the one hand, there is the 'separative' variant, the development of reflective and critical awareness and testing of one's knowing through objectifying the known and distancing oneself from emotional involvement with it. This style is resonant with the Cartesian subject-object distinction and with Enlightenment ideals of objective rationality. On the other hand, Belenky and her co-authors identify a movement into procedural knowing which proceeds by a style they call 'connective' knowing. This is a knowing 'in rapport', a knowing that proceeds toward self-awareness and critical reflection through and by way of participation, relation, and the disciplining of subjectivity through dialogue and reflection. My suggestion is that in describing the movement from the synthetic-conventional to the individuative-reflective stage we have highlighted the 'separative' style of critical reflection and differentiation and have muted the 'connective' pattern. In not fully developing the latter, I believe we have underscored some of our female subjects, and likely, overscored some of our male subjects as well. This is a matter on which we are presently pursuing research, and on which we will welcome the research of others.

Finally, I turn to the theological issues raised by the discussion of faith perspective. I would like to address the following to readers with theological interests and background, both Catholic and Protestant. The most frequent concern expressed by theological commentators on this theory relates to the consistent effort of such books as *Stages of Faith* to focus on the human side of the phenomenon of faith. The language of 'stages' does not intend to negate or deny claims made by Christians or other religionists that faith is the human response to God's grace, that faith is a 'gift' of God. Nor does it aim to replace Christian claims that persons are justified by grace through faith with some kind of naturalism or 'works righteousness.' Though the sequence of faith stages set forth in this theory provides structurally normative developmental distinctions, the effort to study faith as the formation of persons' ways of relating to their neighbours, themselves, and their world in light of their images of an ultimate environment is basically phenomenological in focus. We are not interested in defining or identifying 'saving' or 'justifying' faith, taken in relation to biblical and reformation understandings. This follows from our commitment not to restrict ourselves to studying faith with strictly religious content and orientation. Rather, through eliciting our respondents' articulation of their values, beliefs, and life-sustaining meanings, we want to examine both the contents and the underlying structuring operations by which they shape and integrate their worldviews, without allowing judgments about the truth, adequacy, or orthodoxy of the content or substance of their faith to be the determinative factor. The chapters by William Avery and Richard Osmer in this volume contribute materially to clarifying this set of issues.

In conclusion I should like to comment on a couple of features of this collection of essays that could confuse its readers or contribute to misunderstandings. First, readers should realize that, with the exception of 'The Enlightenment and faith development theory' (paper 1.2) most of the articles by me in this volume are early writings. Only one, 'Religious congregations: varieties of presence in stages of faith' (paper 8.4) reflects aspects of the focus of the three books I have written since *Stages of Faith*, namely, work on practical theology: *Becoming Adult, Becoming Christian* (1984), *Faith Development and Pastoral Care* (1987), and *Weaving the New Creation: stages of faith and the public church* (1991). In those volumes one will find nuances, extensions, and corrections to our early work which many of the critics in this collection have not taken into account. Secondly, the long section included in this volume from the *Manual for Faith Development Research* (paper 1.3) is based upon the 1981 descriptions of stages from *Stages of Faith*. The articulation of criteria for the stages in the *Manual* have a more decidedly Piagetian and Kohlbergian cast than the prose descriptions given in *Stages of Faith*. Moreover, the *Manual* was primarily the work of Romney Moseley and David Jarvis, members of the staff of the Center for Faith Development from 1982–86. Though I approved the *Manual* and helped to refine it, and though it has served to train scorers and has led to fine results as regards inter-relater reliability in our research, it fails to give adequate attention to the interplay of structure and content in faith development theory, and does not give sufficient account of the dynamics of conversion and transformation which are presented in the latter parts of *Stages of Faith* and in other, subsequent writings.

In the three books written subsequent to *Stages of Faith* I have sought to show how the faith stages can be integrated with and made accountable to Christian theological perspectives and norms, and employed in the reshaping of the life and mission of Christian churches. The growing edge in my teaching, writing and research in the last eight years has emphasized these areas of practical theology, though there have been significant articles on faith and moral development in early childhood and relating faith stages to the process of recovery from alcoholism. I am delighted with significant advances in faith development theory and its use represented in the growing number of theses, dissertations, books and articles recorded in the thirty page bibliography compiled at our center by Karen DeNicola, and in the more than 200 research projects on each of the continents using some variant of faith development theory and methods. Both the bibliography and listing of research projects are available upon request. I hope that readers stimulated by the rich collection of articles in this volume will send for the bibliography and research network, so as to pursue this work further.

James W. Fowler
Center for Research in Faith and Moral Development
Candler School of Theology
Emory University
Atlanta, Georgia 30322 USA

Faith development: an overview

Jeff Astley

The work of James Fowler and his associates, first at Harvard and latterly at Emory University, has been centred on understanding the way in which faith develops, and the implications of such development for the concerns of pastoral care and the nurturing of religious understanding and vocation, as well as for 'public church' issues. This introductory essay attempts a brief overview of Fowler's theory and its sources, together with some account of the main criticisms that have been levelled against it, and the practical relevance claimed for it. It is intended for those who may be entirely new to this literature and would therefore value a mapping exercise before embarking on their own journey into the primary sources provided in this volume.[1] References to the papers that follow in the Reader are indicated in square brackets in this introduction.

Psychology and religion

The study of the psychological dimension of religion is often associated in people's minds with the names of Freud and Jung, and with the therapeutic concerns of what is often called 'depth psychology', 'psychoanalysis' or 'psychotherapy'. This approach has much to say about human and religious *development*, and a significant contributor here has been Erik Erikson.[2] Much Christian pastoral work has been strongly influenced by this approach.

Educationalists and practical educators, however, have paid rather more attention to the 'cognitive developmental' psychology or 'cognitive structural' approach initiated by Jean Piaget.[3] This approach describes human development not through stages of social and emotional change determined by our chronological age ('psychosocial stages'), but rather in terms of the development of our structures or patterns of knowing and thinking (cognition) which are not directly age-related. Robert Selman's study of the development of our social perspective-taking is to be included under this heading, as is Lawrence Kohlberg's work on the development of moral reasoning.[4] James Fowler, who was a colleague of Kohlberg for a time, portrays a sequence of development in a number of dimensions or 'aspects of faith' (including logical reasoning, social perspective and moral reasoning) in which a person's structures of understanding and valuing change through various stages as they develop. Although Fowler draws on Erikson to some extent, and like Erikson undertakes to map human development over the entire lifespan, he stands firmly within the cognitive structural approach in his account of 'faith development'. A number of commentators, including both defenders and opponents of faith development theory, regret that depth psychology does not occupy more room in Fowler's account. [See papers 3.1 and 7.1; but also paper 2.3 for a defence of the strengths of the cognitive developmental approach.]

Analysis of 'faith'

Fowler and his associates understand the term 'faith' very broadly. This human faith may or may not be religious. It is essentially a matter of meaning-making: our finding significance and making significance within ourselves and in the world in which we live, move and have our being. Faith is our orientation to life − our life-stance, and as such it incorporates the processes of knowing, feeling, valuing, understanding, experiencing and interpreting. Broadly it constitutes our trust in and loyalty to that (whatever it is) to which we give our hearts and which gives us meaning for our lives.

Fowler draws on the work of a number of theologians and students of religion in this account of faith.[5] He has been particularly influenced by the American theologian H. Richard Niebuhr who gave an account of the variety of people's faith: from faith in those many, little 'gods' to which we ascribe worth, to the radical 'monotheism' of faith in the one true God who transcends all these as an object of our true and total worship [see paper 1.1]. In all these accounts faith is a human activity ('faithing') which may be regarded as universal, for we all make some sort of meaning and find value somewhere. Religious people speak of God as (part of) the *content* of their faith: 'God' is the word that labels their image of what is ultimate in value and power for them, and which plays a central role in the myths and metaphysics by which they live their lives. Others do not use religious concepts in speaking of their centres of value, images of power, and 'master stories'. But Fowler, in any case, is more concerned with the *form* of faith − its 'how' rather than its 'what'. He asks about the ways in which people value, know, and relate to other people and to their own 'ultimate environment' − that which they take to be ultimate. It is the patterns, structures, or processes of faith-knowing which Fowler's work attempts to describe.

He recognizes seven *aspects of faith* or 'windows into faith'. These are interrelated, structured processes that underlie the knowing, valuing and meaning-making that constitute our 'faithing'. [For further detail see paper 1.3.] They are:

a. *form of logic*: the way we think and reason;
b. *perspective-taking*: our ability to adopt another person's perspective;
c. *form of moral judgement*: the way in which we think about moral issues and make moral decisions;
d. *social-awareness*: how and where we set the limits to our own 'community of faith';
e. *relation to authority*: where we find authorities for our lives and faith, and the way in which we relate to them;
f. *form of world-coherence*: our way of holding things together and forming a single, workable 'worldview'; and
g. *symbolic function*: our way of understanding and responding to symbols.

This definition of faith seems rather too broad for many theologically-minded readers, while its aspect-analysis is regarded as restrictively narrow by others. [See papers 2.1 and 2.2, and the papers in section 3.] Fowler's developmental scheme is regarded by many as giving a normative position to 'mature' stage 6: faith which incorporates a particular theological perspective. [See in general the papers in sections 2 and 3.] Many other critical commentators on faith development theory begin with a critique of Fowler's conceptual analysis of faith [see, for example, paper 4.1].

Faith development research

Building on his definition of faith, and the research findings of Piaget, Kohlberg, Selman and others, Fowler developed a semi-clinical interview method in which respondents were asked to talk about their relationships, ideas and ways of valuing and understanding reality, prompted by a number of questions. These interviews can last for up to three hours. The interview transcripts are then coded and scored according to criteria relating to the different aspects of faith. The major claim made on the basis of this research is that faith develops through a sequence of coherent stages (described below).

So far little by way of longitudinal research has been done (that is interviewing the same person over a period of years). But a considerable database of more than five hundred interview studies has been built up (supported by inter-rater reliability tests), together with some related questionnaire studies, which lends credence to Fowler's stage theory. [Papers 6.1, 6.2 and 7.4 in this book provide examples of favourable comments on the reliability and validity of some of the elements of faith development theory.] Some cross-cultural replication has also been done [see paper 5.4].

Nevertheless criticism of Fowler's research method and analysis constitutes one of the main areas of ongoing discussion in the field of faith development. [See especially papers 2.1, 2.2, 2.4, 4.2 and 5.5]

Stages of faith

Fowler claims that faith, as he defines it, 'develops' in the sense that the aspects of faith change over time. People no longer see or relate to others in the ways that they did. They construe reality and treat authority figures differently. They image and understand the content of their faith in changed ways. Fowler makes the claim that six *stages of faith* may be discerned: revealing a sequence of stages through which people move, although some do not progress very far. This sequence is hierarchical and invariant (each stage following the last and building on it, and no stage being missed out), and may well prove to be universal (but Fowler is not willing to claim this much without further cross-cultural study). A faith stage is a 'structural whole' in which there is a measure of equilibrium between the processes of the different aspects of faith. As people develop, however, this balance is upset and they may then be said to experience a longish period of *transition* between faith stages [see paper 5.3 for an attempt to distinguish an additional faith stage in young adulthood].

The descriptive nature of Fowler's account of faith development is to be balanced by the very real sense in which the later stages indicate an increased capacity: not for faithfulness, belief or saintliness, but for a wider and more adequate understanding of experience, and a more consistently humane care for others. No stage is more 'worthy' than another; but later stages are more adequate at meeting the demands and perceptions of the more broadly-based perspective which people often come to adopt. Such an account naturally gives rise to some interesting discussion as to how far the theory can properly claim to be both an 'is' account and an 'ought' account of faith. [See some of the papers in sections 2 and 3.][6]

In the brief summaries of Fowler's faith stages that follow I have employed Fowler's technical terms and then offered some titles which may be appropriate as alternatives to these. The range of chronological ages most commonly found for interviewees who fall into each stage is indicated. A note about the relevance of the different stages for Christian education and ministry has also been added. [For further detail on the stages see the papers in section 1, especially 1.3, and also papers 8.1 and 8.4.]

Stage 0: primal faith

This stage may be described as *nursed faith, foundation faith* (age: 0–4 approximately). This is not so much a stage as a 'pre-stage', and is not really open to empirical investigation. The foundations for faith are laid down in the early experiences of being picked up and nursed, when trust is first formed. This nursing is a real and vital part of any sort of nurture that we might dare to call 'Christian', as we are loved into knowing and feeling.

Stage 1: intuitive-projective faith

This stage may be described as *impressionistic faith*, *imaginative faith*, *unordered faith* (age: 3/4 – 7/8 approximately). At this stage the child's relatively uninhibited imagination yields a chaos of powerful images. Thinking is intuitive and episodic. Reality is perceived as a scrap-book of impressions, as yet not ordered logically. It is a feature of this stage that symbols are viewed magically: they are what they represent. The powerful symbols of Christian liturgy can contribute deep and lasting images in this stage of faith. Hence young children who are excluded from ritual and sacrament – 'because they don't yet understand' – may be being cut off from a vital form of nourishment. Dependable, structured parenting is crucial at this stage for human and Christian growth.

Stage 2: mythic-literal faith

This stage may be described as *ordering faith*, *narrative faith* (age: 6/7 – 11/12 approximately, and some adults). At this stage an individual's power to think logically, to unify experience, and to trace patterns of cause and effect enables that person to order his or her experience. Story-telling is important at this stage, including telling the story of the Christian community to which the child belongs, but meaning can easily be 'trapped' in the narrative. The junior child is keen to belong to some club or group, and self-image is partly constituted by such belonging. He or she has achieved a measure of simple, concrete perspective-taking, overcoming the egocentricity of the very young child.

Stage 3: synthetic-conventional faith

This stage may be described as *conforming faith* (age: 11/12 – 17/18 approximately, and many adults). The ability to think abstractly develops in this stage and there is a new capacity for mutual, interpersonal perspective-taking. What peers, parents, teachers (and sometimes church leaders) say is particularly important. Interpersonal relationships are now very significant; it is a time of going with a particular 'faith-current' or 'faith-crowd'. Those who are at this stage are embedded in their faith outlook, and not yet able to reflect on their beliefs and values. The circle of people we relate to at this stage does so much to provide our meaning-making, and yet we are largely unaware of this process. But our ability to reason in a new and more powerful way can provide Christian educators with exciting opportunities for teaching and discussion.

Stage 4: individuative-reflective faith

This stage may be described as *choosing faith, either/or faith* (age: from approximately 17/18 onwards, or from the 30s or 40s onwards). I am now able to take a 'third person' perspective, 'a transcending standpoint' from which I can evaluate my beliefs and relationships. In this stage I can no longer tolerate having my faith at second hand. I must know who I am for myself, when I am not being defined by my relationships with other people. Beliefs and commitments which previously were rather unexamined can now be consciously adopted. Faith can become one's own. There are dangers in this stage: especially the dangers of an arid over-intellectualism, an unrealistic sense of independence, an over-eagerness to 'close' or resolve untidy issues, and a lack of attention to – or awareness of – the unconscious dynamics of the self. The transition to this stage of faith can be long and traumatic. Christian ministers and educators need to be particularly sensitive here, allowing people space to grow out of one stage of faithing to another.

Stage 5: conjunctive faith

This stage may be described as *balanced faith, inclusive faith, both/and faith* (age: rare before 30). In this stage the unity, coherence and tidiness of stage 4 begin to fade. The stage may emerge through coping with failure and living with the consequences of earlier decisions. One marked feature of it is a new openness to others and their worldviews, and a new ability to keep in tension the paradoxes and polarities of faith and life. Another is a new humility and a recognition of our *inter*dependence. Christian educators need to acknowledge that learners at this stage will appear to be more complex and inclusive than hitherto, and therefore more difficult to control, pigeon-hole or understand.

Stage 6: universalizing faith

This is a very rare stage and something of an extrapolation from stage 5. It may be described as *selfless faith* (age: very rare and usually only in later life). This way of being in faith is essentially a relinquishing and transcending of the self. Stage 6 people go out to transform the world, and often die in the attempt.

Relevance of faith development

Educators and pastors, as well as academic students of each of these practices, have found much of interest in faith development theory. Many have commented on its relevance for decisions about church membership/confirmation, asking at what age – and stage – this should happen. The role of faith 'sponsors' and developmental 'guides' is also important [see the papers in section 7, and 8.2 and 8.3]. Fowler himself has provided some valuable reflections on the congregation and the family as (multi-stage) contexts for faith development [see papers 8.1 and 8.4]. Others have applied these insights to more general questions about dialogue, communication and disagreement within ecclesiastical and educational communities, arguing that many problems in these areas may be illuminated by the recognition that people at different faith stages (or, less tendentiously, with different faith 'styles') may find it difficult to understand one another for specific developmental reasons [compare paper 8.5].[7] We can remember and recognize to some extent the landscape through which we have already passed on our faith journey, but with regard to that which is still before us – 'it does not yet appear what it will be'.

Those who exercise a human and a Christian ministry of care (often in an educational mode) may find further value in faith development theory, although they sometimes regard it as in need of supplementation from other psychological traditions [see, for example, paper 7.1]. It has a place, many claim, in diagnostic pastoral strategies [see papers 7.2, 7.3 and 7.4], and for many this *practical* value provides all that they are looking for as proof of the faith development 'pudding'.

But others are much more cautious and critical: not wishing to apply a theory which they still regard as conceptually, theologically or empirically suspect. And so the debate about faith development continues. The collection of papers in this volume is offered as a contribution to the furthering of that debate.

Notes
1. A fuller introduction may be found in Jeff Astley *et al.*, *How Faith Grows: faith development and Christian education*, London, National Society/Church House Publishing, 1991. Some brief passages in this introduction are taken from that work.
2. See Erik Erikson, *Childhood and Society*, London, Granada, 1977, original edition 1950, especially ch. 7.
3. See Jean Piaget, *Six Psychological Studies*, New York, Random House, 1967; Sara Meadows, 'Piaget's contribution to understanding cognitive development', in Ken Richardson and Sue Sheldon (eds.), *Cognitive Development to Adolescence*, Hove, Open University Press, 1988.
4. See Robert L. Selman, *The Growth of Interpersonal Understanding*, New York, Academic Press, 1980; Lawrence Kohlberg, 'Stage and sequence: the cognitive developmental approach to socialization', in David A. Goslin (ed.), *Handbook of Socialization Theory and Research*, Chicago, Rand McNally, 1969; Lawrence Kohlberg, 'A current statement on some theoretical issues', in S. Modgil

and C. Modgil (eds), *Lawrence Kohlberg: consensus and controversy*, Lewes, Falmer Press, 1985, ch. 30.

5. See, for example, Wilfred Cantwell Smith, *The Meaning and End of Religion*, New York, Macmillan, 1963, chs 6 and 7, and *Faith and Belief*, Princeton, N.J., Princeton University Press, 1979, ch. 1.

6. Some valuable reflections on this topic are to be found in the essays by Fowler and Nipkow in James W. Fowler, Karl Ernst Nipkow and Friedrich Schweitzer (eds), *Stages of Faith and Religious Development*, London, SCM, 1992, pp. 25–26, 33–36, 85–86, 90, 92–98.

7. See also Jeff Astley *et al.*, *How Faith Grows: faith development and Christian education*, London, National Society/Church House Publishing, 1991, pp. 67–69, 76–77.

1. Fowler on Fowler

In this section James Fowler (with his associates) is allowed to speak for himself. In these three essays he offers his own account of the theological, philosophical and psychological framework of faith development theory.

'Faith, liberation and human development' is an early essay, originating as one of the Thirkield-Jones Lectures at Gammon Theological Seminary in Atlanta in 1974. It provides a useful introduction to the understanding of 'faith' used by Fowler, drawing on the writings of theologians and students of religion such as Wilfred Cantwell Smith, Paul Tillich, H. Richard Niebuhr (studied by Fowler for his doctoral research), Richard R. Niebuhr and Bernard Lonergan. This account of the meaning of faith (designated here primarily as 'faith-knowing'), and its inner structure or form, is essentially a conceptual analysis which is both informed by and informs Fowler's theological framework. The essay was first published in the journal of Gammon Theological Seminary, *The Foundation*, vol. 79, 1974, pp. 1–10, and 32.

'The enlightenment and faith development theory' was published fourteen years later. It begins with a brief summary of Fowler's faith stages, and then proceeds to point out similarities between those transformations in the structures of western counsciousness that we call the enlightenment, and the individual's transition between the synthetic-conventional and the individuative-reflective faith stages. Fowler's thesis here is that 'the hard-won structures of rational autonomous consciousness', first shaped during the enlightenment, 'still must be constructed and claimed by persons in contemporary societies'. This involves the development of a critical self-consciousness which is typical of individuative-reflective faith. Fowler describes this in both its strength and its weakness (of overconfidence), touching on the parallels between multi-perspectival post-enlightenment developments of thought and the transition to the conjunctive faith stage. In these ways the philosophical framework and relevance of faith development theory is articulated. This essay was published in the first issue of the *Journal of Empirical Theology*, vol. 1, no. 1, 1988, pp. 29–42.

Our third entry in this section is a series of extracts from the *Manual for Faith Development Research*, written by Romney M. Moseley, David Jarvis and James W. Fowler (Atlanta, Georgia, Center for Faith Development, Candler School of Theology, Emory University, 1986). The complete *Manual* provides the essential information for administering, coding, and scoring the faith development interview. The passages that we have reproduced contain sections summarizing the theological and psychological foundations of faith development theory, the analysis of the interview, and detailed descriptions of the faith aspects and stages.

1.1 Faith, liberation and human development
James W. Fowler

Introduction

It was a distinct honor and privilege to be invited to give the 1974 Thirkield-Jones Lectures at Gammon Theological Seminary on February 26–27, 1974. In offering these lectures in written form I want briefly to establish a context for them and to give readers a clue as to what I am trying to do in them.

The common theme of these three lectures is *faith*. They attempt to focus on and clarify faith, not merely as a religious matter, but as a universal dimension of human knowing, valuing and doing. In each of the lectures, in different ways, I will be asking you to adopt an essentially new perspective on faith – a perspective which we might best describe as a *structural-developmental* point of view. This requires some explanation.

During the twentieth century students of human thought and culture have been flooded with overwhelming amounts of new data in the areas of their interest. This accumulation of data has both necessitated and made possible a method of analysis which enables us to take a comparative look at the development of human mind and culture. Called the *structuralist* point of view, this method has attempted to focus on the underlying *structures* or *operations* of human thought and belief. It tries to understand and define the *laws* or *patterns* the mind employs in constructing the ideas, concepts and beliefs that constitute the *contents* of thinking and valuing.

One of the better-known structuralists, Jean Piaget, a Swiss biologist and psychologist, began about forty years ago to observe that the thinking of children systematically differs in important ways from the thinking of adults. Through years of ingenious research Piaget developed and substantiated an explanatory theory of human mental development. Taking the structuralist viewpoint, he was able to add to it a *genetic* or *developmental* viewpoint. The result was that Piaget showed us that human thinking develops according to certain uniform patterns or structural stages. These stages are universal. That is, they seem – on the basis of many experimental verifications – to occur in all cultures and human groups. Moreover, they occur in the same sequence everywhere, and that sequence is invariant. The growing person cannot skip over a stage. The stages build on each other, and each more advanced stage includes within it the transformed and integrated structures of earlier stages. (I remind you that I am talking now about developmental stages in the *structures underlying or constituting thought,* not in the *content* of thought, which of course is quite variable.)

My friend and colleague at Harvard, Lawrence Kohlberg, has developed across twenty years of research a structural-developmental theory of moral development. He has shown that though there are many different human cultures with highly diverse values, there seems to be a uniform sequence of structurally definable stages − invariant in order − by which persons develop in the capacity for making moral judgments.

Long before I knew about Piaget or Kohlberg I had become interested in faith and its development. During my year at Interpreters' House (1968−69) my work required that I listen to over 150 ministers and lay-persons talk in some depth about their pilgrimages in faith. As I listened to these stories I began to see and expect certain recurring patterns and themes. Erik Erikson's developmental theory of the 'eight ages of man' proved immensely helpful in ordering and sorting out what I was hearing. When I began to teach at Harvard Divinity School I offered a course in which I tried to reflect systematically with students about certain uniformities in the patterns of development in religious orientation and awareness. As I became aware of the theories and research of Piaget and Kohlberg I was able to add more rigor to my own thinking and research. Though our work is still in its early stages I will be employing and sharing with you in these lectures a six-stage, structural-developmental theory of faith which we are constructing. In its present form the stage theory is based on some 115 interviews we have carried out with adults, children and adolescents over the past two years.

Faith as a verb: a preliminary definition

'Faith,' in English, can be employed only as a noun. It can be made into the adjective 'faithful' or the adverb 'faithfully'. But there is no convenient English term for denoting *the activity, the state of being,* or *the quality of participation* that is faith. The first hurdle to be gotten over in understanding what we shall mean by faith here, therefore, consists of beginning to think of faith as a verb.

Here I shall ask you to begin to think of faith *as a way of knowing.* It may also help to think of faith as a way of *construing* or *interpreting* one's experience. At any rate faith, as we shall use it, is an active, constructive, interpretative mode of being.

The kind of *knowing* or *interpreting* that faith is, needs to be clarified further. Faith is that *knowing* or *construing* by which persons or communities recognize themselves as related to the ultimate conditions of their existence. In this sense faith is a knowing or construing which fixes on the relatedness of a person or a community to power(s), boundaries (such as death and finitude), and source(s) of being, value and meaning which impinge on life in a manner not subject to personal control. In theological language, faith is the knowing or construing by which persons apprehend themselves as related to the Transcendent.

Faith understood in this constructive, verb-like sense has one more distinguishing quality. It is a knowing or construing in which *cognition* (the 'rational') is inextricably intertwined with *affectivity* or *valuing* (the 'passional'). In faith one holds a disposition over against the Transcendent. One trusts, gives loyalty, loves and admires the beauty of the Transcendent. Or one fears, resents, distrusts and revolts against it. It is important to see that faith involves both negative and positive moments . . .

Distinguishing faith from religion and belief

In *The Meaning and End of Religion,* Wilfred Cantwell Smith traces how in the West the term *religion* has referred − at varying times and sometimes simultaneously − to four different things:

a. a personal piety or pervasive disposition that permeates and gives coherence to all of a person's strivings and responses;
b. the *ideal* system of beliefs, practices and values that constitute a particular people's piety;
c. the *actual* or *empirical* embodiment of that ideal system in the lives of historical individuals and communities; and/or
d. a generic category referring to a universal dimension of human life and self-consciousness − 'religion in general'. (Smith, 1964, pp. 41−48.)

Readers will note the similarity of the first of Smith's meanings to the previous section's preliminary definition of faith as a 'knowing' or a 'disposition'. Smith employs an understanding of faith very much like ours when he suggests that this first meaning of religion be recognized as *faith*, and that it be kept conceptually distinct from religion as understood in the three other senses. These latter he refers to as the 'cumulative tradition.' He offers us a valuable description of the dialectical movement in faith development between faith and the cumulative tradition:

> If all the matters that we have suggested, theologies, rites, music, dances, congregations, moralities, and much more, the materials of religious history, are in significant part the expressions of the faith of the persons who have produced or maintained them, so also are they, do they become, the ground of faith for those who come after . . . The cumulative tradition is the mundane *result* of the faith of men in the past and is the mundane *cause* of the faith of men in the present. Therefore it is ever changing, ever accumulating, ever fresh. Every religious person is the locus of an interaction between the Transcendent, which is presumably the same for every man . . ., and the cumulative

tradition, which is different for every man ... And every religious person is the active participant, whether little or big, in the dynamics of the tradition's development. (*Ibid.*, p. 168.)

The verb-like, active understanding of faith as a construing or knowing requires that we distinguish it from another closely related phenomenon, namely *belief* or *believing*. In the absence of a verb for *faith* in English, *believe* has come to be taken as the most adequate substitute. But believing – or belief – as Paul Tillich pointed out, is not an adequate synonym for faith.

> The most ordinary misrepresentation of faith is to consider it an act of knowledge that has a low degree of evidence. Something more or less probably is affirmed in spite of the insufficiency of its theoretical substantiation ... This is to speak of *belief* rather than of *faith*. (Tillich, 1957, p. 31.)

Then characterizing faith positively, Tillich refers to it as 'participation in the subject of one's ultimate concern with one's whole being.' (*Ibid.* p. 32.)

H. Richard Niebuhr in his various writings on faith also understood it as a way of being and valuing, as contrasted to merely cognitive or volitional assent to doctrinal propositions. Faith, he wrote, 'is the attitude and action of confidence in, and fidelity to, certain realities as the sources of value and objects of loyalty'. (Niebuhr, 1960, p. 16.) For Niebuhr, as for Tillich, faith is a posture, a disposition toward one's experience of life, that is deeply affected by what or whom one trusts most deeply, and by what or whom one loves or values most. Faith is a knowing in which valuing or the affectional plays an important role.

So far only Protestant, Christian theologians have been cited in our effort to corroborate theologically the understanding of faith taken in this work. Is this way of seeing faith merely a Protestant concern? Some of the more recent research of the comparative religionist, Wilfred Cantwell Smith, leads him to contend that faith, as we have been speaking of it, is a human universal, and that each of the major cumulative traditions holds it as a central concern. In the manuscript of his forthcoming book, *Faith and Belief*, he reports a conclusion from his investigation of the concept faith in the several major world religious traditions:

> I for one am inclined to hold that faith, rather than belief, is *a* or *the* fundamental religious category; and that it has usually been so regarded, both in West and East, including classical Christian understanding.

Though loathe to try to define faith, Smith offers the following contrast of faith and belief in the same manuscript:

> Faith is deeper, richer, more personal. It is usually engendered and sustained by a religious tradition, or at least is meant to be; but it is a

quality of the person, not of the system. It is an orientation of the personality, to oneself, to one's neighbor, to the universe; a total response; a way of seeing whatever one sees and of handling whatever one handles; a capacity to live at a more than mundane level; to see, to feel, to act in terms of a transcendent dimension.

So Smith differentiates faith from religion and belief, and claims that faith is the more primary and more universal of the three. Nonetheless, for him faith 'is usually engendered and sustained by a religious tradition, or at least it is meant to be'.

Richard R. Niebuhr, as did his father and Paul Tillich quoted earlier, writes about *human faith* in a manner that raises the question about the nature of faith *apart* from the tutelage of a cumulative tradition. In *Experimental Religion* Niebuhr writes out of an understanding of faith much like ours in this work:

> We need to compare (faith) to a man's whole way of behaving, or going out of himself and returning. It includes his whole method of taking hold − intellectually, morally, and aesthetically − of the known and 'paying deference to the unknown'. The language of classical theology offers us a word; a man's faith is his persona, the character, the role, or the discipline to which he submits himself and makes the principle of his self-government. (Niebuhr, 1972, p. 38.)

Had he gone no further in characterizing faith I would find myself differing from Niebuhr at two points. In this passage and some following it, he seems to credit faithing man with more selfconsciousness about his faith as *persona* than I do. And secondly, he seems to suggest more autonomous volition in the election or construction of one's faith than seems justifiable to me. (*Ibid.*, pp. 39−41.) These differences between us narrow considerably, however, when Niebuhr turns to his discussion of faith as an *affection*. Faith, as an affection, he says, 'is the basic and all-including frame of mind that gives the whole of personal existence its determinate quality, color, and tone'. He adds:

> It is not sufficient to conceive of faithful man in the world as a rational soul, nor even as rational being whose dignity lies in choosing or willing. He is also an affectional being whose thinking and willing are themselves always qualified by the specific affection or resonance that pervades the whole person-world polarity.

And then he makes a point that meets and underscores my conviction that faith underlies both consciousness and volition rather than resulting from them, and that therefore it is not directly accessible for analysis and control: 'A true affection lies at such a depth in personal existence that it is inaccessible to volition. So much is clear from the fact that it is affection and endows the will with its specific tone and energy.' (*Ibid.*, pp. 45−46.) In a balanced, poetic statement Niebuhr sums up his understanding of affective faith: 'Affective faith is an awakening, a suffering of a whole frame of mind that endows the foundations of his existence. It qualifies all of his interaction with other men, with himself, and with his near and ultimate environment.' (*Ibid.*, p. 47.)

Niebuhr, it seems, is speaking of personal faith as a *human* possibility and necessity, even apart from the tutelage of a given cumulative tradition. Niebuhr is speaking of human faith. I would insist, however, as I think Niebuhr would, that faith does not become aware of itself, does not express or communicate itself, without appropriating or reconstituting something equivalent to religious symbols or rituals.

Let us look briefly at one more recent theological discussion of faith – this one from the writings of the Jesuit systematic theologian, Bernard J. F. Lonergan. Lonergan is speaking less from the phenomenological angle of a Richard R. Niebuhr, and more from the rational-confessional position of a philosophical theologian. But for Lonergan – as for Niebuhr – faith is affectional. In *Method in Theology* he writes:

> Faith is the knowledge born of religious love. First, then, there is a knowledge born of love. Of it Pascal spoke when he remarked that the heart has reasons which reason does not know ... The meaning ... of Pascal's remark would be that, besides the factual knowledge reached by experiencing, understanding and verifying, there is another kind of knowledge reached through the discernment of value and the judgments of value of a person in love. (Lonergan, 1972, p. 115.)

It is very important to underline Lonergan's insistence that faith is a value-knowing – a value-knowing directed toward an adequate source, center or criterion of value:

> To our apprehension of vital, social, cultural, and personal values, there is added an apprehension of transcendent value. This apprehension consists in the experienced fulfilment of our unrestricted thrust to self-transcendence, in our actuated orientation towards the mystery of love and awe.

With the confession of a central element in the content of his own faith, he continues:

> Since that thrust is of intelligence to the intelligible, of reasonableness to the true and the real, of freedom and responsibility to the truly good, the experienced fulfilment of that thrust in its unrestrictedness may be objectified as a clouded revelation of absolute intelligence and intelligibility, absolute truth and reality, absolute goodness and holiness. (*Ibid.*, p. 116.)

Lonergan is clear that faith is a value-knowing. It involves a thrust toward the apprehension of transcendent value. And, he claims, our dim apprehensions of the Transcendent as intelligible, reasonable, true and real, are the grounds for inferring the reality of an absolute source of value. For him, then, faith becomes a matter of decision for or against God so understood: Will I love him in return, or will I refuse? Will I live out of the gift of his love, or will I hold back, turn away, withdraw? In the light of this transcendent value all other values are transformed, magnified, glorified. 'Without faith the originating value is man and the terminal value is the human good man brings about. But in the light of faith, originating value is divine light and love, while terminal value is the whole universe.' (*Ibid.*)

If we step back for a moment from these brief discussions of various theologians' ideas about faith we can draw some general conclusions that will contribute to our clarification of faith. First, in each theologian's position faith is understood as *relational*. It is the response to one's sense of relatedness to the ultimate conditions and depths of existence. It is always *bi-polar* in the sense that faith is the binding of the self and the Transcendent. It is the awareness, the intuition, the conviction of a relatedness to something or someone more than the mundane.

But faith is relational for these theologians in another sense as well. For them, and for us, perhaps it is more accurate to say that faith is *tri-polar*. For it is a sense of relatedness to the ultimate conditions of existence which simultaneously informs *and qualifies our relations and interactions with the mundane, the everyday, the world of other persons and things.*

This leads me to observe that faith has an outer and an inner structure. Though our empirical research will primarily focus on understanding the form of the inner structure of faith-knowing, it is important to point out that faith always has a social or an inter-personal dimension. It is this outer, inter-personal or covenantal structure of faith which I want briefly to look at now.

'World maintenance' and the covenantal structure of faith

About six years ago Gerhard Ebeling, a German Luther-scholar and theologian, preached a memorable sermon in Harvard Memorial Church. His title was a question: 'What happens if God is removed?' Preaching in the midst of the 'Death of God' spasm in the United States, Ebeling tried to depict a world in which any and all awareness of Transcendence is expunged. If you picture that circumstance radically – as the expunging of *every* human vision, revealed and otherwise, of excellence of being – you perhaps can get at least an intellectual sense of what faith is by imagining its absence. Many of us have experienced those times in our lives when the Transcendent is experienced as illusory, a void, or at most a spiteful and arbitrary enemy. We may have been members of communities in which faith is present more by its negation than by its acknowledgement of any vision of excellence of being. If so we know something of the quality of life the bible has in view when it speaks of 'faithless generations'.

I am leading up to this: 'world maintenance' – the holding

together of a shared vision of reality in human communities –
requires interpersonal faith and faithfulness. It also requires, I
maintain, a common awareness of relatedness to the Transcendent.
'World maintenance' involves a tri-polar or covenantal relationship
between persons, and between them and shared visions of excellence
of being. In a real sense the answer to Ebeling's question: 'What
happens if God is removed?' is that the world of interpersonal
faithfulness collapses. Solipsism sets in – both *epistemological*
solipsism, in which each person construes the world and the ultimate
conditions of existence after his/her own fashion; and *moral*
solipsism, in which each person acts solely out of an ethics of
maximizing one's own survival, security and significance. Ralph
Ellison wrote in his book *Shadow and Act,*

> When the belief which nurtures a great social myth declines, large
> sections of society become prey to superstition. For man without myth
> is Othello with Desdemona gone: chaos descends, faith vanishes and
> superstitions prowl the mind. (p. 57.)

And H. Richard Niebuhr, writing sixteen years ago, offers a
disturbingly contemporary observation:

> Questions about faith, faithfulness or fidelity, trust or confidence arise
> in an urgent and tragic form as we view the massive and petty betrayals
> and deceptions of our time – the propaganda of the 'big lie', the
> cultivation of mutual distrust in society as measures of party and
> national policy, the use of pretended loyalty in conspiracies against
> state and civilization, the enlistment of men as faithful followers of
> causes that depend for success on practices of deception. Here the
> question of faith appears in negative form as the problem of the
> meaning of treason. The experiences of the twentieth century have
> brought into view the abyss of faithlessness into which men can fall. We
> see this possibility – that human history could come to its end neither
> in a brotherhood of man nor in a universal death under the blows of
> natural or man-made catastrophe, but in the gangrenous corruption of
> a social life in which every promise, contract, treat, and word of
> dishonor is given and accepted in deception and distrust. If men no
> longer have faith in each other can they exist as men? (Niebuhr, 1957,
> p. 1.)

What I am trying to suggest is now no doubt coming clear. 'Reality'
is a shared construct which is covenantally maintained. (*Covenant*
means a binding of persons in mutual trust and loyalty before and
with a transcendent center of value, toward which each also stands in
a relation of trust and loyalty.) The maintenance of 'reality' requires
constant renewal and transformation. The trust and loyalty to each
other – and to each other in a shared vision of excellence of being –
must consistently be developing and re-vivifying. A principle
contribution of institutional religions in cultures is their generation of
renewing power and passion in the mainly tacit covenant which

sustains a people's interpersonal trust and their shared visions of excellence of being. A society's covenantal maintenance and continual renewal of 'reality' requires faith in a transcendent source and center of being, value and power. It requires the continual emergence of *fresh apprehensions of excellence of being*.

As we turn now to consider the inner structure of form of faith, it is well to alert ourselves to the fact that in the study of faith development we must hold in view a dynamic, dialectical relationship between the outer and the inner structures of faith.

The inner structure of faith, faith as a knowing

Let me direct your attention to that dimension of faith that may be characterized as a kind of *knowing*. This will recall our earlier reference to the verb-like meaning of faith. It also helps us to begin to bring the form or structure of faith, as a way of construing or intepreting life, into view.

To be sure we are all deeply interested in and concerned about faith as a *doing* or a *being*. From time immemorial the *reality* or *genuineness* of faith has been gauged by what it produces in terms of initiatives and responses, heroic sacrifice or leadership, consistent commitment and the like. As the epistle of James says, 'Faith without works is dead.' Matthew's gospel drives at the same point when it says, 'By their fruits you shall know them.' But faith as a *doing* or *being* includes and flows from faith as a kind of *knowing*.

> Initiatives and responses arise out of interpretation — an act of knowing or construing.
> Moral action and responsibility depend upon interpretation and the weighing of norms and values — acts of knowing or construing.
> Faith as orientation to the ultimate conditions of existence, and as orientation to the neighbour and to everyday life in light of relatedness to transcendence, involves interpretation — acts of knowing or construing. (Niebuhr, 1963, chs 1 and 2.)

This brings us now to a difficult spot. I have two affirmations to make and to explicate which may seem, at least initially, to be driving in opposite directions. If I can make clear why they are not mutually contradictory, then we shall have come a long way towards being ready to consider stages in faith development.

The first affirmation has to do with answering the question: 'What kind of knowing is faith?' The affirmation — already foreshadowed in our examination of the theologians' writing about faith — is that faith is a kind of knowing in which *cognition* and *affection* are interwoven. Faith is a knowing which includes loving, caring and valuing, as well as awe, dread and fear. Faith-knowing relates a person or community to the limiting boundaries and depths of experience; to the source, center and standard of valuing or responsibility in life. These are rarely matters of indifference; in relation to them the total self is involved. The self may be disposed negatively or hostilely, distrustfully or rebelliously, or it may be disposed positively and with love, with trust and loyal responsibility. Whitehead wrote in *Religion in the Making*: 'Religion is the transition from God the Void to God the Enemy, and from God the Enemy to God the Companion.' (p. 16.) Faith, which often comes to expression in religion, may apprehend the Transcendent and one's relation to it in terms either of the Void, the Enemy, or the Companion. No one of those interpretations is purely cognitive or rational. Each of them, whether positive or negative, is a *valuing* apprehension, a knowing in which passion and care are invested. Faith-knowing therefore, is simultaneously orientation and arousal, perspective and motivation, indicative and imperative.

This brings us now to the second affirmation, the one which experience tells me often seems to fly in the face of what has just been said. In this work on faith development, and in the stages that are to be presented, we are attending to the *form* or *structural characteristics* of faith-knowing, rather than to its *contents*. We are looking at faith *as a way of knowing and construing*, rather than as *that which is known and construed*. We are looking at *knowing* and *valuing* as *patterned processes* rather than as *knowledge* and *values*.

This focus on the structural character of faith-knowing has its parallels in theories of cognitive and moral development. Piaget's research has concerned itself, not primarily with the child's knowledge of mathematics, physics and logic, but rather with the patterns of thinking and reasoning which the child has developed to organize its experience of the world, and which therefore underlie its knowledge of the physical environment. Similarly, Kohlberg's studies of moral development have focused not primarily on the content and outcomes of moral decisions, but on the forms or structures of thinking evidenced in the justifications or explanations of moral choices.

Faith-knowing has its own structural core. Now undoubtedly it is the highly idiosyncratic content and concreteness of a particular person's faith that most makes it interesting and powerful in its effects on others. It is the beliefs, the values, the symbols, the cultic allegiances of a person which in principal measure give faith its determinativeness for his or her behaviour. But that is not the whole picture. The same or similar content of faith may be appropriate in quite different ways by persons whose faith-knowing is structurally at different stages. Moreover, there is some correlation between structural stages and the possibility of grasping or being grasped by particular beliefs, ritual practices and social-ethical imperatives. Certain types of beliefs, symbols and ritual practices may be fairly stage-specific. While beliefs and practices of faith are almost infinitely variable, our research to date indicates that the structural patterns of faith-knowing show constancies which may not be so variable as regards their form or the sequence of their development in individual lives.

Let me sum up what I am trying to say in this second affirmation. The content — the actual images, values, beliefs, symbols and rituals of a persons' or community's faith — is of central importance in informing their behavior and shaping personality. We are interested in this content of faith in its richness, individuality and concreteness. The interviews we conduct are designed precisely to try to bring it out. Our stage theory, however, focuses on that which is less variable and more constant and capable of comparison between persons and communities, namely, the inner structures or form of faith-knowing.

You should not be unduly disturbed at this point if you find it's difficult to relate my talk of the inner structure or form of faith to anything tangible and familiar from your experience. In a sense I am referring to the *pattern* of emotion-thought which organizes and gives coherence to the data presented to faith-knowing. Human consciousness has trouble making itself aware of the structural operations underlying human consciousness. When we have looked at the stage descriptions and considered some examples I hope that what now seems vague and chimerical may begin to become more clear.

Faith, God and sanctifying grace

The reader of this material may be now quite convinced that the author has 'faith in faith' — that he holds a conviction of the reality of faith as a permeative and consequential part of human knowing and action. Likely there is the question, however, whether the 'Transcendent', the 'ultimate conditions of existence,' or 'God' have only heuristic and functional significance in this writing. While we have spoken of faith as relational — as the linking or binding of the person or faith to the Transcendent — the focus of our analysis has been, and will be, primarily on the human or personward side of that relation. So the question naturally arises whether the author's faith extends beyond faith itself to a Transcendent that is more than a heuristic projection or a functional necessity.

The psychology and sociology of religion can carry out their work without facing this question. Some persons believe that even theology can evade the question and still do its work. With the latter I do not agree. Theology I take to be the ordered inquiry into and reflection upon that which faith apprehends. Faith's apprehensions may be more or less adequate as regards the Other of faith. The criteria of adequacy must *relate* both to the content and the form or structure of faith. Insofar as the criteria deal with the adequacy of the form or structure of faith you are involved, in part at least, in developmental issues. But the overall question of adequacy and its criteria can be answered only in relation to that which is known or construed in faith

– namely human relatedness to the Transcendent. God – and man in relation to God – is the object of theological reflection. Ultimately, theology is to be valued to the degree that it brings that reality, and its implications for our lives, into view.

Here, in closing, I wish to make a simple, perhaps even simplistic affirmation. I am convicted of the actuality, the *a priori* reality, of a transcendent source and center of being, value and power. I am convicted of the belief that human beings are ontically shaped for participation in and realization in their lives of this transcendent being, value and power. Further I am convicted that this source and center exerts, in manifold ways, an attraction, a valence, a drawing into itself of our hunger for excellence of being. That is part, at least, of what western religious traditions have understood when they speak of grace.

Religion, at its best, provides a school for faith. Religion provides particular, concrete symbols, rituals and patterns of personal and corporate living which constitute models *of* and models *for* loving participation in the Transcendent. Though I speak in abstract and formal language here, the nurture of faith in dialectical, constructive relation to a determinant cumulative tradition cannot and must not avoid employing the *particular* contents of such a tradition.

No one of our cumulative traditions is ultimately adequate. Each is only relatively – i.e. *relatedly* – adequate to that which we try to apprehend and participate in through it. It is the grace – sanctifying grace if you will – operative in the attractiveness of the Transcendent, which enlivens and gives saving power to the traditions in which we stand.

References

Ellison, Ralph (1964) *Shadow and Act*, New York, Vintage Books.
Fowler, James W. (1974a) 'Toward a developmental perspective on faith', *Religious Education*, vol. 69, pp. 207–219.
Fowler, James W. (1974b) *To See The Kingdom: the theological vision of H. Richard Niebuhr*, Nashville, Tennessee, Abingdon Press.
Kohlberg, Lawrence (1969) 'Stage and sequence: the cognitive developmental approach to socialization', in D.A. Goslin, (ed.), *Handbook of Socialization Theory and Research*, Chicago, Rand-McNally, pp. 347–480.
Lonergan, B.J.F. (1972) *Method in Theology*, New York, Herder and Herder.
Piaget, Jean and B. Inhelder (1969) *The Psychology of the Child*, New York, Basic Books.
Niebuhr, H. Richard (1941) *The Meaning of Revelation*, New York, Macmillan.
Niebuhr, H. Richard (1960) *Radical Monotheism and Western Culture*, New York, Harper and Brothers.
Niebuhr, H. Richard (1963) *The Responsible Self*, New York, Harper and Row.
Niebuhr, H. Richard (Undated) *Faith on Earth*, (Unpublished book manuscript from the 1950's).
Niebuhr, Richard R. (1972) *Experiential Religion*, New York, Harper and Row.
Smith, Wilfred Cantwell (1964) *The Meaning and End of Religion*, New York, Mentor Books.
Smith, Wilfred Cantwell (1979) *Faith and Belief*, Princeton, N.J., Princeton University Press.
Tillich, Paul (1957) *The Dynamics of Faith*, New York, Harper and Row.
Whitehead, Alfred N. (1926) *Religion in the Making*, New York, Macmillan.

1.2 The Enlightenment and faith development theory

James W. Fowler

Introduction

The Enlightenment as a revolution in western consciousness is primarily associated with the eighteenth century. Though the creation of its decisive breakthroughs was primarily limited, in that century, to an intellectual elite, in the two centuries since its waning it has tranformed European and North American societies. The thinkers of the Enlightenment left virtually no dimension of human activity and self-understanding unchanged. In politics and government they left a powerful legacy to democratic theory, with their doctrines of human equality and human rights, and their legitimation of governments through a variety of versions of social contract theory. In science and technology they built upon the great achievements of the seventeenth century to establish empirical and analytic methods. They completed the severance of physics and cosmology from theology, and initiated the scientific study of psychology and sociology. In religion thinkers of the Enlightenment turned the tools of analytic reason onto the record of biblical faith. Neither doctrinal traditions, priestly hierarchies, nor the bible itself, could withstand the relativizing impact of critical historical study. The Enlightenment pressed for formal and universal criteria for morality and faith, and established rational standpoints from which the particular claims of revealed religion could be held accountable.

Faith development research and theory emerged in the late seventies and early eighties of the present century.[1] It was preceded by the work on the development of moral reasoning of Lawrence Kohlberg and his associates. They, in turn were dependent upon a tradition in philosophical psychology that included centrally the cognitive developmental structuralism of Jean Piaget, the symbolic interactionism of George Herbert Mead, and the genetic epistemology of J. Mark Baldwin. In addition, faith development theory has depended upon the psychosocial theory of ego development offered by Erik H. Erickson. In its theological background it has relied upon the work of Paul Tillich, H. Richard Niebuhr, and the comparative religionist, Wilfred Cantwell Smith.

Faith development theory attempts to account for the operations of knowing, valuing and committing that underlie a person's construal of self-other relations in the context of an explicitly or implicitly coherent image of an ultimate environment. Faith is understood dynamically as involving both the finding of and being found by meaning; both the construction and the reception of beliefs and commitments; and it is meant to include both explicitly religious expressions and enactments of faith, as well as those ways of finding and orienting oneself to coherence in an ultimate environment which are not religious.

In its empirical research and theory building the faith development perspective has identified seven formal, structurally definable stages in the ways persons compose and maintain their life-orienting systems of meaning and valuing. Each stage represents the culmination of a revolution in the patterns of knowing and valuing by which a person finds or makes meaning. The emergence of these stages depends upon development across several structural aspects. These include cognition, social perspective taking, moral reasoning, personal authorization, widening social inclusiveness, cosmological coherence, and symbolic/aesthetic competence (see Fowler, and Keen 1978; Fowler, 1981a, 1986; most comprehensive in Moseley, Jarvis and Fowler, 1986). Development through the stages requires both time and physical maturation, though it is not inexorably tied to either. The sponsorship of traditions, group membership, and the critical relations and experiences arising from interaction in life all affect the rate and extent of a person's ongoing development through the stages. Persons may equilibrate or arrest in a stage or a transition between stages, either for long periods of time or permanently. We believe that the stages are sequential and invariant. We do not have sufficient data to indicate the extent of their universality or cross-cultural validity. The following descriptions will serve as a brief overview of the structural developmental stages of faith. These descriptions are based on a sample of 359 respondents (see table 1).

Primal faith (infancy) A pre-language disposition of trust forms in the mutuality of one's relationships with parent and others to offset the anxiety that results from separations which occur during infant development.[2]

Intuitive-projective faith (early childhood) Imagination, stimulated by stories, gestures, and symbols, and not yet controlled by logical thinking, combines with perception and feelings to create long-lasting images that represent both the protective and threatening powers surrounding one's life.

Mythic-literal faith (childhood and beyond) The developing ability to think logically helps one order the world with categories of causality, space, and time; to enter into the perspectives of others; and to capture life meaning in stories.

Synthetic-conventional faith (adolescence and beyond) New cognitive abilities make mutual perspective-taking possible and require

Table 1: Distribution of stages of faith by age (N = 359)

Stages of faith	Age groups								Percentage of total sample in each stage
	0–6 %	7–12 %	13–20 %	21–30 %	31–40 %	41–50 %	51–60 %	61+ %	%
6	–	–	–	–	–	–	–	1.6	0.3
5–6	–	–	–	–	–	–	–	–	0.0
5	–	–	–	–	14.6	12.5	23.5	16.1	7.0
4–5	–	–	–	3.3	18.8	21.9	5.9	14.5	8.1
4	–	–	5.4	40.0	20.8	56.2	29.4	27.4	24.8
3–4	–	–	28.6	33.3	8.3	–	–	14.5	16.4
3	–	–	50.0	17.8	37.5	9.4	35.3	24.2	24.0
2–3	–	17.2	12.5	4.4	–	–	–	1.6	4.7
2	–	72.4	3.6	1.1	–	–	5.9	–	7.0
1–2	12.0	6.9	–	–	–	–	–	–	1.4
1	88.0	3.4	–	–	–	–	–	–	6.4
	100.0%	100.0%	100.0%	100.0%	100.0%	100.0%	100.0%	100.0%	100.0%*
	(25)	(29)	(56)	(90)	(48)	(32)	(17)	(62)	(359)

*Totals may not equal 100.0% due to rounding errors.   (from Fowler, 1981, p.318)

one to integrate diverse self-images into a coherent identity. A personal and largely unreflective synthesis of beliefs and values evolves to support identity and to unite one in emotional solidarity with others.

Individuative-reflective faith (young adulthood and beyond) Critical reflection upon one's beliefs and values, utilizing third-person perspective taking: understanding of the self and others as part of a social system; the internalization of authority and the assumption of responsibility for making explicit choices of ideology and lifestyle open the way for critically self-aware commitments in relationships and vocation.

Conjunctive faith (early mid-life and beyond) The embrace of polarities in one's life, an alertness to paradox, and the need for multiple interpretations of reality mark this stage. Symbol and story, metaphor and myth (from one's own tradition and others') are newly appreciated (second, or willed naïveté) as vehicles for expressing truth.

Universalizing faith (mid-life and beyond) Beyond paradox and polarities, persons in this stage are grounded in a oneness with the power of being. Their visions and commitments free them for a passionate yet detached spending of the self in love, devoted to overcoming division, oppression and violence, and in effective anticipatory response to an inbreaking commonwealth of love and justice.

We have brought the Enlightenment and the stage theory of faith development together in this introduction in order to lay the groundwork for a special inquiry. In a recent characterization of these stages I pointed to certain structural and functional similarities between the Enlightenment, as a historical time of transformation in the structures of consciousness in western culture, and the transition in the lives of contemporaries from the synthetic-conventional stage to the individuative-reflective stage of faith. In this essay I want to explore in more depth the character of the Enlightenment and test the claim that the construction of the individuative-reflective stage of faith for adults today involves recapitulating, at the personal level, something very like the transformation brought about culturally in the Enlightenment. We will see if, in at least this limited sense, ontogeny must still recapitulate phylogeny.

As we pursue these issues three additional questions will have to be addressed:

a.   to what degree is the faith development research and theory itself an outgrowth of Enlightenment impulses, and thereby caught up both in its strengths and limits?
b.   do we find parallels between the transition to the conjunctive stage of faith and what appears to be a culture-wide struggle toward post-Enlightenment modes of consciousness in the present era?
c.   if so, how do we account for widespread evidence of *regression*, both at societal and personal levels, to pre-Enlightenment and pre-individuative modes of faith and consciousness?

Major characteristics of Enlightenment

In offering his 'model' of the Enlightenment, historian Crane Brinton (1967) proposes three major components:

a.   a passionate commitment to *reason* as the instrument of knowledge and emancipation;
b.   a turn towards *nature* and the *natural* (including human nature) as the central objects of scientific study, and as the source of true insight and norms;
c.   a confidence in *progress*, from the achievement of peace through international law, to the reform of religion, and the conquest of disease in human societies.

Though we will need to add some elements to Brinton's framework, it will serve to organize this brief overview. Immanuel Kant begins his 1784 essay, 'What is Enlightenment?' with the following words (Friedrich, 1949):

> Enlightenment is man's leaving his self-caused immaturity. Immaturity is the incapacity to use one's intelligence without the guidance of another. Such immaturity is self-caused if it is not caused by lack of intelligence, but by lack of determination and courage to use one's intelligence without being guided by another. *Sapere aude!* Have the courage to use your own intelligence! is therefore the motto of the enlightenment.

The instrument of liberation and model of intelligence which the eighteenth century so celebrated was, of course, reason. Ernst Cassirer 1955, p. 5 writes:

> The age senses that a new force is at work within it.... When the eighteenth century wants to characterize this power in a single word, it calls it 'reason'. 'Reason' becomes the unifying and central point of this century, expressing all that it longs and strives for, and all that it achieves.

Through reason, through the disciplined and confident use of rational methods, Enlightenment thinkers anticipated the emancipation of persons and culture from their embeddedness in superstition and unexamined traditions. They intended their liberation from docile obedience to unaccountable forms of governance. And they intended to open the 'ripe' secrets of nature, which had waited so long for penetration and disclosure through the instruments of empirical rationality. Cassirer (1955, pp. 13–14) captures the Enlightenment's grasp of reason as a semi-divine, dynamic force and as an instrument of revelatory power, in the following passage:

> Reason is now looked upon rather as an acquisition than as a heritage. It is not the treasury of the mind in which the truth like a minted coin lies stored; it is rather the original intellectual force which guides the discovery and determination of truth. This determination is the seed and the indispensable presupposition of all real certainty. The whole eighteenth century understands reason in this sense; not as a sound body of knowledge, principles, and truths, but as a kind of energy, a force which is fully comprehensible only in its agency and effects. What reason is, and what it can do, can never be known by its results but only by its function. And its most important function consists in its power to bind and to dissolve. It dissolves everything merely factual, and all simple data of experience, and everything believed on the evidence of revelation, tradition and authority; and it does not rest content until it has analyzed all these things into their simplest component parts and into their last elements of belief and opinion. Following this work of dissolution begins the work of construction. Reason cannot stop with the dispersed parts; it has to build from them a new structure, a true whole. But since reason creates this whole and fits the parts together according to its own

rule, it gains complete knowledge of the structure of its product.

The Enlightenment, building on the astronomy, physics and mathematics of Kepler, Galileo, Newton and others, dissolved classical views of nature. Cassirer (1955, p. 37) writes:

> The clear-cut form of the classical and medieval conception of the world crumbles, and the world ceases to be a 'cosmos' in the sense of an immediately accessible order of things.... One world and one Being are replaced by an infinity of worlds constantly springing from the womb of becoming, each one of which embodies but a single transitory phase of the inexhaustible vital process of the universe.

It is the glory of human reason that it can endure − yes, even execute − this dissolution of its inherited world images, and at the same time assume a stance from which, through probing inquiry and patient synthesis, it can disclose the implicit lawfulness and intricate inter-relatedness that are to be found in nature. In reflecting upon this exhilarating capacity, Enlightenment thinkers became aware of a new intensity and concentration that is fundamental in the nature of mind. Cassirer (1955, pp. 37−38) writes:

> The highest energy and deepest truth of the mind do not consist in going out into the infinite, but in the mind's maintaining itself against the infinite and proving in its pure unity equal to the infinity of being.

In its capacity for maintaining itself against the infinite the mind is capable of enabling us to 'place it (the infinite) within measure and bound, not in order to limit its realm but in order to know it in its all-comprehensive and all-pervasive law. Universal law, which is discovered and formulated in thought, forms the necessary correlate of the intuitively experienced boundlessness of the universe.'

In its reconstruction and rebinding of the world of knowledge the Enlightenment constituted nature and the natural as its horizon. To the realm of nature belongs everything in the sphere accessible by 'natural light' (*lumen natural*). This includes everything whose investigation and understanding requires no other aid than the natural forces of reason. The realm of nature is thus established apart from the realm of grace, where truth is accessible only through the power of revelation. But for the Enlightenment there need be no conflict or opposition between belief and knowledge, between revelation and reason.

The truth of nature is revealed, says to Cassirer (1955, p. 43):

> not in God's word but in his work; it is not based on the testimony of scripture or tradition but is visible to us at all times. But it is understandable only to those who know nature's handwriting and can decipher her text. The truth of nature cannot be expressed in mere words; the only suitable expression lies in mathematical constructions, figures and numbers. And in these symbols nature presents itself in perfect form and clarity.... In nature ... the whole plan of the

universe lies before us in its undivided and inviolable unity, evidently waiting for the human mind to recognise and express it.

Brinton reminds us that not until the seventeenth century does a confidence begin to emerge that the present might be better than the past, and that the future can bring consistent and continuing progress for humankind. The French reformer and *philosophe* Turgot gave a speech at the Sorbonne in 1750 entitled 'On the successive advances of the human mind' which outlined a complete doctrine of progress. His friend and disciple Condorcert recast these ideas in his *Sketch for a Historical Picture of the Human Mind*. This offered an extraordinarily optimistic vision of an utopia of unending progress, leading ultimately to the attainment by all humans of immortality in the flesh on this earth (cited in Brinton, 1967, pp. 521). Most Enlightenment thinkers avoided these excesses, and in fact had realistic conceptions of the ways in which reason can be subordinated to the service of egocentric and selfish passions.[3] Nonetheless, the fundamental spirit of emancipation, coupled with confidence in the potency of education to form persons capable of rationality, gave rise to a great energy of optimism in the age. Not until the bitter excesses of the French Revolution would fundamental questions about the fragility of reason and the power of deeper sources of distortion and perversion in human nature emerge.

Characteristics of the individuative-reflective stage

The thesis of this essay is that the hard-won structures of rational autonomous consciousness, shaped and claimed on behalf of all humans for the first time in the Enlightenment, still must be constructed and claimed by persons in contemporary societies. Though there now exist both cultural models and templates and educational supports for developing post-conventional, critical consciousness, this revolution still requires the courage and determination of which Kant spoke. And it may also require more sponsorship and support than he acknowledged. The civil rights and feminist liberation movements which have emerged, especially during and since the nineteen-sixties, have in large measure been efforts, collectively, to create political, economic, and social space for the claiming by women and ethnic minorities of the full maturity of rational autonomy and its public usage.[4]

In the description of the individuative-reflective stage of faith given in *Faith Development and Pastoral Care* (Fowler, 1987, p. 68) we read:

This stage we find emerging only in young adulthood or beyond.... Specifically, two important movements must occur, together or in sequence. First, the previous stage's tacit system of beliefs, values, and commitments must be critically examined. This means that persons must undergo a sometimes painful disruption of their deeply held but unexamined worldview or belief system. The familiar and taken-for-granted must be (objectified and) made strange. The assumptive configuration of meanings assembled to support their selfhood in its roles and relations must now be allowed to become problematic. Evocative symbols and stories by which lives have been oriented will now be critically questioned and interpreted. So the first movement involves disembedding from the previous stage's assumptive and tacitly held system of beliefs and values (Parenthetical material added).

We see here an effort to describe the awakening of analytic reasoning and the effort to focus it reflectively upon the until-now-implicit body of opinions, beliefs, and values that have constituted and oriented the self. It marks the beginning of a process of assessing the validity of the assumptive foundations and elements of one's worldview in the critical light of one's reflected-upon experience. Structurally this move parallels the Enlightenment's critical dismantling of received systems in theology, philosophy and cosmology. Like the Enlightenment, it is paralleled by a second movement in which the knowing subject makes the self, its capacities and constitution, the object of critical inquiry and reflection. Fowler (1987, p. 68) writes:

Second, the self, previously constituted and sustained by its roles and relationships, must struggle with the question of identity and worth apart from its previously defining connections. This does not mean that the relations (necessarily) have to be broken. Nor does it mean that the roles (necessarily) must be relinquished. Rather, it means that persons must take into themselves much of the authority they previously invested in others for determining and sanctioning their goals and values. It means that definitions of the self dependent upon roles and relationships with others must now be regrounded in terms of a new quality of responsibility that the self takes for defining itself and orchestrating its roles and relations (Parenthetical inserts added to the original).

Just as the Enlightenment's emancipatory thrust derived from a new apprehension of reason, so the groundwork for the double movement in critical reflection, characteristic of the individuative-reflective stage of faith, depends upon new cognitive capacities. In the first place, it requires the full development of what Piaget called 'formal operational' thinking. This means constructing the operations necessary for formulating and manipulating abstract concepts. It means being capable of 'thinking about our thinking'. It means being able to understand and construct mental models of systems of interaction to represent the interrelations of interacting phenomena (Inhelder and Piaget, 1958).

As an intermediate and crucial step towards full formal operational thinking, especially as it can be used in reflecting upon the self and one's implicit system of values and beliefs, one must develop a new level of social perspective taking. We call this level, after Selman (1974, 1976), 'third-person' perspective taking. The synthetic-conventional stage of faith, the one typically arising in early adolescence and just prior to the individuative-reflective stage, is marked by its embeddedness in 'mutual interpersonal' perspective taking. Fowler (1987, pp 68–69) writes:

> In the acute attunement to the expectations and evaluations of significant others that marks ... the synthetic-conventional stage ... persons depend at first upon external relations for confirmation and support of the self. Gradually in that stage the expectations and conforming judgements of valued others become an internalized part of one's personality. These internalized 'voices' of significant others provide guidance and constraint for the interpersonal self. When external or internalized authorities conflict, however, or when their tutelage becomes cramping or constrictive for a developing person, the self must construct a perspective from which both self and the relations with others can be seen from beyond the embeddedness in interpersonal relations. The third-person perspective provides an angle of vision from which evaluations of the expectations of others can be made and from which conflicting claims or expectations can be adjudicated. The use of the third-person perspective provides a basis from which assessments and choices can be made in relation to the beliefs, values, and elements of lifestyle one has evolved.

The third-person perspective opens the way for the use of formal operational abilities to analyze the contents of one's worldview and value system and to see their interrelated elements as part of a system. It may be seen as the epistemological basis for the 'trancendental ego'. It makes possible the movement from being embedded in one's ideology to an at least partial realization of that status of critical self awareness that we could describe as *having* one's ideology (see Kegan, 1982). The third-person perspective also makes possible the construction of self-other relations seen as located in and constrained by the context of systems. This includes the possibility of the awareness of economic and political, as well as familial and religious systems. Ideological and systemic self-awareness may be easier to develop in *some* European contexts and classes than in the United States. This is because primary and secondary education in the United States tend to avoid accentuating ideological and class differences, and, with the media, tend to focus upon the interpersonal realm as the important domain of attention. In European education and politics, in contrast, much more attention is focused on ideological boundaries between parties, classes and religious groups. For university bound students in Europe systematic analysis is encouraged and the groundwork is laid for the kind of step beyond Enlightenment thinking represented by Marxian and Freudian critiques of unconscious and repressed ideologies. This observation leads one to speculate whether the 'modal development level' among educated Europeans may be more nearly at the individuative-reflective stage, whereas for the wider range of educated citizens of the United States it may be more nearly at a transition point between the synthetic-conventional and the individuative-reflective stages.[5]

As a summary for this exploration of structural and functional parallels between the Enlightenment and the transition to individuative-reflective faith, consider another quote from *Faith Development and Pastoral Care* (Fowler, 1987, p. 70):

> The Enlightenment represented a movement in cultural evolution where inherited symbols, beliefs, and traditions were subjected to the scrutiny and evaluation of critical reasoning. Similarly, the development of the Individuative-Reflective stage of faith involves the critical examination and exercise of choice regarding a person or community's previous faith perspectives. In many respects this is a 'demythologizing' stage. Creeds, symbols, stories, and myths from religious traditions are likely to be subjected to analysis and to translation to conceptual formulations ... Paul Tillich pointed out that a symbol that is recognized as a symbol no longer has the power of a symbol. The powerful participation of a symbol in that which it symbolizes, which makes it possible for the symbol to mediate relationship with its reality, is now broken. While the conceptual analysis and translation of the symbol makes its meaning explicit, we may fail to notice that in the process of communicating meanings the initiative has shifted from the symbol to the analyst of the symbol.

The last line of this quote points gently toward the massive over-confidence and blind undersides of the Enlightenment as a movement. In its exhilaration of the emancipatory and critically clarifying power of reason, it failed to anticipate the consequences of enthroning reason without bringing forward the forming and constraining influences of human wisdom in religious and cultural traditions. In its confidence regarding the possibility of dissolving and reconstructing knowledge of reality, and thereby of controlling the complexities of nature, it remained blissfully ignorant of both the social and the psychic unconscious. In its overtrust of its hard-won self-consciousness and rational clarity, it could not measure the degree to which the human soul resents its finitude and strives to ground and defend itself in myopic and self-serving ideologies.

But balance and the wisdom of hindsight are not easy to come by in the midst of a revolution. We need to celebrate the courage and genius of the Enlightenment. We need to celebrate the courage and determination of those who in each generation recapitulate, with their own risky struggles, the Enlightenment's path toward self-conscious possession and public use of their rational autonomy, no matter how much developmental self-deception it necessarily involves.

Conclusion

In conclusion let us give brief address to the three questions identified at the end of our introductory section. First, to what degree is the faith development theory and research itself an expression of Enlightenment impulses, and thereby a participant in both its strengths and limits? Cassirer (1955, pp. 135–136) reminds us that at its core the Enlightenment was not basically irreligious or inimical to religion.

> The strongest intellectual forces of the Enlightenment do not lie in its rejection of belief but rather in the new form of faith which it proclaims, and in the new form of religion which it embodies.... This era is permeated by genuine creative feeling and unquestionable faith in the reformation of the world. And just such a reformation is now expected of religion.... (E)specially among the thinkers of the German Enlightenment the fundamental objective is not the dissolution of religion but its 'transcendental' justification and foundation.

The conception of faith with which faith development theory works is both made necessary by the Enlightenment and is part of the fruit of the Enlightenment's effort to 'reform' religion. This theory and research makes an Enlightenment move when it seeks to provide formal definitions of faith and formal characterizations of 'structuralist' stages. Not until the Enlightenment did this kind of separation of the 'structuring' and the 'content' of ideological perspectives come into play. Though less confident than the Enlightenment about the establishment of rational and ethical bases from which all particular religious traditions can be evaluated, faith development theory does provide a criteriology for assessing the adequacy of a given person's or group's appropriation of its religious content tradition, and the adequacy of the tradition itself. In contrast to the Enlightenment, however, and in ways that show its indebtedness to post-Enlightenment hermeneutics, faith development theory knows that the structural features of faith are at best half the picture, and that any adequate study of lived religious faith must balance the initiative of the interpreter and inquirer with the hermeneutic initiatives of classic traditions.[6] Moreover, faith development theory seeks to acknowledge and systematically account for the important shaping role of the emotions and of the unconscious – personal and social – in the life of faith (Fowler, 1981 b, ch. 5).

Second, do we find parallels between the transition to the conjunctive stage of faith and what appears to be a culture-wide struggle toward post-Enlightenment modes of consciousness in the present era? Were this a much longer essay, it would be fruitful to parallel the discussion of the Enlightenment and the individuative-reflective stage with a similar consideration of the conjunctive stage in relation to a variety of contemporary post-Enlightenment approaches to hermeneutic and philosophy of science. Since the Second World War (anticipated earlier by such thinkers as Einstein, Wittgenstein, Heidegger, Whitehead, and Gadamer) we have been formulating the groundlines of philosophical approaches that will help us to grasp and express the structural features of another revolution in-process in western consciousness – one that will likely prove to be as significant a watershed as did the Enlightenment. Formulations of this new consciousness will have to incorporate the vastly important contributions of the nineteenth century: a full orbed doctrine of evolution and development (biological, cultural, ontological); the critique of ideology and a full grasping of the role of overt as well as covert 'interests' in shaping scientific and philosophical thought and behaviour; an accounting of the 'will to power' and the dynamics of 'resentment' as forces in human behaviour; the social sources of religion, language, and the fundamental categories of thought; and the tremendous cunning of defences and the repressed unconscious in affecting our knowing, valuing and interpreting as well as acting.

But such philosophical perspectives will also have to incorporate the great contributions of twentieth-century reflective experience: the awareness of the fundamental participation of everything in *process*; the relativity to each other, and to what they observe, of all perspectives on the universe and experience; the intrusion into and involvement of any investigator within phenomena being scientifically studied; the ecological interdependence of all systems, including systems of thought and consciousness; the maintenance of the cosmos through the counterpoising pull and force of tensional vectors, giving rise to a unity of such variegated and pluralistic inclusiveness as to challenge the human capacity to fathom, even using a panoply of the infinitely fast computers now available to us for synchronous knowing.[7] Thinkers such as Paul Ricoeur, Michael Polanyi, Jürgen Habermas, and, in theology, David Tracy are pointing the way toward such formulations. In the examination of their work, and that of their co-workers and correspondents, we find characteristics that call for the 'second naïveté', and the dialectical, multi-perspectival structures of knowing and valuing which descriptions of the conjunctive stage of faith have tried to capture. Extensive work in these philosophical sources, combined with fresh empirical investigations of the faith structuring of late-stage respondents promise to lead toward enriched and more precise characterizations of the conjunctive stage.

Times of cultural revolutions in consciousness are un-nerving and frightening, as well as exhilarating. Because of the mal-distribution of wealth, of productive resources, and of life-chances on this globe, considerations of a revolution in cultural consciousness can seem to result in the evasion of the urgent demands of humanitarian relief and the alteration of systems for the equitable delivery of life's necessities. On the other hand, the terrible threat of late-twentieth century nuclear weaponry being controlled by (or controlling) governments that operate on the basis of nineteenth or early twentieth century ethics makes the work of cultural conscientization and modeling exceedingly urgent and imperative.

It seems clear that in face of the complexity and newness of the ways we are being called to think and be, many groups globally are retreating toward the hope of authoritative grounding in the resurgence of pre-Enlightenment religious commitments or the heedlessness of hedonist ideologies. Perhaps it is equally clear that theory and research in faith development, which provides a language and a conceptual system for ordering and speaking intelligibly about the clash of cultural levels of development, has an important contribution to make. At least this should be so for those who, in our time, are trying to bring as much courage and clear-eyed thought to the challenges of our era as the thinkers of the Enlightenment brought to theirs.

Notes

1. The principal statement of faith development theory can be found in the following books by the present author: Fowler, Keen and Berryman (1978, 2nd ed. 1985); Fowler (1981a, 1981b, 1986, 1987). A volume edited by Karl Ernst Nipkow, Friedrich Schweitzer and James Fowler (1988), *Glaubensentwicklung und Erziehung*, Gutersloh, Gutersloher Verlaghaus Gerd Mohn, contains a statement by the present author and a number of critical essays responding to this work and to the research by Prof. Dr Fritz Oser of Friebourg University on the development of religious judgement. The latter volume is published in English under the title, *Stages of Faith and Religious Development: implications for church, education and society*, New York, Crossroads, 1991; London, SCM, 1992.

2. For a detailed study in this stage see this author's article, 'Strength for the journey: early childhood development and faith', in Doris Blazer (ed.) *Faith Development and Early Childhood*, Kansas City, Sheed and Ward, 1988.

3. See Cassirer (1955, pp. 103ff.) 'Voltaire says in his *Treatise on Metaphysics* that without the passions, without the desire for fame, without ambition and vanity, no progress of humanity, no refinement of taste and no improvement of the arts and sciences is thinkable: "It is with this motivating force that God, whom Plato called the eternal geometer, and whom I call the eternal machinist, has animated and embellished nature: the passions are the wheels which make all these machines go."'

4. It is interesting that Kant, in the essay I cited earlier, said, 'All that is required for this enlightenment is freedom; and particularly the least harmful of all that may be called freedom, namely, the freedom for man to make *public* use of his reason in all matters.' (Friedrich, 1949, p. 134.) Though his essay turns out to be more about academic freedom than freedom of speech generally, he articulates well what contemporary liberation movements have been about – the claiming of space in which previously subordinated groups can make *public* use of their freedom and rationality, be they guardians of their own lives and welfare, and be agential participants in shaping the conditions of our common life.

5. These points of comparison are conjectural and speculative, based upon the writer's observations and experiences. For the idea of a 'modal developmental level' in a society of culture, see Kenneth Keniston, 'Psychological development and historical change', in Robert Jay Lifton (ed.) *Explorations in Psycho-history*, New York, Simon and Schuster, 1974, pp. 160–164. The idea refers to the average expectable level of adult development in a given society, culture, or epoch. This paper suggests that the Enlightenment, among many other things, initiated a major shift in the modal developmental level of the national societies in which it took hold.

6.   For Gadamer's conception of the 'classics' as applied to religious traditions see David Tracy, *The Analogical Imagination*, New York, Crossroad, 1981, chs 3, 4 and 5.
7.   For accounts of the new cosmology being shaped by astronomical and particle physicists see two books by Paul Davies, *God and the New Physics*, New York, Simon and Schuster, 1983, and *Superforce*, New York, Simon and Schuster, 1984.

References

Brinton, C. (1967) 'Enlightenment', in P. Edwards (ed.) *The Encyclopedia of Philosophy*, New York, MacMillan, vol. II, pp. 519–525.

Cassirer, E. (1955) *The Philosophy of the Enlightenment*, Boston, Beacon Press (transl. form 1932 German edition by F. C. A. Koelln and J. P. Pettegrove).

Fowler, J. W. (1981a) *Stages of Faith: the psychology of human development and the quest for meaning*, San Francisco, Harper and Row.

Fowler, J. W. (1981b) *Becoming Adult, Becoming Christian*, San Francisco, Harper and Row.

Fowler, J. W. (1986) 'Faith and the structuring of meaning', in C. Dykstra, S. Parks (eds) *Faith Development and Fowler*, Birmingham, Alabama, Religious Education Press, pp. 15–42.

Fowler, J. W. (1987) *Faith Development and Pastoral Care*, Philadelphia, Fortress Press.

Fowler, J. W. and S. Keen (1978) *Life Maps: conversations on the journey of faith*, Waco, Texas, Word Books.

Friedrich, K. J. (ed. and trans.) (1949) *The Philosophy of Kant*, New York, The Modern Library.

Inhelder, B. and J. Piaget (1958) *The Growth of Logical Thinking from Childhood to Adolescence*, New York, Basic Books.

Kegan, R. (1982) *The Evolving Self*, Cambridge, Mass., Harvard University Press.

Moseley, R. M., Jarvis, D. and Fowler, J. W. (1986) *The Manual for Faith Development Research*, Atlanta, Center for Faith Development.

Selman, R. L. (1974) *The Development Conceptions of Interpersonal Relations*, Publication of the Harvard Judge Baker Social Reasoning Project, vol. I and II.

Selman, R. L. (1976) 'Social cognitive understanding', in T. Lickona (ed.), *Moral Development and Behavior*, New York, Holt, Rinehart and Winston.

1.3 Stages of faith

Romney M. Moseley, David Jarvis, and James W. Fowler

Theological and psychological foundations of faith development theory

For the past decade, Dr James W. Fowler has defined faith development as a sequence of stages by which persons shape their relatedness to a transcendent center or centers of value. This identification of faith with meaning-making reflects the influence of H. Richard Niebuhr's theology of radical monotheism. Also evident is the influence of Piaget's constructivist epistemology which suggests a framework for determining the genesis and transformation of cognitive structures. All together, these stages indicate that there is an underlying system of transformations by which the self is constituted as it responds to questions of ultimate meaning.

This manual is intended as a practical instrument for deciphering the intricate and complex process which we refer to as 'faith development'. The criteria or aspects by which the stages are determined reflect the interpenetration of cognition and affect as persons shape their lives around explicit and, in some cases, tacit centers of value.

Piagetian structuralism lends a distinctive character to faith development theory. First, structuralism emphasizes that the whole is greater than the sum of its parts. This means that faith is always more than what is empirically derived through interviews and analytical dissection into a sequence of stages. Theologically speaking, a transcendent function is preserved in the structuring of faith. Secondly, structuralism maintains that a structure is an organized system, i.e. the parts of the whole are structurally integrated. Thus, the aspects are not merely salient features of a stage, but constitute an organized pattern of meaning-making. Thirdly, structures are dynamic. Faith, structurally defined, is a dynamic process. Fourthly, this dynamic process is developmentally ordered.

The term development implies change that eventuates in increasingly complex structures. Hence Piaget, in contrast to Gestalt theorists, focused not only on the existence of organized synchronic structures, but also on their diachronic transformational activities.

The progression from the simple to the complex has important implications for faith development. A pejorative rendering of the theory would stress its hierarchical ordering and increasing sophistication as evidence of cultural imperialism. The claim that faith is always greater than the accumulation of its stages is not a corrective to such misinterpretation. Nevertheless, it must be emphasized that the objective of faith development research is not to 'stage' persons numerically for contrastive or hierarchical purposes. When abstracted from the context of life history such 'scores' are meaningless. Stages refer to an observable pattern of meaning-construction in which specific elements are interrelated. The 'structure' of faith is defined by this system of interrelationships. Structure allows us to predict the emergence of relatively stable patterns in the midst of change. The claim that stages are also normative is supported by these empirical data.

In addition to the four principles cited above, the structuralism also maintains that human behavior is influenced by the confluence of multiple internal and external forces. Stages of faith, therefore, should not be viewed apart from other capabilities developed by persons as they respond to the world. Thus, while stages are hierarchically ordered in a structuralist sense, they are not indicative of an increasing capacity for faithfulness or any other human virtue.

What then is the value of a stage theory of faith development? One value is heuristic. More importantly, faith development theory takes seriously the narrative structure of life history. Here is found an unlimited source of data from which persons gain deeper insight into their lives and foster the development of communities of faith.

In sum, the stages may be viewed as scaffolding for weaving the tapestry of meaning for one's life. The model for faith development is not a linear scaffolding to expedite vertical mobility, but a flexible spiral of interaction between person and society. Like all scaffolding, the stages provide a framework that enables us to appreciate the aesthetics and mystery of human faith.

Structure and function in faith development theory

Piaget's concept of structure as a system of transformations underscores the interdependence of structure and function, both of which are ontogenetically ordered. Functions are the transformational activities, for example, assimilation and accommodation, through which structures emerge. Faith development theory acknowledges the interdependence of structural, functional, and genetic aspects of development. However, faith development theory is not concerned with the construction of *knowledge* but with the construction of *meaning*. The latter is an imaginative activity that cannot be determined simply by identifying an epigenetic sequence of structural stages. We note, therefore, that the notion of structure in faith development theory is extended beyond the strict mathematicological constructs of Piagetian epistemology.

Having argued that structural transformation is an endless process, Piaget arbitrarily restricted the study of cognition to childhood and adolescence. The assumption that cognitive development (not learning) ceases at the acquisition of formal operational logic has not gone unchallenged. In contrast to Piaget's research, the data for faith development research have been gathered from subjects in the adolescent and adult years. These data suggest that what we have defined as faith involves meaning-making activities but are not limited to the mathematicological constructs of formal operational thought but are extended to dialectical thinking at stage five. Our research is more concerned with reconceptualizing the notion of structure as a *metaphor* for the coherence and orderedness evident in the way persons organize their lives around transcending meaning than with proving the existence of post-formal operational stages. (See W. R. Looft: 'Egocentrism and social interaction across the life span,' *Psychological Bulletin*, 1982, 78, 73–92. See also K. F. Riegel: 'Dialectic operations: the final period of cognitive development,' *Human Development*, 1973, 16, 346–370.)

In departing from a strict logico-mathematical notion of structure as a self-regulating system of transformations, we have not abandoned structural analysis. The key issue for structural analysis is that the phenomenon under examination exhibits stability in the midst of change. We are assured by our research findings that the elements of stability and transformation are present in the phenomenon that we have termed faith. In the final analysis, faith development has to do with interpreting the relative stability of human self-understanding in the midst of change. Hence, structural analysis is appropriate. However, not all the activity that we observed is developmental. Rather than isolate the developmental from the psycho-dynamic, as is done by Piaget and Kohlberg, we have attempted to integrate these two forms of activity. In so doing, we have heightened aspects of constructivist espistemology ignored or minimized by Piaget, for example, socio-historical conditions and their impact on the narrative structure of self-understanding. Here, the *relational* character of structuralism is brought to the forefront. Kegan (*The Evolving Self*, Harvard, 1982) provides a helpful constructivist model of the self. This model sharpens what is recognized by faith development theory as the development of social perspective taking.

In addition, faith development theory appropriates the metaphor of covenant in order to underscore the relational and reciprocal aspects of structural activity. These are particularly evident in the ethical imperatives of stages 5 and 6.

Finally, a word about the public and pragmatic components of faith development theory. In a sense, faith *is* what faith *does*.

But what faith does is not to be understood simply as internal transformational activity through which structure emerges. In faith development theory, the idea of function is more comprehensive. We are also concerned about the function of faith in human becoming. What is disclosed in a faith development interview is not merely the private language of a particular individual but public testimony of the transformative and disclosive power of the Transcendent. What stage six describes as the *omega* point of faith development must be understood paradoxically as, on the one hand, evidence of what is optimally desirable for humanity, and, on the other hand, an 'eschatological proviso' for global interdependence.

Coding and scoring system

The process of devising a coding and scoring system[1] for a psychological measure is, to use Jane Loevinger's words, 'a bootstrapping operation' (Jane Loevinger and Ruth Wessler, *Measuring Ego Development*, vol. 1, p. 25), whereby one begins with the basic concepts of the theory, codifies them, and begins to test those initial codifications. This process usually leads to clarification and further refinement of the basic constructs themselves.

As research proceeds, more refined instruments are developed, and more elaborate testing of the theory becomes possible. A theory then becomes more formalized and operationalized. In the case of faith development theory, which is complex, the task of formulating those initial codifications and formalizing the interpretation of interview transcripts to the point where suitable interrater reliability could be attained, has been a lengthy one. This manual represents the results of these initial efforts.

The initial categories for this manual were developed on the basis of a sample of 359 interviews conducted by James W. Fowler and his associates in the years from 1972 to 1983. During this period of time, the conceptual foundations of the theory were worked out, and the basic characteristics of the six stages were outlined.

As the interviewing progressed, several new questions were tried, and different forms of the basic interview guide were tested. The coding and analysis of the interviews was done largely by the individual interviewers themselves during this period, and a research group met regularly to discuss the results. Points of difference concerning the interpretation of the interviews were discussed at these sessions and as a result, the descriptions of the stages were refined, and the sample of interviews were divided by stage.

It was at this point that the desirability of some formalization of the analysis procedures was foreseen and interviews that were thought to be particularly illustrative of general stage characteristics, or those which presented interesting difficulties or questions for the theory were singled out and bound into volumes for further study.

The initial drafts of this scoring manual were based on the further analysis and discussion of this group of interviews, along with others which had been done later but which were not part of the original sample.

The work on the manual began with a careful, response by response analysis of approximately sixty interviews that had been analyzed more generally by the research group. The responses were coded by aspect and staged individually. The result was a group of 'paradigmatic' responses for each aspect at each stage. The initial coding categories for the manual were developed through group discussions about what the various 'paradigmatic responses' had in common, and which theoretical features they illustrated.

With some basic coding categories in place, work was begun attempting to apply these categories to unscored and unanalyzed interviews. In the course of these discussions, the criteria for distinguishing among the aspects, and the criteria for distinguishing between stages for a given aspect were given clearer form. By proceeding in this way, it was hoped to give the individual interview/coder a procedure to follow which would duplicate, as closely as possible, the group process by which interviews were originally analyzed.

There are several methods currently in use by various structural-developmental theories for deriving an overall stage score from the total of individual response scores. The methods are not arbitrary, and each has theoretical implications.

One method that is quite consistent with several interpretations of structural-developmental theory is to take the highest level response that the respondent is able to generate as that respondent's stage score. Under this method, an interview that consisted largely of stage 4 responses, but which contained one or more responses scored stage 5, would be scored as a stage 5 interview. This interpretation and method implies that a 'structure' is something like a competence: that is, something that a respondent is capable of doing but not necessarily something that he or she may do all or most of the time.

Faith development theory, by contrast, has assumed that the structure of faith is a complex unity comprised of the interactions of several components or competencies. If faith is such an overarching structure of meaning-making, a map of the way in which an individual constructs or locates his or her centers of value and images of power, those parts of the personality that are closest to the core of human meaning, then it makes sense to assume that the cognitive and psycho-social competencies described by the aspects of faith, would impinge upon this core process in very different ways among different individuals.

Further, it is reasonable to assume that an average of an individual's functioning across a broad range of cognitive and psycho-social competencies would afford a more telling window into those elusive core structures by which the whole is construed than focusing on any one of these competencies exclusively as the highest-response method of stage scoring would force us to do in an interview of this type.

Some objections have been raised by those with considerable sophistication in psychometric theory, to the use of a simple average to derive the individual's stage score. These objections are well taken, and point toward some of the limitations of an open-ended interview format, at least for psychometric purposes. At the present time, however, there is no theoretical reason to assume that the aspects of faith structuring should be weighted unevenly in any particular manner. Nor has there been a convincing empirical demonstration of the need for more complex scoring algorithms at this time.

It is assumed, and is in fact quite evident from the research that we have done, that there are individual differences in the centrality that the various aspects of faith structuring have in an individual's framing of meaning as a whole. Some persons tend to be more cognitively oriented, for example, either by inclination or by training, and tend to frame their master stories and central meanings in theoretical or metaphoric terms. Others tend to be more interpersonally oriented, while still others tend to orient toward symbols and images. The exact extent to which these differing orientations are characteristics of individuals that are relatively stable throughout portions of the life-cycle, and thus approximate 'personality traits,' or the extent to which they may be stage-specific and seen to vary developmentally, is not known at present.

The fact that these criticisms point to the limits of our present instrument does not decrease their salience or their importance as indications of possible fruitful directions for future research, provided of course that suitably ingenious research methods can be designed to isolate individual factors from the complex matrix of cognitive and psycho-social factors that have a direct bearing on the way individuals frame their meanings.

For the present, however, there are no compelling reasons to assume the seven aspects of faith structuring should not be treated as being of roughly equal importance for the purpose of interview coding and scoring.

Open-ended interview

The criticisms above result, to a certain extent, from some of the strictures imposed by the open-ended, or 'semi-clinical' interview form. While we believe that the current, open-ended form of the interview is still the most appropriate research tool given the current stage of our knowledge of faith development, the person planning to do research with this instrument should be aware of some of its limitations as well as its strengths.

The semi-clinical interview enables us to gather a wider range of data than would be possible with a pencil and paper test, dilemma test, or other format designed to measure structure alone. Along with codable structural data, the open-ended interview yields data on the individual's life history, social relationships and images and thoughts about self that could not be gathered from a test or other instrument that was designed to measure specific structures in isolation. This range of data has been, and continues to be, a fruitful source of insight into the complex ways in which individuals construe their fundamental meanings. It assists the theory building enterprise because it enables us to assess relationships between structural-developmental approaches and other theories aimed at the same phenomena.

In addition, the open-ended format lends itself to modification and revision with comparative ease, thus enabling researchers to devise new interview questions and new lines of inquiry as the need arises. While it is not solely idiographic in intent, this form of interview is most appropriate to the initial stages of research before more specific nomothetic hypotheses are formed.

These benefits of flexibility and contextual richness, however, are necessarily purchased at the expense of some efficiency and formality. The faith development interview, as it currently stands, is rather expensive to administer, and time-consuming to analyze. In addition, exact psychometric comparability of each interview with others is not possible because each one will be unique in some ways, and each will have a differing amount of data for each of the seven aspects of meaning construction that we are studying.

For these reasons, it is doubtful, at present, if the more sophisticated and larger scale studies that would be needed to throw light on some of the issues above, could be done using the interview alone.

There are steps that a researcher can take, however, to work within the instrument's limitations and still produce reliable and comparable data, even if it is lacking in the psychometric exactitude that some projects might demand. For the most part, these steps involve additional care taken in the planning and administering of the interview.

Analysis of the faith development interview instrument

The following section presents the faith development interview in detail, with instructions for the person administering the interview, suggested probes and follow-up questions, etc.

Biographical data and life tapestry exercise

The questions to be asked appear in italics. After each question, there follows, in parentheses, a list of the aspects to which that question is keyed. After many of the questions there are further instructions addressed to the interviewer, suggesting possible variations on the question, or possible probes and follow-up questions. A thorough familiarity with the aspects and with scoring procedures in general will greatly assist the interviewer in formulating his or her own probes and follow-up questions in an actual interview situation. Thus it is recommended that the prospective interviewer should have read the appropriate sections of this manual. Wherever possible, a list of often used probes and follow-ups has been provided with the questions; however, these will not cover all possible situations.

Begin the interview by reviewing the respondent's life tapestry and biographical data sheet. This is a good way to get the interview going, and gives you a chance to warm up to your interviewee as well. In your own review of the respondent's tapestry and biographical data prior to the interview, you have probably formulated some questions that you would like to clarify. This is the best time to ask those questions. Care should be taken, however, to keep this section of the interview as brief as possible. Respondents will sometimes want to expand upon the tapestry in great detail. While this is permissible, you will have to use your judgment as to how much time you want to allow for this first section.

Remember, the life tapestry exercise is not scored directly. However, it can provide considerable information that will be helpful in clarifying some of the responses to the questions themselves when it comes time to score them. Thus you can think of the tapestry as a type of baseline of information over against which the responses to the specific interview questions can be viewed. One possible way to proceed is to allow the respondent as much time as he/she wishes for this part of the interview and then decide whether or not to transcribe this section. A good interview should take 1 to 1½ hours. Beyond this, both interviewer and respondent begin to tire. (aspects: A, B, D, G)

Relationships

1. How do you think of or remember your parents at present? What stands out to you now about your Father or Mother? Can you describe them for me? Have there been any changes in your perceptions of your parents over the years? When? (aspects: B, E)

Interviewer: This question will yield data on the respondent's social perspective taking (aspect B) and relation to authority (aspect E). It is important for you to get a sense of whether or not your respondent is able to construct the interiority of his/her parents, i.e., has some sense of how they think or feel, and can describe things as they might have seen them, etc. Also, probe to see how the respondent constructs the relation of self to parents. Does she have the sense that parents also have an image or impression of her?

To what extent do parents still function as authority figures for the person, at least in her own mind? These questions can be probed by paying particular attention to the respondent's perception of changes in the relationship. What made these changes come about − changes in the parents, changes in the person, or both? It is not necessary that the respondent talk about his/her physical parents if there were other primary caretakers involved. The question applies to both.

2. Are there currently any relationships that seem important to you, either with persons or groups? Why do you think that these are important? (aspects: B, D, E)

Interviewer: Your respondent may experience some discontinuity between this question which asks for present relationships, and the previous one which may include reflection on the past. You may want to preface the question by a remark like, 'Let's go to the present for a moment,' if this seems appropriate. This question assumes that you have looked at the life tapestry, and have noted significant relationships from the past. If you have not talked about these, you might pursue the one or two most important ones as a follow-up to this question.

In probing this question, there are a number of things you will want to learn from your respondent. How is he/she thinking about relationships in general, and in what ways are they important? What is the attitude toward other people? To what extent do others function as authorities for this person? How does this person locate his or her own identity with respect to other persons or groups? How does he or she view their own participation in groups or organizations, etc.?

3. Do you recall any changes in relationships that have had a significant impact on your life or your way of thinking about things? (aspects: B, D, E)

Interviewer: The life tapestry will be of great help to you here. Make notes before the interview of significant relationships and marker events that you wish to follow up. Note that these relationships do not necessarily have to be with persons currently living or with persons whom the respondent has known personally. They could be relationships with writers or thinkers, for example, that the person knows only from books. What is important here is that you get some sense of the way the respondent views these relationships, then and now, and the way in which the respondent thinks about change. This will yield valuable data on how the respondent thinks about other people and groups and about authority.

Present values and commitments

1. Do you feel that your life has meaning at present? What makes life meaningful to you? (aspects: F, A, B, E, D)

Interviewer: This question has the potential to yield data on several aspects because it is so open-ended. It is important that you give the respondent the latitude to answer the question in his/her own way. It is not necessary that you cover all of the aspects on this question, but rather, focus on the one that the respondent's initial thoughts seem to go with. What you are looking for here is the locus of the respondent's meaning-making activities. Does the respondent's sense of meaning or meaninglessness center on interpersonal relations, for example, or upon some set of principles or a world view or on some sense of individual purpose. If the question is answered in the negative, you might probe to find out how the sense that life has no meaning came about, when it occurred, etc.

2. Are there any beliefs, values, or commitments that seem important to your life right now? (aspects: F, D, A)

Interviewer: Here you will want to learn how beliefs, values, and commitments are held, and also how they are enacted in a person's life. You are also interested in who or what supports the respondent's beliefs and values, and who or what might oppose them, how they have been derived and, to a lesser extent, how they may have changed. Some possible probes are: 'Can you give me an example of how that works for you?', 'How did you come to believe that?' or, 'Why do you believe that?', etc.

3. When you think of the future, how does it make you feel? Why? (aspects F, E, D)

Interviewer: This question is projective, and you will want to know what kind of a vision of the world is being disclosed in the respondent's projections of the possible future. It is also important to note the scope of the person's concern. Who comes to mind when he/she thinks about the future: self, family, country, world, etc.? If the initial response to the question is ambiguous, you may wish to probe for more specifics, for example, 'Why do you think that?' or, 'Who do you think will be most affected by that if it comes about?' etc. You are also looking here for signs of how the person assigns responsibility for the future, or whether he/she thinks of humanity as essentially good or evil, etc.

4. When you have an important decision to make, how do you generally go about making it? Can you give me an example? (aspects: C, B, E, D, A)

Interviewer: Here you will want to be sure to probe for a specific example of the person's decision-making process in action. In addition, note who or what functions as authority in an important decision, and where the weight is given − is it an internal or external authority? Note also whose point of view gets considered, and look for evidence, if any, that the respondent is able to think about an important decision from the constructed point of view of others who may be involved or affected by the decision.

5. Do you think that actions can be right or wrong? If so, what makes an action right in your opinion? Are there certain actions or types of actions that are always right under any circumstances? Are there certain moral opinions that you think everyone should agree on? (aspects: C, B, D, E)

Interviewer: It is important to get some sense of the way in which the respondent is thinking of issues like this. The question 'why?' is important.

6. If you have a question which you cannot decide or a very difficult problem to solve, to whom or what would you look for guidance? (aspects: D, E)

7. Do you think that people change significantly as they get older, or do they remain pretty much the same? Why? (aspects: F, A)

Religion

1. Do you think that human life has a purpose? If so, what do you think it is? Is there a plan for our lives, or are we affected by a power or powers beyond our control? (aspects: F, A)

Interviewer: Note that the responses to this question may or may not be given in religious terms. It is important to try to stay within the context that the respondent sets with this question. You may wish to invert questions 2 and 3 and ask question 3 next.

2. What does death mean to you? What happens to us when we die? (aspects: F, A, G)

Interviewer: If the response is 'I don't know', you may wish to probe it further. You might ask the respondent what he or she would hope for or what they think might be possible, etc.

3. Do you consider yourself a religious person? What does this mean to you? (aspects: F, A, G)

Interviewer: Note that if the answer to part one of the question is in the negative, you should still ask part two.

4. Are there any religious ideas, symbols or rituals that are important to you, or have been important to you? If so, what are these and why are they important? (aspects: G, A, F)

Interviewer: In this question you are interested not only in how the respondent thinks about specifically religious symbols, but also how these fit with the respondent's previously stated beliefs and attitudes. It is not necessary that these be presently meaningful. If the initial answer to the question is 'no' you may follow by asking if there have ever been meaningful symbols, rituals, or ideas, if this data is not obvious from the life tapestry. The question of why the idea, symbol, or ritual is important and what it means to the respondent is crucial, because you are also seeking data on how the respondent interprets symbols. If the respondent cannot recall any religious symbols, you might shift the question and ask if any ideas, symbols, or rituals at all are meaningful. If the response is 'no' you can ask the respondent to interpret a common symbol (e.g. the American flag, or the American eagle, etc.).

5. Do you pray, meditate, or perform any other spiritual discipline? (aspects: G, A)

Interviewer: It is important to get some sense of what the spiritual exercise means to the respondent. You might ask 'What do you think is happening when you do this?' or, 'Why do you do this?'

6. Do you think there is such a thing as sin or evil? (aspects: G, A, F, D)

Interviewer: This question also should be probed. If the initial response is negative, you might ask how the respondent accounts for suffering in the world. If the initial response is yes, try to find out what the respondent thinks is the cause of evil, what he/she thinks evil consists of, and how he/she derived his/her present concept of evil.

7. If people disagree about a religious issue, how can conflicts be resolved? (aspects: E, B, D, C, F)

Interviewer: You are looking at several aspects of faith in this question. It is possible that the respondent may answer with a request for a specific example, such as, 'That depends on what kind of conflict you mean' etc. In such cases you may suggest a hypothetical example like 'There are many different religions in the world and they seem to teach different things, what do you make of this?' In other words, one that is fairly general and open-ended is recommended.

You will also wish to consider several of the aspects of faith as the person is answering the question. What is the respondent's sense of how his or her own perspective on the world relates to that of others? Are some beliefs normative for everyone? What are the boundaries of whom he or she is willing to consider in resolving a religious dispute, etc.?

If the question is not meaningful to the respondent when phrased as a question about religious disputes, it may be rephrased as a question about ideas, political views, lifestyle choices, etc.

Crises and peak experiences

1. Have you ever had moments of intense joy or breakthrough experiences that have affirmed or changed your sense of life's meaning?

Interviewer: In this, and the other questions in this section, you may wish to refer to your notes on the individual's life tapestry and question your respondent about specific experiences to which he/she may have previously referred. It is important to try to elicit the respondent's thinking about what he/she thought was going on during the experience, and how the experience may have affected his or her life and thought. It is also important that these breakthrough experiences may not always be positive or interpreted positively by the respondent. They could, for example, be terrifying, demonic, confusing, etc.

2. Have you experienced times of crisis or suffering in your life, or times when you felt profound disillusionment, or that life had no meaning? What happened to you at these times? How have these experiences affected you?

3. Do you feel that you are currently growing or changing in any areas of your life. If so, where do you feel most in need of, or most open to change? What is your 'Growing Edge' at this point?

Interviewer: We recommend that the questions on crises and peak experiences be left until the last section of the interview rather than going into them in detail at the beginning when you are reviewing the life tapestry. This is to give you more flexibility in closing the interview. It is possible that the respondent may wish to discuss this section of the interview at some length, and, if you wish, you can make this time available to him/her. However, if your own time is limited, we suggest that you reach an agreement with the respondent in advance about how long the interview is to take, and stick to the agreed-upon limits.

Whatever you decide, you should close the interview after the respondent has answered question 3 in this section. Close by thanking the respondent, and asking if there is anything further he or she would like to add before you turn off the tape. This is important, as some respondents will want to add to or modify some of their answers to some of the interview questions at this time. It is important to offer the respondent a chance to do this, as it gives a sense of closure to the interview process and avoids the sense of frustration that can come if something is left hanging or not said.

Aspects of faith: a guide to aspect assignments

There is a certain irony in the fact that, after having empha-sized that faith is a structured whole, we must divide it into parts in order to analyze it. This is necessary, however, because the meaning-constitutive structures of knowing are not directly observable, but must be deduced from the ways in which a subject 'operates' on specific content areas. The seven aspects of faith thus represent windows on specific content domains for which the meaning-constitutive operations may be different. Never-theless, there is a dialectic between seeing faith as a whole, and seeing its constitutive parts. This shows up in interviews when one encounters responses that could be coded under several aspects. This is particularly evident in the later stages, where, because of increasing cognitive and affective integration, the boundaries between the aspects become more difficult to establish. One is forced toward a more 'gestaltist' interpretation of the later stages of faith when one observes the interpenetration of the various aspects at these stages.

The aspects of faith are in themselves complex clusters of cognitive skills that are structurally related. For example, one would expect that a person's construction of an object world and sense of the ultimate environment (form of world coherence) would also display a form of logic, and that one's form of moral judgment (aspect C) will be affected by one's ability to take the perspective of the other and by the boundaries of one's social awareness. In many interviews, this means that the aspect assignment will be much less critical than the stage assignment. We have endeavored to make the coding criteria within a given stage as consistent as possible across the aspects. This means that a response coded stage 3 in social perspective taking, for example, would also be coded stage 3 if the coder views it under the aspect of form of moral judgment. Where the aspect assignment becomes more critical is in the assessment of whether an interview indicates transition. We have found that in transitional interviews, the aspects are not as consistent as in more equilibrated interviews. In fact, one or more aspects may lead or lag behind the average by a whole stage. So it becomes necessary to establish a reasonable degree of interrater consistency in aspect assignment.

To do this, we have keyed the questions of the interview to the aspects of faith that they are most likely to elicit. This keying was done on both theoretical and empirical grounds, but we do need more data from this interview format to determine conclusively that this key is completely accurate. The aspects that each question was designed to elicit appear in the order of expected primacy on the interview guide. This can serve as a guide for you in making your initial aspect assignment for a given response. In all cases, however, the final aspect assignment should be made on the basis of your reading of the aspect descriptions, and not solely on the basis of the interview guide.

To assist you in making aspect assignments, we have prepared the following set of general descriptions of the aspects and the type of content that they typically contain. Also are included some questions that are designed to help you to clarify which aspect is the main one being addressed by a given response.

Aspect A: *form of logic*

This aspect describes the characteristic patterns of mental operations the person employs in thinking about the object world. The aspect is based on Piaget's analysis of the development of logical thinking; however it is limited to the generalized features of this development. Stages 1 through 4 follow Piaget's analysis quite closely, although there is some variation in the ages at which the operations appear. Stage 5, however, employs a dialectical form of reasoning that has been termed 'post-formal operational'. Dialectical reasoning can be thought of as a qualitative change in the way formal operations are employed.

Aspect B: social perspective taking

This aspect describes the way in which the person constructs the self, the other, and the relationship between them. To determine if a given response indicates social perspective taking, it is helpful to ask the following question: 'Does the response show how the person is constructing the interiority of the other person? Does it show how the individual is thinking about how the other person is thinking and feeling? Does it show how this relates to the person's knowledge of his or her own internal states?' An answer of 'yes' to any of the above indicates that the response deals with social perspective taking.

Aspect C: form of moral judgment

In assessing the form of moral judgment, we are looking at the patterns of a person's thinking about issues of moral significance including how the person defines what is to be taken as a moral issue and how the person answers the question of why be moral. This aspect answers the question, 'What is the nature of the claims that others have on me, and how are these claims to be weighed?' You will notice, too, that the stages of moral judgment, while similar to Kohlberg's stages of moral reasoning in many ways, also differ in some important ways. In the context of the faith development interview, moral judgment is seen as a complex skill involving not only patterns of reasoning, but grounds of moral justification, the boundaries of social inclusion and exclusion, and social perspective taking. This is due, in part, to the fact that the faith development interview uses a much different approach to data gathering than the Kohlberg moral dilemma test. We are asking more open-ended questions and requesting the respondent to answer them in his or her own way, rather than presenting the respondent with an already-defined moral problem or dilemma. We feel that this approach has the advantage of allowing respondents to formulate what constitutes moral problems on the basis of their own life experiences. However, when this open-ended approach is used, you do get a wider diversity of content material than you might expect on the Kohlberg instrument.

Aspect D: bounds of social awareness

This aspect has several dimensions. The mode of a person's group identification is a central one. It answers the question of how the person is viewing or constructing the group of which he or she is a member. (Note: throughout this manual the term 'group' is used in a broad generic sense. It can mean a family, circle of friends or more formal group affiliation.) It also includes how the person relates to the group to which he or she belongs. In addition, this aspect answers the question of how wide or inclusive is the social world to which a person will respond. Who is the person willing to include in his or her thinking and who remains alien? This aspect will also show the differences in how persons and groups are treated within a given individual's structure of meaning-making. To determine if a given response indicates the bounds of social awareness, ask these questions: Does it show how the person relates to his or her reference group? Does it show how the person views groups other than his or her own? Does it indicate who has a claim on me and to whom and for whom I am responsible?

Aspect E: locus of authority

The aspect, locus of authority, looks at three factors: how authorities are selected, how authorities are held in relationship to the individual, and whether the person responds primarily to internal or external authority. A statement may be coded under locus of authority if it answers any of the following questions: Does the person locate authority internally or externally? To whom or what does the person look for guidance or approval? To whom or what does the person hold himself or herself responsible? How does the person identify authority?

Aspect F: form of world coherence

This aspect describes how a person constructs the object world, including the sense of the ultimate environment. It answers the questions, 'How do things make sense?' or, 'How do the various elements of my experience fit together?' The form of world coherence is a type of cosmology, whether explicit or tacit. It includes the person's world view, but is not limited to that. It also includes the principles by which this world view is constructed, the logical relations by which elements of the world are held together. Strictly speaking, the form of world coherence can include the individual's construction of the social world. However, in actual interview texts, these elements are often better coded under the aspects of social perspective taking or bounds of social awareness.

Aspect G: symbolic function

This aspect of faith is concerned with how the person understands, appropriates, and utilizes symbols and other aspects of language in the process of meaning-making and locating his or her centers of value and images of power. Any passage which reveals how a person interprets symbolic material, particularly those symbols which are important to the individual, can be coded under this aspect.

Relationships among the aspects

One can see from the above that the aspects of faith are interrelated. In fact, they might be said to form clusters of content areas. Form of logic, form of world coherence, and symbolic function express more clearly cognitive content, and thus form one interrelated cluster. Social perspective taking, the bounds of social awareness, and the form of moral judgment represent psychosocial as well as cognitive content, and thus form another interrelated cluster.

The aspects of faith represent complex skills and competences, and as such will sometimes tend to overlap in some content areas. The interrelatedness of the aspects may cause some ambiguity in coding some passages because elements of several aspects may be represented at once. For example, it is difficult to think about moral judgments without employing social perspective taking in some form; however, this is not always true of all types of moral judgment, thus we say the aspects of faith are related, but cannot be collapsed into one another.

With most interviews, aspect coding is less critical than it might at first seem. While it is necessary to assign a given passage to a specific aspect in order to get a stage code, care has been taken to make the stage criteria consistent across aspects within a given stage. Thus, if a given passage could, in theory, be assigned to stage 3 under the aspect of form of world coherence, it should also be scorable as stage 3 under the aspect form of logic. In most cases, aspect assignment will not affect the stage code of a given passage.

Aspect assignment becomes more critical, however, in interviews that display transition. We have found that in transitional interviews, one aspect will often, but not always, lead or lag behind the others, or there may actually be conflict between the aspects. For example, a person may employ a particular form of social perspective taking that leads him to feel that a certain action is correct or right. The form of authority to which the person gives allegiance, however, may not permit the action. Such conflicts or contradictions between aspect domains are usually indicators of stage transition. Thus, in assessing the transitional interview, it is important to achieve interrater consistency in aspect assignment.

Stage 1: intuitive-projective faith

Stage 1 bears the highest correlation with age of any of the stages of faith. Fully 88% of the respondents under six years of age in our original sample were classified as Stage 1. The reason for these high correlations is that the patterns of meaning-making activity that we are calling stage 1 are more directly linked to biological maturation and language acquisition, and less to environmental and social factors than those of the later stages.

Structurally, stage 1 is associated with Piaget's 'pre-operational' stage, that is, the stage prior to the emergence of concrete operations. Because of this, we often have a tendency to think of stage 1 in negative terms, that is, in terms of the things the person at stage 1 cannot do. It is true that the logical capacities of the person at stage 1 seem limited when viewed from the perspective of the later stages. Prior to the emergence of concrete operations, the child has little sense of cause and effect relationships. He or she is not able to think abstractly or to make generalizations from experience. The categories of space and time are not clearly constructed at stage 1, so the person at this stage is not able to order experience in the manner that older children and adults conveniently do. Still, we would do well to resist the impulse to view stage 1 merely as a deficient mode of the later stages. There are complex processes at work at this stage that profoundly influence the ways in which later development unfolds.

What then are the positive features which identify the stage? Stage 1 is marked by egocentric thought. The person at stage 1 does not distinguish readily between fantasy and reality and often will blend the two together. In addition, the person at stage 1 does not differentiate between the object and the way that it appears to him or her. Thus the world of stage 1 is comprised in part by numinous projections and fantasy which make it magical and unpredictable.

There is little ability at stage 1 to take the perspective of the other. The self is not clearly differentiated from the object world at this stage. Interactions with others therefore are largely a matter of moment-to-moment episodes. The primary attachment of the stage 1 person is to the family or primary caretakers.

Thought and language develop along separate but related tracks in early childhood. Thinking first involves 'sensori-motor' knowing while language is acquired later. Only gradually does language come under the service of thought and begin to structure it. Thus the interpersonal interactions of the person at stage 1 are not often as verbal as they become at later stages of development. The child interacts with body and gesture as much as with words. By stage 2 language has become more properly the medium of social interaction.

A further characteristic of stage 1 meaning-making that is quite evident in the faith development interview is that thought at stage 1 is fluid, episodic, and seemingly unconnected. Stage 1 works by moment to moment association, rather than logical construction.

Often its associational images are striking and original. Stage 1 gives a freedom to the imagination that is not present at other stages.

Cognitive processes at stage 1 are typically one-dimensional. By this we mean that the child at stage 1 often sees and responds to phenomena only in parts or fragments. This is because, at the later stages, perception is often 'filled in' by previous experience. We 'see' much more than we perceive. The child at stage 1 appears to be responding only to the immediate effects of stimuli that impinge upon him, and often can be overwhelmed or overloaded by strong or intense stimuli.

Stage 2: mythic-literal faith

With the beginnings of concrete operational thought, which usually takes place in the seventh year, the logical ligatures by which objects and events can be tied together are now in place. This means that the individual, by the time he reaches stage 2, is able to connect events into meaningful patterns, to relate and to classify objects. Thus the episodic and impressionistic world of stage 1 is transformed into a world of order and coherence. At stage 2 the ability to construct a sense of time emerges along with the idea of physical causality.

The world at stage 2 is more ordered and dependable than the episodic world of stage 1. However, it does not yet display the ability to construct collectives that becomes evident at stage 3, nor the rationally systematic qualities that we observe at stage 4. When the person is at stage 2 during childhood (ages 7 – 12) he may typically be a 'young empiricist', interested in the physical characteristics of things, and in the concrete links between things and events. The person at stage 2 is able to distinguish fantasy from reality and is very concerned with making this distinction. The person at this stage begins to rely on his own logic and judgment.

Coupled with the increasing differentiation of thought patterns comes an increasing interest in the way events are connected. The ability to construct space and time at stage 2 gives the person at this stage an increasing fascination with narrative and story and the ability to comprehend and relate stories. Stage 2 persons usually prefer to hear and tell stories that are literal and concrete. Action, adventure and stories that relate to concrete life situations begin to replace fairy tales and fantasy as preferred fare. It is not that fantasy is suppressed at stage 2, but that it has become more concrete and realistic. The stage 2 person projects himself or herself into the myths and stories which he or she creates. In fact, the person at stage 2 cannot separate herself from the narrative texture of the stories she hears and tells. Play becomes enacted narrative. The appropriation of story and myth at this stage is literal, concrete and univocal. The symbols and images of a tradition can make a powerful and lasting impression on a person at this stage.

The interpersonal world also undergoes transformation at stage 2. The social horizon, in our culture at least, typically is widened to include friends, teachers and other members of the wider community. The realm of authority now extends beyond the family and primal others to include teachers, religious leaders, the media, books and the ideas of friends. The person at stage 2 is able to construct the perspective of another, but still in a relatively concrete way.

There is little real notion of the interiority of the other at this stage, but the person at stage 2 will notice, for example, that an object can look different to a person standing on the other side of the room. He has the type of concrete image of the other that is necessary to write a letter, for example. The new perspective taking ability gives the person at stage 2 the ability to evaluate and respond to authorities in more complex ways than at stage 1. Consistency, orthodoxy and the perceived fit between the values and attitudes of significant others become criteria by which the claims of authority are evaluated. The person at stage 2 will consider intentions and motives in evaluating actions, and he or she will ask for reasons when asked to do something.

Stage 3: synthetic-conventional faith

Stage 3 is called synthetic-conventional faith because the person at stage 3 is utilizing advanced perspective taking skills and early formal operational thought to 'synthesize' meanings that are based largely on a felt sense of the attitudes and opinions of others. On the surface, stage 3 can be easily recognized because it is characterized by an intense concern for the building and maintaining of interpersonal relationships. Concrete others and interpersonal harmony become the center of value for the person at stage 3 in his or her faith development. Conventional authority that is perceived to be harmonious with the maintenance of interpersonal relations becomes his or her image of power.

Stage 3 interviews can present unusual difficulties for the interpreter, however, for several reasons. Primarily, because the content issues of stage 3, the concern with the building and maintenance of interpersonal relationships, are pervasive concerns for most human beings throughout life. The question that the interpreter must decide is not simply whether the person is concerned with personal relationships, or even how central a place these concerns may have in the individual's overall structure of meaning-making activity. Rather, the interpreter must direct attention to the patterns of cognitive and affective activity that the individual displays in his or her construction of the sense of relationship itself, of the sense of self and other, and to the types of life experiences that have gone into forming these patterns. It is, thus, very important for the interviewer or coder to be able to distinguish between structure and content when evaluating a stage 3 interview. In order to develop this skill, it is necessary to familiarize oneself with the basic structural features of the stage. In this context, 'structure' may be taken to mean the patterns of mental operations by which content is addressed, appropriated, understood and transformed.

A second source of difficulty in interpreting the stage 3 interview stems from the fact that, in our culture, a considerable number of adults find a more or less permanent equilibration at stage 3. The stage, thus, has both adolescent and adult versions which the coder must bear in mind. We shall point out some of the likely differences between adult and adolescent examples of stage 3 below.

Finally, because our culture generally does not provide a range of ideological alternatives around which stage 4 processes can initially be organized, it has been found to be fairly common for the transition from stage 3 to stage 4 to be a protracted one, often lasting several years. It is quite probable that the researcher will encounter interviews containing mixtures of stages 3 and 4 that cover a wide range of ages, from late adolescence to the mid-thirties and beyond. Thus age alone is not apt to be a very reliable clue for coding an interview above stage 2.

Stage 3 has been labeled 'conventional' and there is the initial temptation to label all interview statements that reflect supposedly conventional attitudes and beliefs as stage 3. It must be borne in mind, however, that 'conventional' is a relative term. It is relative to culture and to the social context within which an individual operates. Thus the political radical, or the adolescent who enjoys 'punk' rock may be conventional when viewed against their own contexts of relationship. The life tapestry should be helpful in locating an individual within a context of social relations. Beyond that, it is necessary to pay attention to how the person's values and commitments have been formed, and the thought processes employed in constructing them.

The type of mutual perspective taking that stage 3 is capable of requires some formal operational thought, and thus the stage is unlikely to emerge before age 12 or 13. The person at stage 3 is capable of constructing a sense of the collective and this requires abstraction. A person may display concern with interpersonal relationships at stage 2, but this concern is characteristically concrete and instrumental. Stage 3 displays a more abstract valuing of relationship for its own sake. It orients toward mutuality and shared feelings and emotions. However, the person at stage 3 is not yet able to place the other, or the sense relationship within the context of a larger system or whole. This capacity does not emerge until stage 4. For the adolescent this sense of the collective or 'generalized other', to use George Herbert Mead's term, is new, precisely because it emerges with formal operations. This fact alone may well account for some of the power that these images usually have for the adolescent at stage 3. For the adolescent, the weight of power and authority is usually given to the other and not to the self. This may not be as noticeable in adult versions of stage 3.

Thinking at stage 3 will not generally display the explicit and rationally mediated system consciousness which stage 4 identifies. Not only does this reflect the limitations of early formal operational thought, but it reflects the fact that at stage 3 the sense of a reflective self that can stand apart from social relations and choose among relational contexts is not yet evident. Stage 3 is concerned with my friends, my family and my group. Thus in attempting to distinguish the stage 3 interview from one that may be stage 4 or 3−4 transitional, it is helpful to ask the question whether the person's stated values and attitudes are likely to reflect a rather straightforward and global or undifferentiated appropriation of the values of his or her group, or whether there is some evidence of the subject having abstracted from these concrete relationships some more abstract sense of general rules of relationship itself which can be applied to others not concretely known.

In the adolescent version of stage 3, we observe a rekindling of the egocentric thought patterns which are similar, but more complex than those observed as stage 1. Stage 3 often displays globally held ideas and concepts that have not been critically examined. There is also a blending of fantasy and reality that often takes the form of grandiose fantasies or the desire to change society.

This adolescent egocentricism is caused by cognitive change, the loss of the sureties of childhood in the widening of the social arena, and the conflict inherent in trying on adult roles. The emergence of formal operational thought brings a new freedom to the mind which can result in the release of fantasy, both grandiose and romantic. Piaget has related adolescent fantasy behavior to the developmental project of trying out adult roles and finding one's place in adult society. 'Grandiose adolescent projects are, in a large majority of cases, a sophisticated game of compensation whose goals are self-assertion, the imitation of adult role models and participation in circles that are actually closed.' In the adult version of stage 3, however, these fantasies are apt to be tempered with age and experience and will not be as evident. They may even be replaced with a sense of resignation or powerlessness which is evidence that the cognitive structures of stage 3 are still operative.

A further distinction between stages 3 and 4 is possible on the basis of how the self is viewed. Persons at both stages are usually concerned with issues of identity, of 'having a self' or of 'being oneself'. At stage 4, however, the sense of self is distinguished from others usually because it is identified with a system of ideas or relationships. Lacking this more abstract locus of identity, stage 3 is not apt to differentiate itself from the relationships in which it is engaged. Rather, it is apt to possess a globally held sense of mutuality and emotional commonality with members of its own group and to project these feelings on other groups 'like us'. So, while the person at stage 3 may be able to say, 'I have a self,' and may in fact appear quite concerned with aspects of selfhood, the sense that accompanies the word 'self' is different at stage 3 than at stage 4.

As Robert Kegan has noted, private relations are the ground of the personality at stage 3, rather than a figure in the object environment. The person functioning at stage 3 orients toward the other, especially with respect to shared internal states, moods, feelings and emotions. Cognitively, the stage synthesizes meanings and values from a composite of valued others, and seeks the approval of these others in order to have a sense of self. Thus there is a strong orientation toward the values of interpersonal harmony and concordance, toward appearances and toward meeting the expectations of others, in particular, the tacit 'generalized other' that the person constructs from the composite of his or her concrete social relations at stage 3.

Stage 4: individuative-reflective faith

Several key characteristics mark the emergence of stage 4 structures of meaning-making. The first of these may be termed individuation: the critical distancing of the individual from the matrix of his or her social relations which forms the derived identity of stage 3. At the same time, we observe a break with the individual's reliance on external, and often tacit, forms of authority. At stage 3, we speak of the person's identity as a derived identity, as one constituted more or less directly by the matrix of social relations. The scope of personal expression that individuals at stage 3 allow themselves is constrained by the norms of the groups to which they belong. Persons at stage 3 are subject to what Sharon Parks terms 'the tyranny of the "they".' Clothing fads and language behavior of persons in the early teenage years is a good example from our culture of what is meant by a derived identity. At stage 3 meaning-making is interpersonal: values and conflicts are located in real relationships between persons. At stage 4, however, the locus of meaning-making shifts, and both values and conflicts move inside. The person at stage 4 typically adopts a more individuated and personal style.

Stage 4 originates in two separate but related developmental factors: the attainment of formal operational thought (typically in early to mid-teens) and the widening of social horizons (in our culture during late adolescence). In interpreting an interview that you suspect might be stage 4, aspects A (form of logic), B (social perspective taking), E (locus of authority), and G (symbolic functioning) are particularly telling.

The change in the stage 4 person's centers of value and images of power is often precipitated by an encounter with groups or persons other than the one which supported the individual at stage 3. A move away to college or getting one's first job often makes it necessary for the individual to relate to persons who are markedly different from those persons to whom he or she is accustomed. This experience can start the move toward 'finding one's own identity.' The interviewer-scorer should note, however, that while this type of encounter is typical of the transition from stage 3 to 4, it is not necessary. Evidence from the life tapestry exercise that such an experience has occurred may give support for interpreting ambiguous passages as suggesting stage 4. The move to break with the derived identity of stage 3 faith will often entail the voluntary adoption of a markedly different worldview or ideology.

Interpersonally, stage 4 is the time of autonomy. The consolidation of formal operational thinking allows the self as a distinct and self-conscious entity to emerge for the first time. At stage 4, the individual is capable of saying, 'I have a self. I have a worldview', conditions which were not clearly recognized at stage 1.

The emergence of this sense of an autonomous self at stage 4 means that the person at this stage will be concerned with defining the boundaries of this 'self,' with disassociating with relationships which controlled the self at stage 3, and with re-establishing relationships with self-selected others and groups. Thus, in a stage 4 interview one would find statements that suggest a recognition of group norms and values as worldviews, as well as a desire to rationally and critically examine these values and norms in order to locate the self with respect to them.

While it is true that the person at stage 4 has typically gone through experiences which have 'disembedded' him or her from the context of primary group relations, this stage is not always individualistic to the point of lacking group affiliations. Rather statements reflecting critical distance from the relationships themselves and attempts to maintain voluntary and self-selected associations are prime indicators of stage 4 thought processes. The person at Stage 4 recognizes that group and class viewpoints are relative and particular, and is able to translate individual and group norms into explicit concepts. This ability itself allows the person at stage 4 to distance himself or herself from the opinions of others and to locate his or her own position with respect to the chosen group. The person at stage 4 knows what he or she believes and is able to express it.

We draw from Erik Erikson the insight that stage 4 faith is characteristically ideological. Since the person at stage 4 is primarily concerned with defining the boundaries of the self, one can expect interviews at stage 4 to involve a rational defense of that person's ideology or worldview. Stage 4 is the time of attempting to work out one's 'philosophy of life,' and the person at stage 4 is often attracted to conceptual systems which promise to encompass the whole of reality. At stage 4 there is always a self-conscious awareness of having a worldview, and of the need to justify this viewpoint in the face of competing ideologies.

Although thinking at stage 4 is critical and rational, the self can often be 'over-identified' with the systems and worldviews it uses to define and maintain its boundaries. Stage 4 thinking can place too much confidence in the power of autonomous reason, and thus tend toward reductionism. The major strengths of this stage are at the same time its major weaknesses. Stage 4 thought is system-oriented and dichotomizing. It seeks to construct and maintain fairly rigid distinctions between subject and object, the knower and the known, the self and the other. It is formalistic in that it understands reality in terms of systems and laws rather than in concrete, particular matters.

The concern with self-definition and boundary maintenance which characterizes stage 4 means that matters of work and career, as well as one's competence and autonomy will also be key issues at this stage. Although these issues in themselves are content and not structure, the interviewer or coder should note that these 'content' issues have a particular salience at stage 4 because they point to special patterns of meaning-making which are indicative of this stage.

The concern with systems and logical relationships at stage 4 extends to the self as well. The self is typically viewed as a 'system' of ideas, needs, drives and potentials that must be directed and controlled. Stage 4 interviews may display a concern with establishing self-chosen standards by which the self is to be evaluated. Persons at stage 4 also govern their relationships with others by abstract rules or laws of relationships. Thus the particular, concrete relationships which govern the self at stage 3 are now brought under the control of self-chosen 'laws of relationship.' Stage 4 is more properly characterized by a commitment to systems and institutions, rather than concrete relationships.

Stage 5: conjunctive faith

Although the pattern of mental operations at stage 5 is difficult to describe succinctly, the visible features of this stage's cognitive style are not difficult to recognize. We have used the word 'dialogical' to summarize the process of meaning-making at stage 5. It is through an ongoing dialogue with reality, characterized by openness and mutuality, that the individual at stage 5 locates his or her images of value and power.

Interview statements that represent stage 5 modes of meaning-making generally display a greater fluidity and lack of concrete boundaries than those of stage 4. Care must be taken, however, not to confuse the open-endedness of meaning-making at stage 5 with the lack of conceptual clarity that one may encounter in interviews from the earlier stages.

Statements reflecting stage 4 patterns generally show a concern with the definition and maintenance of conceptual system boundaries and with identifying with one system of meaning as the definitive one against which others are measured. Stage 5 interviews, however, will generally reflect the awareness that one lives within a plurality of meaning systems and that these may be associated with different employments of the mind or methods. Stage 5 reflects not only an awareness of the possibility of multiple or multi-layered meanings, but an active embracing of this possibility for richness and depth. This embracing of multiple meanings and perspectives, and the attempt to hold these in a critical tension without reductionism is a key characteristic of faith at stage 5.

Broadly understood, phenomenological reflection may be thought of as the characteristic method of stage 5 thinking. Individuals at stage 5 are generally aware of the many modes of meaning-constitutive mental activity and the many perspectives they can generate. The individual at stage 5 does not reject this plurality as a source of confusion nor seek to reduce it to a simpler scheme, but will embrace this feature of reality as a possible source of deeper understanding, allowing reality to present different aspects of itself to awareness.

The person at stage 5 seeks understanding rather than explanation. He or she is less interested in defending a worldview, excluding facts and interpretations from consideration, or fitting them into a pre-existing conceptual framework. Interview statements at Stage 5 generally display a conscious understanding that multiple perspectives are not only possible, but necessary, reflecting the ability to shift from one perspective to another in order to illuminate different aspects of a question or problem.

Statements at stage 5 also display a consciousness of limits: not only the limits of any particular perspective, but the limits of understanding itself. These statements often reflect a rekindled sense of the mystery of being and an increasing sense of the importance of that which remains hidden. Analytical perspectives, worldviews and conceptual systems may illuminate one aspect of a phenomenon only by casting other aspects in shadow. Thus at stage 5 we have the sense that reality is complex and often ambiguous, that human understanding has limits. In a sense stage 5 has reopened the questions which stage 4 had foreclosed. At stage 5 there also will appear the sense that human understanding is mediated, i.e. that it does not represent reality directly, but rather that human cognition is a tool that allows reality to present itself in its own language.

One finds in contemporary philosophy many examples of the general contours of stage 5 thought. The phenomenology of Edmund Husserl, the ontology of Martin Heidegger, the dialogical method of Martin Buber and the philosophical hermeneutics of Hans Georg Gadamer and Paul Ricoeur give us philosophical descriptions of the cognitive patterns of stage 5. It must be emphasized, however, that one need not have a completely articulated philosophical theory to be functioning at stage 5.

A further feature of stage 5 is its willingness to embrace the tensions and polarities that a multi-perspective approach to reality is bound to generate. Stage 5 may have some intuitions of universality that aid in ordering multiple perspectives, or direct one through their use. Stage 5, however, generally resists the temptation to deal with conflict and dissonance by collapsing polarities. Rather it tends to accept them as a necessary feature of reality. This is true for the social, moral and interpersonal world of stage 5 as well. Stage 5 is conscious of the need to balance individual interests with those of the larger community and world.

The sense of limits to understanding which is characteristic of stage 5 may bring with it an increased emphasis on human subjectivity and the need for individual decision in the face of an ambiguous reality. It can also be reflected in an increased awareness of the historical and temporal nature of understanding. The person at stage 5 will usually be aware of himself or herself as standing in a particular culture, tradition or historical epoch, and will take this into account in interpreting and assessing the thoughts and actions of others. Thus stage 5 has a self-critical dimension. The capacity for self-questioning and self-doubt are both present at stage 5 in a more salient way than at stage 4. With this capacity for self-criticism there often appears a genuine openness to the other and the realization that one does not possess all of the truth. The person at stage 5 is willing to engage the other and to be changed by the other in a way that was not possible from the posture of stage 4.

Stage 6: universalizing faith

Stage 6 involves an overcoming of the paradoxes of stage 5. Structurally, we believe it is produced by a furthering of the de-centration process and by the growth of greater inclusiveness in social perspective taking. To state this more clearly, the person at stage 5 acts and thinks from conflict. He or she realizes the limitations of our finite grasp on truth, and further, recognizes that action necessitates often hard choices among competing goods or values. In addition, the person at stage 5 has the awareness that something is lost as well as gained in every such decision. The stage 5 mode of meaning-making is multi-leveled. This means that the claims of self, family, and one's own group can still exert a reasoned, but nevertheless powerful, influence upon the individual. At stage 6, these more narrowly egoic concerns are transcended because they are ordered by an all-encompassing ideal or vision of the good that is indicative of a sense of relationship to and participation in the whole or totality of being.

We need to underscore at the outset that our description of stage 6 is not, strictly speaking, empirically derived. That is, we did not discover a few persons at stage 6 and proceed to deduce the characteristics of the stage from our conversations with them. Would that it were so; but in practice, stage 6 is exceedingly rare.

It is better to think of stage 6 as the teleological (and eschatological) extension of the theory, a type of normative image of what human development can be, and an image that functions teleologically to draw the individual beyond the paradoxes of stage 5. This image is informed partly by a logical extension of the features of cognitive developmental theory (particularly the descriptions of stage 5), partly by the study of the biographies of past and present moral and religious leaders, and partly by the normative images of the major religious traditions.

Because of the teleological nature of our characterization of stage 6, the coder should not expect to find statements of stage 6 consistently throughout an interview. However, in interviewing adults, statements that are possibly stage 6 are often found scattered in an interview that is primarily stage 5, for example. Thus it is necessary to have some criteria for distinguishing statements that are possibly stage 6 if we are to be able to code stages 4 and 5 accurately by our averaging method. We find, in fact, that there are indeed criteria by which statements at stage 6 can be distinguished from those at stage 5, although they must be stated in a more tentative and open-ended manner than some of the criteria for the previous stages.

We have stated that our description of faith at stage 6 is based in part on logical extensions of what can be observed at stage 5. The person at stage 5 lives in the tension between vaguely apprehended universalizing ideas and the concrete demands of an individual, particular existence. One of the central issues that confronts persons at stage 5 is the experience of negation and the resultant consciousness of one's finitude and limitations. It has been said that religion begins with negation, rather than affirmation. Similarly, the transition to stage 6 is not likely to occur without the experience of the negation of one's personhood, either directly or through one's identification with the suffering of others.

The person at stage 5, re-awakened to the depth dimension of human existence and confronted with his or her own limits, has the possibility of experiencing negation of self at many levels and from many sources. If life is to retain meaning in the face of these negations, some way to move beyond them or some way to render them meaningful must be found. This meaning-making appears possible only through a further act of de-centration which enables one's consciousness to transcend the limits of self-concern, thus transcending one side of the paradox. This type of de-centration, however, is not a full resolution. The paradox of individual concerns, versus concerns of the wider community of being, can only be partially mediated by ascetic self-denial. What seems to have occurred in the biographies which suggest lives at stage 6 is an active and conscious giving over of oneself to a relatedness, a participation in a wider community that becomes extended to include all of humankind.

If this move occurs permanently, what results is a radical recentration and reconstruction of one's perceived relationship to the principle of being itself. It is a felt-relationship powerful enough to make all previous loyalties seem relative. It is not that other loyalties, such as the concern for one's own well being, disappear at stage 6, but that previous finite loyalties, centers of value and power are rendered relative to and ordered by emerging loyalty to the principle of being.

It must be borne in mind, however, that the above description of the crisis of persons at stage 5 involves the possibility of a negative as well as a positive resolution. The person at stage 5 must find a way to preserve a sense of life's meaning in the face of negation. If the de-centration mentioned above does not occur, there remain two possibilities: that the person will remain at stage 5 and continue to live in that tension, or that the person will conclude that life is ultimately without meaning and will slip into depression or even madness. The passage to stage 6 is not without risk.

It should be remembered as well that stage 6 is universalizing – and not necessarily universal – faith. We are discussing meaning-making activity by which certain, rare individuals are able to construct a sense of relatedness to, and participation in, the whole. This kind of human maturity, if it comes at all, is not easily won, and is the result of years of struggle well past the middle years of life.

Notes
1. We would like to thank Dr Marvin Acklin of Loyola University in Chicago, Dr Richard Bradley of Ohio State University, and Mr Terrence Kukor of the University of Miami, Ohio, for their most helpful contributions to this part of the project.

2. Fowler evaluated

Much of the rest of this volume falls under the heading of an evaluation of Fowler's faith development theory. In this section we have drawn together four very general critiques: two broadly positive and two that are more negatively critical. They are evaluations that touch on the theological, philosophical and psychological strengths and weaknesses of Fowler's work.

C. Ellis Nelson is a well-known Christian education-alist in the United States, whose own work on Christian formation has been widely appreciated. In his 1982 paper he criticizes Fowler for going too far in relating human faith development to religion, in particular by using the image of the Kingdom of God to give substance to his 'normative' stage 6. For Nelson, Fowler's human 'faith' is best seen as 'the capacity and natural desire of a person to become socialized'. Our *selves* may develop, but we should not speak about the development of human faith — only about our struggle to create meaning. In addition to these criticisms, and others of a broadly theological and conceptual nature, Nelson is also sceptical of Fowler's research method because of the limitations of interview data. (It should be noted that Nelson, with his co-author Daniel Aleshire, scrutinizes Fowler's research in much greater depth in a later study where, while recognizing a number of problems, he concludes that: 'his research methods are, by and large, quite consistent with his structuralist approach'.[1]) Nelson's paper, 'Does faith develop?: An evaluation of Fowler's position', was first published in *Living Light*, vol. 19, pp. 162–173.

The next two papers go together, as Smith's essay is partly a reply to that of Webster. These are both British scholars writing in the mid-1980s and the discussion reveals the early influence of Fowler's work across the

Atlantic. Derek Webster is another religious education-
alist who mounts a broad attack on Fowler's scheme. He
begins with doubts about the reliability of the research
design, the conceptual analysis that produces the seven
aspects of faith (asking 'why are perception, volition
and even humour excluded?'), and the account of faith
'from the human angle'. Many of Webster's questions
relate to the relationship between faith development and
Lawrence Kohlberg's account of the development of moral
judgment. 'James Fowler's theory of faith development'
was first published in *British Journal of Religious Education*, vol. 7, no. 1, 1984, pp. 14–18.

Many of these points are taken up by Marion Smith in
her 'Answers to some questions about faith development'
published in a subsequent issue of *British Journal of
Religious Education* (vol. 8, no. 2, 1986, pp. 79–83).[2] Smith
clarifies and defends Kohlberg's cognitive-developmental
model, as well as Fowler's comments about the relative precedence of moral development and faith development. She
also argues that Fowler's view of faith is not incompatible
with biblical and theological accounts (citing articles by
both Karl Rahner and Rudolf Bultmann).

Sharon Parks's essay, 'Faith development in a changing
world', first published in *The Drew Gateway*, vol. 60, no.
1, 1990, pp. 4–21, brings us back to the North American
debate. She argues that Fowler's work 'both reflects and
addresses some of the central challenges that beset North
American culture'. Parks is a former pupil of Fowler
whose own work on the faith development of young
adults offers an illuminating revision of Fowler's scheme.[3]
In the present essay Parks argues that faith development
theory provides us with a way of speaking of faith that
chimes in with contemporary concerns, particularly with
our concerns about 'the reality of change and pluralism
in a secular world' and with the place of psychology
in providing insight into the human condition. Parks
writes positively both of the potential of faith development theory to relate positively to theological thinking
and of 'the quality of the ethical fiber at the core of
the theory'. But she also usefully surveys the range of

criticisms that have been made of Fowler's concept of faith and of some of the details of his account of its development. She includes here comments from a critical social-political perspective, including those which accuse Fowler of showing gender-bias.

Notes

1. C. Ellis Nelson and Daniel Aleshire, 'Research in faith development', in Craig Dykstra and Sharon Parks (eds), *Faith Development and Fowler*, Birmingham, Alabama, Religious Education Press, 1986, p. 199. For an early critique of Fowler's research procedure, see Alfred McBride, 'Reaction to Fowler: fears about procedure', in Thomas C. Hennessy (ed.), *Values and Moral Development*, New York, Paulist Press, 1976, pp. 211–218.
2. See also Marion Smith, 'Developments in faith', *The Month* (July, 1986) and 'Progress in faith development', *The Month* (March, 1986).
3. See Sharon Parks, *The Critical Years: the young adult search for a faith to live by*, San Francisco, Harper and Row, 1986, and paper 5.3 below.

2.1 Does faith develop? An evaluation of Fowler's position

C. Ellis Nelson

Physical maturation can be documented. We know that physical growth is faster at some stages than others. Yet by middle adolescence the body, including the brain, has completed whatever physical development the genetic code dictated.

Morality is related to age in some fashion. No one would expect four-year-old children to know the long-range implication of their actions. Our law courts do not hold children accountable for their behaviour as they do adults. But how people develop morally, especially beyond adolescence, is not known with any degree of exactness.

When we turn to the spiritual realm, things become even more uncertain. In some ways religious faith is related to the condition and the needs of the body, the state of mental development and training, social conditioning (including religious environment), special events that happen, and the way that people relate all of these matters to their idea of God. Religious faith can grow and it can also decline in importance. None of these statements about the nature of religious faith is new – we could find historical and biblical references to illustrate each one.

Measuring religion

What is fairly new is an effort to measure or give some kind of quantitative judgment about religion, the meaning of religion, or moral behaviour that might be attributed to religion.

Measurement came to religion from psychology. Early efforts to measure intelligence proved fruitful, and such tests were widely used for the first time in the United States during World War I. In the 1920s some religious educators became interested in obtaining empirical data about religion and began to use various methods of measuring. Perhaps the most comprehensive book on this subject was published by Goodwin Watson in 1927, *Experimentation and Measurement in Religious Education*.

During this time and at the same place, Hugh Hartshorne and Mark A. May completed their well known *Studies in the Nature of Character* (1928). Thus was opened the modern era of applying research methods to religious or moral development. Ernest Ligon and Robert Havighurst, each from different perspectives and over a long period of time, engaged in classifying and judging moral development. Ronald Goldman's research, *Religious Thinking from Childhood to Adolescence* (1964), was probably the first thorough application of Jean Piaget's idea of mental development to religious education.

Piaget also influenced Lawrence Kohlberg, the man who has dominated the discussion of moral development in America for the past quarter of a century. Kohlberg has developed and refined a stage theory of moral development. Although there are critics of Kohlberg's stage theory, few alternate theories have received such widespread attention.

According to a biographical note in his book, *Stages of Faith*,[1] James Fowler, while a graduate student at Harvard working in the field of systematic theology, was teaching a 'stage-like' development of faith when some of his students asked if he knew the work of Kohlberg. This comment led to a friendship with Kohlberg and a study of stage development theory.

Over a period of some years Fowler has explored the theory that faith develops in stages somewhat like the stages Kohlberg has proposed for moral development. The book *Stages of Faith* is the first complete report on his work, although Fowler has published many articles describing his theory and citing supporting data.

The purpose of this paper is to make a critical estimate of *Stages of Faith* for Christian education.

Fowler's faith

One is advised to take the title *Stages of Faith* seriously. The subtitle gives the intent of the book: *the psychology of human development and the quest for meaning.*

People with a religious interest will automatically assume that the book is about religious faith, but Fowler is careful to rule out that interpretation. His idea of faith is expressed in these words (p. xiii)[2]:

> I believe that faith is a human universal. We are endowed at birth with nascent capacities for faith. How these capacities are activated and grow depends to a large extent on how we are welcomed into the world and what kind of environments we grow in. Faith is interactive and social; it requires community, language, ritual and nurture. Faith is also shaped by initiatives from beyond us and other people, initiatives of spirit or grace. How these latter initiatives are recognized and imaged, or unperceived and ignored, powerfully affects the shape of faith in our lives.

This definition describes a human quality, not a religious faith. In order to maintain clarity, I will use the term 'human faith' whenever referring to Fowler's theory in order not to confuse it with 'religious faith.'

Human faith to Fowler is a patterned process by which we find life meaningful (p. 3). Human faith is therefore 'not always religious' in its content or context (p. 4). He uses W. C. Smith to make the point that human faith is universal: and on that common human quality, many religious traditions have been formed (pp. 9–12). Human faith, according to Smith, struggles for meaning even if there is no religion to support, enhance or illuminate the quest for meaning (p. 10).

Following Smith, Fowler points out that 'belief' can mean an expression of human faith in the sense of 'setting one's heart on something'; but in our day it has come to mean theological statements that may be detached from human faith (p. 13). Therefore, when people say a creed, they may not, and probably do not, actually believe what they are saying.

I find no special problem with this as an analytical exercise. Jesus put the main idea in his pithy saying: 'For where your treasure is, there will your heart be also' (Matthew 6:21).

Fowler follows Erik Erikson in locating the origin and early development of human faith in the way a baby is treated. But he strikes out on his own to describe three types of human faith-identity. One is polytheism, in which people have a diffuse pattern of human faith. The second is henotheism, in which people have loyalty to one god but a god having no ultimate worth. The third is radical monotheism, in which people have a loyalty to 'the *principle of being* and to the *source and center of all value and power*' (p. 23, emphasis in text).

Here we must pause for a question. Why this discussion of types of human faith? Fowler makes no effort to correlate these three types of faith with the six stages of human faith he will elaborate later on. My guess is that Fowler has begun to realize that, if he has six stages arranged in hierarchical order, the highest stage will have to be established by some method other than by data from interviews. In other words, he is going to construct six stages rather than finding stages as they exist in human beings. I get this clue from his discussion of the third type of human faith where he says it is rarely 'actualized in persons or communities' (p. 23).

His use of human faith to this point has been clear: it is a human quality unrelated to religion. Now he is saying there is a true religion that deserves our allegiance. The true religion – radical monothesism – is a principle. On the surface it seems to be a paraphrase of Paul Tillich's nonsymbolic definition of God as the ground of being. But this is not the case because Fowler's true religion is a principle with attributes – value and power.

Problems with the principle

There is a certain logic to what Fowler has done at this point. If he is going to deal with human faith as a common human attribute, it may be desirable to abstract and escalate it to god-like status. This puts all religions in a subordinate position. It gives him a position beyond history and above criticism from which he can make judgments and towards which he can point his six stages.

Since he has proposed an idealistic religion, we have to deal with it. Here are my problems with his proposal.

First, is the principle something that is abstracted from life? If so, is it always open to new interpretation as life changes? Or is it a fixed principle? Is the principle able to transcend human life in some way so that it helps form the universal community?

What does *source and center* of all value and power mean? Is it a benign characteristic — that is, just a way to say that all we value and all we respect must have a source? If so, what is gained? Values are what people hold dear, things with which they associate their well-being; therefore, witchcraft can qualify as well as many other culturally formed values. Or, is it a dynamic characteristic — that is, a way to say that there is something beyond or in human life that discriminates? If so, what values does this principle hold dear and what is the nature of this power?

The only clue given to answer the above questions is the need to live in 'an inclusive, global community.' Fowler continues: 'It becomes terribly important for us to work with this understanding of faith and to try to formulate and symbolize it so that it exerts truly transformative power over our more parochial faith orientations' (p. 23). We are to formulate and symbolize faith and then it will transform our 'more parochial faith.'

This assignment bewilders me. First, I don't know of a living religion that was created by formula. To think that an abstract principle which we formulate would transform living religions with thousands of years of tradition is hard for me to imagine.

Second, idealism has a role in human life, and hope in a better future here or in the hereafter is an integral part of many religions. But suggesting that people give allegiance to a principle without consideration of other facets of life experienced every day (such as expressions of pride, jealousy and hatred) is not a realistic appraisal of human existence.

Data gathering

At this point in the book, we realize that Fowler is trying to do three things simultaneously. First, he is trying to develop a theory of human faith which matures by stages. He wants this to be true of human beings everywhere – a descriptive account of every person's development – and in the good sense of the word, secular. Second, he is trying to construct an ideal state of affairs for human beings because his research design is an outward and upward process requiring a top stage above common human experience. This ideal state will provide a way to judge religions, philosophies or anything else that claims human allegiance. Third, he is trying to give the Christian religion the best possible interpretation to fit both the stages and the ideal state.

My personal view is that he should have followed the lead of his mentors – Erikson, Piaget, and Kohlberg – who did not attempt to relate their human development theories to religion in a direct way. If he had restricted himself to human faith development as he proposed in the first part of the book, we would not have the complications of dealing with religion in general or with the Christian religion in particular. But he elected to try all three things at once, so the reader has to sort out what is being said and apply it to one of the three tasks. This process is difficult and at times confusing.

Fowler starts with a theory of six stages of human faith development which he has constructed from the works of Piaget, Erikson and Kohlberg. He then interviews people according to a guide covering (1) life review, (2) lifeshaping experience, (3) present values and commitments, and (4) religion. There are 34 questions in the guide (pp. 311–312). The interview takes from two to two-and-a-half hours – a shorter time for children. The interviews are transcribed. People trained by Fowler then study the interviews and judge what stage the interviewee is in.

The interview method is vastly superior to paper and pencil tests commonly used by researchers in moral development. The interview method allows some time to clarify terms, to work through discrepancies and to set a mood of seriousness about the importance of the project. Parts of some of the interviews are duplicated in the book so one can see how the method is used.

We must, however, note the limitations of this method in relation to the purpose of the data gathering.

First, it would be difficult, if not impossible, to learn with any precision from a two-and-a-half hour interview what people mean when they use religious words. In the case of Mary, we have a typical fundamentalist – or do we? Exactly what does Mary mean by all of the religious words she uses? (see chapter 22). Fowler has already said that he is going to follow Smith's idea that beliefs may be in three gradations from basic human faith (p. 13). How can (does) he make judgments about the state of human faith from religious words out of interview data? I think a highly trained psychologist would want many interviews before making even tentative appraisals. Mary uses Christian words. The meaning of these words to her has been fused with her human faith. Also, to some extent the meaning of the Christian words comes from the community of faith that nurtured Mary. Smith says so (pp. 9–10). Under these circumstances, exactly how is the meaning of Christian words sorted out in the case of Mary so as to place her in a stage of *human* faith apart from her understanding of the meaning of these words?

Second, the persons interviewed are not told that, on the basis of their answers, they will be placed in one of six stages of development. Should they be? Sissela Bok thinks that social scientists cannot get accurate data unless they tell their 'subjects' (Fowler also uses this term) how the data are to be used.[3] If the interviewees knew the characteristics of the six stages and that the data would be used to place them in one of those categories, would the resulting conversation be the same as if they did not know? It is a question worth testing.

The fact that the 359 people interviewed represent a sample restricted by geography, age and race is not to my mind a significant factor (pp. 315–317). The crucial matter is how the interviewers are trained and the presuppositions they bring to their task. Additional interviewees can be found to make the sample more representative; but if the interviewers are trained in the system, the resulting data will probably round out what has already been established. This is not a criticism of Fowler. It is simply a recognition of the human factor in this method of data gathering. The same comment has been made about Kohlberg's data gathering – it is inherent in the method of work.

Religion and stages

Given the purpose of this work – the gradation of human faith – the best people to interview would be those who have the least religious background and the least allegiance to any ideology. These cases would greatly reduce or eliminate the problem of interpreting religious language and symbols in order to uncover the structure of human faith. However, Fowler elected to interview Christians and a few Jews. This means he must place Judeo-Christian beliefs which he picks up in the interviews into six stages in order to grade the level of human faith in his interviewees. One example of how he does this is found in interview data from stage two. Millie has just been given the Kohlberg 'Heinz dilemma': Heinz's wife is dying of cancer. A druggist has a new drug that may save the wife's life, but it costs $1,000. Not being able to raise the money, Heinz breaks in and steals the drug.

Millie, a ten-year-old Protestant, performs right on Kohlberg's schedule for stage two – a 'fairness of instrumental exchange.'

Millie uses religious language and Fowler identifies her response as a religious form of human faith at the level of 'reciprocal fairness.' Millie holds out for honesty as a principle rather than allowing the wife's condition to decide the issue (pp. 143–144).

The problems for me in the few paragraphs from this interview are as follows: (1) Millie struggles with the problem: what does this tension mean to her? (2) God's view is important to her: how significant is this in contrast to another ten-year-old child who might make the same moral choice regarding Heinz but has no God concept? Are the two children at the same human faith stage, or does Millie already have a God concept that defines the substance (to some extent) of her human faith?

Although reading backward from the religious language of the interviewees in order to place them in a human faith stage is complex, that is not the most serious problem with this research design. The design arranges six levels of human faith which will be true for humans everywhere regardless of religion or lack of religious beliefs. This requires a description of each stage in language reflecting an increasing ethical achievement toward the principle of love and justice for all in a world community. Since religion is divorced from human faith, religion should not be involved in defining the stages. But Fowler finds that this is not easy to do.

He faces the problem directly but seems to think that the tension between being descriptive (an explanation of the qualities of human faith) and being normative (a statement of what human faith should mean) is a standard hazard for this kind of work. As the project is expanded to include more Hindus, Muslims, and people of other religions, he 'fully expects that our present stage descriptions would undergo a significant process of elimination of Western and Christian biases and that the genuinely structural features will emerge with greater clarity' (p. 298).

It is to Fowler's credit that he documents his lack of clarity. Just a few pages later on, he realizes that a Marxist or a follower of Ayn Rand could qualify at stage four: the individuative-reflective level of human faith. Not liking that prospect, he says that 'philosophical or theological evaluations' will have to be brought in to disqualify these people (p. 301).

The same problem is even more pronounced at the sixth level. This highest level is the incarnation of love and justice in a form of universal faith. Yet, as he describes this stage, he is 'haunted' by the realization that the Revd Jim Jones of Guyana, with his thousand followers giving up all to live in an ideal community, or even the Ayatollah Khomeini might quality. So he adds to the description of stage 6 the idea that people who are at this stage are trying to incarnate love and justice 'in accordance with an intentionality, both divine and transcendent' (p. 201). With this in mind, he lists as models Ghandi, Martin Luther King, Jr, Mother Teresa of Calcutta, Abraham Heschel and others. Throughout this section Fowler says he is searching for the normative – that is, what the highest should be. His proposal is the 'Jewish-Christian image of the Kingdom of God' (p. 204).

My response to Fowler's inability to set up religionless stages is more sympathetic than critical. As a Christian, I am delighted that the Kingdom of God turned out to be the best image for stage 6; but does it really help Fowler's thesis? The Kingdom of God is an image rooted in thousands of years of history and associated with Old Testament prophets and with Christ. How can non-Christians get the hang of it without considerable study and meditation? To use the Kingdom of God to give substance to stage 6 suggests that there may not be a stage 6 of human faith if human faith is honestly interpreted as human without reference to what the Judeo-Christian religion has affirmed.

Dynamics of faith

It is difficult to know exactly how much confidence Fowler places in stages of human faith development. In places he states that stages are 'only half of a much larger and richer picture' (p. 89), or that stages only 'illumine and clarify . . . patterns of faith' (p. 90). Yet the bulk of the book is about stages.

Part V on 'Formation and transformation in faith' is an effort to describe the dynamics of faith, yet how acceptable is this section? The story of Mary is told completely within the language of fundamentalist Christian theology.

Fowler uses the story to show how Mary moved from stage to stage of human faith; but Mary believed that 'the Lord was really working in my life to draw me to himself' (p. 219; see also p. 246). Fowler says that her uses of God, the Lord, and even of Jesus Christ involved a largely unreflective use of these symbols. She had not reflected upon her images or her symbols so as to form concepts. I am inclined to believe that Fowler's hunch is correct, but is it not merely a hunch? The Christian words that Mary uses may have a meaning different from that supplied by the readers of the interview. Moreover, the context of the interview shows that these religious words are precious to her; that is, they are not logical concepts. Fowler faults Mary for not intellectualizing her faith. If she did so, would she have more or better faith?

In the next chapter (23) Fowler, in theorizing about Mary's case and about the role of beliefs in faith, says, 'and we have not taken adequate account of the various patterns of relationship of structure and content in either of two significant kinds of change in faith: *stage change* and *conversion*' (p. 273). So we are left with the affirmation that the research does not deal with the way beliefs relate to the dynamics of change from stage to stage or with the experience of conversion.

Fowler concludes his book with the chapter 'Faith on earth.' This is a complicated postscript attempting to show what his theology is and at the same time denying that his theology influenced the research. For example, he says that (p. 293):

> The stage theory is not a theology. In itself its highly formal stage descriptions have no religious richness or sufficiency to offer. Apart from the stories, the images of power and the centers of value that particular faith traditions can offer, the faith stages are merely scaffolding. What these stages do offer, however, is this: they provide formally normative criteria for determining how adequate, responsible and free of idolatrous distortions our way of appropriating and living from our particular traditions of faith actually are. The stage theory provides a formally descriptive and normative model in relation to which the adequacy of our particular ways of being in faith can be assessed and faced.

The above is a theological statement. In relation to the Christian faith it says that (1) there is something outside the Christian faith (stage theory) that can judge the quality of Christian faith. The Christian religion on the contrary says that God is the judge. (2) Since each stage is higher than the former one, measurement of progress toward the last stage is possible and expected (see p. 296). This is a form of Gnosticism contrary to the Christian conception of faith as a gift from God.

Seeing how Fowler tries to be descriptive and to supply each stage with non-religious normative statements reminds me of Paul Tillich's comment about John Dewey. Tillich appreciated Dewey, especially Dewey's use of experience in philosophy: but Tillich said Dewey's pragmatism would not be possible except in a milieu of Christian idealism. In some other environment it could be demonic.

Ambiguity

Fowler's ambiguity about his research program is best displayed when he writes on 'the dynamic triad of faith' (pp. 91–93). He starts this chapter by saying people have suggested that he use some other term because 'faith' is associated with religion. Those 'who are favorable to religion' proposed that he would be 'more honest' if he described it as 'religious development.' Those 'who fear ... the linkage of faith and religion suggest he call it "belief system formation".' He rejects these suggestions, preferring 'faith' despite its complexity, its likelihood of being misunderstood, and the difficulty of pinning it down precisely (p. 92).

I have no problems on this point. Professors often define terms in certain ways, and Fowler has made it clear in this section and elsewhere that he is talking about faith as a quality indigenous to human beings everywhere. If one wanted to fault Fowler at this point, it would not be that he has insisted on using the word 'faith' but that his definition of human faith is really the whole socialization process: (1) acceptance of a world view, (2) acquisition of cultural values, and (3) formation of a self-image in relation to others in society. To Fowler, human faith is the capacity and natural desire of a person to become socialized. This may or may not include religion.

In this section Fowler mentions objections from two other groups that oppose his use of the word faith in his work: one is from Christians, especially in the Lutheran and the Calvinist traditions, who believe that faith is a gift from God and is related in a unique way to Jesus Christ. Should he not add the Anabaptists and the followers of John Wesley? Would not all Christians affirm that, whatever the psychological or sociological underlying state of human faith may be, the belief that Jesus is the Christ should produce a personality different from the top stage of natural human faith? The fact that this belief does not often do so does not invalidate the point that sainthood is an aspiration beyond the comprehension of people who do not have that possibility on their developmental chart.

The other group of critics is psychologists who say that what Fowler calls faith should properly be labeled ego development because he follows so closely the work of Erikson and Jane Loevinger (p. 92).

Fowler says these two groups oppose his use of faith for 'understandable reasons.' The implication is that he has some sympathy for the reasons, yet he will not accept them. He prefers to go on assuming that faith can be isolated from religion and from ego development. Thus, human faith is an autonomous or semi-autonomous quality of life.

In order to justify and explain his allegiance to the term faith, he uses a story by Flannery O'Connor. The story is about Ruller McFarney, an eleven-year-old boy, who, while playing, finds a wounded turkey. On the way home with his prize he allows three boys to hold it. They run away with the turkey and he is left with feelings of despair. Fowler finds many parallels between the events of this story and an account of life as it happens to most of us. Fowler uses the word God to denote the source of the boy's frustrations, the gift of the turkey, and the despair over losing the bird. He then generalizes to our adult life and points out that events happen to us — such as cancer — which cause us to 'compose images (and perhaps beliefs about and concepts of) the ultimate conditions of our existence' (p. 97).

Fowler's use of this story does illustrate the desire for constructing meaning out of our experiences. But why does Fowler use religion and religious language when he is trying to establish the autonomous state of human faith and development? My feeling is that he does so because he wants to show that religion is a way to respond to human life situations; but underneath is the struggle for faith.

However, to me the use of the story reveals the ambiguous way in which Fowler deals with religion, especially the Christian religion. First, Fowler indicates that Ruller has ideas of God supplied by his parents and grandmother, so that the substance or meaning of human faith is already fused with certain beliefs that have already conditioned his being. The really important question is avoided: to what extent have Ruller's beliefs overshadowed or taken over the underlying psychological base of human faith? What if Ruller had grown up in a strict Muslim family or a Buddist one? Would he not at 11 years of age have had Islamic or Buddhist mental images? At what point is the meaning given to human faith more important than the underlying psychological base of human faith?

The second point is this: why does Fowler give Ruller's experience a vague Judeo-Christian slant? Why not use the story to promote his thesis that human faith advances to newer and higher levels through experience? Since he did supply generalized Judeo-Christian myth as an interpretive motif, we have to deal with it. There are many Christians who would not accept Fowler's theology at this point. Although part of the Christian religion is the living of the Christian story, especially in the sacraments, the Christian religion also affirms that God is concerned with the present. This means that Christians seek guidance as to what should be changed and why – they are not just concerned with making meaning out of what happens.

Issues

Thus far I have been responding to Fowler's work from within the framework of what he reports. In most of the above points I have found that Fowler is aware of the problems and ambiguities about which I have commented.

Stepping back from the book and looking at the enterprise from my own perspective, I recognize the following issues:
Does human faith go through stages, or is human faith a general condition? Notice that I am using faith in Fowler's terms as a non-religious quality of life. Reading this book has forced me to think about the nature of human faith. I am now of the opinion that human faith is like anxiety – it is a general affective state. It probably has its origins in the early years of life as Erikson describes. Then, as persons grow, this general affective state of human faith deals with life situations as they occur. This means that, rather than stages of human faith, we have a struggle to create meaning out of all of the events of life to which persons attach significance.

If this is the case, then the psychologists who said that Fowler was really charting ego development, or the development of the whole self, are right. Human faith from this view does not develop; but our understanding of life and our formation of meaning about life become more adequate for the complexities of life as we mature in the ability to make judgments and to respond to a variety of life experiences.

Can human faith be isolated from religion or beliefs? If so, how? One can think about human faith as separate from religious beliefs. Moreover, we have all seen creative and courageous people who seem to live completely apart from religion. But Fowler does not study such people. He studies people who have a religious faith and attempts to work from their statements back to a stage of human faith. I have already pointed out that this method poses several problems: but one that I have not mentioned before is the generalized content of religion which is carried from one generation to another by our culture. In secular Western society there is so much of the Christian interpretation of life in the environment that Tillich said there was a 'latent church' from which individuals occasionally spoke a prophetic word, individuals who were not in the manifest church (*Theology of Culture,* p. 51).

Fowler's position is that human faith can be disentangled from culture, described, and placed on one of six shelves, each higher than the other. However, as pointed out in the analytical section of this paper, he is unable to sustain his position at levels four and six without recourse to theological statements. He thinks his Western Christian bias (his language) will be reduced when he has more data from people in the East with Buddhist or non-Christian beliefs. But he will still be dealing with religious beliefs.

My feeling is that the enterprise of describing human faith development apart from beliefs is in for more trouble than has already appeared. Somewhere in the growth process human faith becomes fused with religious beliefs or a 'plausibility structure,' secular in nature, emerges. Confidence in these beliefs may and does change, but my point is that fusion does take place. For Fowler to say that this is a definable stage is satisfactory for academic purposes; but the truly important point is that beliefs overwhelm human faith. Belief in an eternal life because one has lived a life of service *may* produce a saint-like character. Belief in eternal life because one has participated in a holy war *may* produce self-sacrificing soldiers. To say that only underlying human faith is important is not enough for those of us who live and work with people who have fused human faith with beliefs to which they give allegiance.

To what extent can Christians utilize a stage theory of human faith? Let us recall again that human faith to Fowler is an ability and desire to make meaning out of life. This meaning is expressed in categories usually associated with the socialization process: world view, values, and self in relation to others. I find the human faith stage development theory of limited value for the following reasons.

The affective element in the Christian faith is not adequately involved in the theory. Human faith as Fowler uses it is a maturation element with strong cognitive elements. Although this theory results in stages 5 and 6, which from a Christian viewpoint can be admired, from that same viewpoint a stage theory can be faulted because it does not adequately involve love and hope. Does love go through six stages, or is love an affection that grows constantly with the right nourishment? The reverse of love is hate, and there is an enormous amount of hatred in many people. Love has a strategy for dealing with hatred. It is displayed in human relations, not entirely in reflection – a major component in Fowler's stages 4, 5 and 6. Another way of focusing attention on love is to ask if a child's love is not as authentic as a mid-life stage 5 person with conjunctive faith including a 'second naïveté.' If so, human faith development may be a necessary condition of Christian faith; but it is not sufficient to produce Christian faith.

Should Christian education limit itself to exactly what a child understands? This is an old issue often associated with memorizing catechisms. Stage theory brings the issue back because of its emphasis in the first three stages on cognitive development. However, Fowler, in his discussion of stage 1 (pp. 3–7) affirms the thesis of Bruno Bettelheim that we should not avoid stories that include fears, hopes and dangers.[4] Because Fowler has affirmed the position that human faith is more than the development of the child's capacity for logical thinking, he is able to recognize other types of mental experience (pp. 101–103). However, since the interview material is mainly about children's concepts, one cannot tell what help this research would be on this issue. The implication is that Christian education should not strain the mental capacity of children, a judgment that is already widely accepted.

Are stages of human development of much value beyond middle adolescence? Christian educators have always used some concept of ages and stages for their printed curricula. They have generally adapted instructional materials to suit the best available psychology of human development.

Today, with data from Piaget and others, there seems to be agreement that the capacity of the mind for logical thinking is formed by middle adolescence. Below this age adaptations have to be made according to mental development, but above this age the important factors are social or situational.

After leaving the three levels of childhood, Fowler projects two more roughly related to age (young adulthood, middle adulthood) and a final stage 6, rarely reached. Why are these necessary?

People respond to experiences that occur and in the process become more mature and capable or less secure and withdrawn. They do so unevenly in different aspects of their life. From the Christian point of view, we want to sponsor maturity of selfhood and responsibility to God. If stages are determined, do we not have our attention diverted to where we are on a predetermined course rather than on what we should be and do in particular life situations?

The Christian religion, I believe, requires that we think in terms of helping people (including ourselves) relate to God and form an allegiance to God's purpose in the world. This allegiance will create a struggle within the self and with demonic forces in society. The mental image of the Christian life by those who have tried to live it has been that of pilgrimage, fighting the good fight, building the Kingdom, or other expressions of involvement in a purpose that has divine sanction. Psychological or human faith development has, at best, been a by-product or a subordinate interest of those who have attempted to live a Christian life.

Let us recall that Fowler has tried to separate his theology from his theory of human faith development. In order to take account of those who insist that the Christian religion is true and that a person can be converted to it, Fowler recognizes an 'x' factor which may account for such an experience (pp. 286–291). This is the only way to deal with factors which do not fit research assumptions.

Christians and adherents of the Jewish religion will demur because they believe God has revealed God's self and God's will at various times. Psychologically, this belief may be grounded in a generalized human faith, but the meaning of that belief does not come from an unknown 'x' factor. The meaning of that belief is that God continues to be, continues to be concerned, and continues to be influential in human life. Such belief has power to shape persons and to help persons make decisions without regard to the stage of their human faith. Probably the best summary of the role of faith in the Christian religion is the book of Hebrews, chapter 11. Here one finds that religious faith is not a generalized human state that assists one to become properly socialized or mature. According to the writer, faith is a way to relate to a known God who has a work agenda for those who believe.

Let's be fair with Fowler. He guesses that his theory accounts for about 50 percent of how human faith develops. He offers no explanation of how religious faith develops. To the extent that religious faith is built on human faith, he may be correct for the first three stages – up to middle adolescence. But after physical growth is complete and the mind has the ability to do abstract reasoning, does religious faith go through stages? I am inclined to believe that people with religious faith have experiences to which they respond. The way they think about these experiences and the way they live and evaluate their beliefs as they live strengthens or weakens their faith in God.

Notes

1. James W. Fowler, *Stages of Faith*, San Francisco, Harper and Row, 1981.
2. Page numbers in this paper refer to pages in *Stages of Faith*.
3. See chapter 13 of Bok's book, *Lying: moral choice in public and private life*, 1978.
4. See Bruno Bettelheim, *The Uses of Enchantment: the meaning and importance of fairy tales*, New York, Alfred A. Knopf, 1976.

2.2 James Fowler's theory of faith development
Derek H. Webster

H. L. Mencken once said: 'To every complex problem there exists a solution which is neat, simple and wrong.' What is offered in James Fowler's theory of faith development is rather like this, according to his critics. His supporters, however, maintain that he is a Triton among the educational minnows of the time. Whatever the truth is, he is certainly in the air. In the USA no collection of papers or any major conference in religious education is complete without a contribution from him and references to his work are now beginning to appear on this side of the Atlantic.[1] His ideas on how faith grows are provoking attention and the publication of his book *Stages of Faith* has made them available in a readable form to a wider audience.[2] Those who imagine that research in religious education is largely a trivial fussing over details, or that researchers are soulless pedants half in love with their own intellectual detritus, should read him: they will be surprised.

The theory of faith development emerged in its first form during 1968 and 1969 when Fowler was an associate director of a religious and cultural centre in North Carolina called Interpreters' House.[3] His counselling work there involved him in listening to the life-histories of scores of people. He saw these accounts as struggles to affirm a meaning for living and discerned within them structures of thinking that were common.[4] A move to Harvard gave him the opportunity to reflect more deeply on these structures. Already in debt to Erikson he now became acquainted with the work of Piaget and Kohlberg and from these 'timbers and foundations' grew an understanding of the ways in which faith matures.[5] Subsequent research has taken many of his profound insights and organized them into a structural-developmental model for which he is seeking scientific validation.

Understanding the theory

Fowler is most anxious to guard against misunderstandings of his theory. There are three which are particularly common. The first concerns the meaning of faith. It is not to be understood simply in its noun form as a system of religious belief. Wider and more active than this it is also a verb indicating a way of 'construing or interpreting experience'.[6] It is that 'way of knowing' which brings order and coherence to life.[7] As an 'orientation of the total person'

77

it has three *foci*: the *self* bound to groups of *others* which are loyal to *what transcends them both*.[8] Despite its complexity and diversity of content it is 'a universal feature of human living recognizably similar everywhere' in structure and including religious as well as non-religious world views.[9]

The second is to see the faith development model as a scientific fact. Rather it is a report of ongoing work, provisional in character and open to new insights. It will change to meet the truth of what it discovers. Fowler's work, though committed to responsible scholarship and the rigorous clarification of ideas, invites those who study it to re-live their own pilgrimage in faith.[10]

The third misunderstanding is to see the stage structure as an instrument for classification in faith terms. The stages, however, are lenses through which to perceive values, not pigeon holes by which to categorize them. They are ways of organizing answering the question: 'How?' rather than a pattern of contents answering the question: 'What?' Though in the earlier stages they are loosely related to age, age is not a sufficient condition for movement through them. Where movement does occur the higher stages reached are not necessarily superior to the lower ones, for people make sense of their experience and their environment in different and not better ways.[11]

The theory of faith development

At first Fowler's explanation of how faith matures looks complex. It is a model which has 'seven operational aspects which are integrated and reintegrated at each of the six levels or stages'.[12] In fact, it is simple, for his grand theory uses seven other theories each of which has six stages. These seven theories concern the development of logical thinking as found in Piaget; the construction of social perspectives, called role-taking, as found in Selman; the form moral judgments take, as found in Kohlberg; the understanding of social reference points, called bounds of awareness; the interpretation of what legitimizes commitments, called locus of authority; the ways of unifying meanings as found in Erikson, called form of world coherence; and the understanding of symbols, called symbolic functioning.

The seven theories 'may best be thought of as windows or apertures into the structures underlying faith'.[13] Each of their six stages is a holistic patterning, a complete network though seen from a differing perspective. The complete cycle of development moves from a phase typical of infants up to three years which is preconceptual, prelinguistic and in which 'trust, courage, hope and love are fused in an undifferentiated way', to stage 1.[14] This is characterized by an *intuitive-projective faith*. It is a phase, usually evident between three and seven years, which has a faith which is episodic, fantasy-filled, unrestrained by logical thought and generated by powerful feelings and images. Its God is magical and pre-anthropomorphic. The ability to engage in concrete operational thinking underlies the transition to the *mythic-literal faith* of stage 2. This is the faith of children between seven and eleven years. It recognizes in a rudimentary way the teachings, symbols and perspectives of the community and appropriates them in a quite literal way. The God of this stage is anthropomorphic, a kingly law-giver whose moral judgments are based on fairness and a consideration of the intention behind action. The *synthetic-conventional faith* of stage 3 does not usually emerge before the twelfth year. Now faith becomes more complex as it is required to integrate wider social experiences, make sense of diverse involvements and 'provide a unifying basis for identity and outlook'.[15] But it does not become objectified and is not made the matter of detached examination. Though rising in adolescence, it is a faith which best describes the majority of adults. Its concepts of God 'tend to be surrounded by mystery and awe' and it places authority outside the individual person.[16]

Stage 4, an *individuating-reflexive faith*, is achieved with a deepening self-awareness and a personal responsibility for values which are integrated into an ideology. Not attained much before eighteen years, it is a demythologizing stage which brings a recognition of the relativity of experience. Its God, a dynamic one who invites humans to become fellow workers with him, is seen most helpfully in the model offered by process theology.[17] Disillusioned with the conceptual clarification of this stage; unhappy with the complexity of life and its compromises; and sensitive to the myths of his culture, a person may be prompted to the *paradoxical-consolidative faith* of stage 5. Not reached until mid-life, it is a stage in which previous boundaries of meaning become porous in the effort to unify contradictions. Aware of the paradox of the truth in opposites, faith here is vulnerable to the strangeness of what is beyond it. It is open to the 'anarchic voices' of the 'deep self' and its God is highly personal.[18] A few exceptional men and women may continue to develop to the final stage 6, a stage of *universalizing faith*. It is seen in the lives and thoughts of Gandhi, Martin Luther King, Mother Teresa, Dag Hammarskjöld, Dietrich Bonhoeffer and Thomas Merton.[19] For persons at this stage the paradoxes of the previous phase have disappeared and they incarnate the spirit of a fulfilled community.[20] They relate to all others with the 'genuine bread of life'[21] creating zones of liberation from 'social, political, economic and ideological shackles'.[22] More lucid, simple and human than others, they have the capacity to participate directly 'in Being'.[23] Their conceptions of God are such as allow for an ultimate union with a transcendent which is manifest in the imminent.

Testing the theory

Fowler tests and develops his theory by means of individual semi-clinical interviews which utilize the approaches of Piaget and Kohlberg. His faith development interview guide takes up to two-and-a-half hours to work through and is a flexible instrument which encourages thought about key values governing living.[24] Up to the publication of *Stages of Faith* nearly 400 subjects had been tested either by Fowler himself or by one of his associates.[25] Within these is a group which will be tested several times over the years in a longitudinal study. The sample of subjects so far is 'overwhelmingly white, largely Christian, evenly divided by sex and distributed through the age categories'.[26] It is also largely confined to North America. Fowler finds that the preliminary evidence from his interviews tends to confirm the predicted pattern of faith development.

It is difficult to assess Fowler's work in any final way, for as he frequently says it is still growing and changing.[27] However, he does wish 'to provoke thought and comment' so perhaps it is fairer to indicate questions prompted by the present shape of the theory rather than a conclusive evaluation.[28] These questions may be resolved as the work progresses. There are at least three broad areas within which they occur. These are experimental design and methodology, moral development and religious belief.

Experimental design and methodology

Fowler's theory is based on a piece of experimental research in human psychology so the criteria relevant to such work apply. How satisfactory is his experiment? There is bound to be some unease that at present no published account exists which sets out the experiment in the usual systematic way and with the appropriate scholarly rigour. It is not clear which hypotheses are being investigated, whether they are theoretically well grounded and if the semi-clinical interview is the most suitable instrument for testing them. Further, it is uncertain what the sample population is and whether it will be representative enough to give results guaranteeing generalizability. Very little statistical support for the theory is offered despite the fact that it is only on this basis that it can be confirmed. It is an unhappy situation when Fowler can present his data only 'in rough form'.[29] Further, it is unfortunate that as it stands his work is very difficult to replicate. A strict application of the experimental criteria can lead to the conclusion that at present there is no objective and empirical basis for the theory of faith development.

Clearer research procedures could reveal other problems, three of which are pressing. The first concerns the number of aspects which characterize each faith stage. Why are there seven of them? Why are perception, volition and even humour excluded?[30] The second concerns the integrity of these aspects. Certainly some overlapping is to be expected, but is there not a sense in which moral reasoning and symbolic understanding are dependent on, not just broadly related to, a prior development of logical thinking? Are not those aspects labelled locus of authority and moral judgment too intimately connected for the distinction that Fowler makes between them to be sustained? Could not the same also be argued for those two aspects called bounds of social awareness and role-taking? The third concerns the use Fowler makes of the existing theories of Piaget, Kohlberg and Selman. His work, though deeply indebted to them, does extend and modify their ideas, he says.[31] Can such a claim properly be made without some prior replication of their experiments which properly establishes the nature of these modifications and indicates their legitimacy? Those who wish to be unsympathetic might suggest that it was a very exceptional experiment indeed which, setting out to achieve a different aim, managed as a secondary by-product to improve on theories with years of patient research supporting them.

Subsequent research by others of the faith development model claims to have confirmed Fowler's thinking.[32] At present this must be a matter of opinion. It is certainly arguable that it exhibits similar methodological and psychometric weaknesses to Fowler's own published work; that it suffers from serious conceptual inadequacy; that it has neither identified nor controlled important variables; and that its attempts to locate the theoretical correlates of faith development are crude.

Moral development and faith development

Fowler's theory incorporates Lawrence Kohlberg's work on moral development. This use prompts many questions, four of which are particularly interesting. Kohlberg maintains that moral development is invariant, sequential and hierarchical. Does this mean that faith development has the same characteristics? If it has not, then it hardly seems to reflect Kohlberg's theory very faithfully. If it has, then it marries oddly with what is known of the experiences of ordinary men and women.[33] Secondly, Kohlberg states that his model of moral development has universal application: does the model of faith development? Kohlberg's claim has been sharply criticized and it is now evident that it is ethnocentrically biased. His cosmopolitanism is more hemispheric than universal. Does this mean that Fowler's model is equally and as ineradicably Western in its understanding of man? Thirdly, Kohlberg himself hypothesizes that moral development precedes development to the parallel faith stage.[34] Fowler takes the reverse view.[35] Neither has empirical data on this but Fowler assumes that his view is the more tenable. But should Kohlberg be right on this point, what effect would such dependence and the resulting uneven development have on any particular faith stage? Finally, there is a crucial question regarding Kohlberg's theory of moral development: how satisfactory is it? The last twenty years has seen widespread debate on it. The emerging consensus seems to confirm Kohlberg's view that there is a cognitive developmental dimension to thought about social relationships, and that for the first three or four stages it is along the lines that he suggests. However, there is considerable doubt that he has offered an adequate theoretical or empirical account of specifically moral development, and there is little agreement on his description of the higher stages.[36] What effect would a more cautious estimate of the validity of Kohlberg's theory have on the model of faith development?

Fowler's use of Piaget's and Selman's theories equally raises questions. If any of the aspects are found to be defective what effect will this have on the theory of faith development? The theories Fowler uses are not all as sophisticated as each other. Those concerning role-taking and moral development have an elaborate research basis, that of symbolic functioning has very little. Do these relative weaknesses and strengths make any difference? But perhaps the major question here relates to Fowler's use of the aspects. Is it legitimate to integrate the stages of completely separate models? Do they genuinely offer unifying links to each other, or are these being forced?

Religious belief and faith development

Those who accept any form of religious belief will have queries for Fowler. Though not as serious in their effects on his model as the methodological questions, they are worth raising.

Initially believers may feel that the word faith selected by Fowler is misleading despite his rather elaborate defence of it. Given their acceptance of his definitions, how do they relate to the believers' understanding of faith within religion? Fowler looks at faith from the human angle. A Christian will probably see his faith from a biblical or theological standpoint. He may wish to say that his faith is given from what transcends him. If he does two questions arise. Is there any necessary or potential relationship between this faith and the faith that emerges as a person quests for meaning with Fowler? Is there any necessary or potential relationship between the Roman Catholic understanding of sufficient and prevenient grace and the model of faith development?

Similarly queries occur when conversion and faith maturation are considered. Is what Baptists call a conversion experience really a stage transition? Is what Anglicans call growing in the faith the consolidation of a particular stage? Is what St John of the Cross calls the dark night of the soul, an experience of anxiety, disintegration and psychic disarray, another account of the breakdown of stage 5 prior to entry on stage 6?[37] Are Martin Luther King and Thomas Merton satisfactory as exemplars of stage 6? Either could be challenged on moral grounds. Their presence is as puzzling as is the association of stage 6 and the Kingdom of God.[38]

Muslims, Hindus, Sikhs, Buddhists and Jews as well as humanists will also have queries from within their own particular stances.

Conclusion

Reading James Fowler is a delightful exercise in admiring the man. For he comes across as a person of great warmth and sincerity, a man who is trying to deal in an honest and sympathetic way with profound and difficult issues. His insights are genuinely helpful and obviously have a creative force. One guesses that he is a superb counsellor. It would be ungracious not to acknowledge the impetus to thinking about faith and its growth which his research has given. It would be ungenerous to overstress its deficiencies: Piaget, too, was somewhat cavalier in these matters. It would be arrogant to deny its potential for churches, schools and counselling clinics. Nevertheless, until a later phase of research chases away the questions, Fowler's work is best seen as an attempt to discern how the self constructs its meanings – and this at the level of practical theology rather than scientific theory.[39]

References
1. O'Leary, D. (ed.) *Religious Education and Young Adults*, Middlegreen, St Paul Publications, 1983, pp. 97–102; Smith, M. 'Developments in faith', *The Month*, June 1983, pp. 222–225; Gallagher, J. 'Theories of development and religious education', *New Review*, Spring 1984, p. 11.
2. Fowler, J. W. *Stages of Faith*, San Francisco, Harper and Row, 1981.
3. Fowler, J. W. and Lawrence, L. 'Stages of faith', *Psychology Today*, vol. 17, no. 11, 1983, p. 56.
4. Howe, L. T. 'A developmental perspective on conversion', *Perkins Journal*, vol. 33, no. 1, 1979, p. 23.
5. Fowler, J. W. *Stages of Faith*, San Francisco, Harper and Row, 1981, p. 39.
6. *ibid.*, p. 175.
7. Fowler, J. W. 'Faith and the structuring of meaning', in C. Brusselmans (convenor), *Toward Moral and Religious Maturity*, Morristown, New Jersey, Silver Burdett Company, 1980, p. 57.
8. Fowler, J. W. *Stages of Faith*, San Francisco, Harper and Row, 1981, p. 14.
9. *ibid.*
10. *ibid.*, p. xii.
11. Fowler, J. W. 'Perspectives on the family from the standpoint of faith development theory', *Perkins Journal*, vol. 33, no. 1, 1979, p. 8.
12. Brusselmans, C. *op. cit.*, pp. 74–75.
13. Fowler, J. W. 'Stages in faith: the structural developmental approach', in T. C.

Hennessy (ed.), *Values and Moral Development*, New York, Paulist Press, 1976, p.186.

14. Fowler, J. W. *Stages of Faith*, San Francisco, Harper and Row, 1981, p. 121.
15. Brusselmans, C. *op. cit.*, p. 70.
16. Haunz, R. A. 'Development of some models of God and suggested relationships to James Fowler's stages of faith development', *Religious Education*, vol. 73, no. 6, 1978, p. 651.
17. *ibid.*, p. 652.
18. Fowler, J. W. 'Life/faith pattern: structures of trust and loyalty', in J. Berryman (ed.), *Life Maps: conversations on the journey of faith*, Waco, Texas, Word Books, 1978, p. 79.
19. Fowler, J. W. 'Stage six and the Kingdom of God', *Religious Education*, vol. 75, no. 3, 1980, p. 237.
20. Brusselmans, C. *op. cit.*, p. 74.
21. Hennessy, T. C. *op. cit.*, p. 185.
22. Fowler, J. W. 'Perspectives on the family from the standpoint of faith development theory', *Perkins Journal*, vol. 33, no. 1, 1979, p. 13.
23. Hennessy. T. C. *op. cit.*, p. 187.
24. Fowler, J. W. *Stages of Faith*, San Francisco, Harper and Row, 1981, pp. 310–312.
25. *ibid.*, p. 307.
26. *ibid.*, p. 317.
27. *ibid.*, p. 323.
28. *ibid.*
29. *ibid.*
30. Loder, J. E. 'Reflections on Fowler's "Stages of Faith"', *Religious Education*, vol. 77, no. 2, 1982, p. 138.
31. Fowler, J. W. *Stages of Faith*, San Francisco, Harper and Row, 1981, pp. 252, 272.
32. Parks, S. D., 'Faith development and imagination in the context of higher education', unpublished ThD thesis, Harvard University, 1980; Chirban, J. 'Intrinsic and extrinsic motivation in faith development', unpublished ThD thesis, Harvard University, 1980; Mischey, E. J. 'Faith development and its relationship to moral reasoning and identity status in young adults', unpublished PhD thesis, Toronto University, 1976; Shulik, R. M. 'Faith development, moral development and old age: an assessment of Fowler's faith development paradigm', unpublished PhD thesis, Chicago University, 1979.
33. Dykstra, C. R. 'Christian education and the moral life: an evaluation of and alternative to Kohlberg', unpublished PhD thesis, Princeton Theological Seminary, 1978, chapters 2 and 3.
34. Kohlberg, L., 'Education, moral development and faith', *Journal of Moral Education*, vol. 4, no. 1, 1974.
35. Hennessy, T. C. *op. cit.*, p. 209.
36. Atherton, T. 'A critique of Lawrence Kohlberg's theories of moral development and moral education', unpublished PhD thesis, Boston University, 1979, chapters 2 and 6. Trainer, E. E. *Dimensions of Moral Thought*, Sydney NSW, New South Wales University Press, 1982, chapter 1.
37. Hennessy, T. C., *op. cit.*, pp. 203–207 is not a satisfactory answer to this question.
38. Fowler, J. W. 'Stage six and the Kingdom of God', *op. cit.*
39. In reaching this conclusion I acknowledge the help received from discussions with my research associate, Mrs M. F. Tickner, and from an unpublished paper by Marion Smith of the Roehampton Institute. It was given at Birmingham University in January 1983 and is entitled 'Some critical reflections on James Fowler's research'.

2.3 Answers to some questions about faith development

Marion Smith

Webster's article on James Fowler's theory of faith development[1] proposes a number of questions, and echoes remarks I made in the seminar paper to which he refers in his last footnote.[2] Since then, however, the study has been taken further. Important clarifications were made in the course of several hours' conversation with Fowler during his visit to Birmingham in the summer of 1983. Barry Miller and I have collaborated in a small piece of research on the development of symbolism (one of Fowler's seven dimensions of faith) and a paper on this was published in October 1984.[3] In addition, an extensive review of Kohlberg's work and its place in religious education has been undertaken in the course of preparation of a chapter contributed to a major evaluation of Kohlberg's theory and its implications.[4] With this material in mind it is thus possible to make some rejoinder to Webster's observations.

In this article only two subjects will be discussed, though they are themselves extensive: the relation between moral and faith development (where Webster calls in question Kohlberg's work, and so Fowler's which incorporates it) and the relation between religious belief and faith development (where Webster calls in question the fundamental connection between the Christian's conception of faith and Fowler's). As I see it, if Webster is really uncertain on these points and can find convincing support for his doubts, then Fowler can be left to fade into oblivion. But there is something to be said in answer to these questions.

The first preliminary and general point concerns the references cited in Webster's article. It was at one time difficult to find the published material in this country, but that is no longer the case. As far as Kohlberg is concerned there is recent and relevant material to be consulted, so that we do not have to rely on an article written in 1974, though what was said at that point is still useful. (We have to remember that Fowler's introduction to Kohlberg's work was about 1969 and that the specific research reported in *Stages of Faith*[5] was conducted between 1973 and 1979.) In 1981 Kohlberg's *Essays on Moral Development* (vol. 1) was published[6] and here, as well as in the volume of papers *Towards Moral and Religious Maturity*, we have a more up-to-date account of his position with work relating to religion contributed by Clark Power. Similarly Fowler's publications in 1980[7] and 1981[5] (or later) must be consulted to establish shifts in his position since 1976. The date of writing is significant when we are considering research theories which are still being tested, modified and reconsidered. Kohlberg's theory has been both refined and deepened over the years, and conversation with Fowler shows that he, too, is constantly re-thinking his position. This openness gives us confidence in the researcher, but it means we have to try to keep up with him.

Moral development and faith development

Kohlberg's cognitive-developmental approach is important in Fowler's theory and not simply for its specific application to the development of moral reasoning. So Webster's queries about Kohlberg, if they are well-founded, need to be answered if we are to take Fowler's work at all seriously. Webster asks whether Kohlberg's theory is satisfactory, almost implying that the widespread debate on it signifies serious doubt. The extensive discussion has arisen because Kohlberg's ideas are of interest to those working in several fields: moral philosophy, psychology, education, religion, penal reform and so on. An important theory generates such testing and challenge, partly to define its scope more precisely.

One of Webster's queries concerns the universal application of Kohlberg's model. He is a little inconsistent here, for a few sentences later he acknowledges consensus over Kohlberg's account of the first four stages. The claim to universality arises, not from empirical research in a range of cultures, but from the role of cognitive development and social perspective-taking (which has a cognitive element) in moral reasoning.

The cognitive dimension in Kohlberg's theory is often not fully appreciated and this is quite understandable if there has been no experience in analysing and grading responses to his interview test, where dilemmas are thoroughly discussed. We are not simply focusing on the reasoning about moral issues as opposed to action. The stages are distinguished, among other criteria, by the specific intellectual capacities shown, or absent, in a discussion. It is these cognitive characteristics which establish the invariant sequence (e.g. egocentrism, complexity of classification, reciprocity, abstraction, hypothesizing, capacity to handle a range of possibilities). The hierarchical nature of the stages is signified by the mode of reasoning which becomes increasingly more adequate, by, for example, taking account of additional considerations and implications. At every stage a particular outcome may be deemed wrong, but at successive stages in the sequence the reasons reflect further decentring, or more complex classification, or wider human implications, or greater abstraction involving principles for action.

Motivations and ideals may certainly be influential in the speed or extent of progression through the stages, and may affect the expression of responses, but, intellectually, the order cannot be otherwise. And as we are speaking about *human* development, it is the hierarchical sequence which grounds the argument for universality. I am not familiar with any work which has established a different *order* in another culture, although, for obvious reasons, we can hardly prove universality by empirical data.

The precise details of the earlier stages will be easier to specify for two reasons. There are many opportunities for empirical study when children and adolescents tend to be progressing rapidly and are, as it were, a captive sample in the school system. But, by definition, the post-conventional stages 5 and 6 cannot be investigated in such detail (there are fewer examples) and, also by definition, at least a stage 5 researcher is needed. To many people, the revisions of the descriptions, and hesitancy over the details of stage 6 give greater rather than less confidence in the quality of the research.

Much the same could be said for the similar and rather vague questioning of Selman and Piaget. Of course we expect details to be corrected and modifications to be made, but these are not difficulties which undermine the whole approach. Selman is a cautious and thorough researcher who makes a very sober statement about the progress of his work.[8] There is a great difference between improvements of technique with consequent corrections in detail (or even in interpretation) and the toppling of a theory. Piaget's work has not yet been wholly over-thrown.

The cognitive-developmental approach of Piaget, Kohlberg and Selman implies an invariant and hierarchical sequence of stages (levels). If we accept that faith includes the strand of recognizing moral issues and reasoning about them, then Fowler's faith stages must also be 'invariant, sequential and hierarchical'. This is what he has claimed, though, so far, the empirical data has not been presented in a way which demonstrates the point.

The second of Webster's comments about faith stages is that the theory 'marries oddly with what is known of the experiences of ordinary men and women'. No detailed evidence for this assertion is presented which is rather odd, for, if it were believed to be true, why should Fowler's work be considered any further? The reference cited is Dykstra's unpublished thesis of 1978. He has since produced an article on the subject[9] from which it appears that he does not use the term moral maturity in the same sense as Kohlberg. He claims that mature moral judgments and actions can be based not on cognitive thinking but on empathy and imaginal thinking. Dykstra is clearly out of sympathy with all that Kohlberg has done but, if we are to use Dykstra as evidence against Fowler, we require some substantial grounds for refutation. From what I have read of Dykstra, and of comment on his doctoral thesis, I take him to be chiefly concerned with moral behaviour and the acquisition of moral virtues. What I have not discovered is any ground for supposing that cognition is unimportant in human development, either for understanding moral issues or for the development of what Fowler means by faith. As we have learned from Selman's work, certain levels of cognitive development are required for comparable levels of empathy and for the use of imagination.

A further question raised by Webster is the apparent conflict between Kohlberg and Fowler on the matter of order of development: Does moral development precede development to the parallel faith stage, or the reverse? I have used the word 'apparent' because, in conversation with Fowler, it was quite clear that there is no such conflict if the precise meaning and scope of the terms used are clarified.

In 1984 Kohlberg wrote: 'Psychologically, I believe that it takes a long time to work out a moral stage in terms of its elaboration as an organized pattern of belief and feeling about the cosmos which Fowler calls a faith stage'.[10] He discusses briefly the position of those who hold that faith comes first because of moral principles which are held on the basis of divine authority or revelation, but, in this case, the 'faith' to which Kohlberg refers is the content of belief, and this does not match Fowler's description, as Kohlberg clearly understands. What Kohlberg means by faith, in relation to moral reasoning, is introduced here, and amplified later[6, 7] in terms of asking questions such as: 'Why exist?' and 'Why act morally?' and of finding that religious faith and affirmation express 'confidence in the ultimate significance of moral action' (Power and Kohlberg, 1980, p. 346).[7]

Some slight empirical support for the precedence of the moral over the parallel faith stage is described by Power and Kohlberg.[7] Kohlberg's moral reasoning interview was used with an adapted form of Fowler's interview. The sample of twenty-one was small but it was selected on the basis of a spread of stages shown by an earlier scoring on Fowler's interview test. In the lower stages 1–3 no divergence was found between the moral and faith stage. In stages 4 and 5 moral reasoning was found one stage ahead, and there was no instance of the reverse. The evidence is much too slight to count as a firm answer to the question of order of development of moral and faith stages but it is a beginning.

So what did Fowler mean by implying that faith development precedes moral development? As I understand it, Fowler is referring to the dynamic quality of faith which is the energy directed towards searching for and constructing meaning in existence and this, obviously, will provide the motivation for meeting moral questions. In that sense, faith precedes the moral decision-making process, but, in this context, Fowler is not referring to the question of stage. The impulse of faith directed towards a moral question may result in decision at the stabilized stage already attained on each dimension, or the outcome may be the creative disturbance leading to a more advanced moral judgment on that particular point. Such an advance, though, will have to be accompanied by many more such outcomes before it is correct to speak of moving into a higher stage (moral or faith). This is precisely the way Kohlberg understands it, and Fowler intends.

Religious beliefs and faith development

The second main aspect to be considered here is the compatibility of Christian faith with Fowler's definition. Presumably, the way in which any particular Christian speaks reflects the stage he has reached in the development of his thinking about faith. Perhaps it may be possible to deny developmental theory, not so much on the grounds of its incompatibility with Christian faith as on the grounds of its incompatibility with Christian faith as that is perceived by a particular Christian. For some of us that would not constitute sufficient reason for setting aside Fowler's theory.

From the Catholic point of view there is no problem at all in accepting the proposition that human beings are so constituted that they search for meaning in existence and that their understanding of the ultimate will develop along with all other aspects of their humanity. Webster suggests there may be biblical and theological difficulties, but the following examples may perhaps dispel that suspicion.

The Catholic Encyclopedia of Theology, *Sacramentum Mundi*,[11] has a number of articles about faith. The first begins with a comment which is immediately relevant. It is said that God has offered 'the supernatural grace of faith as an abiding feature of man's mode of existence as a person' and that it is for every human being who is 'always potentially a believer'.

This entry is written by Karl Rahner, who has commented elsewhere on similar lines. A particularly apt illustration comes from his essay on 'Gradual ascent to Christian perfection'.[12] In this he describes an individual's situation in life and specifies the factors which must be included. These are the 'vital' situation (which includes biological constitution and phase of development); external circumstances not wholly under his control (biological and historical environment, including 'God's sovereign intervention by grace'); preceding situations which are constitutive of the present one and influential in what follows. Here again, the account of the way in which an individual is involved in the spiritual life is entirely compatible with that of Fowler, for Rahner compares the situation of someone who starts the spiritual life in old age, with that of someone who begins in youth. He defines the spiritual life as deciding 'to meet situations in as perfect a way as possible', and points out that the elderly person must meet the situations of old age which the youthful beginner arrives at only after many years.

Powers[13] writing in the *Journal of the American Jesuit Society*, examines the biblical tradition and goes on to say that, for a Christian, the assent which is faith is not 'simply a once-and-for-all intellectual acceptance of the truth of Christian belief statements, but an assent which is lived in the day-to-day experiences of people in community'. A later section of this essay explains how faith can be seen as gift. 'Trusting assent and grounding confidence emerge when personal freedom and courage are committed in the face of events, relationships and other dimensions of one's life process.' As time passes there is found a growing capacity to assent, together with a deeper grounding confidence, and it is the personal past history of assent which creates a greater readiness to assent to the future. This is the mode in which faith is experienced as gift: from one's life, history, fellowmen, and 'from the One who is discovered in the depths and at the limits of one's life'. It is doubtful whether Fowler and Powers have any knowledge of each other, but their views are not opposed.

For a thorough survey of biblical usage we can consult the *Theological Dictionary of the New Testament*[14] and there is much which supports Fowler's approach. Although there are significant distinctions between the Old Testament, Rabbinic Judaism and New Testament usage, the dynamic quality of faith is clear. In the New Testament a present and final act of God in Christ is relied upon rather than the Old Testament reliance on the experience of history, and Christian faith is the act of response to this final act and an attitude which pervades and governs the whole of life. This is an oversimplification of material of great significance and interest, and the article also includes an account of the transformation of 'faith' as an attitude and response to 'the faith' signifying 'what is believed'. Perhaps some fundamentalist Protestants would not approve of the article when it is found that R. Bultmann wrote it, but that would be unfortunate prejudice against a scholarly survey.

Therefore Fowler's account of faith development is not incompatible with reliable biblical and theological sources, both Protestant and Catholic.

The last point which requires comment is the question of conversion in relation to faith stages. There is a whole chapter on the subject in *Stages of Faith*: 'Form and content; stages of faith and conversion' and a list of the possible relations between stage change and conversion.[5] There is also a detailed account of the effects of 'religious conversion' (as the term is popularly understood) and the way in which there can be a recapitulation of the past with a healing effect (an experience of salvation?). The relation between such conversion and an intervention of grace is also discussed (p. 303) so that those who are uncertain of Fowler's position in these matters can refer to his account.

Conclusion

The primary reason for trying to answer some of Webster's queries about Fowler's work is the suspicion that the overall effect of so many unanswered questions could lead the busy educationist to discard Fowler's proposals before they have been properly investigated. This would be unfortunate for the principle of development of faith along with all other aspects of human development is too important to be lightly cast aside.

References

1. Webster, D. H. (1984) 'James Fowler's theory of faith development', *British Journal of Religious Education*, vol. 7, pp. 14–18.
2. Smith, M. (1983) Unpublished seminar paper, Birmingham University.
3. Smith, M. and Miller, B. (1984) 'Symbol and the faith process,' *The Month*, October, pp. 328–332.
4. Smith, M. 'Kohlberg and religious education', in C. Modgil and S. Modgil (eds) *Lawrence Kohlberg: consensus and controversy*, MS completed 1983.
5. Fowler, J. (1981) *Stages of Faith*, London, Harper and Row.
6. Kohlberg, L. (1981) *Essays on Moral Development*, vol. 1, London, Harper and Row.
7. Fowler, J. and Vergote, A. (eds) (1980) *Toward Moral and Religious Maturity*, Morristown, New Jersey, Silver Burdett.
8. Selman, R. (1980) *The Growth of Interpersonal Understanding: development and clinical analysis*, New York, Academic Press.
9. Dykstra, C. (1980) 'Moral virtue or social reasoning', *Religious Education*, vol. 75, pp. 115–128.
10. Kohlberg, L. (1974) 'Education, moral development and faith', *Moral Education*, vol. 4, p. 14.
11. Rahner, K. *et al* (ed.) (1968) *Sacramentum Mundi.*, London, Burns and Oates.
12. Rahner, K. (1984) *Theological Investigations*, vol. 3, London, Darton, Longman and Todd, pp. 3–23.
13. Powers, J. M. (1978) 'Faith, mortality, creativity: toward the art of believing', in *Theological Studies 39 (4) Faith in the Contemporary World*, American Jesuit Society.
14. Kittel, G. and Friedrich, G. (1968) *Theological Dictionary of the New Testament*, Grand Rapids, Michigan, Eerdmans.

2.4 Faith development in a changing world
Sharon Daloz Parks

The occasion of the Vosburgh lectures provides an opportunity to step back and reflect upon the broad context in which we as individuals and as a society now find ourselves. Thoughtful and courageous reflection reveals not simply that we live in a time of change; every time is a time of change. Rather, we seem to be poised at a *pivotal* time in history − a time when our deepest and wisest intuitions compel us to recognize that we seem to be asked to live in one of those apocalyptic eras. Our time is perhaps something like the sixth century, B.C., or the first, fourth, or sixteenth centuries; a time of paradigm shift; a time when patterns we have counted on give way to emerging patterns that we do not yet grasp. Our awareness of this is intensified as we stand on the threshold of the last decade of this millennium; yet most immediately we are now in the last throws of a national election in which the lines − both within each party and between the parties − seem to be most firmly drawn between those who attempt to provide images of leadership which recognize these currents of profound shift and change and those who wish to nurture and exploit the false hope that we, as individuals, as a nation, and as a world, can essentially maintain and sustain our present patterns, our most familiar assumptions and arrangements − and on our terms. Nevertheless, irrespective of the rhetoric and debate of a single election, the evidence keeps mounting, the ground keeps shifting under our feet. We know that we dwell in the context of breaking and broken cultural patterns, and it is these dynamics of cultural shift that shape the challenges which most threaten and inform the church, the university − every major institution in our culture.

This is the context in which you and I are educators, pastors, scholars, theologians, counselors and managers; this is the context in which it is our vocation to cultivate and inform leadership which can with courage and imagination assist in shaping a positive future for the whole human family and the small planet home that we share; this is the context − marked by both fear and hope − in which we meet to reflect upon the themes of wholeness and faith; this is the context in which we gather together to consider how we are making meaning of the times in which we live and how we shall both manifest and reform the faith by which we live.

Introducing faith development theory

As it happens, it is particularly fitting that these lectures coincide with the meeting of the Alumni Association of the Theological School, for I have chosen to engage the issues before us by critically reflecting upon the work of one of the distinguished alumni of Drew's Theological School, James Fowler. As most of you are well aware, Fowler's pioneering theory of faith development has achieved remarkable influence in the life of the American church, both mainline Protestant and Roman Catholic. It is being given significant attention among educators within Reformed Judaism. It has earned respect among some social scientists, and has also received some attention abroad. What I will assert here is that this work has been so widely received precisely because it both reflects and addresses some of the central challenges that beset North American culture at this period in our history. Likewise, however, I contend that when a theory is so widely embraced, it must also command our best critical attention if it is to adequately serve the needs before us; we must resist any naive vulnerability to its inevitable biases and distortions.

Following the work of H. Richard Niebuhr, Paul Tillich, Carlyle Marney, Wilfred Cantwell Smith, Robert Bellah, Jean Piaget, Erik Erikson, and Lawrence Kohlberg, James Fowler has, as a theologian rooted in the Christian, Methodist tradition, joined the conversation between theology and the social sciences so as to formulate an understanding of personality development which interprets and accounts for the indissoluble and continually evolving relationship between the individual, his or her community, and the power of the ultimate reality they share. Appropriating a broad, phenomenological understanding of faith, Fowler has brought together his theological perspective and constructive-developmental psychology, which informed by his own empirical research, has led to the formulation of a theory which describes the development of faith. Outlining a series of six stages which describe the ongoing composing and recomposing of one's sense of self, world, and God, this theory is, above all, a radical response to the central Enlightenment insight − the fact of the composing mind − as it describes the capacity of human beings to receive, relinquish, and re-pattern increasingly adequate apprehensions of the complex reality that we share. In contrast to other psychological-developmental theories, however, the central passion of this theory is to illumine the character and the essential role of the composing of what Niebuhr termed our 'ultimate' or most comprehensive environment and the transcendent and covenantal symbols and relationships upon which all of human being and becoming depends.

Fowler's work became accessible to the public in 1978, just ten years ago; and his central work, *Stages of Faith*, was published in

1982. Don Browning of the University of Chicago begins his review of this work[1] by observing:

> It may be that in our time theology will be revitalized, not by the systematic and foundational theologians, but by the practical theologians, theological ethicists, and religious educators. Although James Fowler's *Stages of Faith* is not actually a book on theology in any sense of the word, it does have enormous relevance to practical theology and through it to the entire body of theological reflection. Its immediate relevance is to the practical theological disciplines of pastoral care and religious education. But it would be a great pity for this book to be relegated to those readers professionally or existentially interested in those endeavors. It is a book of much broader scholarly interest; it is a work that should be of equal interest to the professional theologian and the secular inquirer into the structure and dynamics of human nature.

Building upon Browning's observation, I want to confirm that theology is, indeed, revitalized in the practical and direct response of theologians to the pain, yearning, and possibilities of the cultural-historical currents of a time and people. Faith development theory is serving as just such a response. Since this theory has been cultivated in North American soil, the strength of faith development theory may be manifest in its capacity to respond to key tensions in contemporary North American culture; however, its limits may be prescribed by the myopia inherent in any single culture's view.

For example, the capacity of this theoretical perspective to arrest the attention of so many may be found, in part, in its power to reflect our deepening awareness of the phenomenon of globalization which is now upon us. At the heart of this emerging global consciousness is a heightened awareness and increasingly growing conviction of the interdependence of all life — reflected in the ecumenical, economic, and ecological realities which fundamentally shape the anxieties and hopes of our time. These realities, concentrated most vividly in the threat of nuclear, economic, or ecological holocaust, relativize traditional forms of authority, including religious authority. Yet simultaneously, these very same pressures reveal the limits of relativism, secularization, and polarization. Even the most sophisticated and cynical of folk are compelled to recognize the need for a common faith — a new *public paideia* — by which our culture (which must now be re-conceived in global terms) may renew its common life. This phenomenon of globalization — the expansion of 'what must be taken into account' and its reverberations throughout our common life is, I believe, the central feature of the cultural climate in which faith development theory finds its resonance and makes its most significant contribution.[2]

How is it that faith development theory touches this vital nerve? Faith development theory responds to this phenomenon of globalization and its unprecedented implications in three primary ways. First, it offers a way of speaking of faith so as to hold and affirm traditional religious symbols, stories, and ritual but without foreclosing the conversation about ultimate values and commitments within a pluralistic world. Second, it manifests the conviction that even faith – the centering ground of human trust – can change, undergo transition and transformation, and yet retain its integrity. Third, it does so in a manner which potentially illumines the relationship between the individual and his or her context; thus it offers a way of holding the tension between the claims of the individual and the individual's necessary dependence upon the wider human community – a tension which increasingly assaults the individualistic milieu of western culture.

Fourth, and perhaps most significantly, embedded in each of these three dynamics is an enhanced consciousness of motion, change, and transition – and therefore a way of being with and understanding the profound motion, transition, and potential transformation in which we find ourselves. Indeed, the metaphor of *development*, dominant in western culture and connoting movement, growth, and ongoing transformation, has the power to resonate with both the traditional and contemporary experience of the American immigrant soul. And in the midst of this deepening sense of movement, the understanding of faith in which this theory rests – faith recognized as a broad human phenomenon not exclusively bound by cultic religious control – on one hand liberates the religiously committed imagination and on the other hand serves as a solvent of the secular resistance to religion. In short, faith development theory offers a dynamic language for an understanding of faith and religion which provides one way of addressing the reality of change and pluralism in a secularized world, yet its concern for the quality of mature faith counters the conventional dogma of relativism to which an ideology of pluralism is all too vulnerable.[3]

While these are the primary dynamics which I believe undergird the appeal of this theory, there are other forces at play which should also be mentioned. Surely it must be noted that the attractiveness of faith development theory is attributable in part to its capacity to link religion with psychology. As psychology has become *a* dominant if not *the* dominant way of ordering meaning, composing narrative, and orienting the individual to ultimate reality in the personalistic/individualistic/therapeutic culture of North America, *and* as the limits of psychological interpretation are being felt in the conventional culture at large and even by a growing number of clinicians, faith development theory finds a good deal of its power in both affirming psychological insight and pointing beyond it.

Indeed, faith development theory has the power to point beyond the reigning norms of established psychological practice in five significant ways. First, the Piagetian paradigm which centrally informs this perspective is finally an interactive model, which focuses, not upon the person alone, but rather upon the relation of the person to his or her environment, particularly the social environment. Thus faith development theory presses toward a psycho-*social* conviction and beyond the one-on-one clinical model which currently dominates the healing professions. Second, faith development theory is preoccupied less with a person's past than with the potential of the human life (and it is concerned, therefore, less with the diagnosis of pathology and stands rather in league with a person's direction of growth). Third, the tendency of this psychological and faith perspective is to respect and protect a person's meaning-making capacity, thus holding a bias against any chemical (drug) intervention which would blunt the energy, motion, spirit of the person. Fourth, in contrast to therapies which focus upon the individual as both patient and problem, it draws attention to the fact that both growth and therapy occur in a context − a context that is both ultimate and intimate − and that the character of nurture and healing is dependent upon the adequacy with which persons and their communities construe the character of the ultimate reality in which they dwell. Fifth, faith development theory, therefore, serves as a new conversation between religion and psychology because of its capacity to direct fresh attention to the relationship between the structures of personality and the contents of faith (the symbols, stories, and doctrines) so as to illumine, not only the pathological, but also the adaptive features of religion.

The power of this inter-disciplinary theory is, however, not only on the psychological side but also on the theological side. In addition to its capacity, already mentioned, to mediate religious discourse in a pluralistic world, this theory may potentially contribute to the restoration of the balance of transcendence and immanence in the discourse of theologians. Western culture is slowly becoming aware that theological thought in both its religious and secular forms has been dominated by attention to 'transcendence' at the expense of an adequate recognition of 'immanence.' In its attention to the 'subject' of faith, faith development theory illumines the manifold ways in which faith is mediated through the whole of our environment and alerts the theological imagination to the importance of attention to the immanent as well as to the transcendent. In a climate in which liberation theologies, which are likewise focused upon the immanent dimensions of revelation, are necessarily achieving an increasingly respectful hearing, a part of the intuitive appeal of faith development theory (as well as some of the most vehement resistance to it) is to be found in its resonance with liberation theologies and the potential of this shared address to foundational theology.

In the domain of practical theology, the domain in which faith development theory finds its curricular home, there is a growing awareness that the field is only loosely constituted as a discipline and remains flabby as long as it is composed of artificially reified sub-disciplines – preaching, education, liturgics, counseling, spiritual formation, social concern, program administration, and the rest. Both practitioners and theorists who struggle with the challenges of 'practical theology' have been quick to see the implications of faith development theory for their various domains; but of more importance is the power of faith development theory to foster a serious conversation among them, to forge a direction for a disciplined integration of the practical fields, and to serve the healing of the theory-practice split which distorts and tyrannizes the whole of the western academy.

If faith development theory is, in fact, worthy of such broadly gauged attention and appropriation, it is because of the quality of the ethical fiber at the core of the theory. The potential of the ethical commitments of this work have been expressed most forcefully by the work of Ronald Marstin,[4] who builds upon the work of Fowler to make vivid the correlation between the maturity of faith and the capacity for justice, but it is reflected also in some of Fowler's own most recent addresses to the issues of vocation, the public church, and the formation of a *paideia* which can serve to revision public life.

Critiques of faith development theory

I have outlined the primary strengths of this work, but what are the limitations and perils of this work to which we must also attend? It is not difficult to locate the primary points of the debate which cluster around Fowler's faith development theory. A review of the critical literature clearly reveals five domains of resistance and concern. They are: 1) the definition of faith; 2) the description of stage 6, Fowler's vision of 'mature faith'; 3) the adequacy of the theory in relation to particular religious beliefs; 4) the adequacy of the account of affect, process, the unconscious, and the imagination; 5) the adequacy of the theory vis-à-vis a critical socio-political analysis, especially a gender analysis. It is the first two of these which dominate the discussion to date and the last of these which is gaining increasing attention.

Consider first the critique of Fowler's definition of faith. Fowler defines faith as a human universal, a person's or a community's way-of-being-in-relation to an ultimate environment, anchored in a center or centers of power and value. As such, it includes, permeates, and informs our ways-of-being-in-relation to our neighbors and to the causes and companions of our lives.[5] As Harvey Cox has said in his now oft repeated response to this understanding of faith, 'There is something in this definition of faith to offend everyone.' It seems that it is at once very easy and very difficult for North Americans to hear this definition of faith. Those who in a pluralistic society are reaching for ways to enlarge our present understandings of faith and life so as to join the faith conversation of those different than oneself are intuitively and appreciatively responsive to this perspective. Those, however, with much at stake in traditional definitions of faith are immediately troubled and resistant – a resistance we must respect because, after all, faith itself is at risk.

These latter voices are those whose religious conviction defines faith in terms of a gift to which the human is simply receptive, a phenomenon beyond human control but also beyond human responsibility. This is faith sometimes understood as so radically transcendent as to just 'happen,'[6] and it is generally, but not always, defined in Christian religious terms. Those representing a more secular stance sometimes reflect an equal investment in retaining faith as exclusively transcendent and, therefore, likewise resist an understanding of faith which is integral to the experience of all human beings. While the first group seems to have a stake in defending the *agency* of God, this second group seems to have a stake in insuring the *irrelevancy* of God. The first would prefer to confine a discussion of faith to the subject of 'grace.' The latter would prefer to confine faith to religious categories safely deposited on the margins of society and to label as merely 'ego' the meaning-making, covenantal activity in relation to the ultimate that Fowler – following on Smith, Niebuhr, and Tillich – describes as faith.

Fowler's definition of faith is critiqued also for being too exclusively linked with 'knowing.'[7] It has been observed by one critic that there is a difference between having a center of supreme value and making a psychic commitment to that value,[8] and indeed, though Fowler insists that in faith the rational and the passional are fused, Fowler's emphasis on cognition or knowing may reflect not only Piaget's preoccupation with cognition, but also the split in most of Protestant theology between head and heart, mind and body.

Before we leave this domain of critique we also must note that there are thoughtful voices who press Fowler for a yet richer articulation of the relationship between faith structures and contents. Fowler has set the stage for this work and charted a course by which it may proceed. But I believe that it is fair to say, for instance, that the consequences of the relationships between a given faith content and the differing stage structures have not yet been explicated. For example, if we take seriously that a doctrine such as the Trinity will be grasped quite differently by a concrete operational, mythical-literal (stage 2) child or adult, than it will be by the critically aware, systemically thinking adult described by Fowler's stage 4, then theologians may have a moral obligation to incorporate the insights of a faith development theory into the central considerations of theological methodology. This is to say that, if faith development theory is to realize its potential contribution to the revitalizing of theology, this work will have to become integral to the faith development project.

Having now examined the primary issues surrounding Fowler's understanding of faith, we leave this domain of critique for the moment and turn to the critique of Fowler's 'stage 6.'

The whole first five stages in Fowler's scheme have not begun to receive the force of critique directed to his last stage, universalizing faith, stage 6. Fowler describes this form of faith as marked by an activist incarnation − a making real and tangible − of the imperatives of absolute love and justice. Exceedingly rare, the persons best described as stage 6, he says, have generated faith compositions in which their felt sense of an ultimate environment is inclusive of all being. Embodying a selfless passion for a transformed world, they create zones of liberation from the social, political, economic and ideological shackles we place and endure on human futurity. Living with felt participation in a power that unifies and transforms the world, these persons are often experienced as subversive of the structures by which we sustain our individual and corporate survival, security and significance.[9]

The most caustic of the critiques of Fowler's stage 6 is fostered by the awareness that all theory is to some degree 'biography writ large.' Thus it is remarked that stage 6 is 'elegant, attractive' but also that it seems 'antipluralistic and condescending' and 'too highly shaped by the life world of the theorist,'[10] or that it 'sounds like a professor with a coherent view of the universe',[11] a reflection of an ethos of idealism and intellectualism represented by writers and speakers who conceptualize well.[12]

More systematically, questions are raised regarding the shift in Fowler's methodology which occurs at stage 6. While each of the earlier stages is composed from a range of sources, rooted firmly in the empirical research method of the semi-clinical interview, stage 6 is composed quite differently. Fowler claims only one interview in which stage 6 appears, and draws rather upon biographies and biblical and theological insights and commitments, identifying stage 6 exemplars among well known figures such as Martin Luther King, Jr and Mother Teresa.

Additional critiques of stage 6 cluster around the two following questions: does the fascination with stage 6 preclude adequate attention to the rich implications of stage 5, and detract attention from the need for further empirical research in the faith development of those who are aging beyond 'mid-life'?

Since developmentalists know that we tend to hear only one stage ahead of 'where we are,' (and Fowler is yet only in his forties) it must be supposed that there may be stages of faith beyond Fowler's stage 5 which, while not tied to maturation, may be fostered by the aging-maturation process. In other words, while in constructive-developmental theory maturation is not a determinative factor, Fowler's stages 1 through 5 are influenced by biological maturation as a 'necessary but not sufficient condition' for the development of a given stage. If we are looking at faith across the life-span as well as the development of mature faith, are we to suppose that the conditions for the 'maturity' of faith are in place by middle-age, as supposed by the description of stage 5 and stage 6?[13] Might we find more 'stage 6' persons and might a stage 6 description be significantly recomposed by exploring these questions further as the theorist(s) themselves continue to age-mature? Has Fowler prematurely foreclosed the process of faith development? Some critics have suggested, for example, that Fowler's description of faith development should stop with stage 5, leaving the future open. It can be anticipated that these questions will be pressed harder as the aging population in North America expands.

In fact, Fowler might have done better to leave the questions of development beyond stage 5 open to further research which could remain in continuity with the methodology supporting the first five stages. It must be recognized, however, that it is absolutely incumbent upon Fowler to declare his vision of mature faith, which is precisely what his 'stage 6' does. Theories of human development, do, finally, 'stand on their heads.' The direction and goal of the trajectory envisioned does serve as the primary influence upon what the theorist sees and identifies as significant along the journey. To be responsible as a theorist, Fowler has had to be clear on this matter. But we may ask whether or not his vision of mature faith need to have been titled 'stage 6.'

Fowler has described mature faith in terms of both structure (as just described) and content. But the strongest critiques of stage 6 have been directed consistently at its content, his vision of mature faith. In *Stages of Faith* Fowler described stage 6 in language heavily dependent upon Judaic and Christian imagery – the Kingdom and Sovereignty of God. Further, the example of Jesus has been implicit in his choosing of exemplars: Dietrich Bonhoeffer, Mahatma Ghandi, Dag Hammarskjöld, Martin Luther King, Jr, Thomas Merton, and Mother Teresa. With the exception of Mother Teresa, all are males dead before their time, having in some way given up their life in the affirmation of a larger good, and with the exception of Mahatma Ghandi, all stand within the western Christian tradition. This definition of stage 6 seems to trouble critics primarily because it is an affront to the openness to pluralism which the theory fosters. Fowler's discussion of the 'absoluteness of the particular' does not seem to appease this sense of dissonance.

It should be observed that in *Becoming Adult, Becoming Christian* (published four years after *Stages of Faith*), Fowler's explicitly Christian language is more muted in his discussion of stage 6; he quotes at length a passage from Ghandi which incorporates passages from the *Bhagavad Gita*; and, further, he claims that he could have used examples from Buddhist, Jewish, humanists, and militants as well. This stance may ameliorate some of the critique, but until there is empirical validation in continuity with the methodology underlying the first five stages, 'stage 6' and the question of mature faith will continue to be a primary and crucial point of debate.

What is now most interesting and, I believe, important to note is: the two primary critiques of Fowler's work are directed at the openness of the definition of faith on one hand, and the closedness of the description of stage 6 — mature faith — on the other hand. And some critics address both issues with equal concern. At the risk of appearing to deal too superficially with the issues raised within each of these two critiques, I want to suggest that the tension between these two points of critique may be more important than either critique alone. This tension between an open definition of faith and a particularist vision of mature faith may reflect a deep ambivalence within the North American soul. Is it, perhaps, the case that, consistent with our democratic traditions, we respond to the call to an enlarged vision of the faithful human community (and therefore resist Fowler's seemingly provincial definition of stage 6); yet doesn't our North American culture simultaneously fear the loss of familiar forms of faith — and the loss of privilege those forms support (and therefore resist likewise Fowler's profoundly inclusive definition of faith)?

Against the backdrop of this question, let us note the critiques of faith development theory as they are voiced by particular traditions. We must, indeed, recognize that particularly in relationship to the issue of faith and its content, critique takes form in significant measure along denominational lines. For example, Roman Catholics, prepared by tradition of both natural law and spiritual formation, have responded readily to faith development theory. Unitarian-Universalists have found the theory to be useful in describing both their history of having often 'come out' of other denominations and instructive as a map for moving from a more relativistic stance to engagement with the contents and commitments of faith.

The response of mainline Protestants has been more measured. Protestants tend to hold the suspicion that faith development theory in its attention to the potential of the faithful life is too soft with its anthropology, not taking the pervasiveness of sin and 'the Fall' seriously enough. However, among the mainline denominations, The United Church of Christ, Disciples of Christ, and Methodists have responded significantly to this perspective, the latter encouraged by John Wesley's teaching about sanctification. Presbyterians have been the slowest of the Protestants to be engaged by this perspective. 'Lutherans and Calvinists particularly have been slow to embrace this work because with some conviction and some reason they believe that in some ways Christians can claim the word *faith* in a unique and singular way, and that others have to use the category of religion.'[14]

Although some Evangelicals are drawn to this perspective because it promises pragmatic assistance in terms of evangelism and formation, there is, again, resistance to the generic use of the term 'faith.' In this instance, the resistance is to the relativizing of the notions of scriptural and ecclesial authority and of the claim that there is no salvation apart from the self-disclosure of God in Jesus Christ. As faith development theory is insistent upon a broader notion of faith, these are inevitable and important points of theological debate; they are important, however, not simply in relationship to faith development theory, but because these issues also stand at the heart of the North American struggle with the religious and political pluralism of the contemporary world.

Now let us turn to the last domain of primary critique I outlined, the critique coming from a critical social-political perspective. Those who bring a critical social perspective to faith development theory do not have to look far to find a fitting subject for their reflection. While the word 'faith' may be problematic for theologians, the world 'development' is the first point of sensitivity for critical social theorists, specifically because of its use by economists. The word 'development' evokes a class critique on a global scale when economic development in 'underdeveloped nations' has been equated with the imperialism of North American and Western European interests. Some have suggested that to use this word is already to defeat everything that faith development theory might best serve, reflecting rather than correcting the ritualization of progress which dominates our achievement and consumer obsessed society.[15]

Gabriel Moran, on the other hand, has suggested that the issue of human development is too important to give over either to the psychologist or the economists, or even to the ecologists; he suggests that the word be enriched rather than abandoned.[16] I have suggested that the word 'transformation' might be used in addition to or even preferably. In any case, faith development theory must continue to critically examine its central metaphors as a part of its theological task.

John Broughton has delivered the harshest critique from a social critical perspective. A constructive-developmental psychologist himself who is seeking to be radically informed by critical social theory, he questions whether developmental stages are confounded with existing social hierarchy.[17] He is concerned both with class structures and with gender role arrangements. Specifically, as faith is described in part as a 'knowing,' he reminds us that the sociology of knowledge assists us in recognizing that knowledge is power and that the question of who defines and controls that knowledge is crucial. Accordingly, Broughton asks for greater clarity regarding the adequacy of faith development theory to distinguish, for example, between the person of 'more mature faith' at Fowler's stage 4 and the politically submissive citizen. Since faith development theory is self-consciously normative as well as descriptive work, this sort of critique – particularly that based on an analysis of class, gender, and race – must be taken with utmost seriousness. This work has only begun to emerge (beyond that of Fowler's desire, from the beginning, to be sensitive to these perspectives – especially class and race).

The clearest, most elaborated critique of this sort is coming from a gender analysis. At an informal level, a few *male* critics have asked[18]:

> Even if it is presumed that faith development theory and the theories in which it is rooted represents a male bias in its vision of maturity, is it the case that males necessarily attain the 'illusion of control' represented by Fowler's stage 4? – a critical, systematic, individuated faith which serves to justify an autonomous, powerful, and often isolating vision of faith and competence? Or, is this vision of development reflective merely of the development of the illusions of white, male mastery and privilege which is only modified in the direction of a more profound mutuality *after* stage 4 and the secured achievements of the 'successful mid-life male?'

Yet the most substantial analysis and critique challenging the normativity of developmental models in general has come from *women's* research and analysis. In the field of constructive-developmental theory, this work has been pioneered most forcefully, as many of you are aware, by Carol Gilligan and her colleagues whose research has identified 'a different voice' in the study of moral development, a voice which reflects on moral decision making from an orientation to responsibility and care rather than in terms of rights and the limitations of powers.[19] This work has dramatized the differences between the story of human development understood in terms of individuation of the self and that understood in terms of relation and the formation of a responsive self.

Fowler is well aware of Gilligan's work which he has discussed at length both appreciatively and critically in his book *Becoming Adult, Becoming Christian*. Yet it must be observed that when he follows this discussion with a fresh description of the stages of faith development, the dynamics of the individuating self (in contrast to the connective self) continue to dominate the description, even when examples from women's lives are used.

If we pursued this line of critique, we might begin by returning to Fowler's description of stage 6, mature faith, observing that not only are his examples predominately males, dead before their time, they are also those whose relationships with women may be perceived as problematic. Further, these men may be perceived as defined over-against community rather than as participating in the daily creation and sustaining of vital living community. Fowler characterizes them as having undergone a unique 'negation of ties'[20], language which women do and *do not* identify with our deepest impulses toward faithfulness. In this same vein, a male critic, Paul Philbert, has commented[21]:

> Fowler's conception of the end-term of development as probably leading to lonely prophetic martyrdom rather than to mutually enlivening community raises some underlying questions.... Are there socio-historical allegiances controlling the individualistic focus of these stages which will only reinforce the competitiveness and isolation characteristic of our present [North American] world? ... His last word on development portrays a strangely isolated hero. How ironic that a vehicle which serves so well as a metaphor for the integration of challenging concepts of growth still divides us at the very foundational level of imagination which Fowler likes to name *faith*.

Until such time as stage 6 exemplars are identified by methodology (and therefore sample controls) in continuity with the other stages, might persons who sustain covenantal commitments to marriage and/or community also be candidates for stage 6?

Perhaps socio-political critique finally most compellingly demands that we recognize that it is not easy and is perhaps inappropriate for any of us as individuals to think in adequately inclusive modes, and that therefore, the impact of a gender, race, and class analysis will not have its full effect until the composing of theory itself becomes a more egalitarian, shared enterprise, a matter which would require the more mature development of our political, academic, and social structures in the direction of the interdependent truth which is our ultimate reality. To put it in another way, we might say that inclusive modes of theory building, especially in the realm of theology, may be dependent upon the formation among us of a yet more mature faith.

In the meantime, we can recognize with respect and appreciation that within a mere decade and a half, James Fowler has fostered a conversation which, though it takes form at the cross-roads of religion and psychology, has not been confined to that sphere. Faith development theory now engages not only psychologists and theologians, but also ethicists, historians, clinicians, educators across disciplines and across the life-span — both parochial and public — spiritual directors, pastors, social theorists, social activists and many others. Not all of these conversations yet take place in the fullness of their potential strength; but it is not too much to say that something significant in human experience and human hope has been touched by this work. Therefore, it will continue to require our most vigorous and faithful critique, in North America and wherever its influence stirs the faithful imagination, specifically because it meets us where we are, in our fear and in our hope, in our desire to conserve the strength of our traditional faith and in our willingness to be invited into the promised potential of our shared and perhaps more faithful future.

Notes
1. Don Browning, Book review: *Stages of Faith: the psychology of human development and the quest for meaning*, by James Fowler, in *Anglican Theological Review*, vol. 65, 1983, pp. 124–127.
2. See James W. Fowler, 'Pluralism, particularity and paideia,' *Journal of Law and Religion*, vol 2, 1984, pp. 263–307. See also, Sharon Parks, 'Global complexity and young adult formation: implications for religious and professional education,' *Religion and Intellectual Life*, vol. 3, no. 3, 1987.
3. These dynamics correspond with the growing emphasis upon metaphor and faith language within religious-theological discourse which increasingly finds its voice in the language of 'meaning' and 'story' (narrative).
4. Ronald Marstin, *Beyond Our Tribal Gods: the maturing of faith*, Maryknoll, New York, Orbis Books, 1979.
5. James W. Fowler and Sam Keen, *Life Maps: conversations on the journey of faith*, (ed. Jerome Berryman), Waco, Texas, Word Books, 1978, p. 21.
6. Dwayne Huebner, 'Christian growth in faith,' *Religious Education*, vol. 81, no. 4, 1986, p. 516.
7. See especially James W. Fowler and Sam Keen, 'Body/faith: trust, dissolution and grace,' in *Life Maps: conversations on the journey of faith*, (ed. Jerome Berryman), Waco, Texas, Word Books, 1978, ch. 3.
8. Ernest Wallwork, 'Religious development,' in J. Broughton (ed.) *Cognitive Developmental Psychology of James Mark Baldwin*, Norwood, New Jersey, Abler Publishing Co. 1982, p. 375. A related issue is voiced by a few who raise the question of the relation of knowing and action-participation in the domain of faith. In this press for a more articulated role for 'obedient action' in faith, Dykstra offers a useful model by which the whole critique of Fowler's definition of faith may proceed. He urges Fowler's critics to recognize that there have always been many definitions of faith, and one must be as careful as Fowler is in saying *if* faith is this, *then....* Craig Dykstra, 'What is faith?: an experiment in the hypothetical mode,' in Craig Dykstra and Sharon Parks (eds), *Faith Development and Fowler*, Birmingham, Alabama, Religious Education Press, 1986, ch. 2.
9. James W. Fowler, *Stages of Faith*, San Francisco, Harper and Row, 1981, pp. 200–201.
10. Richard A. Hoehn, Book review: *Stages of Faith*, in *Review of Religious Research*, vol. 25, no. 1, 1983, p. 79.
11. Sam Keen, 'Body/faith,' *op.cit.*, p. 103.
12. Steven Ivy, Book review: *Stages of Faith*, in *The Journal of Pastoral Care*, vol. 23, no. 4., p. 272.
13. See Constance H. Buchanan, 'The fall of Icarus: gender, religion and the aging society,' in C.H. Buchanan *et al* (eds), *Shaping New Vision: gender and values in American culture*, UMI Research Press, 1987.
14. James W. Fowler, 'Critique and future directions in the study of faith development,' unpublished lecture, Harvard Divinity School, Fall, 1984.
15. Dwayne Huebner, unpublished response, Conference on faith development, Auburn Theological Seminary, March, 1982. J.E. Loder and J.W. Fowler, 'Conversations on Fowler's *Stages of Faith* and Loder's *The Transforming Moment*', *Religious Education*, vol. 77, no. 2, 1982, pp. 13–18.
16. Gabriel Moran, *Religious Education Development: images for the future*, Minneapolis, Winston Press, 1983, pp. 1–27.
17. John Broughton, 'The political psychology of faith development theory,' in Craig Dykstra and Sharon Parks (eds), *Faith Development and Fowler*, Birmingham, Alabama, Religious Education Press, 1986, p. 97.
18. Craig Dykstra, unpublished response, Conference on faith development, Auburn Theological Seminary, March, 1982, and Constance H. Buchanan, 'The fall of Icarus: gender, religion, and the aging society,' *op.cit.*

19. Carol Gilligan, *In a Different Voice: psychological theory and women's development*, Cambridge, Harvard University Press, 1982.
20. James Fowler, *Becoming Adult, Becoming Christian*, San Francisco, Harper and Row, 1985, p. 73.
21. Paul J. Philbert, 'Symposium review: *Stages of Faith*,' *Horizons*, p. 122.

3. Theology and faith development

In this section we have included three essays that express broadly theological criticisms of Fowler's account of faith and its development.

Mary Ford-Grabowsky offers a 'theoretical alternative to faith development more in keeping with traditional biblical and dogmatic understandings'. Her essay, 'The journey of a pilgrim: an alternative to Fowler', which first appeared in *Living Light*, vol. 24, 1988, pp. 242–254, criticizes Fowler's reliance on developmental ego psychology as neglecting the biblical image of the inner self. She seeks to correct this inbalance with contributions from Jungian depth psychology and the 'theology of faith' of the twelfth century Benedictine abbess, Hildegard of Bingen. She concludes that there is 'more to Christian development than [an account of] ego growth' that is devoid of content and mystery and ignores the restraining power of evil.[1]

The other two papers offer criticisms of Fowler's definition of faith from traditional Protestant perspectives. They were both published in vol. 85, no. 1 (1990) of the journal *Religious Education*. William Avery's piece, 'A Lutheran examines James Fowler' (pp. 69–83), is in some ways the more positive of the two. While accepting *both* that Fowler's account of faith is the only definition Fowler can allow himself within the framework of the social sciences, *and* that this concept must be rejected from the standpoint of the Lutheran theology of justification, Avery re-interprets Fowler's work as an account of 'different ways of living in one's baptism' – and welcomes it as such.

Richard Osmer has been associated with faith development thinking over a number of years.[2] In his paper 'James W. Fowler and the Reformed Tradition: an exercise in theological reflection in religious education' (*op. cit.*, pp. 51–68), he attempts to assess the theological issues at stake in criticisms of Fowler that arise from a Reformed theological perspective. Drawing on Calvin and H. Richard Niebuhr, a theologian who has greatly influenced Fowler's work,[3] Osmer initially postulates that Fowler's work is consistent with the Reformed tradition as being 'simply a depiction of natural piety'. But Fowler's understanding of faith departs from the cardinal insights of such a theology in his formal account of faith and in his implicit theology both of the Fall and of the relationship between nature and grace. Osmer recognizes, however, that these insights themselves are (or should be) the subject of profound debate within Reformed theology.[4]

Notes

1. See also Mary Ford-Grabowsky, 'The fullness of the Christian faith experience: dimensions missing in faith development theory', *The Journal of Pastoral Care*, vol. 41, no. 1, 1987, pp. 39–47, and 'Flaws in faith development theory', *Religious Education*, vol. 82, no. 1, 1987, pp. 80–93.
2. See his joint essay with Fowler, 'Childhood and adolescence: a faith development perspective', in Robert J. Wicks, Richard D. Parsons and Donald Capps (eds), *Clinical Handbook of Pastoral Counseling*, New York, Paulist Press, 1985.
3. See Stuart D. McLean, 'Basic sources and new possibilities: H. Richard Niebuhr's influence on faith development theory', in Craig Dykstra and Sharon Parks (eds), *Faith Development and Fowler*, Birmingham, Alabama, Religious Education Press, 1986, pp. 157–179.
4. For other theological critiques of Fowler's work, see also Dwayne Huebner, 'Christian growth in faith', *Religious Education*, vol. 81, no. 4, 1986, pp. 511–521, Clyde J. Steckel, 'The emergence of morality and faith in stages: a theological critique of developmental theories', in Paul W. Pruyser (ed.), *Changing Views of the Human Condition*, Macon, Georgia, Mercer University Press, 1987, pp. 159–177 and Sam Keen in Jim Fowler and Sam Keen, *Life Maps*, Waco, Texas, Word Books, 1978.

3.1 The journey of a pilgrim: an alternative to Fowler

Mary Ford-Grabowsky

Although the value of James Fowler's research is undeniable, the post-modern era is challenging his model of faith development as theologically deficient, inadequate to account for the depths of the Christian faith life. Fowler impoverishes the concept of faith by focussing on what he calls the 'human side' of faith without reference to the revealed 'divine side,'[1] thus neglecting the transtemporal aspect of faith, the Christian trinitarian confession, and the faith-destroying work of sin and evil. Grounding his concept of the person in the development ego psychology of Piaget and Kohlberg, he perpetuates a cognitive bias and structural reductionism of the personality that loses the biblical image of the *esō anthrōpos* (inner self), the whole man or woman alive in Christ.

This paper uses the analytical psychology of C. G. Jung and the Pauline theology of Hildegard of Bingen to propose a theoretical alternative to faith development more in keeping with traditional biblical and dogmatic understandings. A case study taken with a 'Christian faith interview' (C.F.I.) intended to supplant the Fowler interview instrument in Christian faith research demonstrates the validity of this approach.[2] Whereas Fowler's interview format asks only what a subject thinks, thus cutting off much of the person, the C.F.I. looks for the full participation of the personality in faith.

Jung's idea of spiritual development

A 'second reading' of Jung[3] is needed to replace the partly overcritical, partly uncritical, first Christian reading. The new study should be governed by a principle of selectivity that prescinds from the gnostic and reductionistic elements in Jung's thought to utilize those elements compatible with Christian ideas. This paper will adhere to the principle of selectivity by using a core distinction he grounds in Paul.

In defining human personality Jung differentiates between the ego and the self. Ego refers to the individual's center of consciousness, self to the psychic totality composed of conscious and unconscious elements. As the source of one's sense of identity and continuity, the ego develops through interaction with the environment in the first half of life whereas the self is potentially present at birth as the complete person one is meant to become. The two constructs thus relate like part to whole and concrete reality to ideal reality. Whereas the ego is the perceptible part of the personality, the self is a 'transcendental postulate' ultimately unknowable, a portion of its contents and dynamics remaining unexperienced even in psychoanalysis. The unrepresentable self often takes the form in individual dream symbolism of a mandala delineated in the circular or quadratic structures symbolic of wholeness.

Jung considers the ego 'mortal,' the self 'immortal.' While any of his ideas contains less meaning than the corresponding Christian concept, his notion of 'immortality' at least implies a grasp of the transtemporal dimension of reality missing in Fowler. The self is 'immortal' because it is an archetype, a bipolar construct anchored on one 'side' in eternity, and on the other in time. The archetype's double nature is suggested in its etymology, *arché* meaning place of origin, principle, or cause, and *typos*, imprint. The German word *sinnbild* (symbol), with which Jung designates the self, breaks down in the same way, its first syllable indicating the imperishable world of meaning, its second syllable an image in the *bios* (life). While the transhistorical aspect of the archetypal self pre-exists consciousness as an abstract imperceptible *Gestalt*, its historical aspect is capable of unique differentiation in concrete, material attributes. Jung seems at times to equate the potential pole of the self with the biblical *eikōn theou* (image of God), the actual pole with the *homoiōsis theou* (likeness of God), the former with Plato's *eidos* (form), the latter with the *eidōlon* (idol), (despite critics' charge that he thus confuses psychology with philosophy).

Jung believes that the psyche is structured in syzygies, pairs of opposites subject to a conflicting tendency, the ego driving toward the splitting up of the opposites, the self toward a *coniunctio oppositorum* (joining of opposites). An innate 'transcendent function' strives to overcome the ego's preference for 'onesidedness' however by bringing the opposites into relationship so that they may be held in tension, neither side repressed. The unconscious pole of a pair is joined to the conscious pole by means of a 'uniting symbol.' Ongoing participation in the consciousness/unconsciousness dialectic through symbol interpretation not only grants knowledge of the opposites but of the self, since the self is the medium of the *commixtio oppositorum* (mixing of opposites) and one who knows the opposites knows the self. (Jung would not agree of course with the Christian doctrine that one who knows the opposites knows Christ.)[4]

Whereas the ego is merely the 'gatekeeper' to unconsciousness the self participates in the 'collective unconscious,' the repository of the archetypes, and incorporates a 'personal unconscious,' the 'acquisitions of personal life, everything forgotten, repressed, subliminally perceived, thought, felt.' The personal unconscious contains two archetypes, the shadow or negative side of personality and the anima/us or contrasexual compotent of the psyche.

Jung's distinction between the personal ego and the transpersonal self, traceable through the Church Fathers to the Pauline writings, where the *exō anthrōpos*, or outer self, is frequently compared and contrasted with the *esō anthrōpos*, or inmost self. Paul explains these designations primarily through a series of analogies. The *exō anthrōpos* relates to the *esō anthrōpos* as flesh to spirit for example or as the unregenerate self to the regenerate self, the sin nature to the new nature, the unspiritual person to the spiritual person, the old self to the new self (Romans 6:6, 7:22; I Corinthians 2:14, Ephesians 3:16, 4:24; Colossians 3:10). The *exō anthrōpos* and the *esō anthrōpos* should not be seen as exact theological equivalents of Jung's psychological terms (ego and self) but the close correspondence between the two pairs justifies a comparison, since the ego like the *exō anthrōpos* connotes the narcissistic psyche guilty of original *hybris* (pride) while the self like the *esō anthrōpos* suggests the pneumatic man or woman.

Jung conceives of spiritual growth as recurrent transformation on what he calls the ego/self 'axis,' meaning that individuals alternate throughout the course of the human lifespan between ego-centeredness and the higher life of the self. He metaphorically calls the process by which the ego is dislodged from its place of psychic centrality and shifted to the periphery of the psyche 'ego crucifixion,' since the birth of the self means a defeat for the ego. Like the regeneration myths of Osiris, Dionysius, and Persephone, the redemption narrative of Hercules, or Jesus' message to Nicodemus, Jung's transformation model moves through darkness to light. But the dynamic unfolds in an endless pattern of dying and becoming, repeated because life experience inevitably brings about renewed egocentricity and renewed need for rebirth. Cycles of centering/decentering/recentering accumulate on the spiral of spiritual development in a pattern called 'circumambulation around the center,'[5] a sound psychological equivalent of the biblical journey *in Christo*.[6]

Jung explains failed transformation on the ego-self axis with a concept of satan, or evil, interpreted as the arresting power that blocks not only individual spiritual development but the growth of the cosmos as well. 'Satan' causes in the human psyche a state of hubristic 'ego inflation'[7] that impedes self-actualization. This prideful self-centeredness blind to God and neighbor prevents realization of the *esō anthrōpos* causing the *exō anthrōpos* to dominate one's attitudes and existence. Thus satan and inflation relate to each other in Jung as evil to sin in Christian theology

In the same context, Jung saw a causal relationship between his era's increasing narcissism and agnosticism. Only self-actualization, he argued, could cut through the ego's selfishness and reopen humanity to knowledge of God.

Jung's depth psychology undergirds a Christian theology of faith more adequately than does Fowler's ego psychology, not only because it brings in a conception of the transtemporal and a fuller understanding of the person, but also because the idea of 'Satan' helps to account for the absence of faith. Fowler thinks everyone always has faith but biblical faith is a gift rejected and lost as well as received.

A theology of faith

Hildegard of Bingen, a Benedictine abbess of the twelfth century celebrated in her time as a theologian, prophet, preacher and reformer, refers repeatedly in her writings to the Pauline *exō anthrōpos* and *esō anthrōpos*, translated as the *homo exterior*, outer man, and the *homo interior*, inner man.[8] These two personality designations differ first in that the *homo exterior* (like the ego in Jung) has a tendency to become inflated with pride[9] whereas the *homo interior* (like the self in Jung) is characterized by humility and a capacity for sacrifice.[10] Whereas the *homo exterior* is unreceptive to 'divine things'[11] *the homo interior* knows God in faith and experience as the Living Light, the Word heard and seen. Hildegard conveys the *homo exterior's* inability to know God with the image of blindness: 'The outer eyes can not see' the incomprehensible Deity perceptible to the *homo interior's* 'contemplative eye.'[12] The *homo exterior* resists grace[13] and succumbs to sin[14] while the *homo interior* appropriates grace and struggles against evil. The former 'consents to fleshly desires,'[15] the latter lives the *imitatio Christi*. The former fails in goodness by 'exercising the will in liberty,'[16] the latter overcomes wilfulness by surrender to God's will. The two relate as prelapsarian to postlapsarian[17] and, her most important point, Christian faith is a function of the *homo interior*: 'Some people know through the inner eye what is hidden from the outer sight and in this they believe with certainty not doubting. Now this is faith.'[18] The *homo exterior* 'has no wish to believe,'[19] but the *homo interior* 'finds life in salvation because he or she believes.'[19] What does the *homo interior* believe? Hildegard's short formula for the confessional aspect of faith is 'true belief in the Trinity,' a gift granted at baptism independently of one's potential for the stadial evolution of cognitive ego structures essential to Fowler. Ironically in Fowler's system the *homo exterior* (ego) is the bearer of faith and the *homo interior* (self), the biblical subject of faith, does not enter into the discussion (although it is implicitly there in stages).[20]

Since baptism holds no guarantee of either lifelong faith or the *homo interior's* altruistic attitude, Hildegard talks about 'working God's work with God' to sustain or recover both. We include in this category (1) her theology of grace, (2) her sacramentology, and

(3) her hermeneutic of evil and sin. Who 'works God's work with God' by appropriating grace, receiving the sacraments, and resisting the power of negative energy will know Christ in faith and the self-*in-Christo*. 'Humankind is called to assist God,' she says, 'to co-create,'[21] not in the sense of a synergy doctrine where humanity and God are equal partners in the divine work, but as a finite creature cooperating with an infinite creator, while acknowledging that even our own contribution to our salvation is a gift of God. We will look briefly now at each aspect of 'working God's work with God.'

Hildegard's theology of grace interweaves the concepts of freedom and predestination. A passage on the functions of grace says it uplifts, energizes, heals, converts, transforms, grants goodness, elicits repentance, opens, resolves conflict, potentiates free choice and faith.[22] Her belief that grace actualizes the *homo interior* is implicit here; in faith the 'uplifting' operation alone pinpoints the transformation through what Hildegard's Benedictine order calls the 'ascent of humility' and the 'ascent of faith,' the image of upward movement communicating transition to the 'higher' life of the self.

For Hildegard, grace and freedom relate (1) reciprocally, and (2) paradoxically. As to the first, were there no prior freedom on which grace could act, grace would be inoperative; conversely were there no grace to act on freedom, freedom would be inoperative: freedom is the condition for grace, grace the condition for freedom. The paradoxicality surfaces in the context of the 'problem' of grace: its limited efficacy, the failure of many people to ever acquire the self's broad viewpoint. 'Here is the struggle,' she writes, 'that what (grace) gives attains to its end or not.'[23] She believes that there is at the point of coincidence between grace and freedom a 'Struggle,' a decision-making process that feels like a tug of war: one can appropriate grace or spurn it; some people decide to 'follow God's will,' others to 'precipitate themselves toward death.'[24] If we make the first choice, it is all God's doing; if we make the second, it is all our own doing. *Omne bonum a Deo, omne malum ab homine* (every good from God, every evil from man). She highlights the paradoxicality by insisting that when we follow God's will it is 'whether we wish to or not,'[25] since the Holy Spirit acts within us to accomplish what we could not unaided by grace.

Hildegard uses the word 'predestination,' but it does not mean that the predicament of the faithless *homo exterior* is willed by God, nor that the divine omnipotence disempowers humanity, nor that there is either double predestination or predestination to sin. Rather, the word alludes to the divine love that calls to salvation, the 'elect,' (apparently all people although many ignore the call)[26]:

> God works ... through the Only-begotten, in the love of the church,
> to bring to the consummation of the last day everything predestined
> before creation ... God draws it back to himself confirmed ... and
> completed in the highest perfection.

Here is a Pauline cosmic soteriology, not the doctrine of the
apokatastasis (restoration). Hildegard's doctrine of hope extends
to only those who respond to God's will, not to all people. She
uses the image of 'compelled sheep' (see John 10:1–42, 1:29) for
those ordained in the eternal counsel for salvation, those whom
'God compels against their wills ... to leave inquiry.'[27] The divine
constraint is more like a lure or incentive however than a force that
would violate human freedom, a point illustrated with pericopes like
Ecclesiasticus 15:16: 'God has placed before you fire and water;
stretch out your hand for whichever you wish.' In respect to those
instances when God's correction is painful she quotes passages like
Wisdom 3:4–5:

> Though in the sight of people they were punished,
> their hope is full of immortality,
> having been disciplined a little,
> they will receive great good,
> like gold in the furnace God tried them,
> like a sacrificial burnt offering God accepted them.

The trial by fire pictured here as gold refining is a good metaphor for
the suffering often concomitant with the *homo exterior/interior* conversion. Jung uses the same figure to denote transformation on the
ego/self axis (anchoring his argument in pagan alchemy however).
Hildegard distinguishes between suffering God (1) 'imposes' and (2)
'allows,' the first referring to predestination and the positive will of
God, the second to foreknowledge and the permitting will of God.
Imposed pain is rare and linked to original sin since flawed people
are sometimes unable to 'stand firm' in the *homo interior* posture
without this divine reminder.

Hildegard's sacramentology, the second aspect of 'working God's
work with God,' is too large a topic to be treated thoroughly here but
a summary follows. In essence the seven Roman Catholic sacraments
constitute the principle means of grace for undergirding the *homo
interior* and faith. In particular, baptism, 'the sacrament of the
true unity,' (see Matthew 28:19) and eucharist call forth the
Christian-self. Baptism launches people in the right direction but
some, feeling weighed down by the baptismal garment, discard
it while others, finding it light, retain it by (1) confessing 'true
belief in the Trinity,' and (2) performing acts of service, and (3)
keeping the creature/creator covenant. Exegeting Mark 16:16 (One
who believes and is baptized shall be saved, but one who does not
believe shall be condemned), Hildegard writes that 'the Holy Spirit
awakens the soul to life through the pouring of the water.'[28] Baptism

grants faith, faith the knowledge of God, knowledge of God the stilling of desire, the stilling of desire a rebirth that issues in the life of the *homo interior*. Thus regenerated in the font, restored to purity by remission of original sin, one becomes free enough to walk in grace — that some choose another way is a matter of evil and sin.

Hildegard's theology of the eucharist is connected to her theology of the light. The light (which has nothing to do with the medieval light metaphysic, a neo-platonic emanation doctrine) signals two realities: *Deus Lux Vivens* (God living light) and the spiritual light created four days before the sun's physical light. Christ's real presence in the eucharist 'bathes communicants in light' reinforcing faith, *scientia Dei* (knowledge of God), healing and the *homo interior's* will to live as a light to the world.[29] To communicants, she says, 'Ihr sollt ein brennendes Licht sein und die Wahrheit im Nahmen der Dreifaltigkeit lehren.' (You have to be a burning light and learn the truth in the name of the Trinity.)[30]

The concept, 'working God's work with God,' incorporates as its third element Hildegard's hermeneutic of evil and sin. Like Jung, she symbolizes evil with the figure of 'satan,' who fortifies the *homo exterior's Weltanschauung* (outer man's world view), thus impeding development of the *homo interior* capable of faith. 'You who desire your salvation,' she counsels, 'who have received baptism and are the anointed mountain of God, *resist* satan.'[31] But the evil one seduces the *homo exterior* into prideful non-resistance[32] drawing him or her from 'the true way of righteousness' (Job 17:9) onto the 'by-ways' of sin.

Heinrich Schipperges notices the attention Hildegard gives to the *retardierende Kraft* (restraining power) of evil, the arresting power by which negative energy hinders, knocks off course, or blocks totally the development of the *homo interior* and the natural world.[33] This concept coincides theologically with Jung's psychological idea of satan as the demonic fixating force that fosters hubristic ego-centeredness, thwarting the growth of the self. For Jung, satan reverses the 'directional self-actualizing tendency' of the teleological structures inherent in human and cosmic being. To make the same point, Hildegard allegorizes satan's work as a 'reversal of *viriditas*,' meaning the 'greenness' of both nature and grace: 'Satan's power extends to the source of the wind,' she writes. 'He seems to set the air in motion, to bring forth fire, to cause lightning, thunder, and hail-storms to fall.... He seems to rob the forests of their greenness, to give them a new sap.'[34] Just as he stops the free forward flow of life, so the course of faith: Satan beclouds the inner eye of the *homo interior* so that the *homo exterior* will see with the 'outer eye' only 'what it likes to see, ignoring the invisible that exists eternally in God and can be understood through true faith alone.'[35] Hildegard's central metaphor for sin, the *tumor mentis*, or swelling of the mind, resembles both biblical *hybris* (pride) and what Jung means by 'ego inflation' (discussed above). 'Because of the swelling of the mind,' she writes, people 'do not seek the remedy of salvation.... While they are able to find God, they do not seek.'[36] Humanity stands at the crossroads of decision, able despite the seductive power of evil to choose the 'wrong way' or the 'right way,' ego-centeredness or God-centeredness, faithlessness or faith. Who 'works God's work with God' will select the 'right way.'

We will now look at Hildegard's idea of faith development, which departs radically from Fowler's. For her, an innate desire to know God activates all human growth. The search for God goes on in memory and time, backwards in longing for our lost homeland, forwards in striving towards the eschaton. When 'the good and the bad are separated at the Last Judgment,' she writes, 'it will be clear how either in infancy or in childhood or in youth or in old age or at the end of life one sought God.'[37] In any lifecycle era, faith entails exertion in four areas: (1) to not forget God, (2) to turn to God in the mirror of faith (I Corinthians 13:12), (3) to surrender to God's presence, and (4) to confess belief in the Trinity present in scripture, reason, conscience, and nature to the 'contemplative eye' of the *homo interior*. But faith development properly speaking has to do with two factors: (1) learning more about one's faith, its doctrines, rites, and traditions for example and (2) increasing one's zeal. Hildegard wrote her theological trilogy, *Scivias*, to contribute to precisely those two goals: to teach the Christian faith to her ignorant contemporaries and transmute their lukewarm commitment into fervor.[38]

Since, for Hildegard, faith is a function of the *homo interior*, faith development also relates to transformation on the *homo exterior/homo interior* pole, the Jungian ego/self axis. Her theological correlate to Jung's 'circumambulation around the center' is an updated-Augustinian interpretation of the Platonic, Neoplatonic 'journey of the pilgrim soul.'[39] A biblical image of the faith journey as concerned with the divine 'object' of faith as with the human subject, it indirectly questions Fowler's reduction of faith into the non-biblical language of developmental psychology.

'The journey of a pilgrim' allegorizes both humanity's and the individual's plight as 'being underway' between creation and return to God, between *exitus* (going out) and *reditus* (returning). The voyage begins with the infusion of life soon followed by birth into the 'shadow of death' (Isaiah 9:2; Matthew 4:16; Luke 1:79) where the anguished pilgrim laments this 'fall' and longs for 'paradise lost.' Although baptism relieves the human predicament by kindling hope of going back on a straight and narrow path to Mother Zion, the wanderer soon strays off the way of salvation into the by-way of sin in the 'Zone of Evil.' Captured there by the enemy, subjected to servitude, the wounded traveller comes to know the suffering.

The suffering turns out to be purposeful however since it induces the captive to take responsibility for his/her role in the entrapment and to repent. Immediately divine consolation comes, and soon the pilgrim is freed to wander onward. Nevertheless 'whirlwinds' of conflict quickly assail the struggling wayfarer causing new detours. Eventually, however, one arrives at the 'Zone of Christ' where manna provides strength to resist the enemy's tempting onslaughts. A voice is now heard saying[40]:

> The ineffable Trinity revealed itself when God sent into the world the Only-begotten, conceived by the Holy Spirit and born of Mary in order that men and women ... might be brought back to the way of truth.

Only constant effort to meet Hildegard's four requirements for the faith life (remembering God, turning to God in the mirror of faith, surrender, and acknowledging the Trinity), will empower the voyager to stay on the right road. If no promise comes of perfect future adherence to the way of justice and human weakness makes likely another fall from grace, hope nevertheless assures fresh repentance and God's help. The pilgrim's journey ends with joyful anticipation of death and resurrection at the Last Judgment.

Hildegard punctuates her 'Pilgrim's Progress' with biblical citations like Ezekiel 18:31: 'Cast away from you all the transgressions which you have committed against me, and get yourself a new heart and a new spirit.'[41] The three-step *itinerarium* implicit here, moving from (1) sin to (2) repentance to (3) salvation in ever-reoccurring cycles, does not unfold in a linear pattern like Fowler's stages but takes the spiralling course called by Jung 'circumambulation around the center.' The voyage swings forward and backward between the 'Zone of Evil' and the 'Zone of Christ,' the two cardinal points on Hildegard's map of the spiritual life, offering opposite enticements to the traveller, who succumbs first to one then to the other until the voyage finally ends in the final triumph of grace. Here Hildegard's (Augustinian) conceptualization of the spiritual life coincides with Jungian 'centering/decentering/recentering': a sojourn in the 'Christ Zone' means centering, imprisonment in the 'Evil Zone' decentering, return to the holy zone recentering. These interludes parallel alternations on the ego/self axis.

An idea central to Hildegard's doctrine of the spiritual life and implicit in her story of the itinerant Christian holds that God requires of every Christian 'a martyrdom of you against yourself' in imitation of Christ's crucifixion.[42] Comparable theologically to Jung's concept of the 'ego crucifixion' needed to set free the pneumatic self, 'you against yourself' refers to the battle for psychic dominance ongoing between the *homo interior* and the *homo exterior*. There is an advance in meaning of course between

Jung's idea of the self and Hildegard's concept of the *homo interior* or Christian-self, and her vision of spiritual progress goes far beyond Jungian self-actualization to the Pauline goal of life *in Christo*.

An analysis of a Christian faith interview (C.F.I) will verify the Jung/Hildegard study.[43]

Case study

A typical modern American pilgrim, 'John' wandered from his native Midwestern town to Europe, India, and the Far East in search of his lost faith. In France a depression climaxed with a powerful spiritual experience that guided him, not only to rejoin the Church, but to become a monk and take holy orders. At the time of the interview John had been a priest for eleven years, nine spent at a New England Monastery, the last two at a West Coast University in a doctoral program.

In the monastery he had experienced profoundly Christ's love. Communal liturgy and prayer 'open a deep dynamic,' he said, 'the power of symbolic action, the power of being present to each other. . . . Things happen (in liturgy and prayer) that I've not experienced otherwise. . . . It leads us into dimensions of love, . . . an experience of love that I think is rare. . . . It's very, very deep.' (3) Like Hildegard's *homo interior* he was 'strongly God-centered,' (11) sensing divine 'arms around the community,' (5) feeling God knew him 'through and through . . . like a crystal' accepting even what he found unacceptable in himself (6–7).

When John moved to the West Coast he underwent 'a time of real crisis.' (11) Separated from his brother monks and isolated, feelings of loneliness, anxiety and anger overtook him until he lost 'the center of his existence,' (14) Christ. When love and hope waned the 'deepest period of doubt' he had ever undergone (31) turned his former focus on God into 'thinking of self,' (11) causing a regression to precisely what Jung means by the 'ego,' Hildegard by the *homo exterior*. (Notice that John himself makes an experiential association between 'doubt' and 'thinking of self,' thus bearing out Hildegard's pairing of faithlessness and ego at one end of a spectrum, faith and the *homo interior* at the other end.) John's monastic 'centering' formation had clashed with a 'decentering' situation able to reverse conversion. A 'recentering' dynamic would restore his faith, hope, and love but not until a painful year had gone by.

Forced by the pain he was undergoing to search for his lost 'center,' John began to practice what for Hildegard are the four criteria of the faith life (see above) by looking for people with whom he could talk about Christ and for a community where he could recite the Hours. He discovered a Catholic high school where 'the community of Christ is experienced' (21) and he could regularly celebrate the eucharist, then formed a university student group to pray the psalms, another to meet for mass on Wednesdays. 'Now it's back to being a very rich experience of God,' (11) he said, 'The most important thing, what gives my life meaning, is (once again) love.... Feeling it. Giving it. Being it.' (50) The key to John's healing lay in (1) recreating in the new environment a community as supportive as his monastery and (2) rediscovering the power of the eucharist as 'God's presence, ... forgiveness, acceptance, the way we accept each other, God's love.' (23) Slowly, faith replaced self-concern until he sensed Christ 'the center of (his) existence' restored. (14)

John encapsulated his experience by defining faith as 'surrender to God's presence,' (56) unknowingly echoing one of the four factors Hildegard connects to faith and refuting Fowler's contention that faith grows in proportion to maturation.

During his first two years on the West Coast John completed a cycle in what Jung and Hildegard understand as *spiritual development:* 'Circumambulation around the center'; transformation on the ego/self axis; centering, decentering, recentering. In the process he came to conceive of *faith development* in terms of exactly the two elements Hildegard isolates, depth of understanding (53) and commitment (51). Transferred unwillingly back to his monastery after five years on the West Coast, strongly reluctant to leave his new friendships, John slipped again into the *homo exterior* stance. Since he tends, however, when life circumstances assail his faith to 'stretch out his hand' for 'water' rather than for 'fire,' it is not unrealistic to predict another mounting *rotatio* on the spiral of spiritual growth.

Concluding critique

John's interview exemplifies 'the journey of a pilgrim' much as St Hildegard envisioned it 800 years ago, Jung at mid-century. His story also supports our Jung/Hildegard survey (and biblical ideas) by demonstrating that there is more to a person than an ego, more to reality than the 'human side,' and more to Christian development than ego growth. It also shows how the *retardierende Kraft* of evil works to reverse spiritual advancement and destroy faith.

It would seem that Fowler will have to incorporate into his research the kinds of factors Jung and Hildegard treat if he wants to reach conclusions about faith as Christians have understood it for nearly two millenia. A few concluding observations will make the point.

First, whereas Hildegard connects faith to every life era, Fowler thinks that stages of faith reached later in life contain a 'more true' kind of knowing than earlier ones and are therefore superior.[44] This minimization of youthful faith is questioned by the C.F.I. John for example in his boyhood, adolescent and monastic years had deep religious experiences of being 'wrapped in God's arms' sensing the oneness and goodness of creation. Spiritual experience began for him at 'four, five, six,' he said, 'Those childhood years were very rich for me that way.' (53–55) Biographies of child saints like Therese of Lisieux also show that faith is not a chronological more-is-better matter.

Second, Fowler's theory is based on a purely formal 'logic of conviction'[45] devoid of content, but according to Hildegard faith deprived of the creed cannot be Christian faith.

Third, he maintains that humanity is 'genetically potentiated'[46] for faith, but we are gifted with faith at baptism not birth. Hildegard would fault his reduction of 'true belief in the Trinity' into genetic categories void of mystery and computerized.

Fourth, Fowler calls the structuralist systems informing his thought and by extension his own system 'philosophical psychologies,'[47] setting up their standards as absolute measures, with his own model as normative rather than descriptive. This elevation of an epistemological enterprise to ontological levels is unjustifiable however, especially transposed to the field of faith. As a relation of being-to-Being faith is indeed an ontological matter, but a system dealing with the evolving structures of human knowing is not an ontology.

More than once Hildegard summarizes her understanding of faith by alluding to St Paul: 'If you confess with your lips that Jesus is Lord and believe that God raised him from the dead you will be saved' (Romans 10:9). Because the bible grounds and pervades her thinking about faith, 'the journey of a pilgrim' would seem to offer a more appropriate approach to faith than Fowler's mathematico-logical propositions.

Notes

1. J. W. Fowler, *Stages of Faith*, San Francisco, Harper and Row, 1981, p. 32.
2. About 60 of these interviews have been gathered. Their findings will be reported on elsewhere.
3. P. Homans speaks of a 'second reading' of Freud in *Theology After Freud*, Indianapolis, Indiana, Bobbs-Merrill, 1970.
4. See E. Cousins, *Bonaventure and the Coincidence of Opposites*, Chicago, Franciscan Herald Press, 1978.
5. C. G. Jung, *Alchemical Studies* (Collected Works, vol. 13), Princeton, Princeton University Press, 1967, par. 38f.
6. For a comparison of the Jungian and Christian mystical journey, see J. Welch, *Spiritual Pilgrims: Carl Jung and Teresa of Avila*, New York, Paulist Press, 1982.
7. C. G. Jung, *The Archetypes and the Collective Unconscious* (Collected Works, vol. 9), Princeton, Princeton University Press, 1967, par. 254.
8. References in this section will pertain to *Scivias*, Tr. A. Fuhrkotter. Corpus Christionorum Continuatio Mediaevalis (Turnholti: Brepols, 1978).
9. Sc. III, 8, 8, 440–41.
10. Implicit in Sc. III, 8, 1; III, 5, 16, 451–54.
11. Sc. II, 3, 30, 645–46.
12. Sc. II, 1, 93–94.
13. Sc. I, 4, 30, 933–34.
14. Sc. III, 87, 8, 265–66.

15. Sc. III, 5, 16, 455.
16. Sc. III, 8, 8, 492–93.
17. Sc. III, 8, 15, 667–713.
18. Sc. II. 3, 30, 639–44.
19. Sc. II. 3, 30, 663–64.
20. On Fowler's confusion of two tracks of human development see M. Ford-Grabowsky, 'What developmental phenomenon is Fowler studying?' *Journal of Psychology and Christianity*, vol. 5, no. 3, 1986, pp. 5–13.
21. Quoted in G. Uhlein, *Meditations with Hildegard of Bingen*, Santa Fe, Bear and Co., 1982, p. 106.
22. Sc. III, 8, 8.
23. Sc. III, 8, 8, 238.
24. Sc. I, 6, 4, 127–36.
25. Sc. III, 8, 8, 251.
26. Sc. III, 10, 32, 905–12.
27. Sc. III, 4, 17, 465.
28. Sc. II, 3, 30.
29. Sc. II, 6, 24.
30. Hildegard of Bingen, *Welt und Mensch*, trans. H. Schipperges, Salzburg, Otto Muller Verlag, 1965, p. 209.
31. Sc. II, 7, 22, 538–40.
32. Sc. II, 7, 21.
33. Hildegard of Bingen, *op.cit.*, p. 327.
34. Sc. III, 11, 27, 553f.
35. *Ibid.*
36. Sc. II, 6, 86, 2432–36.
37. Sc. III, 12, 7, 194–97; WW p. 348.
38. Sc. I, 1, 32–45.
39. Sc. I, 4, 8.
40. Sc. I, 4, 8, 388–94.
41. Sc. I, 4, 12, 480–81.
42. Sc. III, 10, 2, 107; WW, p. 312.
43. This interview is in my doctoral dissertation (Princeton Theological Seminary, 1985) 252–62. Numbers in parentheses indicate responses.
44. Fowler, *op. cit.*, p. 101.
45. *ibid.*, p. 98.
46. *ibid.*, p. 303.
47. *ibid.*, p. 101.

3.2 A Lutheran examines James W. Fowler
William O. Avery

In 1981 James W. Fowler published his epoch-making book, *Stages of Faith*.[1] In the years since then, the theory set forth in that book has received worldwide attention, general acceptance among many religious scholars and groups, and wide-ranging criticism from others.[2] Lutherans and Presbyterians have been the denominations most hostile to Fowler's theory. Fowler has said:[3]

> Lutherans and Calvinists particularly have been slow to embrace this sort of work because with some conviction and some reason they believe that in some ways Christians can claim the word *faith* in a unique and singular way, and that others have to use the category of religion.

In my opinion Lutherans, Presbyterians, and others who resist Fowler's contributions because of his way of defining faith ought to re-examine his theory. In this article I will propose a way around the 'faith' obstacle, which keeps some Christians from realizing the benefits to be gained by using Fowler's insights.

To substantiate my argument, I will do the following. First I will show how Fowler tries to stand in two distinct disciplines, in social scientific research and in practical theology, and tries to build bridges connecting the two. Second, I will describe Fowler's concept of faith and explain why it is the only definition of faith he can allow as a social scientist. Third, I will state the Lutheran view of justification and why such a view rejects Fowler's concept of faith. Fourth, I will list the seven aspects Fowler uses in his interviews to measure faith development. I will argue that the seven aspects measured by the faith development interview more accurately measure different ways of living in one's baptism than they measure different stages of faith. If what Fowler's interviews measure can appropriately be seen as ways of living in one's baptism, then it is possible for Lutherans, Presbyterians, and others, who cannot accept Fowler's definition of faith, to appropriate the many benefits from using his theory. Finally, I will list the benefits of Fowler's theory for the Christian Church as he described them to me in a recent conversation.

Two distinct strands in Fowler's work

On the one hand, Fowler works as an empirical social scientist presenting a structural-developmental stage theory. He has collected and organized some relevant data according to the canons of the social sciences. On the other hand, Fowler works as a practical theologian whose theory makes a rich contribution to theological anthropology. The 1981 publication of *Stages of Faith* laid out his structural-developmental stage theory. In his work since 1981, Fowler has consciously brought his stage theory into the theoretical framework of a concept of practical theology and applied it to Christian education and pastoral care.[4]

As a social scientist, Fowler draws on two distinct but related families of life-span developmental theories: psychosocial theories and constructive developmental theories.[5] Psychosocial theories go back to the work of Sigmund Freud, who wrote about psychosexual development, and Erik Erikson, who developed an eight-stage theory of psychosocial development. Significantly, Erikson's stages of development continue throughout adulthood, dividing adulthood into 20–25 year eras.[6] Psychosocial theories were refined and popularized by researchers such as Daniel Levinson and associates, *Seasons of A Man's Life*, Gail Sheehey, *Passages*, and many others.

Constructive-developmental theories focus significantly on cognitive processes by which knowing is achieved. Fowler's work is especially indebted to Jean Piaget's four-part stage theory of cognitive development and Lawrence Kohlberg's 30-year study of moral development. Fowler says that 'faith development theory, while indebted to the psychosocial theory of Erikson, finds its principal theoretical grounding in the constructivist tradition.'[7] In his scientific mode, Fowler claims to be doing empirical research that is not dependent upon Christianity in that he attempts to develop a universalist theory of human faith.

At the same time, Fowler works as a Christian theologian who is very cognizant of the impact of his theological assumptions on his theory. He writes as follows[8]:

> The stage theory of faith development indisputably rests upon theological assumptions and reasoning. These assumptions have convictional status, and finally rest upon the faith commitments of the theorist and of faith tradition of which he is a part. They can be rationally explicated, however, and are subject to statement in largely formal and functional terms. To a degree not yet fully tested, they seem capable of being stated in terms derived from other traditions and cultures not Christian or western. The acknowledgement and rational explication of these broadly theological foundations do not jeopardize the theory's claim to scientific integrity. In this regard there are parallels with the conviction-laden philosophical rationales for normative and descriptive theories of cognitive development, and for developmental theories of moral and religious reasoning.

In other words, Fowler maintains that all theories have normative endpoints for their theories, and these are essentially contested conceptions. He continues[9]:

> Whether we speak of Habermas's ideal of an undistorted communications situation, Marx's vision of the classless society, Piaget's utopia of formal operational thinking, or Kohlberg's 'universalizing principles of justice,' we are dealing with normative visions deriving from particular philosophical commitments and traditions.

The goal of mature faith, which Fowler sets forth as his highest stage, does influence what he identifies as significant in the other stages. But Fowler says that acknowledging these theological foundations does not jeopardize the theory's claim to scientific integrity.

Not only is Fowler's theory rooted in theological foundations, but in recent years he has moved to develop the implications of his theory for Christianity. In the 1970s Fowler worked on a universalist theory of human faith. In the 1980s he is developing a specific theory of Christian faith development. In so doing, Fowler maintains a dialectical relationship (a 'mutually critical correlation' to use the term he has borrowed from David Tracy) between his normative theology interests and his theory as social scientific research.

Fowler's definition of faith

The most criticized aspect of Fowler's theory, especially among Lutherans and Presbyterians, is his broad definition of faith. Fowler asserts that faith is a human universal, recognizably the same phenomenon in Christians, Marxists, Hindus, and Dinkas, and is a disposition involving both emotions and a kind of knowing or cognition. His definition states that[10]:

> In the language of constructive developmental psychologies, faith is a construing, a construing of the conditions of existence. It is a special kind of construing, for it attempts to make sense of our mundane experience in the light of some accounting for the ultimate conditions of existence.

Faith involves a person in three different kinds of construal: (1) faith involves a patterned knowing (belief); (2) faith involves a patterned valuing (commitment or loyalty); (3) faith involves a patterned construction of meaning usually in the form of an underlying narrative or story. This construing is partially and growingly conscious but is in large degree unconscious.[11]

Fowler's definition of faith suggests that faith is determined by development processes and is a construction of human understanding. He posits that people progress on a ladder of development through certain structural features of faith even though the content of one person's faith at any stage may be quite different from others at that same stage. That is to say, Fowler says his stages are not primarily matters of the contents of faith.

Stages account for differences in the styles, the operations of knowing and valuing.[12] Thus, Fowler claims that faith stages meet the structural-developmental criteria for stages. They provide generalizable, formal descriptions of integrated sets of operations of knowing and valuing. The stages are related in an invariant sequence, because each new stage carries forward the operations of all the previous stages.[13]

In a recent presentation, Fowler summarized his concept of faith this way[14]:

> I sought to evoke an awareness of faith as a multidimensional, central form of human action and construction. It involves both conscious and unconscious processes, and holds together both rational and passional dynamics. Faith, as I conceptualize it, holds together both religious and non-religious directions and forms.

Fowler's definition of faith is absolutely critical to his theory, if it is to be a theory of faith development. Fowler never really argues for his view of the nature of faith. He distinguishes what faith is from religion and belief, but he never considers other possibilities for how faith might be understood. Craig Dykstra has pointed out that Fowler uses a 'since ... then' method of arguing. 'Since faith is ... faith can be described developmentally in the following ways.' Dykstra concludes that the most fundamental reason Fowler considers no alternatives is that 'a structural developmental theory of the nature of growth or change in faith requires precisely the kind of understanding of faith that Fowler in fact presents.'[15]

Therefore, faith as a model is not limited to any particular religion. Structurally and dynamically, faith means the same things in every religion. Only the 'contents' change from faith to faith. Faith need not even be religious. Fowler can use universal, generic, structural, and developmental categories to talk about faith growth and change. The underlying structure of a person's faith, rather than the 'contents,' becomes the primary norm. Fowler cannot define faith any differently and still have a structural developmental theory of growth or change in faith.[16]

As a social scientist, Fowler is directly dependent on Piaget's four stages of cognitive development and Kohlberg's six stagelike positions in the development of moral reasoning. However, Fowler's faith stages are more complex than Piaget's and Kohlberg's stages, because his faith stage theory does not separate cognition from emotion or affection or the role of imagination.

Fowler defines faith stages as follows[17]:

> Following Piaget and Kohlberg, we think of a stage as an integrated system of operations (structures) of thought and valuing which makes for an equilibrated constitutive-knowing of the person's relevant environment. A stage, as a 'structural whole,' is organismic, i.e., it is a dynamic unity constituted by internal connections among its

differentiated aspects. In constructivist theories, successive stages are thought of as manifesting qualitative transformations issuing in more complex inner differentiations, more elaborate operations (operations upon operations), wider comprehensiveness, and greater overall flexibility of functioning.

Thus, Fowler's theory meets the structural developmental criteria for stages.

Faith stages are identified in terms of seven operational aspects, which are integrated and reintegrated at each of the six levels or stages. The seven aspects are (1) form of logic; (2) roletaking; (3) form of moral judgment; (4) bounds of social awareness; (5) locus of authority; (6) form of world coherence; and (7) symbolic functioning.[18] These seven categories are so broad as to encompass a person's general orientation to reality. One question to be asked is whether these seven aspects measure 'faith' as Fowler defines this term. I think they do, but this is not my question. My question is whether these seven aspects measure faith as Lutherans and many others define that term. I contend the answer to this question is 'No.'

A Lutheran response to Fowler's concept of faith

The strength of the theological stance of the Lutheran Church is its emphasis on the gospel. Lutherans help Christians focus on the fact that the center of Christianity is the good news of what God has done for us in the death and resurrection of Jesus, God's Son. Lutherans speak of this center as the doctrine of justification by grace through faith. God accepts humans into relationship not on the merit of their own lives but solely on the merit of God's own love. Robert Kysar, a Lutheran, has said[19]:

> The Lutheran church holds this prize possession close to its heart. Its whole tradition revolves around this hub. This is not to say that other Christian denominations have no claim upon this truth.... Yet no other denominational tradition takes its lifeblood so exclusively from [justification by grace through faith] as does Lutheranism. Unlike any other Christian body, Lutherans are perpetually called back to that 'good news.' Like the flower must have the life-sustaining rays of the sun lest it wither and die, Lutheranism has sustained its life by constant exposure to the rays of this fundamental affirmation.

The other side of the Lutheran focus on justification is a lack of emphasis on sanctification. Lutherans are so concerned that Christians hear the free gift of the gospel that they are suspicious of all attempts to prepare for or to grow in this gift as examples of works' righteousness. There is a very sound reason for the Lutheran suspicion. It is easy and tempting to put conditions on the gospel, to change the gospel into law. The history of Christianity provides numerous examples of this outcome.

The issue of development in Christian life surfaces in seminary and parishes especially over the issue of spiritual formation. Lutherans say that if faith is a gift, the human attempt to develop one's faith is inappropriate. Christians can only make themselves available for this gift through Word and Sacrament since the gospel always comes from outside oneself. Yet a hunger for growth and sustenance in Christian life persists. One example of this hunger is the fact that the most requested topic for presentation at meetings of interns and their supervisors is 'spirituality' — what it is, how it can be developed in a way to still be true to the Lutheran heritage.

The issue of the development of Christians' discipleship is also critical, because the vast majority of persons at worship and church school on any given day have been baptized and want to be supported and strengthened in the Christian life. These members have questions such as, 'How do we grow and change in our Christian discipleship?' People do change. Their spirituality, their understanding of God's word, the appreciation for the sacrament, the meaning of life in this world and life eternal change throughout their lives. How are Lutheran pastors to respond to the concern for growth and change?

However, Lutherans are not helped by Fowler's concept of faith as a construing of the conditions of existence. Because Fowler's concept makes faith a human act, it undercuts the radical primacy of the gospel. Therefore, a Lutheran definition of faith must differ from Fowler's concept and requires an alternative definition of faith.

First, faith is a gift from God and not a human achievement. Fowler says the capacity for faith may be built on the prevenient grace of God, but his acknowledgement does not go far enough in recognizing the reality of sin that makes it impossible for humans in their own power to believe in God. Faith is a gift from outside that tears apart all our attempts for self-achievement or self-fulfillment and lets us acknowledge this gift that we cannot control.

Second, faith cannot be separated from the object of faith. The object of one's faith determines what faith is. Much of what Fowler defines as expressions of faith Christianity has traditionally called idolatry. People can be and often are unfaithful. Fowler's definition of faith does not allow for idolatry or unfaithfulness.

Third, the hierarchical nature of Fowler's faith stages is the opposite of my understanding of faith. Jesus rebuked the disciples when they sought to keep the people from bringing children to him, saying 'whoever does not receive the kingdom of God like a child shall not enter it' (Mark 10:14–15 and parallels). There is a radical difference between the human drive for self-actualization or self-authentication and the Christian gift of faith. Fowler's theory is a hierarchical stage theory and, as such, is part of the story of human self-actualization, humans reaching toward their potential. I say this about Fowler's theory even though, as a theologian, Fowler rejects self-authentication as a Christian goal.

Faith is essentially a revelatory act of God. It is God meeting the person. One cannot know anything of God unless and until God meets the person. Within certain Christian traditions, such as the Lutheran tradition, it is believed that God meets the person in baptism. That is, the Lutheran Church baptizes infants because baptism is God's act not contingent on any response by the child. If an essential aspect of baptism were the response of the person, then the church should not baptize infants. We baptize infants because faith is God's gift given in baptism and the gift is God himself. In this sense, faith is an event, a happening. It is what God gives, what God claims as his own. Then the baptismal life is always asking questions such as, What is this meeting about (when God meets me in baptism)? What does it claim of me? What does it mean for me? To express this in a corporate sense is to say that life in baptism is the life of a pilgrim people asking, musing, and praying about what it is to be the people of God whom God has claimed as his own.

In his most recent work, Fowler acknowledges an almost exact parallel between his 'stages of faith' and 'stages of selfhood' as presented in the work of one of his former students, Robert Kegan.[20] In fact, the parallels are so total that in this recent book, Fowler himself describes his stages as 'stages of faith and selfhood.'[21] Do Fowler's stages measure faith or do they measure selfhood? Are faith and selfhood synonymous?

For those of us whose concept of faith is radically different from Fowler's and who wonder how Fowler himself can say his stages measure faith and selfhood, there is a way to employ the benefits of Fowler's stages. We can apply what is being measured by Fowler's seven aspects, not to faith development but to different ways of living in one's baptism. Living in one's baptism includes one's concept of selfhood but also encompasses one's entire life as a baptized child of God. I believe it is proper to see the stages Fowler delineates as growing out of baptism, because baptism is the cornerstone of a Christian's whole life.

Baptism and the Christian life

Baptism is the chief act of the Church of Jesus Christ. This statement does not mean that baptism is primarily a human act; it is God's work and God's gracious and free gift to us. In the World Council of Churches document, *Baptism, Eucharist and Ministry,* the meaning of baptism is described as follows[22]:

> Baptism is the sign of new life through Jesus Christ. It unites the one baptized with Christ and with his people. The New Testament scriptures and the liturgy of the Church unfold the meaning of

baptism in various images which express the riches of Christ and the gifts of his salvation.... Baptism is participation in Christ's death and resurrection (Romans 6:3–5; Colossians 2:12); a reclothing in Christ (Galatians 3:27); a renewal by the Spirit (Titus 3:5); the experience of salvation from the flood (1 Peter 3:20–21); and exodus from bondage (1 Corinthians 10:1–2) and a liberation into a new humanity in which barriers of division whether of sex or race or social status are transcended (Galatians 3:27–28; 1 Corinthians 12:13). The images are many but the reality is one.

Baptism is a life-long sacrament. That is to say, humans spend their whole lives living into the status they have already been given in their baptism. Daily, humans return to their baptism. Daily they die to sin anew and are reborn in God. Physical death is the final dying to sin and one's resurrection is the final rebirth. In the *Large Catechism*, Martin Luther expressed it this way[23]:

In baptism, therefore, every Christian has enough to study and to practise all his life. He always has enough to do to believe firmly what baptism promises and brings – victory over death and the devil, forgiveness of sin, God's grace, the entire Christ, and the Holy Spirit with his gifts. In short, the blessings of baptism are so boundless that if timid nature considers them, it may well doubt whether they could all be true.

Luther also claimed that when we feel that God has deserted us or when we feel oppressed by our sins, then we ought to take our baptismal certificate out of the bureau drawer and say, 'I am baptized! I am baptized! Therefore I have the promise that I will be saved and have eternal life.'

To live as a Christian is to live out of the foundation of one's baptism. Hearing the Word of God and partaking of the eucharistic meal are ways to renew our baptismal covenant. Luther said that in baptism, 'the old man daily decreases until he is finally destroyed. This is what it means to plunge into baptism and daily come forth again.'[24]

Baptism is the daily garment that the Christian is to wear all the time. Luther continues[25]:

Every day [the Christian] should be found in faith and amid its fruits, every day he should be suppressing the old man and growing up in the new.... But if anybody falls away from his baptism let him return to it.... As we have once obtained forgiveness of sins in baptism, so forgiveness remains day by day as long as we live, that is, as long as we carry the old Adam about our necks.

Most importantly, all grace for a Christian is given in his or her baptism. There is no need to add anything to the baptism. It is to the sufficiency of this gift that the Christian returns again and again throughout his or her life. At the same time, one can also acknowledge that people respond to their baptism in different ways that can be grouped into 'stages' or 'styles.'

The advantages of viewing Fowler's model as a model of the ways Christians live in their baptismal relationship are many. Such a change allows faith to have the specific and explicitly Christian definition rather than as a generic human universal. It enables faith to be seen as God's gift rather than a fruit of human development. It allows for the possibility of idolatry and unfaith. To speak of different ways of living in baptism removes much of the sting of Fowler's hierarchical stages, because the grace of baptism is always sufficient.

Such a change also enables one to admit that Christians respond to different people and events in different ways. Instead of claiming that Christians are in all aspects of their lives at a certain level, the baptismal imagery enables one to see that a person may be at different 'levels' or 'stages' in regard to various persons, events, issues, or dilemmas. A person may function at the mythic-literal stage with regard to a particular person or event and at the conjunctive level with another person or event. In the complex make-up of a person, that person does not usually function completely within one hierarchical level.

We will no longer talk about development in any other context than a Christian context. Fowler has been criticized for claiming more than his research warrants in saying that his stages of faith are possibly universal.[26] Finally, by changing the foundation to ways of living in one's baptism, we blur the total separation Fowler wants to make between 'structure' and 'content.' I remain very skeptical of Fowler's attempt to provide an account of faith development that is independent of content. One simply cannot completely separate the 'structural level' of faith from its content.

Benefits of Fowler's theory

By setting Fowler's theory into the context of baptism rather than faith development, Lutherans, Presbyterians, and others can obtain the benefits to be gained from his theory.

Recently, I had the opportunity to ask Fowler what were the benefits of his development theory for the Christian Church. Because of limitation of space, I will only sketch the outline of our conversation.

First, Fowler said his theory makes tacit aspects of experience explicit. It provides a language for discussing, understanding, and taking responsibility for an aspect of our common experience. The theory takes hold as a language system, and awareness is connected to language. That is, people may not be aware of experience until they put it in words. At the same time, awareness of the stages is not the awareness to which people are completely strangers. Upon being exposed to his theory, there is a sense of validation of their intuitive feelings about people. As such, Fowler sees his theory as empowering as well as threatening.

Second, Fowler said his theory gives a hermeneutical or interpretive frame for understanding religious and interpersonal interaction. It helps us understand others' views when they argue not only from different premises and basic assumptions but also from fundamentally different sets of 'operations.' His theory offers a third-person perspective on pastoral encounters and results in a kind of appropriate detachment that serves effectively to keep the pastor from getting hooked inappropriately.

Third, Fowler sees his theory assisting education and counseling by providing a new set of lenses for understanding dis-ease or transitions in a person's life. Some changes, not all, are stage changes. When stage change is involved, the ways of intervening are very different for adults in the transition from the mythic-literal stage to the synthetic-conventional stage than for adults in transition from the individuative-reflective to the conjunctive stage and so forth. Using the stage level in fully appropriate ways, one is led to a fuller understanding of the way change is perceived differently by different people. Fowler noted his theory also provides a non-pathological language and conceptual system for diagnosis.

Fourth, Fowler believes his theory makes a major contribution to theological anthropology. Although the contribution has not yet been fully developed, he claims the theme of 'becoming a subject before God' gives an everyperson story about the revolutions in consciousness that people in a society like ours are likely to undergo, and it provides for a sequencing of these series. It poses for Christians this question: How does conversion to Christ-formed consciousness occur or re-occur in each of the stages? In terms of theological anthropology, Fowler said this theory provides an empirical and theoretical point of reference for such traditional doctrines as justification, regeneration, and sanctification and has potential for enriching the notions of sin and grace and resistance to grace.

Fifth, Fowler said his theory provides a paradigm making linkages between theology and social science and contributes to a missing area of social scientific enquiry. At the very least it presents a new paradigm in developmental psychology.

Sixth, Fowler believes his theory may take its place with other movements in society toward a cultural evolution. He sees Western society in a new watershed period with a revolution in consciousness at the cultural level, the likes of which have not occurred since the enlightenment. The culture is in the process of a change from the individuative-reflective to the conjunctive stage but with many people and groups of people resisting and retreating to the synthetic-conventional or even the mythic-literal stage.

As the cultural shift is occurring, the church needs to ask itself,

With what cultural paradigm is it connected? Is the Church involved in enmity toward God's future? Is change part of God's future? Can one link the new cultural stage with growth toward the Kingdom of God (defined as God's power of the future)? Is God luring us to the future for greater participation? His theory can help address these questions.[27]

Fowler does not claim all things for his development theory. Rather he sees his theory as only 'one constituent component of a more comprehensive practical theory for Christian formation and transformation.'[28] Developmental change is only one of three kinds of change in individuals. He knows his developmental theory deals with individual change but that Christianity is concerned also with social, systemic, and historical change.[29] He realizes that 'developmental stages can constitute plateaus of augmented defensiveness or self-groundedness, and can represent only a sequence of more sophisticated patterns of self-deceiving world-construal.'[30] Fowler has long recognized the distinction between development and conversion and the necessity of both for the Christian.[31] He admits his stages are not stages in soteriology and that a person at a lower state should never be considered less of a Christian because of his or her level. Pushing people to higher stages is not the goal of Christian education or pastoral care, although providing an open environment in which such change can more easily take place is.[32]

Conclusion

While Fowler's contribution is only one part of a theory of Christian (trans)formation, this article has argued that his theory can be very helpful in assisting Christians to live fruitfully in their baptismal relationship to God and to one another. The Lutheran Church has been strong and focused on justification by grace through faith but weak and unfocused on what it means to live and grow as a Christian. Closer attention to Fowler's development theory can help rectify this deficiency.

Lutherans and others have rejected the contributions of Fowler's theory because of his definition of faith. This article suggests a way out of such a rejection by arguing that what Fowler is measuring in his seven aspects is not faith development but stages or ways of living in one's baptism. This article makes clear that humans do not need to add anything to their baptism in order to complete it but does suggest that one can change, grow, and develop in one's understanding of what it means to live as a Christian and how to actually do so.

One need not go as far as Fowler does, in suggesting that Western society is in a period of cultural evolution from the individuative-reflective to the conjunctive stage, in order to agree that he has outlined important benefits to be gained by using his development theory. Fowler himself is beginning to develop the contributions of his theory for theological anthropology, an area fraught with implications and possibilities.[33]

In short, Fowler's theory has an important contribution to make to theology, liturgics, pastoral care, homiletics, and Christian education and ought not to be ignored by denominations or individuals who reject his concept of faith. This article provides a way past that obstacle so that the many benefits of his theory can be employed by a larger number of Christians.

Notes

1. James W. Fowler, *Stages of Faith*, San Francisco, Harper and Row. 1981.
2. An unpublished manuscript and address given by Sharon Parks, 'A summary of the main points of the North American critique of James Fowler's theory of faith development,' at the International Symposium on Religious Development and Education, Blaubeuren, University of Tübingen, June 12–17, 1987, pp. 14–15.
3. As quoted by Sharon Parks, p. 15.
4. See an unpublished manuscript and address given by Karl Ernst Nipkow, 'Stage theories of faith development as a challenge to religious education and practical theology,' at the International Symposium on Religious Development and Education, Blaubeuren, University of Tübingen, June 12–17, 1987.
5. See James W. Fowler, 'Stages of faith and adult life cycles,' in Kenneth Stokes (ed.), *Faith Development in the Adult Life Cycle*, New York, W. H. Sadlier, 1983, pp. 181–187.
6. Erik H. Erikson, *Childhood and Society* (2nd ed), New York, W. W. Norton and Co., 1963; Erik H. Erikson, *Identity*, New York, W. W. Norton and Co., 1968.
7. An unpublished manuscript and address given by James F. Fowler, 'The vocation of faith development theory: directions and modifications since 1981,' at the International Symposium on Religious Development and Education, Blaubeuren, University of Tubingen, June 12–17, 1987.
8. Fowler, 'Vocation,' p. 19.
9. Fowler, 'Vocation,' p. 22.
10. James W. Fowler in a lecture given at the Association for Clinical Pastoral Education, October 1986 in Atlanta. The lecture subsequently became a chapter in Fowler, *Faith Development and Pastoral Care*, Philadelphia, Fortress Press, 1987, p. 56.
11. Fowler, Lecture in Atlanta and *Faith Development and Pastoral Care*, p. 56.
12. Fowler, *Stages of Faith*, p. 52.
13. Fowler, *Stages of Faith*, pp. 99–100.
14. Fowler, 'Vocation,' p. 5.
15. Craig Dykstra, 'What is faith?: an experiment in the hypothetical mode,' in Craig Dykstra and Sharon Parks (eds), *Faith Development and Fowler*, Birmingham, Alabama, Religious Education Press, 1986, p. 51.
16. See Dykstra for a more complete argument regarding this point.
17. James W. Fowler, 'Faith and the structuring of meaning,' in Craig Dykstra and Sharon Parks (eds), *Faith Development and Fowler*, Birmingham, Alabama, Religious Education Press, 1986, p. 31.
18. See Romney M. Moseley, David Jarvis, and James W. Fowler, *Manual for Faith Development Research*, Atlanta, Center for Faith Development for the Candler School of Theology, 1986.
19. Robert Kysar, 'I chose to change,' *The Lutheran*, vol. 18, no. 19, 1980, p. 11.
20. Robert Kegan, *The Evolving Self*, Cambridge, Mass., Harvard University Press, 1982.
21. Fowler, *Faith Development and Pastoral Care*, pp. 53–77.

22. *Baptism, Eucharist, and Ministry*, Geneva, World Council of Churches, 1982, p. 2.
23. Martin Luther, 'The Large Catechism,' *The Book of Concord*, tr. Theodore G. Tappert, Philadelphia, Fortress Press, 1959, pp. 441–442.
24. Luther, p. 445.
25. Luther, p. 446.
26. See, for example, John M. Broughton, 'The political psychology of faith development theory,' in Craig Dykstra and Sharon Parks (eds), *Faith Development and Fowler*, Birmingham, Alabama, Religious Education Press, 1986, pp. 93–94.
27. A conversation held in Fowler's office at Candler School of Theology, Emory University, Atlanta, Georgia, on September 25, 1987.
28. Fowler, 'Vocation,' p. 1.
29. Fowler, *Faith Development and Pastoral Care*, pp. 99–111.
30. Fowler, 'Vocation,' p. 12.
31. Fowler, *Stages of Faith*, pp. 281–286 and *Becoming Adult, Becoming Christian*, pp. 138–141.
32. Fowler, *Faith Development and Pastoral Care*, pp. 80–82.
33. See especially Fowler's books, *Becoming Adult, Becoming Christian*, and *Faith Development and Pastoral Care*.

3.3 James W. Fowler and the Reformed tradition: an exercise in theological reflection in religious education

Richard R. Osmer

Every theory of influence deserves the critical reflection of colleagues in the same field. Such is the case with the work of James Fowler. In *Stages of Faith* and in other publications, Fowler has formulated a theory that describes different stages through which faith might move as it develops. While challenged by a variety of sources, Fowler's work has received some of its severest criticisms from representatives of the Reformed tradition. Ellis Nelson, for example, has written that Fowler gives human faith a 'god-like status,' which 'gives him a position beyond history and above criticism from which he can make judgments.'[1] The exchanges between James Loder and Fowler are well known, with Loder arguing that Fowler's work has little to do with a biblical understanding of faith.[2] Craig Dykstra has argued that Fowler operates with two distinctive understandings of faith in his theory, giving rise to a fundamental incongruence between his descriptions of the early stages and his descriptions of the later stages.[3]

Clearly a theological interest is at work in these criticisms, an interest that brings the critics into conflict with the theological convictions that undergird Fowler's theory. This focus on fundamental theological issues is proper. Indeed, it is a level of reflection and discussion that is badly needed among religious educators.

This article attempts to sort out the theological issues at stake in the criticisms most frequently made of Fowler by representatives of the Reformed tradition. A counter-question of sorts will be raised of these critics: Are they truly representative of the full range of Reformed thought? Are there dimensions of that tradition that would lead to a more appreciative response to Fowler's work?

In a sense, this entire discussion is an attempt to show the relevance of theological reflection to religious education. Fowler's theory of faith development must be assessed on theological grounds, as Nelson, Loder, and Dykstra clearly recognize. It also confronts us with the reality of particularity in religious education, something this field frequently seeks to avoid in generalized notions of religion and education. Theology is never theology in general. It involves choices and commitments that invariably reflect the particularity of the theological heritage of the theologian. Thus it is proper and fitting for members of the Reformed tradition to raise questions of Fowler from the standpoint of their own theological tradition. It is equally proper, however, to hold them accountable to the riches of their community's heritage.

Part one

Ironically, Fowler, a United Methodist, is deeply influenced by one of the foremost representatives of contemporary Reformed thought, H. Richard Niebuhr. This is an important point of departure, for often Fowler's work is viewed as a simple extension of the Piaget-Kohlberg school of structural developmental psychology.[4] Criticisms made of Piaget's and Kohlberg's work are automatically applied to Fowler.[5] This is a mistake. There are, in fact, three central sources of faith development theory: Piagetian structuralism, Erik Erikson's ego psychology, and the theological ethics of H. Richard Niebuhr. Niebuhr, about whom Fowler wrote his dissertation and first book, is by far the most important of these three.[6] It is from Niebuhr that Fowler gains his basic understanding of faith and his depiction of the endpoint of faith development, something that is deeply influenced by Niebuhr's understanding of radically monotheistic faith.[7]

More important for our purposes, however, is Fowler's appropriation of Niebuhr's transformational understanding of the pattern of grace.[8] It is here that certain themes, which are central to the Reformed tradition, inform Fowler's thought. What is meant by a transformational pattern of grace? Niebuhr presents grace as standing in a transformational relationship to the created-but-fallen order.[9] Grace does not eradicate this order, nor does it merely perfect it; rather, it converts some aspect of the created order in ways that allow it to regain its proper orientation under the sovereignty of God. To use Niebuhr's own words: 'The problem of culture is therefore the problem of its conversion, but of its replacement by a new creation.'[10] In Niebuhr's view, this transformational pattern of grace underlies the thought of Augustine and Calvin.[11]

The contrast between a position in which grace is seen as transforming culture and one in which it is merely perfecting it is particularly important for our purposes. The latter represents the position of the third type, 'Christ Above Culture,' described by Niebuhr in *Christ and Culture*. This position attempts to synthesize Christ and culture, presenting grace as adding spiritual dimensions that are not present in the created order as it is. Grace thus perfects nature or culture by bringing its various dimensions into a harmonious relationship under the Lordship of Christ. Thomas Aquinas is the theologian of this position *par excellence*.

In contrast, the transformationist position found in the fifth type, 'Christ the Transformer of Culture,' takes the radicality of the Fall more seriously. Grace is presented as bringing about a genuine conversion of the world, involving a reordering of life that does far more than merely raising it to a higher, harmonious level. In the face of the reality of evil, radical transformation is called for, a transformation that remains eschatological, for the conversion effected by grace continues to exist within a finite, sinful world that, at its best, mirrors God's Kingdom provisionally.

It is important to keep this distinction in mind as we examine Fowler's work. Does he come closer to a synthetic, perfection-of-culture position, or does he take over a genuinely transformational pattern of grace from Niebuhr? In Niebuhr's own thought, the attempt is made to use a transformational pattern to describe the relationship between human faith and Christian faith. He does so, I believe, in a manner that is deeply dependent on the thought of John Calvin. Calvin begins the *Institutes* with a description of human faith that is given in creation, a kind of natural piety if you will. As he puts it in the first book of the *Institutes*, God 'has sown in men's minds that seed of religion.'[12] Human beings are created for relationship with God, and they are incomplete or twisted without that relationship.

Calvin goes on to describe the distorting effects of the Fall on natural human faith. The longing of natural piety for God after the Fall gives rise to the perverse construction of idols to fill the void, which is created when persons turn away from their Creator. Calvin goes on to take a third step in the *Institutes*: What human beings cannot do themselves, God in Christ has done in their stead, bearing the cost of disobedience and proffering the gift of faith. Faith, while a gift of God and the work of the Holy Spirit, involves the conversion of natural piety given in creation. God is restored to the rightful position of sovereign Lord over every facet of a person's life.[13]

Niebuhr follows a similar pattern in his depiction of the relationship of natural piety of the gift of faith.[14] In *Radical Monotheism and Western Culture*, he describes faith as a human universal.[15] All persons construct centers of value and meaning to which they give their trust and loyalty. As human beings, they have faith of some sort, for it is a constitutive dimension of human existence. Here, as in the first chapters of the *Institutes*, he is pointing to the reality of natural piety.

Like Calvin, moreover, he always follows his depiction of human faith with a discussion of sin.[16] Human beings construct centers of value and meaning which focus on items other than the sovereign God.[17] He goes on to describe the crucial role of Jesus Christ in the transformation of idolatrous human faith. Christ's disclosure of the absolute trustworthiness of God frees persons from an anxious clinging to the lesser gods, which they have perversely constructed in God's place.

What we have here is a transformational pattern of grace in the realm of human faith. Natural piety, which is corrupted under the impress of sin, is transformed under the influence of the Mediator, Jesus Christ. It is precisely this transformational pattern of grace that Fowler has appropriated from Niebuhr to inform his work. It provides the larger context in which Fowler would have us understand his stages of faith described in formal structuralist terms.

Following Niebuhr, Fowler begins by describing faith as a human universal.[18] At this point, he uses highly formal, nontheological language. Persons are described as inevitably constructing centers of value and meaning that shape their basic orientation to life. This is Fowler's equivalent to Niebuhr's and Calvin's understanding of natural piety. He typically goes on to appropriate Niebuhr's understanding of natural human faith's distortion in sin, describing it in terms of henotheistic and polytheistic faith styles.[19] This in turn is followed by a description of the transformation of human faith toward Christian faith. As Fowler wrote in one of his earliest articles, 'To become Christian means the conversion of our human faith toward Christian faith, and development in Christian faith involves the gradual conversion, by formation and *metanoia,* of our human faith toward faith mediated by companionship of Jesus Christ.'[20]

Thus, on the surface, a strong case can be made that the theological assumptions undergirding Fowler's work are consistent with the Reformed tradition as it has been interpreted by H. Richard Niebuhr. His depiction of the stages of faith in formal language is simply a depiction of natural piety, something that stands in need of transformation.

This initial evaluation, however, cannot be sustained in the face of three major issues that emerge out of Fowler's appropriation of Niebuhr's transformational pattern of grace. They force us to ask whether Fowler violates this pattern in serious ways, leading to the kinds of criticism people like Nelson, Loder, and Dykstra have raised.

These issues can be formulated as three questions: (1) Is Fowler's use of a developmental paradigm adequate to the radical discontinuities and disruptions that are implied in a genuinely transformational pattern? Is the radicality of the Fall taken seriously enough to point to the wrenching nature of conversion? (2) Does Fowler's preoccupation with natural piety in his stage descriptions rest on an inadequate understanding of the relationship between nature and grace? (3) Does Fowler's use of structuralism to describe faith, even in its natural form, lead him to distort this phenomenon? Can faith ever be described without reference to its object and to the distinctive convictions of particular communities by which that object is mediated?

In the remainder of this article, each of these questions will be explicated. What we will find is a genuine tension between Fowler's work and certain strands of the Reformed tradition. We will also find, however, that these questions represent tension points within the Reformed tradition itself. It is conceivable that members of this tradition who come down on these issues in ways that differ from Loder, Nelson, and Dykstra would evaluate Fowler's work in a more positive light.

As Alasdair MacIntyre once noted, a living tradition is always engaged in an ongoing argument.[21] When genuine conflict between different parties within a tradition ceases, traditionalism of some sort prevails, and the living tradition is dead or dying. To the extent that the Reformed tradition is engaged in such an ongoing argument, the theological convictions of only one side have been articulated by religious educators in their evaluation of Fowler to this point. Our task is to complicate this theological conversation.

Part two

The first question raised above is an important one: Is Fowler's use of a developmental paradigm adequate to the radical discontinuities inherent in the transformation of natural faith to Christian faith? To a large extent, this is the basic criticism that Loder makes of Fowler. In a more extended form, the criticism goes something like this: A developmental pattern, when used to describe the religious life, inevitably diminishes a recognition of the reality of sin and leads to an understanding of the pattern of grace as a kind of naturalistic, evolutionary process that focuses on the increasing differentiation and reintegration of structural competencies. In contrast, a more adequate description of the religious life recognizes that natural piety faces a crisis when confronted by the Word of God, a crisis that interrupts and reorients natural developmental processes.

This kind of criticism harks back to important theological issues that came to the fore in religious education with the emergence of the conflict between liberalism and neo-orthodoxy. In this country, persons like George Albert Coe, the dean of the religious education movement, made great use of a developmental paradigm, under the influence of Boston personalism, to describe the pattern of grace in social and individual processes.[22] As Shelton Smith clearly saw, this use of developmentalism rested on a theology that severely underestimated the reality of sin, had an insufficient understanding of the reconciling work of Christ, and possessed virtually no eschatology whatsoever.[23] Smith contrasted what he called Coe's 'growth pattern' of grace with a 'crisis pattern,' which he found more consistent with biblical religion.[24]

The use of a crisis pattern of grace was, of course, widespread among those theologians who were attempting to break free of the liberal theological paradigm. From Bultmann to Tillich to Barth to Reinhold Niebuhr, we see variations on this theme at different points in their thought.[25] Barth and Reinhold Niebuhr remain paradigmatic for many contemporary Reformed theologians and pastors. In recent years, however, questions have been raised about the adequacy of a crisis paradigm to describe the religious life.

A variety of persons has called attention to the problematical nature of this approach. One of the most important criticisms has been raised by Stanley Hauerwas, who points out that a crisis pattern lends itself to a kind of 'occasionalism.'[26] God's commands and actions are viewed so exclusively in terms of discrete events that it becomes virtually impossible to describe the elements of continuity of the religious life.

A Christian's moral life, for example, is reduced to moments of decision or obedience in response to God's commands. Little focus is given to those enduring patterns of communal and personal existence that are so determinative of the basic orientation of the moral life. Similarly, the ecclesiology, which a crisis pattern engenders, is problematical. The church is not just an 'event,' a periodic gathering of persons who have come together in response to the Word of God.[27] It is also a people with an ongoing life that takes on cultural and institutional form through time.

At no point, moreover, has a crisis pattern been the exclusive way of understanding grace's operation for the entire Reformed tradition. Other than the neo-orthodox theologians (at certain points in their thought), it is Reformed pietists who have tended to employ a crisis pattern most frequently in their focus on individual conversion. As George Marsden points out, doctrinalist and culturalist strands of the Reformed tradition in this country have focused on very different theological emphases.[28]

If we turn to Calvin's thought, we look in vain for an exclusive preoccupation with the crisis of an individual's conversion. Rather, various crises of the individual religious life are located in a broader pattern that centers on the church as a means of grace and the covenantal community into which the child is baptized as an infant and through which he or she is encouraged to grow in faith throughout life. Indeed, developmental patterns correlate quite nicely with certain dimensions of this understanding of the religious life.

As one modern Reformed theologian, Donald Dawe, has pointed out, the developmental dimensions of Calvin's thought are best understood if they are located within the two languages he uses to describe the Christian life: 'status' language and 'process' language.[29] Status language refers to our standing in relationship to God. It is used to point to the restoration of a right relationship with God, which has been given to us in Jesus Christ, typically dealt with under the doctrine of justification. Process language refers to the actualization of our status as forgiven sinners. It is typically found under the rubric of sanctification. This sort of language frequently is characterized by paradox, referring simultaneously to the divine initiative and human effort, to transforming moments and slow, steady growth. It is in process language that we find developmental themes in Calvin's work.

The transformation of natural, sinful faith is described as an ongoing, lifelong process that takes place through constant exposure to the means of grace.

Calvin describes justification and sanctification as benefits of Christ's grace, which flow simultaneously to believers. It is impossible to discuss the new life given in Christ without also discussing the free gift of forgiveness by which we are justified. A kind of reductionism takes place when one or the other of these emphases becomes dominant or their interrelation is not kept in view. Too frequently, the argument between advocates of a crisis pattern of grace and a developmental pattern has engaged in just such a reductionism.

It is one thing to claim that our status is a free gift of God through Jesus Christ. It is quite another to transpose the giftedness of this status into experiential terms, making a crisis pattern the exclusive mode by which to describe the process by which grace is appropriated in the Christian life. This essentially is the kind of reductionism that takes place in the thought of James Loder.[30]

Fowler also has difficulty properly distinguishing these two languages in his work. This leads him to distort the transformational pattern that he seeks to take over from Niebuhr. His stages of faith, beginning in childhood and extending all the way to universalizing faith, amalgamate natural piety and sanctification. These two distinctive realities are placed together on a single continuum. Qualities of the self that clearly are morally and religiously desirable – qualities that are properly described by the process language of sanctification – are presented as the upper stages of a developmental sequence of natural piety. This makes for confusion, because the crucial term in a transformational pattern of grace is missing: the acceptance of the status given freely in Jesus Christ. We end up with a partial, formalistic description of the process of sanctification that is not integrally related to justification.

It is little wonder that representatives of the Reformed tradition have raised questions about Fowler's work. They sense a violation of the 'deep structure' of a transformational pattern of grace as found in Niebuhr and Calvin. To this point, however, these Reformed critics have not adequately taken into account the developmental themes that are consistent with their own tradition, something that would lead them to a more complex evaluation of Fowler's potential contribution.[31]

Part three

This leads to the second, closely related tension between Fowler's work and the Reformed tradition, put in the form of the second question: Does Fowler's preoccupation with natural piety in his stage descriptions rest on an inadequate understanding of the relationship between nature and grace? Throughout his theory, Fowler calls attention to the various natural human capacities that undergird the process of faith development: the ability to reason, to take the perspective of others, to understand symbols, and so forth. Advances in these domains lead to advances in faith stages. Does this not rest on an inadequate understanding of the relationship of nature and grace? It seems that grace is made to conform to natural developmental processes. Human growth and human effort seem to be given too large a role.

At various points, Fowler has articulated a theological position, which lends itself to this interpretation. In his most recent book, for example, *Becoming Adult, Becoming Christian*, he draws on the concept of synergy, found in the Eastern Orthodox tradition, to describe the relationship between the human potentials given in creation and God's activity. He writes:[32]

> My own position on these matters is the following: I believe that grace, as the presence and power of creative spirit working for human wholeness, is given and operative in creation from the beginning. In that sense, I agree with that theological tradition that argues that the 'natural' or a 'state of nature' are fictional concepts, corresponding to nothing in history or the present. Human development towards wholeness is, I believe, always the product of a certain synergy between human potentials, given in creation, and the presence and activity of Spirit as mediated through many channels.

Fowler seems to be much closer to his own Methodist heritage at this point than to Niebuhr or Calvin. Typically, synergy implies cooperation between human potentials given in creation and the divine. Nature and grace are held together in a way that stands in real tension with Reformed thought, especially in its more recent Barthian formulation. Since Barth's well-known *Nein!* to Emil Brunner, many Reformed theologians have viewed with great suspicion any theological position that seems to affirm a role for nature in the reception or development of God's free gift of grace.

But here, once again, we are confronted with an issue that has been and continues to be argued in the Reformed tradition. Barth's understanding of the relationship between nature and grace is not normative for the Reformed tradition as a whole. While a concept of synergy, such as Fowler uses above, is foreign to the Reformed tradition, this does not mean that the only alternative is a Barthian understanding of the relationship between nature and grace. A strong case can be made that Calvin's thought is more complex and more adequate than Barth's on this issue.

There can be no question that Calvin placed great emphasis on God's sovereignty in relation to the created order. Grace clearly takes priority over nature. Saving knowledge is a gift of grace, not an outgrowth of natural piety. Even the workings of the natural order are seen by Calvin as the result of God's providential governance, the special intervention of God at every moment.[33] However, Calvin never rejected creation outright. Redemption is always the redemption of creation. This is a crucial assumption in a truly transformational pattern of grace. Grace brings about a restoration of the original and proper orientation of nature under the sovereignty of God.

The recent work of the Calvin scholar, Ford Lewis Battles, on Calvin's use of the theme of accommodation is quite suggestive in this regard.[34] Calling attention to Calvin's education in classical rhetoric, Battles argues that Calvin's basic model of the relationship between God and the created order is based on the rhetorical principle of accommodation. This principle urges the speaker to adapt verbal representations to the capacities of the people who are being addressed.

Key words in Calvin's use of this theme are 'capacity' and 'measure.' Through an act of divine condescension, God overcomes the gap separating him from his creatures by adapting to their capacities. As Battles puts it, 'It is God who knows the incalculable difference in measure between His infinity and our finiteness, and accordingly accommodates the one to the other in the way in which He reveals Himself to us.'[35]

What is so suggestive about Battles' development of this theme is the way that it holds together divine accommodation and human capacity. God knows our measure and accommodates accordingly. This is far different from a synergistic understanding of this relationship as proposed by Fowler. But it does not lapse into a rejection of the proper role of the created order as the scene of divine activity. It may well be that Battles' explication of this theme in Calvin's thought is the most adequate way of conceptualizing the relationship between God's activity and the created order in a transformational pattern of grace. God does not overrule human capacities given in creation, nor does God merely uplift them. Rather, God accommodates to human capacities in ways that reorder them to their rightful place.

Viewed along these lines, the stages of faith that Fowler describes might be seen as providing some insight into the kinds of human capacities to which God accommodates. They describe certain features of natural piety that are transformed through the divine accommodation. When an adolescent experiences a profound and deeply meaningful conversion experience, for example, that does not mean that he or she stops being an adolescent and all that that entails.[36] It may very well be that he or she views God in highly personalistic terms, something that is quite understandable in terms of Fowler's description of the synthetic-conventional stage of faith.

It is not inconceivable, thus, that Fowler's stages of faith, if placed in a theological framework that is somewhat different from that which he himself offers, could be appropriated by members of the Reformed tradition. Reformed critics of Fowler's work have not yet addressed the complex theological issues involved in describing the relationship between nature and grace. It may well be that a fuller assessment of the convictions of their own particular heritage might provide them with a more nuanced evaluation of the structures of development that Fowler has uncovered.

Part four

This brings us to the third and final critical question members of the Reformed tradition have raised about Fowler's work: Does his use of structuralism to describe faith, even in its natural form, lead him to distort this phenomenon? Is it not impossible to describe faith without reference to its object and to the concrete beliefs and practices of particular communities by which that object is mediated?

On the surface, this criticism focuses on Fowler's acceptance of the structure-content distinction, which is an important part of Piagetian structuralism. By describing faith in terms of its structuring activity, so the argument goes, Fowler leaves out those contents, such as beliefs about God, that constitute the heart of faith. Fowler could counter by arguing that his structuralist account of faith is actually in the service of a theological understanding of this phenomenon taken over from Niebuhr and, to a lesser extent, from Tillich, in which human beings are portrayed as inevitably giving 'deity-significance' to centers of value and meaning.

The issue goes deeper, however. It has to do with whether there really is a phenomenon, faith, that exists universally. In large part, the answer to this question hinges on whether it is possible to identify universal features of human existence that cut across distinctive cultural communities. The attempt to identify such universal structures or processes is an inherent part of structuralism, in both the synchronic approach of Levi-Strauss and the diachronic approach of Jean Piaget. It is important to locate this argument in current theological trends.

Within recent theology and ethics, a vigorous conversation has emerged between those who argue that theology must develop a public language in order to participate meaningfully in a pluralistic world and those who argue that Christian theology must primarily seek to be faithful to the distinctive narratives and beliefs by which it is constituted as a community. Members of the Reformed tradition come down on both sides of this argument.

Representatives of public theology, such as David Tracy (a Roman Catholic) and Don Browning (a Disciple of Christ), have typically argued for a universal structure to practical moral reason as a way of grounding the possibility of public discourse. Browning, for example, draws explicitly on the work of John Rawls and Ronald Green in this regard.[37]

Those who argue against this position claim, on philosophical and theological grounds, that the existence of a universal structure of practical reason is a pipe dream. It is the misguided legacy of what Alasdair MacIntyre calls the 'enlightenment project': the attempt to ground morality in universal forms of reason and not the concrete (supposedly parochial) beliefs of particular religious or moral communities.[38]

In contrast, they argue that practical reason is always 'narrative-dependent.' It is based on those particular stories and beliefs that determine a community's basic notions of the Good and what it means to live a virtuous life. Different communities project different, even incommensurable, visions of the Good, growing out of the beliefs and practices flowing from the underlying narrative that holds a particular community together. In theological circles, Stanely Hauerwas and George Lindbeck have offered two of the most eloquent and passionate presentations of this perspective.[39] They both explicitly reject a liberal, Kantian understanding of reason and attempt to offer a 'postliberal' alternative.

Members of this position might look at Fowler's structuralist account of faith and charge it with abstractionism of the worst sort. Faith can only be defined from within the distinctive beliefs and practices of a particular community. Any effort to define faith in general invariably results in a kind of cultural imperialism. At best, there are 'family resemblances' in what faith means in different religious communities, as Wittgenstein pointed out in other domains.[40]

This is precisely the kind of critique of Fowler's definition of faith that recently has been offered by Craig Dykstra, who is sympathetic with both Hauerwas' and Lindbeck's perspectives. Drawing on categories from Lindbeck's book *The Nature of Doctrine*, he portrays Fowler as a variant of the 'experiential-expressivist' approach to religion, an approach in which religion is seen as the expression of internal, universal religious experience.[41] In contrast, he seeks to offer a definition of faith that grows out of an explicitly Christian perspective, a definition, he notes, that may or may not be compatible with that of other religious communities.[42]

Once more, however, we find ourselves confronting an issue that is not clearly settled within the Reformed tradition. One could just as easily ask whether Dykstra's appropriation of Wittgensteinian philosophy, by way of Lindbeck, overwhelms his theology at crucial points. Some members of the Reformed tradition, beginning with Calvin, have been wont to ask whether they could find universal structures in the created order. They seek such structures in large part because of their conviction of the universal sovereignty of God.

A major problem with the perspective advocated by Dykstra, Hauerwas, Lindbeck, and others is whether it inevitably leads us to a position of radical cultural relativism, certainly the spirit of modernity. Do these persons end up offering us little more than a highly sophisticated version of culture-Protestantism? If their perspective is taken at face value, we may be able to settle moral issues within the framework of a particular religious or moral community, but it is very difficult to see how questions could be adjudicated between different communities. If the underlying narratives that make moral and theological discourse possible really are incommensurable, then there seems to be no ground for common discussion, much less moral agreement. It is unclear however, whether the Reformed tradition is inclined in this direction. A strong case can be made that it is not.

As we have already noted, Calvin was no advocate of natural theology. He rejected the idea that persons could know God in a saving way through the workings of reason alone after the Fall. Calvin's evaluation of the natural law, however, continues to be an arguable question in the Reformed tradition, as the well-known exchange between Barth and Brunner made clear.

Even relatively conservative interpreters of Calvin like Niesel acknowledge that his theology portrays Christians, whose eyes have been corrected by the knowledge of faith, as able to see the 'inner law which is written and as it were impressed upon the hearts of all.'[43] Gustafson goes even further, calling attention to the fact that Calvin stresses in his discussion of the law the continuity between the natural moral law, the Decalogue, and the moral teachings of Jesus.[44] Similarly, an editorial note in the Westminster edition of the *Institutes* states, 'Calvin's view of the Commandments as a divinely authorized text expressing and clarifying the natural law engraved on all hearts is the traditional one.'[45]

All of this is to say that while radical cultural relativism is foreign to certain strands of the Reformed tradition, the search for universal structures of human existence is not. There is no question that there are key differences between a theologically interested search for such structures and one that is based on Enlightenment modes of thought. The former makes no claim to operate out of a position of neutrality in which reason functions in a pure fashion. Rather, reason is seen as based on the principles and metaphors that are provided it by scripture and tradition. The search for universal structures of life, which exist under the sovereign God, begins with this starting point.

If I have pointed to the theology underlying faith development theory with any cogency, then it may very well be that Fowler searches for universal structures of faith in human life in just this fashion. His stage descriptions are clearly theologically interested. To the present, he has not dealt with the complex question of how a theory can be descriptive and theologically normative at the same time. Nonetheless, his attempt to identify universal structures of human faith development is not inherently antithetical to every strand of the Reformed tradition and, in some ways, may even be roughly analogous to the universalism that many Calvin scholars believe is present in Calvin's view of the natural moral law.

Once more, we confront an issue that is arguable in the Reformed tradition, one of increasing import in the face of the work of Lindbeck, Hauerwas, and Dykstra. Fowler's work stands as an important counter-question to representatives of this approach. Can the Reformed tradition be satisfied with a version of cultural relativism, or does it have a stake in the search for universal structures of human existence under the sovereign God? The debate on this issue is just beginning to unfold. But after all, such a debate is the mark of a living tradition.

Part five

The intent of this article has been not only to determine the underlying theological issues at stake in the differences between Fowler and his critics in the Reformed tradition but also to make a point about the importance of theology itself in religious education. It is impossible to understand what is at stake in the argument about faith development theory without examining the issues on *theological* grounds. Undoubtedly, persons who are not members of the Reformed tradition will have experienced the ins and outs of this argument as outsiders. This is not their tradition; its basic theological convictions and sensitivities are not ones to which they subscribe.

But this is precisely the point. Conversation in religious education cannot always assume commonalities without sacrificing that which is frequently most important: distinctive notions of God and the faith community that are deeply rooted in a particular religious tradition. Acknowledgement of this fact may make conversation more difficult. But it does not make it impossible. It may well be that a re-entry of theological particularity into religious education would force those of us who write, teach, and practice in this field to appropriate more fully the traditions of our own faith communities, traditions that do not preclude conversation with others but are the condition of its possibility.

Notes

1. Ellis Nelson. 'Does faith develop? an evaluation of Fowler's position,' *Living Light*, vol. 19, 1982, p. 164.
2. James Loder, 'Reflections on Fowler's *Stages of Faith*', *Religious Education*, vol. 77, 1982, pp. 133–39.
3. Craig Dykstra, 'Faith development and Christian education', presented at The Institute for Faith Development Studies, Emory University, June 28-July 2, 1982, pp. 14–16. Cf. 'What is faith? An experiment in the hypothetical mode,' in Craig Dykstra and Shàron Parks (eds), *Faith Development and Fowler*, Birmingham, Alabama, Religious Education Press, 1986.
4. In the article cited above, for example, Nelson seems to view Fowler strictly in terms of Piaget and Kohlberg, with a minimal acknowledgement of Erikson's influence. He goes so far as to write that Fowler 'strikes out on his own' when he describes styles of faith in terms of polytheism, henotheism, and radical monotheism (p. 164). Nelson clearly misses Niebuhr's influence at this point, as he does throughout the article as a whole.
5. One of the best places to see Fowler's critical appropriation of Piaget is in 'Faith and the structuring of meaning,' in J. W Fowler and A. Vergote (eds), *Toward Moral and Religious Maturity*, Morristown, NJ, Silver Burdett Company, 1980, especially pp. 57–64.
6. James Fowler, *To See the Kingdom: the theological vision of H. Richard Niebuhr*, Nashville, Abingdon Press, 1974.
7. For Fowler's own discussion of his appropriation of radical monotheism to describe universalizing faith (stage 6) see his book, *Stages of Faith: the psychology of human development and the quest for meaning*, San Francisco, Harper and Row, 1981, pp. 204ff.
8. See *Stages of Faith*, chs 23–24.
9. Niebuhr's most extended discussion of this theme is in his classic, *Christ and Culture*, New York, Harper Torchbooks, 1951, chapter six. As Ottati, Kliever, and others have pointed out, Niebuhr adopts the transformational type in his own theology. See Douglas Ottati, *Meaning and Method in H.Richard Niebuhr's Theology*, Washington, University Press of America, 1982, p. 121; Lonnie Kliever, *H. Richard Niebuhr*, Waco, Texas, Word Books, 1977, pp. 57–8.
10. Niebuhr, *Christ and Culture*, p. 194.
11. *Ibid.*, pp. 217–18.
12. John Calvin, *The Institutes of the Christian Religion*, ed. John T. McNeill, Philadelphia, The Westminster Press, 1960, 1.5.1.
13. Faith is not identical with natural piety, as Edward Dowey makes clear in *The Knowledge of God in Calvin's Theology*, New York, Columbia University Press, 1952. Faith involves knowledge not given in creation which becomes available only through scripture as it witnesses to Jesus Christ. Of special importance in this regard is faith's trust in the gratuitous mercy of God shown in Christ. Faith, however, is not totally distinct from natural piety, for it involves a restoration of the fundamental intentionality of that piety, reordering human affections and cognition under the sovereign God. See also James Gustafson's discussion of Calvin and Augustine on this point in *Ethics from a Theocentric Perspective*, volume 1, Chicago, University of Chicago Press, 1981, pp. 165, 171, and François Wendel, *Calvin: the origins and development of his religious thought*, tr. Mairet, New York, Harper and Row, 1950, p. 191.
14. Lonnie Kliever's discussion of this is quite helpful, in his *H. Richard Niebuhr*, ch. 2.
15. H. Richard Niebuhr, *Radical Monotheism and Western Culture*, New York, Harper Torchbooks, 1943. See especially chapters 2 and 3 of the supplementary essays.
16. See, for example, pp. 119ff. which follow a discussion of faith as human centers of value and meaning. For an extended treatment of sin, see his essay, 'Man the sinner' in *Journal of Religion*, vol. 15, pp. 272ff.
17. Niebuhr even offers us a kind of typology in this regard, differentiating

henotheistic faith and polytheistic faith. In contrast to both of these styles of faith, he describes radically monotheistic faith.

18. Fowler, *Stages of Faith*, 'Part One.'
19. *Ibid.*, pp. 19–20.
20. James Fowler, 'Faith development and the catechesis of children,' unpublished lecture given at Boston College.
21. Alasdair MacIntyre, *After Virtue*, Notre Dame, University of Notre Dame Press, 1981, p. 206.
22. George Albert Coe, *Religion in Education and Morals*, Chicago, Fleming H. Revell Company, 1904; *A Social Theory of Religious Education* (1927), rpt., New York, Arno Press, 1969. Coe continues to have a real, but chastened, personalism in *What Is Christian Education*, New York, Charles Scribner's Sons, 1929.
23. H. Shelton Smith, *Faith and Nurture*, New York, Charles Scribner's Sons, 1948.
24. *Ibid.*, pp. 61ff.
25. An interesting collection of the early writings of these persons can be found in James Robinson (ed.), *The Beginnings of Dialectic Theology*, Richard, John Knox Press, 1968.
26. Stanley Hauerwas, *Character and the Christian Life: a study in theological ethics*, San Antonio, Texas, Trinity University Press, 1975, ch 1. Herbert Hartwell, a sympathetic interpreter of Barth, describes this as Barth's 'actualism,' pointing out that 'Thus, the Word of God is always an act of God, that is, event, and that act takes place in the freedom of His grace.' *(The Theology of Karl Barth: an introduction,* London, Gerald Duckworth and Co., 1964, p. 34.)
27. Hartwell describes Barth's understanding of the church as follows: 'Thus to Barth the Church is not an institution but an event that by the free grace of God in Jesus Christ and in the power of His Holy Spirit must continually happen afresh in order that there may be the true Church of Jesus Christ' *(Ibid.,* p. 144).
28. George Marsden, 'Reformed and American,' in David Wells (ed.), *Reformed Theology in America: a history of its modern development*, Grand Rapids, Eerdmans, 1985, pp. 1–12.
29. The reflections which follow are indebted to various personal conversations which I have had with my colleague at Union, Donald Dawe.
30. James Loder, *The Transforming Moment: understanding convictional experiences*, San Francisco, Harper and Row, 1981.
31. There is far more potential compatibility between the religious socialization model engendered by Ellis Nelson in *Where Faith Begins* and the ethics of character advocated by Craig Dykstra in *Vision and Character* than they have acknowledged. Socialization can be construed as a developmental process, as we see in the work of George Herbert Mead. Character can be seen as based on certain developmental patterns.
32. James Fowler, *Becoming Adult, Becoming Christian*, San Francisco, Harper and Row, 1984, p. 74.
33. See Edward Dowey's excellent discussion of this in *The Knowledge of God*, pp. 129ff.
34. Ford Lewis Battles, 'God was accommodating himself to human capacity,' in Donald McKim (ed.), *Readings in Calvin's Theology*, Grand Rapids, Baker, 1984, ch. 7.
35. *Ibid.*, p. 35.
36. Fowler, building on the work of Romney Moseley, has identified a number of ways that conversion can be related to stage change. Cf. *Stages of Faith*, pp. 285–6.
37. Don Browning, *Religious Ethics and Pastoral Care*, Philadelphia, Fortress Press, 1983, pp. 63–68. In a similar fashion, McCann and Strain draw on the work of Jurgen Habermas to describe the possibility of theology's participation in public discourse. See Dennis McCann and Charles Strain, *Polity and Praxis*, Minneapolis, Winston Press, 1985.
38. MacIntyre, *After Virtue*, chs 1–6.
39. Stanley Hauerwas (with Bondi and Burrell), *Truthfulness and Tragedy*, Notre Dame, University of Notre Dame Press, 1977; *A Community of Character:*

toward a constructive Christian social ethic, Notre Dame, University of Notre Dame Press, 1981; George Lindbeck, *The Nature of Doctrine: religion and theology in a postliberal age*, Philadelphia, The Westminister Press, 1984.

40. Ludwig Wittgenstein, *The Blue Book*, New York, Harper Torchbooks, 1955; *Philosophical Investigations*, tr. G. E. M. Anscombe, New York, Macmillan Publishing Company, 1952.
41. Dykstra, 'What is faith?', pp. 51ff.
42. *Ibid.*, p 54.
43. Quoted in Wilhelm Niesel, *The Theology of Calvin*, tr. Harold Knight, Philadelphia, The Westminister Press, 1938, p. 102.
44. James Gustafson, *Protestant and Roman Catholic Ethics: prospects for rapprochement*, Chicago, University of Chicago Press, 1978, pp. 18–20.
45. Calvin, *Institutes*, n. 5, p. 367.

4. Philosophy and faith development

Critical assessment of Fowler's concept of faith, like his own justification for the use of that concept itself, inevitably takes the form largely of conceptual analysis. In this sense it may be broadly defined as 'philosophical critique', particularly where such assessment is concerned primarily with questions of coherence and consistency, and with drawing out the logical implications of the concept.[1] In this section we have included two papers which both have a rather different justification for appearing in this category. They represent a philosophical focus in their concern for epistemological issues, and for the 'logic of faith'.

David Heywood's paper, 'Piaget and faith development: a true marriage of minds?', was first published in *British Journal of Religious Education*, vol. 8, no. 2, 1986, pp. 72–78. As its title suggests, it is essentially a critique of Fowler's use of Piaget (via Kohlberg). Heywood criticizes Fowler not only on the grounds that Piaget's theory has not been empirically verified, but also and more centrally because 'the philosophy underlying Piaget's work ... is fundamentally antithetical to some of Fowler's most important emphases'. Piaget's structuralist assumptions are here criticized; and Fowler's attempt to broaden Piaget's 'logic of rational certainty' into a broader and more holistic 'logic of conviction' rejected as incoherent.

Romney Moseley served for a time as Associate Director of the Center for the Study of Faith Development at Emory University. His doctoral research was in the area of faith development and conversion.[2] In his essay 'Forms of logic in faith development theory', *Pastoral Psychology*, vol. 39, no. 3, 1991, pp. 143–152, Moseley also focuses on Fowler's 'logic of conviction', arguing that this metaphorical extension of the term *logic* 'radically shifts the theory of faith development away from Piagetian structuralism and towards dialectical psychology'. Here Moseley proposes a radical revision of faith development theory which dispenses with the concept of a stage of faith, or rather understands this concept metaphorically, stressing primarily the heuristic function of faith development theory in making intelligible the activity of human imagination in relation to the transcendent.

Notes
1. For further analyses of Fowler's concept of faith see Craig Dykstra, 'What is faith?: an experiment in the hypothetical mode', and J. Harry Fernhout, 'Where is faith?: searching for the core of the cube', in Craig Dykstra and Sharon Parks (eds), *Faith Development and Fowler*, Birmingham, Alabama, Religious Education Press, 1986, pp. 45–64 and 65–89. See also Gary L. Chamberlain, 'Faith as knowing: a study of the epistemology in faith development theory', *Iliff Review*, vol. 38, 1981, pp. 3–14.
2. See his essays 'Faith development and conversion in the catechumenate', in Robert D. Duggan (ed.), *Conversion and the Catechumenate*, New York, Paulist Press, 1984, pp. 145–163, and (with Ken Brockenbrough) 'Faith development in the pre-school years', in David Ratcliff (ed.), *Handbook of Preschool Religious Education*, Birmingham, Alabama, Religious Education Press, 1988, pp. 101–124.

4.1 Piaget and faith development: a true marriage of minds?

David Heywood

One cannot read very far into the literature of faith development without encountering the name of Jean Piaget. Of the variety of sources in the fields of theology and psychology which form the basis for faith development theory, the work of Piaget is among the most influential. As developed by James Fowler over the last ten years, faith development is one of a family of structural developmental theories of human development based on Piaget's work, the other most prominent being that of Lawrence Kohlberg. When Fowler writes that a stage is to be understood as a 'structural whole' and that stages are 'sequential and hierarchical in their relationship to each other', he is consciously building on the foundations laid by Piaget in his studies of cognitive development in children, extending over a period of nearly fifty years.

At first sight, it would seem strange to use a theory of child development, whose final stage is completed by the age of sixteen, as the basis for a theory of development extending throughout adulthood. Equally strange is the use of a theory explicitly and narrowly confined to cognitive development as the basis for something as wide-ranging as a study of faith. Moreover, some of the major criticisms made of Fowler's work, the seemingly arbitrary choice of the 'variables' said to comprise a faith stage, the excessive eclecticism, and the problems arising from the separation of form and content, also arise to a great extent from his dependence on Piaget.[1]

This article probes into the relationship between Fowler's work and Piaget's theory and arrives at two main conclusions. First, Piaget's work does not have the unchallenged empirical status taken for granted in faith development literature. Secondly, the philosophy underlying Piaget's work on cognitive development is fundamentally antithetical to some of Fowler's most important emphases, and this requires him to find an alternative theory to explain the process by which stage-transition takes place. If we ask whether such an alternative theory is available, we find within the field of learning theory a wide range of different models of the process of learning and meaning-making, some of which are quite familiar with the concept which Fowler labels 'faith'. Above all, it should be realized that the activity of 'structuring' in the sense of attempting to provide for oneself a coherent view of the world, by no means presupposes the existence of 'structures' in the Piagetian sense.

Faith's 'inner structure'

The area of development on which we are focusing is the area Fowler calls the 'inner structure' of faith. This is the realm of psychological, 'inner' development. It is distinguished from the 'outer structure' of faith, which is the sphere of 'world maintenance', of shared values and beliefs. This distinction enables Fowler to develop a theory of faith development which is semi-independent of specific belief content. It is the existential dimension of faith by which the 'outer structure' and the 'inner structure' are maintained in relationship. The description of this existential dimension is drawn from Tillich, where faith is described as 'ultimate concern'. Tillich's concept of ultimate concern unites the inward, subjective condition of faith and its outward, concrete object. In the same way, Fowler uses the concept of 'the ultimate conditions of existence' to establish the relationship between outward beliefs and inward faith, between 'what faith knows' and 'how faith knows'. The root of this threefold treatment of faith is already to be found in Fowler's work on H. Richard Niebuhr, under the headings of 'interpersonal structure', 'organic structure' and 'existential analysis'.[2] This article focuses on the 'inner structure' or 'organic structure' and in particular the use of Piagetian structural developmentalism in this context.

Piaget's work has several important advantages as the basis for faith development. In the first place, the rigid separation of form and content in structural developmentalism coincides exactly with the distinction between the inner structure and the outer structure of faith. According to Piaget, cognitive development proceeds entirely according to its own inbuilt laws. It is not altered in its course, but only retarded or accelerated by the specific content of learning experiences. In the same way, faith development is said to proceed uniformly, regardless of particular belief content, although accelerated or retarded by specific experience. Another advantage of the structural developmental paradigm is the universality of its application. Piaget and his associates have done comparatively little in the way of cross-cultural comparison, but for the Piagetian the universal validity of his conclusions is guaranteed by the structuralist philosophy which underlies the theory of cognitive development. For Fowler, such inherent universal validity is the ideal basis for a theory of faith development encompassing men and women of all religious persuasions and none. Finally, the extent of Piaget's work, its fifty-year history, the range of subjects covered and the sheer quantity of his experimental work and its detailed description make it appear not only fully empirically verified, but a sound basis for future development.

Empirical problems

The status of Piaget's work appears to be one of the major foundations of confidence in the validity of faith development. However, the result of this is that Piaget's conclusions are being used to provide a short cut to the empirical verification of faith development. Introducing his work in 1974, Fowler wrote that 'I hypothesize that these stages, understood as *structural wholes*, are *sequential* and *hierarchical* in their relationship to each other.'[3] Already it can be seen that the idea of stages is the dominating concern of the work, to the relative neglect of the process behind development. The major problem with this sentence, however, lies with the words, 'I hypothesize ...'. The understanding of stages as hierarchical and sequential structural wholes is, strictly speaking, not one of Fowler's hypotheses. It is a description of stage formation drawn directly from the structural-developmental model of cognitive and moral development. In Fowler's work, it has much more of the character of a presupposition than that of an hypothesis.

An extract from Fowler's own account of his work makes this clear[4]:

> A faith stage is a structural whole. To break open the metaphor a bit we may say that a stage is organismic – a flexible organization of inter-related patterns of operation. When one analyses a faith interview, one wants to read or hear 'through' to the structural whole underlying the beliefs, values, attitudes and actions described in the linear prose of the respondent. The problem is to read or hear and comprehend in such a way that the content becomes clear, at one level; but on another level one wants to let the structure of a person's faith 'precipitate' out of the content that has been offered.

In Fowler's research, the data is looked at 'through' the theory. The aim is to *describe* stages which are *presumed* to exist. The belief that 'a faith stage is a structural whole' is the basic presupposition on which the whole theory rests. This belief is not actually being tested by the method of research Fowler describes. To test it adequately would require a coherent theory of the process behind faith development which theoretically could be disconfirmed by the data from the interviews. Instead, the supposed empirical verification of Piaget's theory, with its account of the process of structural development, is being used to provide faith development with its empirical base.[5]

However, the validity of Piaget's work is far from unquestioned. In the last ten years in particular, it has been subject to both theoretical revision and empirical disconfirmation. In a fascinating little book, entitled *Children's Minds*, Professor Margaret Donaldson of Edinburgh University describes the results of experiments into object permanence, class inclusion, transitive reasoning, decentering and a wide range of other aspects of cognitive development, all of which cast serious doubt on Piaget's conclusions and invite reinterpretation of his own experimental findings.[6] Perhaps even more damaging are the results of experiments with adults. Piaget's claim is that what he calls 'formal operations', that is abstract, hypothetical thinking, is a necessary and inevitable final stage, to which all thinking tends by the process of equilibration underlying stage progression. A large number of studies with adults, however, show the subjects failing to perform at the level of formal operations and a percentage of older subjects appearing to regress in their reasoning ability. The problems of adulthood were considered by Piaget in a paper of 1972 in which he was forced to conclude that although logically the performance of formal operations and the specific content to which they are applied is distinct, in practice this is not the case. Ability to engage in formal reasoning is frequently restricted to specific specialist areas, even for highly educated people, such as lawyers and doctors. He hypothesized that although all normal subjects attain formal operations, they generally do so only in areas which concern them. Lawyers can reason formally about law, but not about physics, and so forth. The question raised by Piaget's concessions to aptitude and content specialization is that of the logical independence of abstract thinking from its specific content, in other words, that separation of form and content which is basic to structural developmentalism. Despite his attempts to reconcile the findings with adults with his earlier work, the fact remains that the fundamental philosophical orientation of Piaget's theory excludes content, interest and aptitude as significant variables. The discovery of the importance of these factors invites alternative explanations of cognitive functioning and cognitive development.[7]

Piaget's theory

It is important to be aware that Piaget's theory of cognitive development, which he calls 'genetic epistemology', arises from an underlying philosophical standpoint, namely structuralism, on which it is dependent.[8] Piaget himself would have disputed the description of structuralism as a philosophy, preferring to think of it as a scientific methodology. However, his scientific work is based on a certain approach to reality, an ontology, in which 'reality' is said to consist of structures. The structuralist approach to reality is an alternative to atomism and its psychological analogue, associationism, as well as to Gestalt holism. For Piaget, the physical world and the biological world were to be interpreted in terms of structures, and in psychology the possibility of knowledge was dependent on the development of the appropriate cognitive structures. The bridge across the 'epistemological gap', the guarantee that the knowledge of the world which is made possible by cognitive development corresponds to the world as it is in itself, is provided by the analogy between the structures of the physical world and those of the mind. Both types of structures obey the same rules of development and so the knowledge made possible by the structures of the mind will correspond to reality, which is made up of physical and biological structures. Such a situation applies, however, only when the structures in the mind are complete, that is when formal operations are attained. The achievement of formal operations is the natural culmination of the process of stage development, a final and fundamental decentering toward the possibility of complete objectivity, the ability to perceive and interpret the world as it really is. 'Objectivity' is guaranteed by the perfect reversibility of the structures of formal operations and such objectivity alone guarantees the validity of scientific conclusions.

'Piaget's theory' is thus not *simply* a theory of child development, nor even *mainly* a theory of child development. It is principally a theory of evolution, which embraces a fully developed ontology and epistemology. Without this background, the theory of cognitive development cannot properly be understood or evaluated. In several crucial respects, Piaget's theory of child development draws on the philosophy of structuralism. One of the most important of these is the assumption that all thinking is governed by logical form, logic itself being an axiomization of biological structures which are genetically present in DNA. His interpretation of the evidence supplied by the numerous and wide-ranging experiments into children's thinking is based on the assumption that the child is responding to the logical form of the task set. Failure to perform the task indicates failure to comprehend its logical form which indicates a lack of the requisite mental structure. Piaget and his fellow-workers have thus imported their philosophical assumptions into their interpretation of the evidence to an extraordinary degree.

The evidence reviewed by Professor Donaldson, however, demonstrates the serious distortion caused by these assumptions. Many of these experiments involve simple variations on Piagetian tasks. The logical form of the task is the same as that of the Piagetian experiment but the content and overall situation is varied. They show not only that young children are able to perform a wide variety of mental operations of which Piaget pronounced them incapable but also that in many cases it is variation in the content of the experiment rather than in the form of the task which has the greater effect. The children respond not simply to the logical form of the task but to a construction of its overall meaning which involves several other factors, the perceived intention of the experimenter, the verbal form of the instructions, the difficulty of the task, the salience of different parts of the content, and so on. These experiments have the effect of disconfirming a series of hypotheses which could not be said to have been proved by Piaget and his team of researchers, since their interpretations are seen to rest so heavily on their philosophical assumptions.

Taken simply as a theory of child development or even as a model of cognitive structure, the breadth and inclusiveness of Piaget's work appear impressive. The range and subtlety of his hypotheses, the construction of the experiments and the fruitfulness of the questions he raises indicate a powerful and original creative mind. Moreover, the integration of the experimental results into an overall philosophical system makes his interpretation appear not simply persuasive, but assured. However, to view the work on child psychology from the point of view of philosophical structuralism is to become aware of the immensity of the presuppositions which lie behind the construction of the experiments and the interpretation of the results. It must, therefore, be held to be a major criticism of the faith development movement that it treats Piaget's work as an assured foundation in isolation from the philosophical standpoint on which the interpretation of his work rests.[9]

The logic of conviction

Fowler's own main criticism of Piaget concerns the narrowness of his cognitive focus. Fowler maintains that 'knowing' extends far beyond the strictly cognitive field to involve a person's total orientation. He credits Piaget with having given a satisfactory explanation of the 'logic of rational certainty', the purely cognitive aspect of the knowing process, and includes Piaget's theory of cognitive development as the first of his series of seven variables. But Fowler wishes to extend the application of the structural-developmental hypothesis beyond the field of cognition. He sees himself as working towards a broadening of Piaget's narrow focus, a process already begun by Kohlberg in his theory of moral development. To this end, Piaget's strictly rational emphasis is to be placed in the context of a broader 'logic of conviction' which derives from a person's fundamental faith-orientation.[10] The problems begin, however, when we ask how this 'logic of conviction' is related to the process of faith development, which Fowler wants to explain in structuralist terms. With which of the seven variables are we to associate it, if not with the form of logic? Can the idea of a 'logic of conviction' be reconciled with structural-developmentalism at all?

The answer Piaget himself would have given to this last question is quite clear. In his account of the process of cognitive development the idea of any sort of 'logic of conviction' is ruled out entirely. In Fowler's explanation, the logic of conviction arises from the construction of what is known and the construction of the self in relation to what is known. In Piagetian theory, the understanding or construction of the personal self plays no part in cognitive development. The structures which govern mental operations are the property of what is called the epistemic or epistemologic subject, which is carefully distinguished from the individual human or personal subject. The personal subject is the conscious reflective self, of which one is more or less aware. The epistemological subject, on the other hand, is entirely unconscious. It corresponds to the 'cognitive nucleus common to all subjects', similar to and deriving from Kant's description of the innate and unconscious structuring activity of the mind. The development of logical structures is the work of the epistemological subject and is an unconscious process.

By the separation of the epistemological from the personal subject, Piaget splits the whole world of experience into two distinct regions; on the one hand, concrete, empirically verifiable facts, on the other, subjectively formed meanings and values. The human subject is unavoidably involved in the everyday world of decision-making and interpersonal relationships, the world of the 'fragmentary and frequently distorting grasp of consciousness'.[11] This is the world of subjectively inherited values which go beyond the limits of actual knowledge. The task of co-ordinating these systems of value with the objective conditions of knowledge is the work of philosophy, and the product of philosophy is what Piaget calls a 'wisdom', a rational co-ordination of values. Since this activity is not tied to the objective conditions of the real world the number of possible conclusions for philosophy is variable, in contrast with the one, scientifically established model of genetic epistemology. 'There can be several wisdoms while there exists only one truth.'[12]

For Piaget, the achievement of objective, scientific knowledge requires a decentering away from the involvements of the individual personal subject into the world of the epistemological subject. The logic of conviction, in Fowler's sense, bears no relation to the achievement of rational certainty. That which underlies rational certainty is the development of the operational structures which make knowledge possible. His description of the process of development rules out entirely the existence of an underlying 'logic of conviction'. Such a thing is mere subjectivity, a penumbra of distorting value judgments surrounding the solid core of objectively perceived fact.

The process of development

In order to broaden Piaget's theory into a theory of faith, Fowler must bypass its structuralist assumptions. Although his understanding of stages is dependent on Piaget, a new account of the process of development is required. However, a further weakness is exposed at this point since, in Piaget's theory, the description of the stages, and in fact the very existence of definable stages, is an outcome of the process of development. According to Piaget, the theory of stages rests on the observations (1) that there are structures; (2) that these are constructed; (3) that their construction is a gradual process.[13] In other words, the idea of stages of development is not separable from the theory of process, which is itself dependent on the philosophy of structuralism. This theory we saw to be fundamentally antithetical to the idea of the construction of the self in relation to the known, a crucial part of Fowler's definition of faith. What, then, is left of the idea of stages in relation to faith?

If the development of faith is to be linked with cognitive and emotional development and with the process of socialization and personal maturity some alternative theory of the process behind such development is required. If we begin to look for such alternatives, there is no difficulty in locating them. Piaget's is by no means the only theory even of cognitive development. The process of criticism and reinterpretation of Piaget's work has gone far enough to indicate that as far as cognitive development goes, we are now into the post-Piagetian period. Nor does this take account of those theories opposed to Piaget or independent of his influence. The need for such alternative models is seen clearly enough in the descriptions of cognitive functioning attached to Fowler's stages 4, 5 and 6. The extension of a 'dichotomizing' cognitive style to 'dialectical' and then 'synthesizing', although described as an extension of Piaget's work, is actually based not on developments of Piaget but on different accounts of cognitive structure, different accounts of logic and even of ontology. Alternative models of development are offered by analysis in terms of systems rather than of structures on the Piagetian model, and from the school of psycholinguistics, which is especially concerned with the structuring of meaning. The activity of 'structuring' by no means presupposes Piagetian structures.[14]

The Kohlberg connection

This paper began with the question why Piaget's theory of cognitive development should have been adopted as the basic paradigm in faith development theory and will conclude by suggesting that the answer lies in the influence of Kohlberg. It was Kohlberg himself who first introduced Fowler to the work of Piaget,[15] yet between Kohlberg and Piaget are several crucial differences, all of which are important elements of Fowler's work also.

In the first place, Kohlberg's description of moral development, while using the Piagetian model of hierarchical stages, departs from Piaget's description of morality. Kohlberg moves the province of morality away from social interaction, that is, in his interpretation, an affective sphere, toward a reasoned philosophical ideal. He explicitly claims that it is ways of knowing which lie behind ways of behaving. In Kohlberg's description, the evolutionary basis for stage development gives way to a philosophical basis and the emphasis shifts from structure towards development. The idea of sequential and hierarchical stages forms the starting point and basic assumption of Kohlberg's work, just as it does for Fowler. Moreover, the process norm behind stage transition of Piaget's work is replaced by Kohlberg by an end point norm. For both Kohlberg and Fowler, Stage 6 is a final form which informs the whole process of development. Finally, it is to Kohlberg that we must attribute the link between Dewey and structural development, even though Dewey's understanding of the process of development was completely different from Piaget's. With the link with Dewey, however, comes the change in emphasis toward the desirability of development, rather than, with Piaget, its inevitability.[16]

It seems clear that Fowler is using Kohlberg's version of Piaget, rather than Piaget himself as the basis of his theory. Fowler interprets Kohlberg as having broadened the basis of Piaget's structural developmentalism by introducing more aspects of human behaviour, including affectivity.[17] From this has developed the view, which seems generally accepted in faith development literature, of Piaget as having provided an empirically verified theory of cognitive development capable of being broadened into other areas. The conclusion of this paper, on the other hand, is that Piaget's theory is not empirically verified and not capable of being extended into other areas, in particular not into the domain of faith. It is suggested that structural developmentalism is not the model of cognitive functioning best suited to the explanation of the structuring of meaning, and those concerned with the shortcomings of faith development as it stands at present might care to look in alternative directions. As to the marriage of Piaget and faith development, it seems justifiable to admit impediment.

References
1. James E. Loder, in J. E Loder and J. W. Fowler, 'Conversations on *Stages of Faith* and *The Transforming Moment*', *Religious Education*, vol. 77, 1982, p. 138; John L. Elias, *Psychology and Religious Education,* Bethlehem, Penn, Booksellers of Bethlehem, 1979, pp. 124–125; Gabriel Moran, *Religious Education Development: images for the future*, Minneapolis, Minnesota, Winston Press, 1974, p. 110.
2. Fowler, *Stages of Faith*, San Francisco, Harper and Row, 1981, pp. 92–93; 'Toward a developmental perspective on faith', *Religious Education*, vol. 69, 1974, pp. 208–213; *To See the Kingdom*, Nashville, Abingdon, 1974, pp. 209–224.
3. 'Toward a developmental perspective on faith', p. 213.
4. 'Stages in faith: the structural developmental approach', in T. C. Hennessy (ed.), *Values and Moral Development*, New York, Paulist, 1976, p. 186.
5. See the comments of A. McBride, 'Reaction to Fowler: doubts about procedure', in T. C. Hennessy (ed.), *Values and Moral Development*, New York, Paulist, 1976, pp. 211–218.
6. Margaret Donaldson, *Children's Minds,* Glasgow, Fontana, 1978. See also: Theodore Mischel (ed.), *Cognitive Development and Epistemology*, New York, Academic Press, 1971; Brian Rotman, *Jean Piaget: psychologist of the real*, Hassocks, Sussex, Harvester Press, 1977; Linda S. Siegel and Charles J. Brainerd,

Alternatives to Piaget: critical essays on the theory, London, Academic Press, 1978; Johan Modgil, Celia Modgil and Geoffrey Brown (eds), *Jean Piaget: an interdisciplinary critique*, London, Routledge and Kegan Paul, 1983; J. Modgil and C. Modgil (eds), *Jean Piaget: consensus and controversy*, New York, Holt, Rinehart and Winston, 1982.

7. H. Long, K. McCrary and S. Ackerman, 'Adult cognition: Piagetian-based research findings', *Adult Education*, vol. 30, 1979; Jean Piaget, 'Intellectual evolution from adolescence to adulthood', tr. J. Bliss and H. Firth, *Human Development*, vol. 15, 1972, pp. 1–12.

8. Jean Piaget, *Structuralism*, tr. Chaninah Maschler, London, Routledge and Kegan Paul, 1971; French edition, 1968.

9. Charles Taylor comments that such an approach is likely to lead only to sterility. 'What is involved in a genetic epistemology?', in Mischel, *op. cit.*, pp. 415–416.

10. Fowler, 'Faith and the structuring of meaning', in J. Fowler and A. Vergote (eds), *Toward Moral and Religious Maturity*, Morristown, NJ, Silver Burdett, 1980, pp. 60–63.

11. *Structuralism*, p. 139.

12. Piaget, *Insights and Illusions of Philosophy*, tr. Wolfe Mays, London, Routledge and Kegan Paul, 1971; French edition, 1965, p. 210. The description of Piaget's epistemology is based on *Structuralism* and *Insights and Illusions*.

13. 'Piaget's theory', in P. A. Mussern (ed.), *Carmichael's Manual of Child Psychology*, New York, John Wiley and Sons, 3rd ed., 1970, p. 710.

14. Klaus F. Reigel, 'Dialectical operations: the final period of cognitive development', *Human Development*, vol. 16, 1973, pp. 346–370; Morris L. Bigge, *Learning Theories for Teachers*, 4th ed., New York, Harper and Row, 1982; Frank Smith, *Comprehension and Learning*, New York, Holt, Rinehart and Winston, 1975; R. D. Anderson (ed.), *Schooling and the Acquisition of Knowledge*, New York, John Wiley and Son, 1977.

15. Fowler, *Stages of Faith*, San Francisco, Harper and Row, 1981, p. 38.

16. Lawrence Kohlberg, 'Development as the aim of education', 'From is to ought' and 'Justice as reversibility', in *The Philosophy of Moral Development, vol. 1*, New York, Harper and Row, 1981.

17. 'Toward a developmental perspective', p. 213.

4.2 Forms of logic in faith development theory

Romney M. Moseley

Fowler defines faith as an *activity* by which we compose our relation to a transcendent center of meaning and value (Fowler, 1980). This definition of faith is strongly influenced by H. Richard Niebuhr's theology and ethics. Piagetian structuralism (constructivism) provides a psychogenetic framework for mapping the transformation of cognitive and affective processes by which faith develops. By basing his stages of faith on Piagetian constructivism, Fowler adopts the position that faith follows a logical progress of development. Vidal notes that early in the formulation of his theory of cognitive development Piaget regarded the religious history of humanity as a process of objectivization by which 'individual thought subjects itself to a simultaneously logical and moral norm that transcends it, and which is for the logician the true object of religious experience' (Piaget, 1921, p. 412).

Evidently, Fowler agrees with Piaget that it is possible to demonstrate, from the perspective of individual psychological development, the logical parallelism that exists between the evolution of religious and moral values and the stadial development of cognitive processes from egocentric to abstract logical operations. The concept of *structure* is the key concept upon which rests claims of logical development, for example, the hierarchical and invariant sequence of stages. Most importantly for our discussion, the distinction between *structure* and *content* allows the structuralists to focus on equilibrated structures as the definitive characteristic of a stage. Contradictions in beliefs and values are treated as matters of content that are secondary to the principle of equilibrium.

The priority of structure over content leads to the further distinction between 'hard' and 'soft' stages (Power and Kohlberg, 1980; Power, 1987). Fowler himself does not consider his stages as 'soft.' As far as he is concerned, his stages are logically ordered and empirically validated. He proposes two forms of logic that correspond to the structure/content dualism, namely, a 'logic of rational certainty' and a 'logic of conviction.' His intent is 'to grasp the inner dialectic of rational logic in the dynamics of a larger, more comprehensive logic of convictional orientation' (Fowler, 1986, p. 25). This view of a wider context of knowing and valuing is decisive for his definition of faith as a contextually and relationally grounded activity. Given the Kantian influences on Piaget's theory of knowledge and Kohlberg's theory

163

of moral development, one can understand why Fowler does not want faith to be seen in the same light as Kant's view of religion, that is, as primarily concerned with rational ideas (Kohlberg and Power, 1981).

The problem arises when Fowler insists on using the language of structuralism to explain both the 'rational logic' of cognitive structures and the 'comprehensive logic of convictional orientation.' To accommodate both forms of logic, Fowler declares that he is using the term logic 'in a metaphorical sense, designating two major kinds of structuring activity which interact in the constitutive-knowing that is faith' (Fowler, 1986, p. 23). In other words, logic is not to be understood in the Aristotelian sense of deriving logical contradictions. On the one hand, Fowler's use of the term logic is consistent with Piaget's understanding of the development of demonstrable logic – the logic governing the evolution of structures which are necessary for the construction of concepts of physical reality, for example, concepts of time, volume, number, etc. (Piaget, 1926). On the other hand, the progression of the stages indicates a widening nexus of self-other and self-transcendent relationships that culminate in the stage of 'universalizing faith.'

While the self-transcendent relationship is the ontological matrix of faith development theory, Fowler provides neither an explicit theory of the formation and transformation of the self nor an exposition of the nature of the transcendent. He relies on Niebuhr's theological anthropology for a normative formulation of the triadic and covenantal relationship between the self, others and the 'One beyond the many' (Niebuhr, 1960, p. 32).

Niebuhr's radical monotheism is consistent with his coherence theory of truth and value. A coherence theory of truth establishes truth on the basis of a coherent relation that exists between the parts of a larger system (Grant, 1984, p. 40). It is not surprising then that Fowler speaks of 'a larger, more comprehensive system of convictional orientation.' In contrast, Piagetian epistemology follows a correspondence theory of truth. Truth is established on the basis of its correspondence to the data of physical reality. Piaget is primarily concerned with the genesis of logico-mathematical structures (genetic psychology) and the genesis of scientific knowledge (genetic epistemology). Stages are 'structured wholes' (*structures d'ensemble*). Each stage is a logical configuration of structures and functions.

In faith development theory, this configuration of structures and functions is demonstrated in the relationship between the seven 'aspects' or constitutive elements of a stage of faith: form of logic, social perspective-taking, moral judgment, bounds of social awareness, locus of authority, form of world coherence, and symbolic functioning. It is to be expected that as the stages of faith move away from Piaget's stages (1 through 4) there is a shift from a correspondence to a coherence theory of meaning and value. Not surprisingly, 'world coherence' — 'the logical relations by which elements of the world are "held together"' — becomes increasingly important in the progression of the stages (Moseley, Jarvis, and Fowler, 1986).

In a word, Fowler is caught between the empiricist demands of structuralism and the metapsychological and metaethical concerns of liberal Protestant theology. Given the propensity of structuralism to subsume the domain of faith to the narrow concerns of psychological equilibrium, Fowler recasts the concept of structure so that it can accommodate the moral and religious factors that comprise the domain of faith. Of particular concern is the need to show how the relation to a transcendent source of meaning is structured. This proposition is itself a *religious* conviction. Fowler tries to maintain a clear distinction between faith and religion on the basis of Wilfred Cantwell Smith's (1960) explorations in etymology and the history of religions, but this is offset by the theory's theological presuppositions. Fowler adheres to a liberal Protestant belief that the substance of religion is the experience of transcendence (the sacred, ultimate concern, etc.).

There is another way in which religion is critical to faith development theory. This is seen in Fowler's assertion that faith involves a more comprehensive form of logic than is found in Piagetian constructivism. This raises the question of language. An extensive discussion of this subject is beyond the scope of this paper. It is sufficient to note Lindbeck's observation that we need to consider how religion functions as a 'cultural and/or linguistic framework or medium that shapes the entirety of life and thought' (Lindbeck, 1984, p. 32). In this regard, 'symbolic functioning,' one of the vectors by which a stage of faith is identified, is relevant to our discussion. In the *Manual*, we pointed out that 'this aspect of faith is concerned with how the person understands, appropriates and utilizes symbols and other aspects of language in the process of meaning-making and locating his or her centers of value and images of power' (Moseley, Jarvis and Fowler, 1986, p. 54). In the faith development interviews, we discovered that religion is critical to symbolic functioning. Not only does religion provide symbolic content for the structure of faith but, as Lindbeck argues, religion is a cultural/linguistic interpretive scheme from which meaning is derived. It seems to me that this is what Fowler means by 'the structuring power of the *contents* of faith' (Fowler, 1981, p. 276). In the domain of faith, what counts is not only the processes by which meaning is composed but also the cultural and symbolic systems from which persons derive meaning and value. The human quest for meaning takes place within this larger historical-cultural context. In effect,

Fowler breaks down the structuralist epistemological dualism of structure and content.

Structure and teleology

Borrowed from Gestalt psychology, *structure* refers to a covert system of operations that is inferred from the observation of patterns of behavior. The hallmark of Piaget's theory of cognitive development is the proposition that knowledge is constructed by the interaction of innate cognitive structures and assimilable data from the environment. Assimilation and accommodation are two complementary cognitive activities. Assimilation refers to the process by which data are incorporated by cognitive structures; accommodation is the process by which internal structures are transformed by the assimilation of data.

According to Piaget, a stage of development is a configuration of cognitive structures that are in equilibrium at a given age level. The biological development of new cognitive structures results in equilibration or rebalancing at a higher stage. Cognitive operations that are logically related to each other result in knowledge of the physical world − for example, the development of concepts of time, number, volume, etc. In sum, structure is a metaphor for the logical relationship that exists between the elements of cognition.

In explicating the forms of logic in faith development theory, it is evident that developmental transformation is determined not only by the historical progression of stages but also by the end-point toward which development progresses. The preeminence of the final stage is deeply rooted in the theological foundations of faith development theory. Fowler maintains that the progression of stages is governed by a specific *telos*, namely, a normative covenantal community of persons-in-relation to each other and to a transcendent One. How this telic vision shapes the progression of the stages is yet to be determined.

Piaget, in contrast, is less concerned with teleology. Wartofsky (1971) suggests that Piaget's theory is 'teleonomic' rather than teleological since there is no conscious goal that is being sought by the developing organism. Given the preeminence of teleology in faith development theory, we can understand why Fowler's stages extend beyond Piaget's final stage of formal operational logic. Up to the development of this stage, parallelism exists between Fowler's and Piaget's stages. The stage of sensorimotor operations correlates with 'primal faith;' preoperational or intuitive logic with stage 1, 'undifferentiated faith;' concrete operations with stage 2, 'mythic-literal faith;' and formal operations with stage 3, 'synthetic-conventional faith.' Fowler divides formal operations into *partial* operations at stage 3 and *full* operations at stage 4, 'individuative-reflective faith'. He argues that this differentiation is based on the difference between *inductive* and *deductive* logic. And so, in the *Manual*, we declare (Moseley, Jarvis and Fowler, 1986, p. 108):

> the person at stage 3 can recognize inferences and systems, but generally, he or she will not be able to produce such systems spontaneously. This makes stage 3 the stage of inductive rather than deductive operations. The person at stage 3 is able to reason from particular facts and events to more general laws and rules, but he or she cannot yet produce the laws and rules by purely abstract processes. To use Piaget's language, the formal operations do not yet function as 'anticipatory schemata' at stage 3, particularly in the years of early adolescence.

In making this claim we were influenced by the inclination of persons at stage 3 to organize the world around issues of interpersonal harmony rather than rigorous conceptual abstractions. This apparent inability to plumb the depths of theories and systems led to the conclusion that formal operations were not fully formed at this stage. In contrast, 'the person at stage 4 can construct systems and analyze multidimensional problems.... At stage 4 the self is more closely identified with systems of ideas and systematic thought processes' (Moseley, Jarvis and Fowler, 1986, p. 136).

In summary, we arbitrarily selected certain functions of formal operations to make our case for a post-formal operations form of logic.

Dialectic and paradox

Having broken down formal operations into two discrete stages, Fowler proposes yet a fifth stage of logic, namely, 'dialectical thinking' as a qualitative advance beyond Piaget's last stage of formal operations. At stage 5, 'conjunctive faith,' ideational systems are brought into dialogue with each other. In the early formulations of faith development theory, stage 5 was termed 'dialectical-paradoxical faith.' This description aptly captured Riegel's (1976) notion of dialectical thought as the basis of dialogue. The dynamics of this stage revolve around the assimilation and accommodation of conflicting truth claims. This stage describes the emergence of genuine interreligious dialogue, hence has important implications for the public, pluralistic and ecumenical character of the Church.

In defining human development in terms of dialectical psychology, Riegel was not merely proposing a form of logic beyond Piaget's stage of formal operations. Rather, he was criticizing Piaget for limiting the notion of dialectic to the complementary processes of assimilation and accommodation. From Riegel's point of view, dialectic points to the ongoing relationship between the changing self and the changing world. A key proposition is that persons are producers of their own world, always generating new possibilities for the transformation of the world. Hence, Riegel was not interested in identifying stages but in showing the limitations of Piagetian logic in charting transformations which extend throughout the life-span. Fowler's use of dialectical thinking as a distinct stage beyond formal operations differs considerably from Riegel's understanding of dialectical thinking. At stage 5, dialectical thinking is linked to a dialogical form of multiple perspective-taking. According to Moseley, Jarvis and Fowler (1986, p. 156):

> Stage 5 logic is characterized by an openness to reality and to different perspectives on it. It looks to the interplay or dialogue between perspectives or approaches to generate insight into a problem or question.... It may be said that stage 5 logic has noticed the limitations of explanation in the formal sense and has ceased to be as concerned with achieving closure around a limited or chosen set of concepts or ideas. It should also be noted that logic at stage 5 orients toward processes rather than toward systems.

The distinction between 'processes' and 'systems' parallels the differentiation of structure and content. Stage 5 does not promulgate any one truth claim. Rather, it exemplifies the ongoing process of discerning meaning and truth from multiple perspectives. Here, Fowler is closer to Riegel's life-span approach to human development. Nevertheless, he misses the most important point of Riegel's approach to human development — there is no final stage, indeed stages do not exist.

The heart of the problem is Fowler's understanding of dialectic and paradox, both of which have to do with conflict. Faith development theory recognizes that persons exist in a world of conflicting systems of beliefs and values and multiple points of reference for meaning-making. Dialectical thinking describes a level of complementarity (assimilation and accommodation) that is required for holding together conflicting systems of beliefs and values. But this is the extent of Fowler's use of Riegel. Riegel's realism which centers on the changing self-world relationship is overshadowed by a stronger Hegelian idealism. This is seen in the general description of 'conjunctive faith' as a conjunction of opposites (*conjunctio oppositorum*) that are sublated into a higher synthesis or overarching 'whole' at stage 6, 'universalizing faith.' Fowler refers to this stage as a 'centering located in the Ultimate' (Fowler, 1986, p. 31). In the *Manual* (Moseley, Jarvis and Fowler, 1986, p. 182), we described the form of logic in this final stage as follows:

> The person at stage 6 is able to use the logical forms of all previous stages, but will not necessarily be limited to any one of them. One might expect statements at stage 6 to display a functional ordering of logical forms; that is, the use of the logic that the individual considers most appropriate to the subject matter involved. Beyond this, however, one would also expect to see the ability to reason

'synthetically.' This form of reasoning would transcend or resolve the paradoxes and dialectical tensions of stage 5, not through suppression of paradox and difference, but by the apprehension of hidden principles of unity which underlie paradoxes.

The 'synthetic' logic of this stage is not empirically derived but reflects a philosophical bias toward a neo-Hegelian understanding of 'hidden principles of unity that underlie paradoxes.' How this unity is embodied in particular persons is perhaps the most problematical aspect of faith development theory. It should be pointed out that the empirical validity of stage 6 is yet to be validated, hence the transition from the 'dialectical logic' of stage 5 to the 'synthetic logic' of stage 6 cannot be interpreted as a structural change in Piaget's sense of the term. It is even more important to note that those named as paradigms of 'universalizing faith' − Martin Luther King, Jr, Mother Teresa and Mahatma Gandhi were not subjected to the clinical interviews and coding procedures by which a stage of faith is determined.

Dialectic and metaphor

My revision of faith development theory rests heavily on Riegel's view of the self-world relationship as a *continuous* process of interaction between a changing self and a changing world that persists throughout the life span. This retrieval of dialectic as the art of dialogue between conflicting arenas of experience heightens the significance of defining faith as a composing of meaning. Dialectical transformations bring into focus the hard contours of life that form the matrix of faith − the arduous task of composing meaning out of chaos, conflict, suffering, and meaninglessness. It seems to me the most that a mere mortal can do is to bring whatever wholeness that comes from the process of relating to a transcendent center or centers of meaning into dialogue with other arenas of experience that are always changing and evoking transformations of the self and world.

The problem in raising dialectic to prominence as a root metaphor of transformation is that dialectical psychology does not entertain a closed system of stages. We therefore need to recast what is meant by a stage of faith, if this is at all an appropriate description of transformations in the self-transcendent relationship. I, for one, would gladly dispense with the concept of a stage of faith since it is heavily laden with elitist images of faithful human beings. At the same time, I find that there is merit in describing the configuration of cognitive and affective dynamics that are observable in the self-transcendent relationship. To say that a stage of faith is a 'logically' ordered configuration of psychological processes tells us little about the self that is being formed and transformed at a particular time in the life span.

Fowler's argument for a 'metaphorical' understanding of the term logic indicates that a stage of faith is more comprehensive than its cognitive-developmental operations. But this is a strange use of metaphor. There is a need for a systematic linguistic analysis of the distinction between the terms logic and metaphor in faith development theory, especially since these terms reflect the two different languages of psychology and religion. In asking us to adopt a metaphorical understanding of logic, Fowler indirectly illumines a basic paradox in faith development theory. Simply put, a stage is and is not what is observed (Streib-Weickum, 1989, p. 165). Preserving this metaphorical tension is essential if we are to avoid reducing the domain of faith to the rigid requirements of empirical psychology. Recognizing this, Fowler offers yet another definition of faith as an activity of the imagination. I suggest that the imaginative activity of faith has to do with its religious functioning. On this point, Garrett Green is helpful. To paraphrase Green (1989, p. 54), a stage of faith is at most a normative model or exemplar of what the relationship to the transcendent 'is *like*'. A major characteristic of metaphors is that they function analogically. We could also say that a stage functions both as a scientific and a religious paradigm. Scientifically, it is a logical configuration of meaning-making activities. Religiously, it exemplifies the self-transcendent relationship. I am adopting Green's definition of a paradigm. A paradigm is 'an exemplar or ideal type – because it shows forth a pattern, a coherent nexus of relations, in a simple and straightforward manner. Paradigms function heuristically by revealing the constitutive patterns in more complex aspects of our experience that might otherwise remain recalcitrant, incoherent, or bewildering' (1989, p. 53). Faith is one such phenomenon.

A metaphorical reading of stages allows us to preserve the tension between scientific and religious paradigms in faith development theory. If we accept the proposition that the primary value of faith development theory is heuristic, then we would be less inclined to see faith development theory as a theory of personality development. In the final analysis, faith development theory makes intelligible a mysterious activity of the imagination, namely the relation to the transcendent, for which there is no corresponding literal equivalent. Hence, each stage, including the final stage, embodies a 'not-yet' quality, an eschatological proviso that human becoming remains unfinished. While dialectical psychology does not embrace the self-transcendent relationship as a core experience of the self or maintain an explicit eschatological posture, it is oriented toward transformations of the self that are yet to occur. In a sense, dialectical psychology emulates an essential paradox of struggle and surrender that is camouflaged by the structural-developmental emphasis on hierarchically ordered stages. The absence of stages points to impermanence of any form of attainment. Whatever is, is not yet. Altogether, the tentativeness and paradox of dialectical psychology and metaphorical theology (McFague, 1982) offset the potential misuse of faith development theory as a theory of personality development and as a tool for expediting religious triumphalists on their journey of becoming perfecters of faith.

Conclusion

In conclusion, a metaphorical interpretation of forms of logic in faith development theory requires that we revise the theory to reflect the imagistic, symbolic, and affective dimensions of human development and the tentativeness of experience, including the experience of transcendence. In this effort, both dialectical psychology and metaphorical theology are helpful. Both take seriously the problem of paradox without seeking its resolution in a *coincidentia oppositorum*. Their rejection of Hegelian idealist logic and historicism is a refreshing challenge to the quest for an overarching Whole into which paradox is eventually sublated. Most importantly, dialectical psychology and metaphorical theology are conversation partners who liberate faith from its entombment in structural-developmental logic. Together, they provide hermeneutical lenses for viewing the paradox of struggle and surrender in the self-transcendent relationship. Ultimately, the very effort to make or compose meaning reaches its fullest expression in the renunciation of effort. To define such striving for meaning as faith development makes sense only if we understand the paradox of struggle and surrender: in other words, when we understand faith as a paradox of grace.

Notes
1. An earlier version of this paper was read at the Annual Meeting of the Society for the Scientific Study of Religion and the Religious Research Association in Salt Lake City, Utah, October 29, 1989. I am indebted to Professor L.B. Brown from the University of New South Wales, Australia for his helpful comments on an earlier draft of this paper.

References
Fowler, James W. (1981) *Stages of Faith*, San Francisco, Harper and Row.
Fowler, James W. (1986) 'Faith and the structuring of meaning', in C. Dykstra and S. Parks (eds), *Faith Development and Fowler*, Birmingham, Alabama, Religious Education Press.
Grant, David (1984) *God: the center of value*, Fort Worth, Texas Christian University.
Green, Garrett (1989) *Imagining God*, New York, Harper and Row.
Kohlberg, Lawrence and Power, F. Clark (1981) 'Moral development, religious thinking and the question of a seventh stage,' in L. Kohlberg, *Essays in Moral Development*, vol. II, San Francisco, Harper and Row, pp. 212–319.
Lindbeck, George (1984) *The Nature of Doctrine: religion and theology in a postliberal age*, Philadelphia, Westminster Press.
McFague, Sallie (1982) *Metaphorical Theology: Models of God in religious language*, Philadelphia, Fortress.
Moseley, Romney M., Jarvis, D. and Fowler, J. W. (1986) *Manual for Faith Development Research*, Atlanta, Center for Research in Faith and Moral Development, Candler School of Theology, Emory University, Atlanta.
Niebuhr, H. Richard (1960) *Radical Monotheism and Western Culture*, New York, Harper and Row.

Piaget, Jean (1921) 'L'orientation de la philosophie religieuse en Suisse romande,' *La Semaine Litteraire*, p. 412. Cited by Fernando Vidal, 'Jean Piaget and the liberal Protestant tradition', in M. G. Ash and W. R. Woodward (1987) *Psychology in Twentieth Century Thought and Society*, New York, Cambridge University Press, p. 284.

Piaget, Jean (1923) 'La psychologie et les valuers religieuses,' *Sainte Croix* 1922, Lausanne, La Concorde.

Piaget, Jean (1926) *La Representation du Monde chez l'Enfant*, Paris, Alcan.

Power, F. Clark and Kohlberg, Lawrence (1980) 'Religion, morality and ego development,' in J. W. Fowler and A. Vergote (eds), *Toward Moral and Religious Maturity*, Morristown, New Jersey, Silver Burdett'.

Power, F. Clark (1987) 'Hard versus soft stages of faith and religious development. A Piagetian critique,' paper delivered at the International Symposium on Religious Development and Religious Education, Blauberen, University of Tubingen, June 12–17.

Riegel, Klaus (1976) *Dialectical Psychology*, New York, Academic Press.

Smith, Wilfred Cantwell (1963) *The Meaning and End of Religion*, New York, Macmillan. Smith's interpretation of religion fits Lindbeck's 'experiential-expressive' approach to religion by which the external features of religion are derived from inner experience.

Streib-Weickum, Heinz (1989) *Hermeneutics of metaphor, symbol and narrative in faith development theory*, unpublished Ph.D. dissertation, Emory University, Atlanta.

Wartofsky, Marx (1971) 'From praxis to logos,' in T. Mischel (ed.), *Cognitive Development and Epistemology*, New York, Academic Press, pp. 129–147.

5. Interview data and faith development

The next two sections take us firmly into the empirical realm where psychologists of religion have critiqued and extended faith development theory in the light of data from their own researches. As Fowler's work is so dependent on data from extended semi-clinical interviews it is not surprising that much of the critical literature that has an empirical flavour is derived from the use of a similar interview method.

Eugene Mischey's paper, together with the comments by Jerome W. Berryman, Richard E. Davies and Henry C. Simmons, was first published as early as 1981 in *Character Potential: a record of research*, vol. 9, pp. 175–191. As the title 'Faith, identity and morality in late adolescence' suggests, the study seeks to clarify the forms of faith expression shown by late adolescents, and the ways in which these interact with morality and identity constructs. Interviews with thirty-two subjects were scored for faith stage. Additionally an assessment was made of their responses to specific questions about 'existential challenges' such as illness, puberty and responsibility, and to three Kohlbergian moral dilemmas. The results showed that these late adolescents fell into four distinct groups. Mischey draws a number of interesting conclusions from this analysis, in particular that 'identity achievement is the back-bone of, or key to, higher forms of both faith development and moral development'.

Sharon Parks's paper 'Young adult faith development: teaching in the context of theological education', first published in *Religious Education*, vol. 77, no. 6, 1982, pp. 657–672, focuses on young adults. On the basis of her own study sample of college students and the research work of others, Parks hypothesizes an identifiable developmental stage between Fowler's faith stages

3 and 4 (or 'within' stage 4).[1] This stage of (somewhat fragile) 'young adult faith' is compared with Kenneth Keniston's recognition of a developmental stage between 'adolescence' and 'adulthood'. In a more practical section to the paper the implications for teaching such adults in the context of theological education is then explored.

Randall Furushima's paper on 'Faith development in a cross-cultural perspective', first published in *Religious Education*, vol. 80, no. 3, 1985, pp. 414–420, provides a rare example of an attempt to replicate Fowler's work in a very different cultural milieu. Twelve adult Buddhists from Hawaii (mainly of Japanese descent) were interviewed using Fowler's research instrument. After some wide-ranging comments based on this data, Furushima concludes that the 'claim of universality for faith development theory can be partially substantiated' by this study.

Susan Kwilecki's study in the journal *Religion*, Vol. 18, 1988, pp. 231–253, is entitled 'Personal religious belief development: the "articulate authoritarian" type'. The interview studies reported here[2] have convinced her that Fowler's scheme fails 'to portray the variety and cultural relativity of individual religious striving'. Preferring a broader notion of religious development (as 'the unfolding in a life of ... an awareness of a sacred dimension'), Kwilecki argues that developmental patterns in this area may be discerned in particular religious outcomes in particular cultures. Her account of one such phenomenon – the 'articulate authoritarian' style of fundamentalist religious belief and its development – is presented with rich illustrative detail. This account challenges the assumption (which she claims to be made by Fowler and others) that dogmatic conviction is always developmentally immature. Certainly 'religious absolutism did not block intellectual activity' in many of her interviewees. Kwilecki argues that the type is found in many cultures, and includes Newman among the exemplars of it.[3]

Notes
1. See her book *The Critical Years: the young adult search for a faith to live by*, San Francisco, Harper and Row, 1986.
2. See also her 'A scientific approach to religious development: proposals and a

case illustration', *Journal for the Scientific Study of Religion*, vol. 27, no. 3, 1988, pp. 307–325.

3. Other interview studies include John Snarey's 'Faith development, moral development, and nontheistic Judaism: a construct validity study', in William M. Kurtines and Jacob L. Gerwitz (eds), *Handbook of Moral Behavior and Development*, Hillsdale, N.J., Lawrence Erlbaum, 1991, pp. 279–305.

5.1 Faith, identity, and morality in late adolescence

Eugene J. Mischey

A fundamental, common preoccupation of late adolescence is the quest for and expression of a viable, psychosocial identity capable of rendering a life-perspective that provides a meaningful existence. This search has been made more difficult by the complexity of a society which is characterized by pluralism, secularization, and the relativization of values.

The sheer complexity of contemporary society makes a developmental analysis of late adolescence very laborious. It has been especially difficult to carry out a *global*, developmental analysis of this age-group in an empirical fashion. With the exception of researchers such as Marcia, studies describing late adolescence often address themselves to a series of inter-connected specifics along a single continuum (e.g., cognition, morality or religiosity).[1] Such studies usually provide a detailed description of a specific variable in outright succession, although what is really occurring manifests a different logic, a logic of constant interaction among many variables.

However, many educators and psychologists, in describing late adolescence, have tended to stress only one aspect of reality, often to the detriment of all others. Studies in adolescent cognition after Jean Piaget, or on role-taking ability in adolescence after Robert Selman, or on adolescent morality after Lawrence Kohlberg, are examples of focusing developmentally and with great precision upon a single aspect at the expense of a more global description of adolescence.

While such ground-breaking efforts are a necessary prerequisite for any categorical examination, the dynamic interplay of those several aspects is often virtually smothered. This is ironical, when one considers that this period of ideological development can, at the very least, be described as interactive. In focusing upon young adults and their progression from adolescence, one frequently is left with only fragmented perspectives on how and why this group of selves comes to be. Such fragmentation has been additionally augmented by studies that do *not* focus upon either individual lives or life-histories.

The recent research on faith development tends to involve a more global description of human development. Dr James W. Fowler of the Candler School of Theology at Emory University in Atlanta,

Georgia, has established and refined a structural developmental theory of faith which focuses empirically on the whole 'gestalt of being.' Fowler views faith as 'a mode of being in relation to the ultimate environment' and, so, postulates six stages or developmental levels of 'faithing,' through which every individual gives form and coherence to life by coming to understand and relate to a sense of individuality, others, the surrounding world, and a form of Transcendence.[2]

One of the most important attributes of this theory is that Fowler describes a universal phenomenon that reflects an individual's *integrated* system of operations, in which many types of competencies are employed: e.g., moral reasoning, role-taking ability, symbolic formation, bounds of social awareness, locus of authority, form of world coherence and form of logic.[3] These integrated systems are what Fowler calls 'windows' into the structures underlying faith; they allow the researcher to bring an individual's total character and life-history into sharper relief. Because it encompasses so much, faith development theory logically lends itself to a more global view of any area of concentration.

In an attempt to shed more light on how late adolescents search for and come to express a meaningful life-perspective, research into their faith development was begun several years ago. Beside the more global perspective offered by faith development theory, it was felt that an in-depth analysis of identity formation and moral reasoning would aid in producing a three-dimensional picture of late adolescents.

In addition, several theoretical questions about the developmental relationship amongst these variables were also addressed. For instance, are there exact parallels between moral stages and faith stages, or does one precede the development of the other? Furthermore, is identity achievement a prerequisite for or a simultaneous occurrence with certain stages of faith and moral development? While the general relationship amongst faith, morality and identity has been confronted by Fowler, from a theoretical perspective, and by Mischey, from a young-adult standpoint, it seemed that a comparison of these constructs across a shorter age-span and during an even more malleable time-period (e.g., one where initial ideological formation and ontological expression occurs) would allow one to learn more about how they do interact.[4,5] Moreover, knowledge of that interaction might explain why growth in these developmental areas occurs for some individuals, but not for others.

The initial concern was, therefore, to understand the concept of faith in its delineation in the life of late adolescents. A secondary concern was to attempt to probe into the relationship between faith, identity and morality. A tertiary concern was to identify any factors which seem to either stimulate or impede development. Thus, this study addressed three specific questions.

a. What form of faith expression do late adolescents generally exhibit?
b. How do the developmental constructs of faith, morality and identity interact during late adolescence?
c. What factors, if any, play an important role in stimulating faith development during late adolescence?

Method for this study

Subjects

Thirty-two late adolescents were interviewed. There were eighteen males and fourteen females, and they ranged in age from eighteen to twenty-two years. All belonged to one of two major groups in the London, Ontario, area: late adolescents working towards college degrees at the University of Western Ontario, and late adolescents engaged in various occupations. Of the twenty late adolescents who were students, fifteen were Catholics, two were Protestants, and three were non-believers. Of the twelve late adolescents who were working, six were Protestants, two were Jews, and four were non-believers. Both groups reflected a fair degree of ethnic and social-class diversity.

Procedure

Each subject was interviewed according to Fowler's open-ended, semi-clinical format. Each faith-status interview was loosely structured around fifteen, straightforward questions incorporating such faith-issues as death, meaning of life, loyalties and commitments, evil, symbols, guilt and shame. These fifteen questions attempted to bring into focus the individual's presently held world-view, as well as their developmental evolution to a now-held perspective: e.g., the probes were directed at the structure of thought, not at the content. Moreover, depending on whether or not the respondent answered in religious or non-religious terms, subsequent queries were modified to suit the individual's preferred terminology. All espoused beliefs and principles were checked against examples of actual patterns of behaviour and action, as offered by the respondent.

Each interview was taped and scored for a Fowler faith stage by the author and one other scorer. The scoring was done directly from the tapes, according to a modified auditory-scoring system devised by the author in an earlier study of young adults.[6] The system used in this study was composed of thirty-two indices representative of the major, qualitative progressions in Fowler's seven general variables. Each tape was scored once for stage description and twice by variable progression. Each subject had a graphic chart exemplifying his stage and variable score, as well as a list of general comments which aided

Table 1: Examples of stage 3 and stage 4 combinations in the Mischey study of late adolescents

Stage description	Notation used	Value assigned
pure stage 3	3	3.00
major stage 3 [minor stage 4]	3(4)	3.25
pure transition	3 – 4	3.50
major stage 4 [minor stage 3]	(3) – 4	3.75
pure stage 4	4	4.00

in composing the individual's personality. Inter-judge agreement on the author's auditory-scoring system was beyond 83%

The scoring analysis for transitional and mixed stages of faith was reflective of the network presented in Table 1.

Consideration was also given to one other important aspect in the maturation of faith, the prototypical challenges, which are described by Fowler as 'existential challenges with which faith must deal.'[7] Based on the role that this factor played in structuring the faith of both young adults and adolescents, it was decided to seek a further clarification of its inter-relatedness to structural-developmental gains.[8,9] Therefore, each subject was asked to report and to reflect upon such issues as sickness, accidents, death, puberty and responsibility. There was a strong feeling that these conflicts were incentives for the structuring of more encompassing and meaningful life-perspectives. The average length of a faith interview was two hours.

At the end of each interview, individuals were asked to fill out a moral dilemmas questionnaire. The three moral dilemmas of Kohlberg's form A were used. Assessment of moral judgment was based on Kohlberg's aspect-scoring system, with stage mixtures following a format similar to the one used for scoring faith stages (i.e., they were handled by intuitively weighting a dominant and minor stage of response). The limits of aspect-scoring, as outlined by Kohlberg, were taken into consideration.[10] Where possible, the standardized issue-scoring manual devised by Kohlberg and his colleagues was used as a check, but significant discrepancies were not encountered.[11] Inter-judge agreement with one other scorer was above 85%.

The basic probes for the information necessary to determine a subject's identity status, according to Marcia, were included in the faith-status interview.[12] Occupational goals and ideological beliefs (i.e., religion and politics) were categorized on two criteria: crisis and commitment. Each individual was given an identity rating indicative of identity achievement, or diffusion, or foreclosure, or moratorium on each of these three areas. These ratings were then averaged to

Table 2: Summary of faith scores, moral reasoning scores, and identity status by faith stage delineation. *

Faith group:	Mean for Faith stage scores:	Number in the group:	Mean age in years for the group:	Mean for the moral reasoning scores:	Identity status for the groups:
I	2.75	03	18.3	2.91	diffused
II	3.00	17	19.7	2.94	foreclosure [diffused][a]
III	3.50	04	20.5	3.50	Mixed
IV	3.75	08	20.7	3.66	identity achieved [moratorium][b]

WHERE: * = Subjects scoring a Major 3 and a Minor 4 in faith were not found in the sample used for this study.

   [a] = Five subjects in this group were scored as Diffused.

   [b] = Four subjects in this group were scored as Moratorium.

compute an overall identity status. However, an overall rating was given when at least two of the three areas exemplified similar forms of expression (e.g., foreclosure in politics and religion — the subject was rated as 'foreclosure'). An individual who tended to score differently in all three areas was placed into an overall 'mixed' category. Total agreement between the author and one other scorer was used as the criterion for all such assignments.

Results from this study

Based on a delineation of faith stages, table 2 indicates that the faith statuses of these late adolescents tend to fall into four groupings.

Globally speaking, table 2 indicates that the mean score for faith development for late adolescence is predominantly a stage 3 (i.e., the synthetic-conventional faith stage), with a slight emergence of stage 4 (i.e., the individuative-reflexive faith stage). The mean faith score for the entire sample was 3.23, which means that the way these individuals certify meaning in their lives rests on the sanction of properly designated people, or by the authority of consensus among those people who 'really count.' There is a conventional understanding of what life is all about. The presence of eight individuals exhibiting at least 50% of individuating faith (i.e., (3)−4) shows that late adolescence is also a time when life-perspective begins to be tempered by the realization that life must encompass the hardship of taking on responsibility for one's own beliefs, disposition, and life-style. Apparently, a beyond-conforming understanding of life begins to emerge as one *attempts* to synthesize many, divergent perspectives into some form of personal unity.

The form of moral reasoning for this sample was also conventionally bound. The mean moral reasoning score for the entire sample
was 3.19. In terms of reasons for doing 'what is right,' there was
a general desire to maintain those rules and that authority which
supported stereotypical, good behaviour. In many cases, subjects
also stressed the need to uphold the social system, as well as a desire
to meet any defined obligations, as dictated by one's conscience (i.e.,
Kohlberg's stage 4).

There was an extremely high correlation between the faith scores
and the moral reasoning scores of these late adolescents, as scored by
the author (i.e., $r = 0.81$). A test of significance for this correlation
coefficient was highly significant (i.e., $t = 7.60$; $df = 30$; p is less
than .001). The two measures were extremely dependent.

The t-test was also used to test whether this sample scored similarly
on faith and morality. As a result, the null hypothesis was retained,
since the t-value indicated no significant difference between mean
scores (i.e., $t = 1.33$; $df = 31$; p is not significant). Thus, it
can be assumed that late adolescents are developmentally oriented
towards conventional authority both in faith and in morality.
Differences between males and females, late adolescent students
and late adolescent workers were non-significant.

In terms of identity status, significant results were obtained. A
developmental trend from low identity status (i.e., diffusion and
foreclosure − basically, faith-groups I and II) to high identity status
(i.e., identity achievement and moratorium − basically, faith groups
III and IV) can be seen in table 2. Moreover, there was a strong
statistical difference on how high identity and low identity late
adolescents scored on faith and morality. A significant difference
at better than the .001 level of confidence was found (i.e., $t =
12.10$, and $df = 30$), when the mean faith-score of high identity
subjects (i.e., 3.70) was compared to the mean faith-score of low
identity subjects (i.e., 3.01). Similarly, a significant difference at
better than the .001 level of confidence was found (i.e., $t = 8.12$,
and $df = 30$), when the mean moral reasoning scores of high and low
identity status subjects were compared (i.e., 'high' subjects' mean $=
3.68$, and 'low' subjects' mean $= 2.97$). Generally speaking, it seems
that late adolescents who have formed, or who are on the verge of
structuring, an identity tend *towards* exhibiting a post-conventional
or individuating faith. These same individuals also express a higher
form of conventional moral reasoning, although not a single person
reflected Kohlberg's principled level of thinking.

Two additional results must also be noted. First, there was
a strong degree of correlation between faith and prototypical
challenges (i.e., $r_{pb} = 0.55$), as well as between morality and
prototypical challenges (i.e., $r_{pb} = 0.64$). Tests of significance for
these correlations indicated the existence of significant association:
(i) for faith and prototypical challenge, $t = 3.60$; $df = 30$; p is less

than .01, and (ii) for morality and prototypical challenge, t = 4.56; df = 30; p is less than .001. The implication seems to be that subjects with higher expressions of faith and moral development discussed and reflected upon past and present experiences of conflict and tension, whereas their counterparts rarely did. This result was not surprising, in light of the greater degree of personal investment and active involvement that characterized high identity status individuals (i.e., 100% of faith-group IV and 50% of faith-group III).

Second, a most surprising result occurred when the scores of subjects expressing a religious faith orientation were compared with the scores of non-believers. A significant difference at approximately the .02 level of confidence was found (t = 2.45; df = 30). The faith-scores of believers with a mean of 3.30 were significantly higher than the faith-scores of non-believers with a mean of 2.96. This was unusual, since faith development theory posits structural factors and not content factors (such as religious orientation) as responsible for progression. While these results may be mere coincidence (e.g., the non-believers in this sample were simply lower in their faith-orientation), the possibility of a 'content interaction' must not be quickly discarded.

Qualitative analysis and discussion of this study

A purely quantitative analysis of how late adolescents structure a meaningful world-view does not do justice to the intricacies and complexities that characterize each of these personalities as they interact with their historical and temporal situations. The idiosyncratic, human qualities that come to be expressed during faith-status interview deserve a qualitative analysis, based on description and indexed by intuitive insight. While statistical analysis may connotate precision of conclusions, the down-play of non-significant results or the over-emphasis of significant results may skew the reality. This possible lack of qualitative precision, however, can be down-played when clearly qualitative instruments are used in an attempt to measure equally clearly qualitative aspects of reality.

Fowler's use of seven general variables in his description of 'faithing' gives the researcher of ontological issues the confidence of qualitative control. Moreover, his description of variable progression across stages allows one to tease out subtle differences that may symbolize a given stage for a particular individual, group or community. This feature of Fowler's faith development theory has provided this author with a more encompassing view of development by allowing him to identify four distinct faith-groups within a relatively short period of time. Although the following section offers only a brief glimpse of the 'faithing' of late adolescence, at least three dominant motifs seem evident, each of which has educational and social implications. Since this finding reflects the subjective impressions of the author and one scorer, it is hoped that further research will underscore the following contentions.

Four faith groups in late adolescence

Faith-group I was marked by a sense of confusion, passive commitment, a negative-like identity, and an uncritical life-perspective. While expressing a trust in the administration of church, government and education, faith-group I individuals found it difficult to explain why. Involvements in the various theaters of life were minimal, and any meaningful synthesis of these external realities were sporadic and passive. Written and oral responses to questions like, 'What is right?' took on Kohlberg's good-boy orientation, although deeper probes could not elicit any logical elaboration as to why certain acts were morally correct. All the individuals in faith-group I lacked any formal exposure to traditional religions (e.g., discussions pertaining to religion or any other form of ideology were absent in their homes). The subjects had a difficult time describing 'who they were' and, consequently, frequently responded in terms of who they were *not*. Their faith-perspectives were, in essence, an extension of their parents', although there was a smorgasbord flavour underlying their views: e.g., they occasionally spoke of and related to a 'mixed bag' of ideological systems. They described their lives as basically uneventful, and probes to uncover any occurrence of conflict or tension in such forms as accidents, death and responsibility were left unanswered. (Statistical analysis confirmed this assertion.)

Generally speaking, analysis of faith-group I shows that, while transition from faith stage 2 to faith stage 3 may appear as early as eleven or twelve years of age, there are adolescents as old as nineteen who have not yet structured a coherent organization of experiences beyond their primary social groups. Attitudes towards life are still semi-consciously observed, adopted and imitated. With the fear of such diffusion towards self and life becoming increasingly evident in some social realms, it behooves educators and psychologists to re-examine the importance of social role definitions as guide-lines for growing youth.[13] Two thematic questions pervaded the responses of the individuals in faith-group I: (i) 'What do they [i.e., parents, employers and school] expect of me?' and (ii) 'Why do they [e.g., school] expect me to major in my second year already?' Without a sense of direction or a feeling of self-definition, and lacking a social structure for purposes of self-worth, this faith-group I category may become larger in future research studies.

Faith-group II was marked by conformity, a sense of ease, happiness, and an orderly life-perspective. Expressing a pure synthetic-conventional faith, this largest group discussed their now-held perspectives very systematically and conveyed the impression that life-events, though often seemingly ambiguous, can be understood and validated, if one correctly chose the 'proper pinnacle of competency' for guidance. Experiences with one's environment were qualitatively more encompassing than those of faith-group I, although there remained a very rigid loyalty to one's chosen religion or ideology in that environment. Perspectives on truth, righteousness and meaningfulness were based on authoritarian statements of philosophy, church or government. 'Authority through consensus and conformity to authority' was the underlying rule to which these life-perspectives adhered, and their moral reasoning scores supported such conformity.

Deeper probes into the commitments of faith-group II revealed an unquestionable acceptance of their own views and a relatively unconcerned tolerance of opposing viewpoints. It became evident that these subjects unemotionally compartmentalized (or 'shelved') dissonant views; even more importantly, they exhibited a lack of personal, active involvement in sifting out pluralistic viewpoints and solidifying their own world-views. It became apparent that these personal ideologies and philosophies were imprints or carbon copies of the faith perspectives of their parents, or other significant authority figures (e.g., any responsibility for their views rested in a passive acceptance and an equally passive organization).

As was true of faith-group I, evidence of conflict, sorrow and tension were relatively nonexistent. The entire group was very comfortable in discussing all issues that were raised during the faith status interviews. The challenge of synthesizing world differences was seemingly circumvented on purpose.

This second faith-group qualifies any educational implications stemming from the first one. If we ought to re-examine social role guidelines, for instance, how are educators to help? And how do we foster life-styles that are self-finding and reflective *beyond* moral conformity and faith conventionality? Gorman has suggested that we consciously expose students 'to different viewpoints and through discussion and reflection encourage them to appreciate the rights, needs, hopes and desires of those with backgrounds different from theirs.'[14] The extremely complacent attitude of faith-group II, as well as the uncritical disposition of faith-group I, suggests that both the quality and the degree of encouragement may be important, if compartmentalization is not to continue. It seems that a curriculum should not only 'stimulate' cognitive conflict by introducing culturally meaningful challenges but, also, qualify those challenges. Mildly yet meaningfully frustrated adolescents may want to work with perseverance towards a solution to challenges that motivate genuine, active participation in different communities. Erikson has addressed this use of frustration for some time, noting that adolescents would profit educationally if they were gently but firmly led to discover that learning to search out can achieve results and accomplish things that otherwise would never have been attained by one's thoughts or through the imitation of others.[15] In much the same way, Fowler has noted that active involvement is a prerequisite for an individuating faith. It seems that resolutions must be accompanied with considerable effort, and that active participation is a requirement of ideological formation.

Both faith-group III and faith-group IV were curious and explorative, responsible, actively searching for or expressing a stable sense of self-hood, and critical in their life-perspectives.[16] In terms of their faith development, both groups were beginning to express an individuating faith. While there was still a felt affinity to chosen, external authorities, the criteria for their acceptance was beginning to be based on matters of personal, indepth experience (e.g., there was a conscious effort to pull together theory and practice into some intelligible, meaningful unity). Various attitudes and beliefs were being explored and tempered by a critical self-awareness. Compared to faith-group II, the views of these twelve subjects seemed less rigid. In fact, flexibility tended to dominate the beginnings of a lasting world-view. The seemingly irrational urge to conform, manifested by faith-groups I and II, was beginning to disappear, and a significant degree of autonomy was starting to appear. Interpersonal interaction was more global and effective and, while values and ideologies of parents or significant authorities were occasionally echoed, deeper probes revealed the fact that the resemblance was a function of active choice. Their structure of moral reasoning was beginning to be tinged with the imperative of conscience and, with the exception of one individual, all faiths were religiously based.

One of the most decisive things that differentiated faith-groups III and IV from faith-groups I and II was the notion of prototypical challenges. As suspected, the experience and subsequent in-depth reflection upon such events as the death of a friend or relative, family poverty, immigration, serious ailments, failure and defeat, and major responbilities early in life, pervaded the life-histories of these individuals. While some mention of similar conflicts was made by members of faith-groups I and II, the frequency and the quality differed greatly. Moreover, the impression that these challenges left upon the lives of the members of faith-groups I and II was less striking. There was no doubt that the members of faith-groups III and IV not only experienced greater conflicts but, also, internalized with greater earnestness the meaningfulness of life's challenges. At the very least, such occurrences tended to become an incentive for reflection and reorganization: as one subject put it, 'It started me thinking about what life was all about.' (Statistical analysis significantly confirmed the inclusion of such challenges in their life-histories.)

Discussion of the qualitative analysis

If challenges in life are truly incentives towards higher forms of faith expression (or for expressions beyond strict conformity) during late adolescence, then a qualifier for Erikson's educational frustration hypothesis seems in order. While only educational research can confirm the importance of this variable, it seems safe to suggest that the experience of frustrating challenges ought to be vicariously 'lived out,' in terms of a structured curriculum. Although it may be argued that the value of a frustrating challenge comes to fruition only if it is naturally encountered, some form of educational exposure may at least stimulate a serious awareness. Research in faith development strongly confirms that many adults lack such a critical self-awareness.

While some secondary and post-secondary systems have tried to incorporate challenging topics (e.g., through courses such as human development, values education, and interpersonal relations), the question that this study implicitly addresses is a structural one. A mere knowledge or discussion of content areas such as the meaning of life, death, and justice may not be sufficient to structure a post-conventional mode of thinking. If, however, patterns of socialization that complement such topics are instilled through *active* participation, then the meaningfulness of life's challenges may become internalized with greater sobriety. Educationally speaking, the life-perspectives of late adolescents ought to be gently coerced into actively experiencing the critical issues and events of life. As Gorman implies, curriculums should be so structured that 'contagious,' first-hand exposure to poverty, prisons, hospitals, judicial proceedings, different cultures and religious traditions has the opportunity to complement an already growing theoretical ideology.[17] As faith-groups III and IV show, becoming involved with the mentally retarded, the aged, or with the sick as a 'candy-striper,' tends to enable the individual to more completely absorb the emotional impact of such experiences, rather than solely the cognitive aspects, which is important, since learning must occur in the affective domain as well as in the cognitive domain.[18] Such exposure may indeed induce students to incorporate one of Fowler's marks of an individuating faith, which is 'the serious burden of responsibility for one's own commitments, life-style, beliefs and attitudes.'

A second, unanticipated factor that needs to be considered is the contribution that the content of traditional religions may make in structuring a faith-perspective. While past research on faith development has shown conclusively that high forms of faith-expression need not be religiously oriented, the significantly higher scores of believers in this study re-opens the question of the function of religiosity. Although further clarifying research is required, it is possible that traditional religions may serve a preparatory function in the construction of higher forms of faith.

This possibility was initially viewed as paradoxical. It was originally felt that individuals nurtured by religious tradition would remain more conventional in their outlooks, while those who experienced a lack of an established groundwork would more quickly be forced into a critical analysis of life. However, in view of the present results, one might argue that a religious environment may provide a milieu in which individuals are encouraged or, even, forced to grapple with abstract symbolism so that they may clarify their life-perspectives. Such a grappling may lead to a realization of the relativity of many faith-orientations and, hence, to a more encompassing and personal perspective.

Given the presumption that successful challenges are rooted in some form of security, an established religious community may work as a type of fail-safe system. Such a community may give the individual a sense of security, *within which it is safe* to 'try out' different ideologies. This trial and error experimentation may, then, be carried out in an anxiety-controlled fashion with the full awareness that extremely threatening experiences can be withdrawn from, emotionally and cognitively.

Regardless of whether traditional religions foster a sense of security or a perception of challenge, the possibility that they may enhance participation and active commitment towards structural-developmental gains in faith seems to exist for late adolescents. However, one must ask why so many adults are best described as expressing a Fowler stage 3 or a Fowler stage 3–4 religious faith-orientation. Why are faiths that manifest the qualities described by Fowler's stage 5 or stage 6 such a rarity? The answer, it seems, may well be three-fold:

a.   the relativizing nature of genetic endowment and temperament may be a factor;
b.   as the present results strongly indicate, the experience and meaningful internalization of prototypical challenges may be lacking;
c.   traditional religions, as Fowler cautions, may fail to provide 'an openness toward and sponsorship for continuing stage development in general.'[19]

Consideration of the interdependency of faith, identity and morality

In an earlier study of young adults between the ages of twenty and thirty-five, sufficient empirical data was gathered to suggest that a *temporal* relationship exists amongst the concepts of identity formation, faith development and moral reasoning.[20] That study implied that an individual's identity formation may be a prerequisite, or necessary condition, for a 'serious' or autonomous type of faith-orientation. It was reasoned that identity (i.e., the consideration of and commitment to alternative ideologies) must first provide meaning to the self in relation to society *before* a faith-perspective could give coherence to the self and, thereby, provide for a meaning of one's existence in that society. The present study underscores this assertion, both qualitatively and quantitatively.

An identity must be achieved, or at least be in the process of formation (moratorium), before the beginning of independent faithing of a Fowler stage 4 starts to emerge. Of the twelve individuals in faith-groups III and IV who were beginning to express an individuating faith, five were classified as identity achieved, while five were in a state of moratorium. The majority of subjects categorized as either foreclosure or diffuse (i.e., faith-groups I and II) manifested a synthetic-conventional faith.

Higher forms of moral reasoning also seem to accompany the formation of identity. The present study, however, questions the general assertions of James Marcia and several other ego-development researchers.[21] Their contention that individuals high in identity tend to function at principled levels of moral reasoning, while subjects lower in identity tend to function at preconventional and conventional levels, seem partially unjustified. The present study, while indicating that low identity subjects do score conventionally (or lower), does not provide any evidence that high identity subjects reflect principled reasoning. The resolution of this issue may be *temporal* in nature.

For example, it could be hypothesized that identity formation is a necessary-but-not-sufficient condition for post-conventional moral reasoning. That is, a sound identity must be accompanied and nurtured by the appropriate environmental circumstances before traces of principled reasoning begin to appear. To some extent, this idea is in agreement with Kohlberg's constant claim that the development of higher moral structures is independent of, but subtly entails, features of ego development.

It does appear that identity achievement is the back-bone of, or key to, higher forms of both faith development and moral development. In terms of theoretical interplay, identity formation might well be viewed as a major prototypical challenge for faith development, as well as a standardizer for moral development. For educational purposes, the fostering of self-understanding ought to be a major concern of both curriculum development and counselling. Such a focus at the secondary and post-secondary levels should contribute to the curtailing of student discontent with education, student drop-out rates, student isolation and confusion, and an uncertain student morale.[22] At the very least, such a concern would not impede individuals from moving towards more autonomous expressions of faith and morality.

The results of the present study also suggest that the concepts of faith and morality are chronologically related. While the studies by Gorman, Mischey, Power, and by Fowler himself have shown that faith and moral stages roughly parallel each other, there was some evidence to suggest that development in faith precedes development in morality.[23,24,25,26] The present study gives further credibility to this assertion, although the statistical analysis does *not* corroborate this idea.

Qualitatively viewed, those individuals showing evidence of individuating faith, or the growth of autonomous reasoning and affectivity, tended to lag behind in terms of moral reasoning (i.e., they remained conventionally oriented); yet, while they were conforming in terms of the domain of righteousness, they were also beginning to break away towards independence in terms of a meaningful life-perspective. This seeming paradox suggests that faith may provide the milieu in which one comes to structure the cognitive ability to reason at a higher moral stage. It seems that issues of faith 'pull' the way in which one ought to behave or, perhaps, that 'faithing' motivates a person to be moral. Conversely, it seems that an autonomous faith may be a necessary condition for the higher forms of morality.

The educational relevance of this chronological relationship involves the validity of the claim that religious education can be a strong developer of morality. Kohlberg continues to defend, for instance, his concern that public moral education should have a structure and foundation independent of religion. He continues to argue that the substance of religious teachings with its ontological questions (e.g., 'What is the meaning of life?') does not address the concept of morality on logical or rational grounds. In his pursuit of a specifically moral domain in the process of human development, Kohlberg notes that questions of theodicy become 'psychologically serious' only after an individual has attained moral principles. In a quest to stress the unique characteristics of moral structures, he has emphasized that stages of moral development *exclusively precede* the development of ontological thinking. In other words, Kohlberg feels that questions relating to morality and religious ontology are mutually exclusive: ideas about God and life are independent of true moral development.

However, Fowler's faith development theory is, to a significant degree, a theory of ontological development. This study of late adolescents indicates that ontological and epistemological perspectives are an integral part of the 'developing, autonomous, personality.' An individuating faith interweaves these perspectives in a way that demands an attempt to understand the rights and situations of other individuals in the community – to this extent, faith must and does reflect a type of moral standard. *Given the likelihood of faith precedence, it seems logical to assume that an individual initially seeks out answers to questions surrounding their existence as a human being and the general purpose of life before they realize the need for or the desire to be ethically responsible in society. Practically, the claim to separate religious faithing from morality seems unwarranted, since faith may be the motivation for moral reasoning.*

Since many religious educators address ontological questions which are, by definition, Fowler's faith-issues, a suppression of such teaching is unjustified. For many people, such content seems to be a foundation for structural-developmental gains in faith and, thus, a precursor of moral development. To this extent, religious education is moral education. However, whether religious education can lead individuals towards post-conventional perspectives depends on the degree to which it structurally reflects the signposts of faith development theory.

Notes

1. Marcia, James E., 'Identity in adolescence,' unpublished manuscript, Simon Frazer University, 1978.
2. For a detailed presentation of Fowler's theory see: Jim Fowler and Sam Keen (edited by Jerome Berryman), *Life Maps: conversations on the journey of faith*, Waco, Texas, Word Books, 1978.
3. For further details see *Life Maps, op. cit.*,
4. Fowler, James W., 'Faith and the structuring of meaning,' unpublished paper presented to section 39 of the convention of the American Psychological Association, August 26, 1977, in San Francisco, California.
5. Mischey, Eugene J., 'The relationship of faith development to moral reasoning and identity status in young adults,' unpublished paper presented to section 39 of the convention of the American Psychological Association, August 26, 1977, in San Francisco, California.
6. For a more detailed description of this type of scoring system, see: Eugene J. Mischey, 'Faith development and its relationship to moral reasoning and identity status in young adults,' unpublished Ph.D. dissertation, University of Toronto, 1976.
7. Fowler, James W., 'Faith stage profiles by variables,' unpublished manuscript, Harvard Divinity School, 1975.
8. See Mischey, *op. cit.*, 1976.
9. See Margaret Gorman, 'Moral and faith development in 17 year old students,' *Religious Education*, vol. 72, no. 5, 1977, pp. 491–504.
10. See Thomas Lickona (ed.), *Moral Development and Behavior*, New York, Holt, Rinehart, and Winston, 1976, pages 42, 43.
11. See Lawrence Kohlberg, *et. al.*, *Standard Form Scoring Manual – Form A*, Cambridge, Mass., Center for Moral Education, Harvard University, 1979.
12. For a recent outline of the identity status interview, see: James E. Marcia, 'Studies in ego development,' unpublished manuscript, Simon Frazer University, 1976.
13. See James E. Marcia, *op. cit.*, 1978.
14. See Margaret Gorman, *op. cit.*, 1977.
15. See Erik H. Erikson, *Identity, Youth and Crisis*, New York, W. W. Norton, 1968.
16. For purposes of discussion, faith-group III and faith-group IV are linked.

However, it should be noted that the expression of these features was less pronounced in faith-group III.

17. Gary L. Chamberlain articulates a similar viewpoint in terms of community participation and faith development theory. See: Gary L. Chamberlain, 'Faith development and campus ministry,' *Religious Education*, vol. 64, no. 3, 1979, pp. 314–324. For an additional discussion of the role of action and exposure in faith development, see: Mischey, *op. cit.*, 1976, pp. 200–215.

18. For an elaboration of how the notion of affect may play an important role in the solidification of an individuating faith, see: Mischey, *op. cit.*, 1976, pp. 200–215.

19. See James W. Fowler, 'Faith development theory and the aims of religious socialization,' in G. Durka and J. Smith (eds), *Emerging Issues in Religious Education*, New York, Paulist Press, 1976.

20. See Eugene J. Mischey, *op. cit.*, 1976.

21. On this point, see the following sources: James E. Marcia, *op. cit.*, 1978; M. H. Podd, 'Ego identity status and morality: the relationship between two developmental constructs,' *Developmental Psychology*, vol. 6, 1972, pp. 497–507; P. J. Poppen, 'The development of sex differences in moral judgment for college males and females,' unpublished Ph.D. dissertation, Cornell University, 1974; I. Rowe, 'Ego identity status, cognitive development and levels of moral reasoning,' unpublished M. A. thesis, Simon Frazer University, 1978.

22. A majority of the late adolescents who were working (in the sample drawn for this study) strongly emphasized their perception of a lack of concern by their former teachers: that is, a lack of concern for their inner discontents beyond curriculum involvement.

23. See Margaret Gorman, *op. cit.*, 1977.

24. See Eugene J. Mischey, *op. cit.*, 1976.

25. See Clark Power, 'Faith and morality: a cognitive developmental perspective,' unpublished paper presented to Section 39 of the convention of the American Psychological Association, August 26, 1977, in San Francisco, California.

26. See James W. Fowler, 'Stages in faith,' in Thomas Hennessy (ed.), *Values and Moral Education*, New York, Paulist Press, 1976.

5.2 Comments on the article by Eugene J. Mischey

Jerome W. Berryman, Richard E. Davies and Henry C. Simmons

Jerome W. Berryman

I enjoyed and much appreciated Dr Mischey's article. It is important not only for itself but, also, because it makes Fowler's method and theory more explicit and public by putting it to the empirical test.[1] Too little about Fowler's own research has been published by Fowler and others which is *specific enough methodologically* for an informed discussion or a fair replication to take place. Perhaps this will be remedied by the publication of Fowler's forthcoming book, sometime in the Spring of 1981.

My response will be to the single issue of the perceived theoretical ambiguity underlying Mischey's study and its relation to problems in Fowler's work (to date), upon which Mischey's study is based. I will discuss what I see as the cause of this lack of clarity, the questions it raises, and the research tradition I see Fowler and Mischey tending to stand within. I will then conclude with an alternative way to organize the data of faith which does not attempt to crowd the whole phenomenon into one model. This suggestion is not made as a final statement, but in order to provide raw material for a continuing discussion.

Probing a perceived problem

Ambiguity glitters in both the introduction and the interpretative sections of Mischey's article. The subject matter of the study – a 'preoccupation of late adolescence' – is defined as 'the quest for and expression of a viable, psychosocial identity capable of rendering a life-perspective that provides a meaningful existence.' Once stated, this definition begins to shift in expression among such semantic indicators as: 'gestalt of being,' 'mode of being,' 'the individual's personality,' 'pull,' 'milieu,' and other words for the phenomenon which Fowler calls 'faith.' As the article is concluding, Mischey confides to us that Fowler *really* is describing, to a large extent, 'ontological development.' The ambiguity comes from not knowing whether Mischey and Fowler are talking about the *same* model or event, and that uncertainty makes an evaluation of Mischey's correlation study involving the two additional models of Erikson and Kohlberg little better than guesswork.

The ambiguity of the language used to define the subject matter of the study could be clarified if we could tell whether the study is using scientific, philosophical or religious language. Those languages draw on their own paradigms to give a contextual meaning to them. For example, the word *faith* means something different and involves a different tradition and model, in religion and in science. Do Fowler and Mischey collapse or merge the paradigms of religion and science? (For the moment, we can leave aside the question of the philosophical and other paradigms which might also be mixed in this discussion.)

Fowler and Mischey need to face the question of what the relationship *is* between religion and science and, as well, what each of these paradigms for knowing are like. To my knowledge, this has not been made explicit in print, although Fowler is not unaware of the paradigm issue.[2]

What is needed is a comparison between religion and science in terms of assumptions, language usage, logic, research method, research exemplars (e.g., Jesus vs Piaget, or Moses vs Freud), and other similar paradigm indicators. Mischey's effort to be precise empirically has, for instance, demonstrated how very practical good theory can be.

This question of the paradigm is important because, as Kuhn has demonstrated about paradigm change in science, the *worldview transitions* from Aristotle to Galileo to Newton to Einstein were not so much based on empirical verification or falsification but, rather, on commitment shifts.[3] If this is true within the general paradigm of science, then it must be more true when one shifts *from* the paradigm of religion *to* the paradigm of science.

It seems there are *at least* five questions that cannot be evaluated, much less answered, before decisions are made about the paradigm issue. It seems to me that we must ask questions like the five which follow.

First, can the Fowler, Erikson and Kohlberg models be correlated across paradigm lines? If so, how? Is comparing Fowler and Erikson like comparing an apple and an onion rolling down an inclined plane? Both are 'global' but the center, taste, classification and covering are so different that the meaning of the measurement can be questioned, despite one's ability to perform it.

Second, if Fowler is not needed to provide the correlation of a religious model and a scientific model − leaving aside whether this is possible − why use Fowler's model at all? Loevinger provides a developmental, structuralist model of ego development from within the scientific tradition to correlate with the neo-Freudian model of Erikson.[4] Loevinger has made her theoretical position clear within science, and both she and Erikson are studying ego development. They provide two 'windows' into the *same* room. The introduction of a faith model causes one to wonder if a correlation of Fowler and Erikson does not provide 'windows' into *different* rooms.

Third, to be specific about Fowler's model, we might ask if the Piagetiän method – of which Fowler uses only the verbal part – is appropriate for the stages of development which extend beyond Piaget's formal operations? Or has Fowler tried to do something like weighing someone with a thermometer? If we do not know how the religious and scientific paradigms are functioning in this study, as we have said, then the definition of 'faith' cannot be clarified. Not only is this true across the paradigm lines but, in addition, it is also true within the individual models themselves. The phenomenon changes so much in both Erikson and Fowler that one wonders if the same methods of investigation are appropriate at the later stages which were appropriate earlier. In the two models this question has to be evaluated differently, since Erikson's model is expressed in more literary and philosophical terms, while Fowler's model seems more intended for specific quantification.

Fourth, are Fowler's stages similar to compounds of diverse elements (e.g., water is a compound of oxygen and hydrogen), or are they unstable mixtures (e.g., the mixture of oil and water)? Here the issue of the paradigm must enter into any discussion of Fowler's stages. If those stages are really unstable mixtures of religion and science, can a mathematical average of seven such stage-variables be taken? Or if taken, can such an average be meaningfully termed a 'stage'? We must ask how such a questionable 'stage' can be correlated with a *different kind* of 'stage' from Erikson?

Fifth, if Fowler's model includes parts of Erikson, Piaget, Kohlberg, Selman and others, is a correlation between Fowler's stages and part of a Kohlberg stage, for example, simply redundant? If such a correlation is neither redundant nor a tautology, what can we expect to learn from it? Is it possible that stage-stage correlation will be able to show anything *more* than whether Fowler either (i) changed the used model or (ii) changed the testing method for a used model *after* he had incorporated it into his own model? These are important questions, and they need answers.

These five questions illustrate a larger need. We need to know whether Mischey and Fowler see themselves as (i) empirical theologians or (ii) social scientists who use religious language, in a rather up-rooted and inconsistent fashion, mixed with scientific language.

I would like to suggest that both Mischey and Fowler are really empirical theologians. The reason I make that suggestion is because of the *values* expressed in Fowler's model. Piaget valued the scientific method as epistemology, and he enthroned it in his final stage of formal operations. Kohlberg valued Rawls philosophical ethics, and he enthroned its principles in his final stage. Fowler's final stages seem to extend Piaget's formal operations into *stages* of paradox, dialectic and an ultimately paradoxical universalizing which is, at the same time, the most centered and the most open and diffuse stage. This final stage in Fowler's model places that model well within the realm of values characteristic of the Western tradition of spirituality. In the Eastern tradition of spirituality, for example, a final stage would have involved a dissolving into the One.

The tradition of Western spirituality *is* the research tradition associated with the Western religious paradigm. Now, *if* it is true that both Fowler and Mischey stand within that religious paradigm and, so, are not primarily dealing just with value and power in society, *then* the relationship between the religious paradigms and its own tradition of research needs to be critically and historically worked out.

Alternative theoretical organization for faith research

My own use of Fowler's model has suggested that *too much* has been crowded into it, probably during an early, enthusiastic stage of model development. The interest in language, developmental structures *and* personality theory is just too much for the Fowler model to carry. In my own work, I have separated these three areas of interest, so that methods of measurement can also be separated, and I have added the dimension of the creative process. As a result, it seems possible to study the relationship with God from within the religious paradigm along the following lines.

1. Faith is, therefore, the relationship of the creature (and of creatures) with the Creator.
2. Reality is, then, experienced in relationships. Among these relationships are those we know as religion and science. Both religion and science have their own paradigms, in which reality both creates and is created by language, in paradigm-dependent ways.
3. The creature-Creator relationship of the religious paradigm has, it seems, four dimensions.
   a. Faith development *structures* make explicit the relationships of life in community in relation to the Creator. A 'stage' is, then, a model for organizing masses of data for communication purposes, rather than being a mirror of total reality in itself.
   b. Faith *style* is how the personality expresses and encounters the Creator in life. Tillich's inward-tending/outward-tending distinction and his will-feelings-thinking continuum model or, at the least, offer a preliminary sketch of a personality model for faith research.[5] This is where genetics seems to fit.

c. Faith *process* is the creative process. While the process itself has five parts, one can enter that process at any point and work in both directions to fill out the whole transformation, either in an inter-stage or in an intra-stage manner. The five parts of the process are:

i. living with a conflict;

ii. scanning for a solution;

iii. a felt intuition that a solution is present, even if not consciously so;

iv. a conscious working out of the solution's details;

v. a testing of the solution's re-framing of the conflict for coherence and social usefulness.[6]

It is this kind of a faith *process* that Mischey needs to address in his discussion of stages and sub-stages, rather than limiting his attention to the correlation of conceptual apples and onions.

d. Faith *language* that is appropriate for both knowing and for knowing about faith needs to be organized into its functions. Probably these functions are what we know as parable, myth and liturgy and, perhaps, translating such a faith language into other forms does *not* improve its ability to communicate meaning. Religious language was, after all, intuitively developed by the species for this very purpose. Mischey's observations about religious language being required to move into the Fowler stages beyond the Piaget stages in Fowler's model is, therefore, redundant, since these 'upper' Fowler stages are based on religious values in the tradition of Western spirituality. One would not, indeed could not, expect the models of Piaget, Kohlberg or Erikson to capture those values in the same way.

Conclusion

It has been my intention to sketch some questions about, and an alternative solution for, the theoretical ambiguity in Mischey's study and the Fowler model upon which he relies. In a certain sense, I have been talking to myself in this Comment, since I am indebted to both Fowler and Mischey for their pioneering work, parts of which I use daily in my own research.

Richard E. Davies

Mischey's article is one of those relatively rare reports of research that challenges the imagination and helps set the stage for the application of theory, in addition to reporting results. We all should look forward to further studies by Mischey. We also should look forward to complementary studies by researchers working independently of Mischey. The exploratory study that is reported in this article raises concerns that are so significant that they should be investigated further. However, I do want to make four comments as a specific response to Mischey's article.

First, let us not overlook the *exploratory nature* of this research. When the measures seem to uncover four distinct groups, and one group consists of only three individuals, while another includes only four, one is *not* in a position to make firm generalizations, either quantitative or qualitative. At this point, we must recognize that the material under Mischey's section heading, 'Qualitative analysis and discussion of this study,' constitutes a series of elaborated hypotheses.

Second, of course, and quite understandably, *small samples* are characteristic of much 'developmental' research, because the stages have been defined in relation to complicated interview schedules. A number of attempts have been made, with some success, to develop valid, short measures of Kohlberg's stages.[7] No doubt, we can look forward to similar work with Fowler's stages. Then it will be more practical to study larger samples.

Third, in either doing or reading about the *statistical analyses* of this or similar 'developmental' studies we must continually remind ourselves of a fundamental point: stage scores are ordinal, not interval. The caution inherent in this comment is not for the author, but for the reader. For example: in the table entitled, 'Examples of stage 3 and stage 4 combinations in the Mischey study of late adolescents,' the author assigns commonly accepted values to the stages; however, we must remember that they *are* only ordinal values. Then, in table 2, 'Summary of faith scores, moral reasoning scores by faith stage delineation,' we see that some of the values 'drop out' of the sample Mischey studied, so that there is a clear clustering into two groups. However, it is useful to remember that because the values are ordinal, the clustering is not quite as clear cut as it may appear. I do *not* believe that this invalidates any of Mischey's conclusions, but a word of caution is appropriate. We all must be careful that we do not read more into the numbers than is justified.

Fourth, Mischey's finding that reflection on prototypical challenges *promotes* faith development should be pursued. Various structured training programs such as Outward Bound, the Chicago Urban Training Center and, possibly, even Clinical Pastoral Education have employed some such notion for a long time. Still, we must ask such questions as: What experiences are best? How are those experiences best assimilated? What are the limits, if any, on such experiences? To what degree can vicarious experiences substitute for actual experiences?

It seems to me that Lorimer's 1971 article in the *Canadian Journal of Behavioral Science* and Hood's 1977 article in the

Journal for the Scientific Study of Religion provide examples of related research.[8]

Henry C. Simmons

Both my comments on Eugene J. Mischey's article, 'Faith, identity and morality in late adolescence,' concern community: that group of persons with whom I am in intimate relationship of life and meaning.

First, I note that absence of a community of life and meaning may explain why, in Mischey's sample, the scores of non-believers were significantly lower than the scores of believers. Fowler's faith development theory posits that structural, and not content, factors are responsible for progression; but Mischey asks us not to discard quickly the possibility of 'content interaction.' It seems possible to interpret both Fowler's position and Mischey's findings in another way.

Faith, whether religious or not, has for Fowler a strongly *communitarian* component: it is both my and our way of relating to what we together consider to be the transcendent. It seems to me that for Mischey's sample (and, perhaps, more generally in society) there is little systematic communitarian basis for non-religious faith. Non-religious faith is more likely to result from a negative stance than from a positive 'standing with community.' Thus, it seems possible to qualify both Fowler's and Mischey's positions by stressing again that progression in faith depends on 'content interaction' only to *the extent that* this 'content interaction' is dynamic interaction with the others with whom I am in relation to the transcendent.

Second, Mischey's findings are of less use to the educator than might first appear, unless he is able to tell us the precise shape of the community experience of the practice of religion and religious education which these adolescents identify as bringing them to their present faith perspectives. In his presentation, Mischey makes a substantial contribution by challenging Kohlberg's contention that ideas about God and life are independent of true moral development. Mischey's findings indicate, on the contrary, that faith is the motivation for moral reasoning. Religionists who might like to take comfort in this idea should recognize, however, that at many periods of history the traditional religions have failed to provide an openness towards and sponsorship for continuing stage development in general. It appears, then, that it is *not simply* religious faith as such which makes the difference, but religious faith of a certain type, or religious faith presented in a certain way.

In Mischey's sample, the faith of all save one of the individuals in faith-groups III and IV was religiously based. But it is precisely here that Mischey's presentation is incomplete, for he does *not* tell us the shape of the community's religious practice and education, which the adolescents identify as bringing them to their present position. For example, was Mischey able to ascertain that those in the higher faith-groups did, as a matter of fact, experience a different type of education than those in the lower faith-groups? Did attendance at a denominational school make a difference? Does current religious practice make a difference? And, if so, how? These are, it seems to me, important questions, if we are to understand the relationship between faith development and moral reasoning.

Much current religious education practice in the area from which Mischey's sample came has been at least modestly renewed in the direction of both fostering self-awareness and opening up towards a larger sense of community and world. Generally, it moves towards a more personal sense of commitment, rather than concentrating on simple adherence to rules or to a group. However, we can only reshape educational practice in the way in which Mischey suggests (i.e., in order to foster a sense of self) *if* we know the real shape of the real community which gave rise to the real progress made by the adolescents in the higher faith-groups.

From the perspective of the religionist, a critical issue is the development of a strong sense of self within the group or community. Moreover, that community's life-perspective must be broader than the small local community itself. We *need* to know from Mischey (and other researchers) the precise *quality* and *substance* of the religious practice and education which all the students in his sample lived, and by which they were formed, so that we can continue to shape the kinds of communities which foster authentic human growth.

Notes

1. Fowler relied on Mischey's earlier work with young adults in his chapter, 'Moral stages and the development of faith,' in Brenda M. Munsey (ed.), *Moral Development, Education and Kohlberg*, Birmingham, Alabama, Religious Education Press, 1980.
2. Fowler took a major part in the colloquium convened by Christiane Brusselmans that resulted in the book entitled, *Toward Moral and Religious Maturity*, Morristown, New Jersey, Silver Burdett Co., 1980. In that book this point is specifically implied.
3. See Thomas S. Kuhn, *The Structure of Scientific Revolutions*, Chicago, Ill., University of Chicago Press, 1962.
4. See Jane Loevinger, *Ego Development*, San Francisco, Jossey-Bass, 1976. In this book, Loevinger is careful to distinguish and discuss her work in relation to Kohlberg, as well as to the work of J. M. Broughton, 'The development of natural epistemology in adolescence and early adulthood,' unpublished doctoral dissertation, Harvard Univ., 1975, esp. see pp. 441–446.
5. See Paul Tillich, *Dynamics of Faith*, New York, Harper Torchbooks, 1957. In this book, Tillich deals with the following three topics, each of which is apropos of this question of faith and person: the *types of faith* – see esp. pp. 55–73; the *centered act of a whole personality* – see esp. pp. 30–40; the *power of personality's integration* – see esp. p. 105 and pp. 111 ff.
6. James E. Loder has, for example, argued for a similar kind of process, which he calls 'transformation.' See Loder's chapter, 'Negation and transformation: a study in theology and human development,' in J. W. Fowler and A. Vergote (eds), *Toward Moral and Religious Maturity*, Morristown, New Jersey, Silver

Burdett Co., 1980. Also see Loder's inagural address in *The Princeton Seminary Bulletin*, vol. 3, no. 1, new series, 1980, pp. 11–25.

7.   For an example of such a short measure of Kohlberg's stages, see the *Journal of Personality Assessment*, vol. 41, 1977, pp. 396–401.

8.   For Lorimer's article, see *Canadian Journal of Behavioral Science*, vol. 3, 1971, pp 1–10. For Hood's article, see *Journal for the Scientific Study of Religion*, vol. 16, 1977, pp. 155–163.

5.3 Young adult faith development: teaching in the context of theological education

Sharon Parks

A young woman in her senior year of college was reflecting on her faith journey. Her story was one of a rocky voyage from freshman year through senior year. The turbulence had swirled around the issues of individuation from family and the cognitive dissonance between traditional religious knowing and academic study – all cast in a series of romances that raised further questions regarding role definitions for herself as a woman. Seeming to have arrived at some new shore of understanding and anticipating entering graduate studies at a prestigious university, she says of her sense of her present and future faith experience:

> I'm open to being a believer but I'm ... I'm comfortable and aware now that whatever I come up with will not be the traditional and that's O.K. It can still be bona fide even though I know everyone doesn't have to fit into a niche. So I'm working it through and it feels comfortable and it feels like it'll come.

A professor of religious education and graduate of the same school to which she was heading remarked after reading her story, 'I bet she'll go through the same thing all over again.'

I suggest that the study of faith development gives us some means by which to confirm both her intuitive confidence and his intuitive pessimism. I submit the hypothesis that becoming adult in faith is a process more complex than has traditionally been recognized either by bar/bat mitzvah, 8th grade confirmation rites, religiously oriented colleges, seminaries, or other centers of graduate study.

Young adult faith development

The multi-disciplinary study of faith development is informed by a broad phenomenological understanding of faith. Wilfred Cantwell Smith, H. R. Niebuhr and others have helped us to recognize faith as a dynamic, on-going, composing activity – the activity of meaning-making, the seeking of pattern and order in the chaos of disparate elements of lived experience. In this perspective the word 'faith' is not only a noun, it is also a verb. Faith is the activity of composing our conviction of the character of the force field of life. Faith composes our convictions of value and trustworthiness. Faith is the patterning activity that orders our sense of the ultimate nature of the cosmos of being.[1]

Faith development study brings this understanding of faith into dialogue with developmental psychology (Piaget and Erikson) and in so doing is able to discern and describe a predictable sequence of patterns in the on-going dynamic construing activity that is the journey of faith.

James Fowler, the primary pioneer in this work, has identified a sequence of six 'stages' in the development of faith. His third stage is a pattern of faith knowing which typically emerges in the post-pubertal teenage adolescent years, but which may also be characteristic of many persons through the whole of their post teenage lives. This particular faith pattern he describes as 'conventional' and characteristically it is evidenced in part by the 'tacit' character of its faith knowing. In contrast, the following developmental era (individuating − stage 4) is characterized by an 'explicit' system of knowing; one self-consciously takes responsibility for one's faith construction. One is no longer content simply to assume that one knows 'how it is' by virtue of one's confidence in the knowing of others. Fowler has not found this particular transition to occur before the age of seventeen; it may typically occur later (sometimes even coinciding with mid-life transitions).

I contend that in consideration of this movement from con-ventional to a post-conventional faith knowing, one of the most significant aspects of faith structure is what Fowler terms the 'locus of authority.' This dimension of faith describes the manner in which persons 'interpret and rely upon sources of authoritative insight or "truth"'[2] regarding the ultimate character of their environment. 'It suggests the operational criteria ... employed − consciously or unconsciously − at each stage for discerning reliable authority and for choosing among competing sources.'[3]

In the transition from conventional to post-conventional faith the locus of authority shifts from 'outside' to 'inside.' Authority which was previously invested in *assumed* centers of trust 'outside' the self, i.e. parents, peers, teachers, cultural 'heroes,' religious authorities, 'those who count' − is now self-consciously located 'within' as one comes to recognize that one must take responsibility for one's own knowing, one's own choices − even at the level of religious faith.[4]

This description of the movement from tacit to explicit knowing and from 'outside' to 'inner' authority may appear to best describe 'cognitive' dimensions of faith experience. However, the same movement may be recognized in affective experience. Robert Kegan observes that we gain access to affective life when we orient our descriptive activity to the perspective of the one making the tran-sition.[5] Therefore, I suggest that the transition under consideration here is experienced affectively as a movement from 'dependence' (upon trusted others 'out there') to 'inner-dependence' (a trusting within).[6]

Table 1: Characteristics of faith stages 3 and 4

Faith aspect	Stage 3 conventional	Stage 4 individuating
form of world coherence	tacit system of knowing	explicit system of knowing
locus of authority	those who count	self
form of dependence	authoritarian dependence	inner- dependence

We may chart these strands of development, as we have discussed them thus far, in table 1.

In my earlier experience as a college chaplain and teacher, I assumed that it could be expected that in the college years persons would essentially accomplish this transition and thereby secure the achievement of 'adulthood.' Indeed, persons of twenty-one or twenty-two could be recognized as exercising an inner agency and appeared emancipated from an earlier dependence upon outside sources of authority for the construing of self, world, and God. They were ready (were they not?) to assume adult roles and responsibility in society.

What puzzled me was that even the most 'mature' students continued, even after graduation, to exhibit a mixture of both 'dependent' and 'inner-dependent' behaviors. These students on one hand expressed 'post-conventional' commitments with a responsible and self-aware sense of choice and consequence. At the same time they returned to sources of leadership and reassurance in a manner reminiscent of the very young child who ventures into new space only to return periodically to 'touch' the parent as a means of maintaining a sense of confidence and trust.

In light of this seeming contradiction I have subsequently 'listened' more carefully to undergraduate and graduate students. Giving particular attention to a small study sample of college seniors (20) and informed specifically by Perry (1968), Keniston (1973) and Gilligan (1980) I now hypothesize that there is an identifiable developmental 'stage' or era between the 'adolescent' and 'adult' eras, between Fowler's third and fourth stages. I believe that this era is important to an understanding of the whole of faith education and worthy of the particular attention of those who teach in graduate school settings. I name this era 'young adulthood.'

The threshold of adulthood is problematic in the culture of the United States. The varying age requirements relating to drivers licenses, drinking, voting, military service, marriage, and the right to medical care without parental consent, are all in some measure indicators both of adulthood and the culture's ambivalence regarding the timing of its emergence. This awareness is heightened when we recognize that for many 'adulthood' is not really assumed until one 'has a job,' is married, and/or is financially independent. Therefore, 'adolescence' appears to be extending into the late twenties and early thirties. For some, this term may be appropriately applied. I am suggesting, however, that the term 'young adulthood' as I wish to describe it may be more adequate. Let us see how this may be so.

Erik Erikson is helpful to us in the quest to determine the threshold of adulthood. He describes 'self-identity' as having 'a claim to recognition as the adolescent ego's most important accomplishment.'[7] I suggest that the achievement that is 'the central accomplishment of adolescence' may appropriately mark its completion. According to Erikson 'self-identity' is accomplished as differing role images, or what Fowler would term 'derived selves,' are successfully reintegrated in an ensemble of roles which also secure social recognition. Such 'identity' is an extraordinary achievement because 'it helps simultaneously in the containing of the post-pubertal id and in the balancing of the then newly invoked super-ego as well as appeasing the often rather lofty ego ideal – all in the light of a forseeable future structured by an ideological world image.'[8]

Of particular importance to our understanding of this developmental accomplishment is the recognition that this self-system named identity is 'self-conscious.' Loevinger, in discussing the same period of development, writes of the emergence of the 'self-aware self.'[9] Here one becomes responsible for the composing of one's self in relationship to others. One becomes self-conscious, self-aware. It is this achievement, the emergence of the 'self-aware self' that I propose may appropriately mark the completion of adolescence and the beginning of adulthood.

If this be so, then according to Fowler's scheme, persons who selfconsciously compose their sense of self would also exhibit a confident inner-dependence, evidenced by a consistent exercise of an agency, the authority for which lies within. I did not find such inner-dependence characteristic of college juniors and seniors nor of young-alumni-now-graduate-students. Students I thought had 'left the nest' with mature wings seemed to require yet a further degree of support and leadership. I was puzzled.

The puzzle begins to be simplified if one looks carefully at the conclusions of William Perry's study of college students. Perry has mapped the epistemological journey from the simple authoritarian and dualistic world of 'right and wrong,' 'we and they' through relativism toward commitment within relativism, and finds them a position of 'initial commitment.' The place of commitment is 'a place to stand,' 'a new faith,' on the other side of relativism. But

Perry helps us to see that this movement toward commitment first takes a form I wish to call 'probing commitment' prior to a period of 'tested adult commitment.'[10] This movement is illustrated in it following chart of progression:

authoritarian dualism	→	relativism	→	probing commitment	→	tested commitment

I have also found it of interest to note discrepancies in Fowler's descriptions of the character of these developmental eras. At one time Fowler suggested that the 'explicit system' characteristic of individuating (stage 4) faith was 'ideological' in character and evidenced by dichotomous thinking which tended to collapse the dichotomy in one direction. (For example, one would finally feel compelled to choose between individual and community values.) In later writing he indicated that the tension of the dichotomy was maintained.[11]

Of further interest were Fowler's observations regarding the transition from conventional to individuating faith. He wrote, 'Frequently the transition from stage 3 to stage 4 is a somewhat protracted affair. The transition may begin around ages 17–18, though we rarely find well-equilibrated stage 4 characteristics before the early twenties. It is not uncommon to interview adults at all ages who are best described as 3–4 transitional types and who give evidence of having been there for a number of years.'[12] Elsewhere he noted that 'we find a quite large group of adults in our sample who are best described as "equilibrated transitionals"'[13] between the Conventional and Individuative stages.

Kenneth Keniston's work offers further insight into the puzzles of this post-adolescent era. Keniston, who is calling for the recognition of a developmental stage between 'adolescence' and 'adulthood,' asserts that[14]:

> psychological development results from a complex interplay of constitutional givens (including the rates and phases of biological maturation) and the changing familial, social, educational, economic and political conditions that constitute the matrix in which children persons develop.... Some social and historical conditions demonstrably slow, retard or block development, while others stimulate, speed and encourage it. A prolongation and extension of development, then, including the emergence of 'new' stages of life, can result from altered social, economic and historical conditions.

Keniston is contending that just as major transformations in American society after the Civil War effected such real change in human experience that 'adolescence' emerged as a recognizable stage in human development, the same magnitude of change has subsequently occurred, 'creating' yet another recognizable stage in the human life cycle. Among the changes he cites are the shift in the percentage of students who finish high school and begin college, and 'a rate of social change so rapid that it threatens to make obsolete all institutions, values, methodologies and technologies within the lifetime of each generation; a technology that has created not only prosperity and longevity, but power to destroy the planet, whether through warfare or violation of nature's balance; a world of extraordinary complex social organization, instantaneous communication and constant revolution.'[15]

Keniston offers the possibility that many young persons who seem both to react against and also to reflect the shape of contemporary society are not adequately described as either 'adolescent' or 'adult.' He states that[16]:

> For the twenty-four-year-old seeker, political activist, graduate student often turns out to have been *through* a period of adolescent rebellion ten years before, to be all too formed in his or her views, to have a stable [equilibrated] sense of self, and to be much further along in ... psychological development than his or her fourteen-year-old high school brother or sister.

Keniston observes a significant contrast between such young persons and other post-adolescents whose place in society is settled, who are married and parents, and fully committed to an occupation. He wants to characterize the post-adolescent-not-yet-adult as not having 'settled the questions whose answers once defined adulthood: questions of relationship to the existing society, questions of vocation, questions of social role and life style.'[17] Of course many have described such phenomena as 'protracted adolescence,' certainly a pejorative description at best (though in some instances undoubtedly accurate). Yet, in light of the evidence, such a description appears both inadequate and inaccurate. For as Keniston states[18]:

> While some young men and women are indeed victims of the psychological malady of 'stretched adolescence' many others are less impelled by juvenile grandiosity than by rather accurate analysis of the perils and injustices of the world in which they live.

As he describes the characteristics of this 'new stage' of development, the stage 3−4 transitional puzzle becomes clarified; I hypothesize that within Fowler's stage 4, two separate, identifiable stages can be distinguished. For it becomes apparent that the post-adolescent persons Keniston describes have indeed achieved a 'self-aware self,' individuated from family; but this new self is as yet 'over-against' society or 'the-world-as-it-is.' The new self is not yet a full participant in the 'adult world.' Yet the new self is aware of its identity, values and integrity as distinguished from societal conventional norms. The person Keniston describes is able to 'sense who he or she is and thus to recognize the possibility, conflict and disparity between his or her emerging selfhood and his or her social order.'[19]

Thus far, Fowler's stage 4 may be interpreted as inclusive of

Keniston's 'new stage.' However, what is of most striking and illuminating significance for our purposes, is Keniston's identification of the *'pervasive ambivalence* [of this stage] toward *both* self and society.'[20] There is a self-aware self to be ambivalent about − but it does not have the 'fully equilibrated' character of Fowler's individuated stage four. Yet, it appears substantive enough to be more than 'transitional.' Let us examine this new self more closely.

Keniston makes clear that this 'ambivalence' about self and society does not necessarily presume social activism. It may take the form of *rejection of society* or the world-as-it-is. But it may also take the form of *rejection of self*. This self-rejection or, better, ambivalence, may be manifest in 'major efforts as self transformation employing the methodologies of personal transformation that are available in any cultural era: monasticism, meditation, psychoanalysis, prayer, hallucinogenic drugs, hard work, religious conversion, introspection, and so forth.'[21]

Erikson described the emergence of self-identity or the self-aware self as a task integrally related to the issue of effectiveness in society.[22] What Keniston's insights suggest is that in another era these two tasks may have been achieved simultaneously. Now, however, the construction of a self which is effective in society may occur in a series of two stages. The self may emerge from embeddedness in the family in an identifiably self-aware form and indeed necessitate the *encounter* with the issue of effectiveness in society. But the further task of the new self-aware is the integration or reconciliation of the two poles of self and society. This developmental era, therefore, 'involves a characteristic stance vis-à-vis both self and world, perhaps best described by the concept of *wary probe*,' (reminiscent of our earlier discussion of 'probing commitment' and 'ambivalence'). This wary probing is qualitatively different from adolescent experimentation in search of self definition. The probing of the post-adolescent is a serious exploration of the adult world, through which society's 'vulnerability, strength, integrity, and possibilities are assayed.' A corresponding self-probing tests the strength, vulnerability, capacity of the self to withstand or use what society will make, ask, and allow.[23]

Keniston asserts that when a 'new stage' such as he describes appears in history, a re-examination of previous periods of history will reveal persons who 'had shown hallmarks of this stage long before it was identified and named.'[24] Evidence of the same is found in a study by Howard Brinton, the Quaker historian. Examining three hundred Quaker journals from the seventeenth and eighteenth centuries, he has identified four stages in Quaker faith experience. The first he identifies as a period in childhood from the ages of about 7−12 in which children experience the presence of God in forms which seem to correspond with Fowler's stage 2. The second period is that of 'youthful frivolity' and is characterized by desire for 'airy friends' and fashionable clothes – Quaker taboos. This period may correspond with Fowler's conventional stage 3. Of the most interest here is the next period; this period begins in the mid-teens and Brinton describes it as 'the divided self' – a description significantly resonant with Keniston's 'ambivalent self.' Brinton finds here a sense of inner tensions, struggle, and experience of 'wilderness.' This period comes to an end for the Quaker when the decision is made to follow the Inner Light; such a choice meant identification with a community (society) now known as The Society of Friends. The average age at which Quakers first spoke in meeting signifying the decision to follow the Inner Light and be 'at one' was 26 years.[25]

I am suggesting, then, on the basis of my own observations and research, Keniston's studies, Brinton's analysis of historical data, and Fowler's identification of 'equilibrated transitionals' between stages three and four in faith development, that a distinction must be made between the 'adolescent,' the 'young adult' and the 'adult.' I propose that 'young adult' faith be recognized as self-aware but ambivalent in relation to self and society. The 'adult,' as we will see, has resolved this tension and is more confident. One's self-awareness has seasoned and is a more robust 'self-reflection.'

When the above observations and insights are brought together, we may describe the 'young adult' as evidencing a self-awareness that is yet 'fragile.' By 'fragile' I do not mean puny or weak but rather fragile in the sense that a young plant is fragile – vulnerable yet full of promise. Thus the young adult may be characterized by a 'fragile inner-dependence.' This form of dependence effects the dynamics relative to the 'locus of authority.'

Locus of authority revisited

As noted earlier, Fowler's work delineates the transition of authority from 'those who count' – assumed authorities 'out there' – to authority 'within.' It now becomes significant to our discussion to note that he also comments that the emergence of stage 4 is often facilitated by a charismatic person or group. This latter comment in conjunction with Keniston's work again invites us to recognize the transition into adulthood as a two-step process. The locus of authority shifts first from those *assumed* sources of authority 'out there' that one has appropriated unselfconsciously, to an authority out there that one *chooses*, and then in a second movement, to an authority located within. The authority that is both 'out there' *and* 'chosen' will be 'charismatic' in that it captures the imagination of the emerging self and 'calls out' or 'answers' the yearnings of one's own becoming.

Such leadership offers a vision of self, world, and 'God' which appears worthy as a fitting form for the holding and shaping of new being.

Not surprisingly, then, the faith of the young adult seeks the 'ideal,' in the sense of that which is authentic, consistent, pure – worthy of the emerging self. This seeking of the 'ideal' is empowered in part by the emergence of full formal operational thought (the capacity for abstract thought as delineated in Piaget). This new found power of the mind to transcend more concrete modes of knowing conspires with the quest for the 'ideal' to create a faith stance which is 'over-against the world-as-it-is and nurtures a vision of the world-as-it-must-become;'[26] and we can expect such faith to have an 'ideological' quality.

If we are to recognize the full implications of these phenomena for teaching in the context of theological education, it is important to attend also to the aspect of development Fowler terms 'bounds of social awareness' and which I wish to term 'form of community.' This aspect of faith development helps us to describe in each era the character of one's 'network of belonging.' In Fowler's scheme, the individuating shift in the bounds of social awareness is a movement from conventional/assumed 'ascription groups' to a 'self-selected class or group.' I perceive that a distinction can be made between the affiliative style of the 'young adult' and the 'adult.' The young adult's affiliative group is to some degree self-consciously chosen and is therefore a 'self-selected class or group.' But the group is felt to be in some sense set apart from, or over-against, the world-as-it-is. Further, the group claiming the young adult's allegiance is a powerful shaper of the emerging self it both calls forth and forms. The 'adult', on the other hand, affiliates with a 'self-selected class or group,' which finds its place within the world-as-it-is – even if only as a strategy for transforming the world-as-it-is. And the 'adult's' authority within is confirmed by, but not located in, the group. (It may assist in putting this phenomenon in perspective to note that Robert Kegan suggests the irony that the self-aware self may actually require a group to come into being.)[27] The strands of development described here may be traced in Table 2.

If in light of this discussion we return to the young woman with whose reflections we began, we can hypothesize the following: the college years have served to enable the voyage from her conventional faith knowing, through her individuation from family-societal values; she has arrived on a 'new shore' in that she now feels 'comfortable;' yet she has not yet fully formed a new explicit faith – she knows only that it 'won't be the traditional' and it 'feels like it'll come.' She appears to be a young adult – self-aware, both fragile and full of promise. How will her graduate school meet her in her on-going exploration toward adult faith?

Table 2: *Characteristics of adolescent, young adult and adult faith stages*

Faith aspect	Adolescent	Young adult	Adult
form of world coherence	tacit system	explicit system (ideological-ideal)	explicit system (pragmatic-ideal)
form of logic	early formal operations	full formal operations (dichotomizing: collapsing)	full formal operations (dichotomizing: maintaining tension)
form of intellectual development	authoritarian dualism	probing commitment	tested commitment
locus of authority	those who count	charismatic person and/or group (confirmed within)	self (confirmed without)
form of dependence	dependent/counter dependent	fragile inner dependence	confident inner-dependence
form of self	derivative	self-aware (ambivalent)	self-reflective (centred)
form of community	conventional	ideologically compatible communities world rejecting	self-selected class or group (within world-as-it-is)

Implications for teaching in the context of theological education

All of the foregoing argues that it may typically be the case that persons coming to graduate school are still in the process of adult faith formation, particularly, but not exclusively, those who come directly from their undergraduate experience. They may be either still in the disequilibrium of the transition from conventional/adolescent to young adult faith, or they may be exploring the 'new shore' of young adult faith. In either case, these persons are in search of and vulnerable to ideological interpretations of self, world, and God which serve to call out and give place to the emerging self. Such students are particularly responsive to images of the 'ideal' – while also seeking a relationship of integrity to society – a fitting vocation.

Daniel Levinson describes this era in development as 'early

adulthood' and refers to the person in this era as the 'novice' adult.[28] American society tends to send its 'novices' predominately to the contemporary monastery or convent – the halls of higher education.[29] Higher education provides the framework for a time set apart for vocation formation. To be formed in vocation in its fullest sense is inevitably to be engaged in spiritual or faith formation. The young adult must compose a sense of knowing and being which will form the basis of lived adult faith. Many areas of study in higher education may object to such an analysis. However, those of us who teach in seminary contexts cannot escape the recognition that, if not to other graduate schools, surely to ours do persons come who are self-consciously seeking an explicit and worthy faith in the service of delineating a vocational path.

These persons seem to give ample evidence of the 'ambivalence' of young adult faith in their relationship to professional preparation for a religious vocation. Studies, religious affiliation, and even ordination are engaged by many as a very 'wary probe.' But the questions posed to us, or the assertions made somehow 'too strongly,' each ask overtly or obliquely, What is the character of life? What can I believe? What can I have confidence in? Who am I to become? Am I alone? What is ultimately worthy of my energies and fidelity? In what or whom may I hope? Is it possible for me to find a place of integrity (and a salary) in society?

We must come to a renewed awareness that to be a professor is to be both a scholar and a spiritual guide – truly educators in the sense of ones who 'lead out.' 'Professor,' which at one time meant 'church member,' is in its primary definition 'a person who professes something; esp.., one who openly declares his (or her) sentiments, religious beliefs, etc.'[30] To take such a definition of professor seriously is to recognize again that those who teach in a seminary context not only serve as spiritual guides, but each syllabus becomes a 'confession of faith.' Every syllabus makes a statement regarding what the one who professes has found to be worthy of value in the journey toward more adequate knowing and being.

To suggest that the academic enterprise is confessional in character may appear to contradict the notion of 'academic objectivity.' How may the professor/scholar in the context of theological education proceed with integrity, when 'academic objectivity' is interpreted in a manner which has seemed to sponsor critical awareness in a form precluding participation in a self-conscious affirmation of transcendent values, meanings, faith? Does not 'responsible teaching' seem to require a dispassionate presentation of 'fact,' the drawing of distinctions for the purpose of critique, and the mere laying out of multiple points of view upon which students may in turn 'objectively reflect?' Has not a reified Kantian epistemology led the contemporary academy into a dogmatic relativism from which theological education is not immune?

George Rupp is addressing the task of theology in the context of pluralism and relativism. He posits the inadequacy of composing what I have termed 'adult' commitments either upon a position which can claim to be immune to relativism or by accepting unqualified relativism as unavoidable. He perceives both of these positions to assume a Kantian epistemology, and he asserts on the basis of a Hegelian critique, that a strict dichotomy between phenomenal knowledge and noumenal reality is untenable.[31] For Rupp interprets Hegel's critique as enabling us to recognize that 'it is, to be sure useful and even necessary to distinguish between the object as it is in the consciousness of the knower and the thing in itself. But while the intention of this distinction is to call attention to the limitations of a given claim to knowledge, its effect is to drive the knower toward more adequate comprehension.'[32] The epistemological model is not, then, one of the knower on one side of an impenetrable barrier and reality on the other. Instead there is an ongoing process of interaction between the knower and the real, a process which in principle acknowledges no limits even if in practice it can never attain a totally adequate comprehension of what Hegel termed 'absolute knowledge' or 'the truth.'[33]

This third (Hegelian-Rupp) position, then, is a resource for rejecting both uncritical conventional dogmatism and unqualified relativism, for 'it recognizes the rootedness of every position in particular personal, social, and cultural conditions. Yet because the various partial and incomplete perspectives are attempts at grasping or comprehending the one reality there is, it is possible to make judgments as to their measure of validity.'[34] Therefore, though the task this suggests is obviously extremely complex, yet 'because the reality toward which claims of truth are directed is not by definition completely inaccessible, this task is not proscribed in principle.'[35] Rupp is delineating an epistemological model in which the impenetrable barrier between the knower and 'the one reality there is' is in principle dismantled and replaced by an on-going dynamic process between the knower and the real – a process resonate with the dynamic character of faith activity as earlier defined.

In light of our analysis of the dynamics of young adult faith formation, such an epistemological model suggests that the 'on-going dynamic process between the knower and the real' yet requires for the 'young adult' the accompaniment of a true 'professor.' Truth, the real, is still mediated by another who compellingly 'leads out.' The professor serves as a 'locus of authority' and the bearer of an 'ideology' which the young adult's yet dependent imagination appropriates in its quest for a 'new faith.'

Such an awareness invites us to reflection upon both the content and the method of our teaching. Thomas Groome asserts that for Christians and Jews educating activity that is religious is not only 'for faith' but 'for the Kingdom and for freedom.'[36] If educators in the context of theological education have among their students young adults who by the definitions here have particular receptivity to the 'ideal,' then we have among our students those who dwell in the developmental era which provides the optimum readiness for envisioning the Kingdom, a New Age, – the world-as-it-may-become. This is the era in which one can hear and see and invest one's heart in a profoundly transcendent vision – intimations of Life's wholeness, oneness, justice – the possibilities of Being. Are the 'ideologies' we present adequate to center the emerging fragile self? Are the images we make accessible for the formation of young adult faith worthy of the potential energies of the young adult soul? Are the curriculums we present and the manner of their presentations adequate to form the faith of the contemporary young adult? Do we share and guide a pilgrimage that is an on-going, dynamic process between the knower and the real?

If, as Erikson has contended, the developmental era we have focused on here is one which holds the promise of renewal in every generation,[37] then I suggest that the characteristic dynamics of this Young Adult era compel our attention. And if our teaching serves to enable such renewal perhaps a faith development perspective may empower our own vocation.

I close with words written from a theological student to a professor:

> Gentle art that speaks my soul ...
> Come find me in this lostness and
>   guide me through ...
> Hear the prayer that cannot form ...
> O Sound of Life, please teach me mine.

Notes

1. James W. Fowler, *Stages of Faith: the psychology of human development and the quest for meaning*, San Francisco, Harper and Row, 1981, Part I.
2. James W. Fowler and Sam Keen (edited by Jerome Berryman), *Life Maps: conversations on the journey of faith*, Waco, Texas, Word Books, 1978, p. 40.
3. *Ibid.*
4. See William G. Perry, *Forms of Intellectual and Ethical Development in the College Years: a scheme*, New York, Holt, Rinehart and Winston, 1968.
5. Robert Kegan, *The Evolving Self: problem and process in human development*, Cambridge, Mass., Harvard University Press, 1982, p. 169.
6. My essential understanding of the dynamics of dependence in relationship to development has been most substantively informed by William Weyerhauser, 'One person's view of conscience with special reverence to his therapy,' unpublished Ph.D. dissertation, Fuller Graduate School of Psychology, 1975; and William R. Rogers, 'Dependence and counter-dependency in psychoanalysis and religious faith,' *Zygon*, vol. 9, 1974, pp. 190–201.
7. Erik Erikson, *Identity, Youth and Crisis*, New York, W. W. Norton and Co., 1968, p. 211.

8. *Ibid.*
9. Jane Loevinger, *Ego Development*, San Francisco, Jossey-Bass, 1976, p. 19.
10. William G. Perry, *Intellectual and Ethical Development in the College Years: a scheme*, New York, Holt, Rinehart and Winston, 1968, pp. 156–158.
11. James W. Fowler, 'Aims of religious socialization,' p. 11; and 'Stages in faith,' p. 184.
12. James W. Fowler, *Life Maps, op.cit.*, p. 70.
13. James W. Fowler, 'Faith and the structuring of meaning,' paper presented to section 39 of the convention of the American Psychological Association, August 26, 1977, in San Francisco, California, p. 20.
14. Kenneth Keniston, 'The struggle of conscience in youth,' in C. Ellis Nelson (ed.), *Conscience*, New York, Newman Press, 1973, p. 335.
15. *Ibid.*, pp. 332–333.
16. *Ibid.*, p. 333 (the language has been modified to be inclusive).
17. *Ibid.*
18. *Ibid.*, p. 334.
19. *Ibid.*, p. 336 (the language has been modified to be inclusive).
20. *Ibid.* (emphasis added).
21. *Ibid.*
22. Erik Erikson, *Identity, Youth and Crisis, op.cit.*, p. 211.
23. Kenneth Keniston, 'The struggle of conscience in youth,' *op.cit.*, p. 336.
24. *Ibid.*
25. Howard Brinton, *Quaker Journals: varieties of religious experience among friends*, Wallingford, PA, Pendle Hill Publications, 1972, p. 36.
26. In light of Keniston's earlier observations, it should be noted that the ambivalent young adult self also stands over-against the self-as-it-is in loyalty to the self-as-it-may-become.
27. Robert Kegan, *The Evolving Self, op.cit.*, p. 102.
28. Daniel Levinson, *The Seasons of a Man's Life*, New York, Alfred Knopf, 1978, p. 28.
29. This statement may seem to presuppose equal access to higher education for all, which is not the case. It should therefore also be noted that the military is another institution charged with the task of 'adult formation.'
30. *Webster's New World Dictionary, second edition*, s.v. professor. For additional discussion of professor as spiritual guide see *Theological Education*, vol. 17, no. 1, 1980, which focuses on 'mission, spirituality, and scholarship.'
31. George Rupp, *Beyond Existentialism and Zen: religion in pluralistic world*, New York, Oxford University Press, 1979, pp. 8–9.
32. *Ibid.*, p. 9.
33. *Ibid.*
34. *Ibid.*
35. *Ibid.*
36. Thomas H. Groome, *Christian Religious Education*, New York, Harper and Row, 1980.
37. Erik Erikson, *Insight and Responsibility*, New York, W. W. Norton and Co., 1964, p. 126.

5.4 Faith development in a cross-cultural perspective
Randall Y. Furushima

James Fowler's faith development theory, with other developmental theories in psychology, usually view *stages* as sequential, invariant, hierarchical, and universal. Sequential means that stages occur in the same order and never in reverse; invariant means that the sequence is necessary, i.e., stages cannot be skipped; hierarchical means that each new stage emerges from the previous stage and transforms and integrates the structures of earlier stages; and universal means that the particular stages hold sequence, invariance, and hierarchy everywhere.[1]

Fowler claims that there are underlying structures in the way people live in faith, and that these patterns, or systems of organization, occur in a sequential, invariant, hierarchical, and perhaps universal fashion. These present claims and projected claim of universality were examined in a research project completed in 1983, which this paper summarizes.

Although there appears to be an even distribution across sex and age categories in interviews conducted thus far in faith development research, there is an imbalance which is weighted toward a white and Christian data sampling. Of the total respondents to date, 97.8% are white, 81.5% are either Protestant or Catholic, 11.2% are Jewish, 3.6% are Orthodox, and 3.6% are of other orientations.[2]

Significant cross-cultural research data have yet to play a part in the formulation and refinement of faith development theory.[3] If the universality of faith development theory is to be claimed, then cross-cultural data would need to be gathered and analyzed within the existing stage and aspect schemes. Fowler believes that the inclusion of such data would have a significant impact upon the present description and structural features of his theory.[4]

This is a report of the conclusions of a study which examined faith development theory's projected claim of universality through cross-cultural research among adult Buddhists in Hawaii. The study included twelve interviews with adults of the Jodoshinshu, or Shin, sect of Buddhism. Most of the interviewees were born in Hawaii, while all were raised and reside in Hawaii. Of the twelve, there were nine women and three men, ranging in age from twenty-eight to fifty-nine. The respondents spanned two generations, including seven second-generation Japanese (*nisei*), four third-generation Japanese (*sansei*), and one second-generation Chinese-Hawaiian. All twelve are native speakers of English, and although several are bilingual in Japanese, the interviews were conducted in English. Fowler's method of interviewing was consistently applied throughout the project, which is a semi-clinical, open-ended interview process which utilizes a uniform set of questions.

The analysis of the data involved three aspects, viz., the identification of significant content and structural features which were revealed in the interview; to the extent possible, the schematization of these features within the framework of faith development theory's stages and aspects; and the critical consideration of this schematization in light of any significant features, or cultural forms, not accounted for by the given framework. An attempt was made to preserve the criteria of the present stage and aspect schemes, while introducing and utilizing different categories of analysis, especially the specific sociocultural, ethnic, and religious qualities which have affected the lives of the interviewed.

Regarding the issue of universality, the interview data and analysis suggest that there are areas of faith which can be accounted for within the present faith development framework among those interviewed in this study. Specifically, the stage identities of the interviewees of this study are within the range of adult faith stages, found between and inclusive of stages 3 and 6. In four of the interviews, significant aspect features of numerically higher and lower stages were revealed. Although each of the four respondents could be located within a particular stage identity, significant features of the aspect scheme within other stages were present.

Of the interviewees within the *nisei* group, there are four in stage 3, two in stage 3−4 transition, one in stage 4−5 transition, and another in stage 5. Of those in the *sansei* group, three are in stage 4, and one is in stage 5. These stage indications reflect qualities of faith which can be found in the interviews of this study. However, they do not exhaustively account for the data. There are features within the interviews which disclose other dimensions of the present aspects of faith, in addition to other ideas which are applicable toward the refinement of faith development theory. The following is a composite summary of ten features of the analysis, generalized toward the end of contributing constructively to the assessment of the claim of universality.

The first feature involves the *social aspect of faith*. In the present scheme, the aspect of bounds of social awareness is limited within a definition of faith-construing marked by a personal knowledge of self in relation to others. There is a dimension of social reality which this aspect cannot include by its very definition. Bounds of social awareness is an aspect of faith which accounts for the widening community which creates and sustains meaning for the participant. Centers of social meaning, however, involve more than a mentalistic orientation to the development and sustenance of faith. Focusing on the depth of social relationships and experiences within particular work, family, or religious communities, an aspect broadened around this active dimension of faith would more accurately frame the data of this study. It has been suggested in the data that the social roots of faith are essential qualities of present valuing and imaging. The social aspect of faith then becomes a constitutive dimension of faith-knowing.

The second feature concerns the *assumed rational-critical approach* of stages 4 and 5. Rational reflection plays a significant role in faith-knowing.[5] Built upon a logic of rational certainty and a logic of conviction, Fowler claims that in faith, the latter is more inclusive that the former.[6] Nevertheless, the critical orientation of stages 4 and 5 reflected especially in the social awareness and authority aspects cannot be assumed cross-culturally. Several interviewees in this study have indicated stages 6 features while embracing other stage aspects. With one interviewee, his particular faith orientation appeared to be centered on stage 3 while at the same time characterizing stage 6. The power of rational criticism appears to be a necessary quality of persons moving beyond stage 3, with the exception of stage 6. A focus on the relationship between stages 3 and 6 is necessary to account for some of the data, as well as the less rational approaches of others who also display characteristics of stage 6.

The third feature expands upon the symbolic aspect and involves the *metaphoric-poetic dimensions of faith imagination*. More than a depiction of the role of symbols, the metaphoric-poetic aspect draws upon the natural, artistic, and religious forms which communicate the holy as well as the mundane. These forms were no more centrally reflected than in the artistic vocations of two artists who were interviewed. One was an *ikebana* artist who specialized in flower arrangements, while the other's art was modernistic. The poetic paradigm was also the narrative frame-work upon which some persons spoke of their families, relationships with others, and religious faith. Meaning-making as *homo poeta* thus involves a creative performance derived from a different sort of language competence.

Related to the third, the fourth feature involves the *variety of forms available in the expressions of faith*. Styles, or modes, of communication are a substantive quality of faith-knowing and perception. In the interviews of this study, stories, anecdotes, and art were employed to communicate mindfully and visually the faith essence of individuals. The available social, historical, and religious sensitivities which contribute to the narrative quality of personal faith expressions would appear to be developmental in nature, increasing in depth through the lifespan.

The fifth feature involves the *critical impact of history* upon personal and social faith identities. In this study, the impact of World War II, and the subsequent sociohistorical conditions affecting the lives of Hawaii's Japanese-Americans were significant screens through which decisions of faith were viewed. With several persons, specific observations regarding this issue were raised. Their particular stances regarding the past, involving the reintegration of events and circumstances to their present conditions, is a fruitful aspect of faith worth further exploration.

The data strongly suggest that faith reflects *cultural forms and dispositions*. As the sixth feature of the analysis, the specific contextual ingredients of the Japanese qualities of obligation, pride, face, self-restraint, and humility were framed within the interview responses. Additional dispositions of gratitude, appreciation, and patience were evident in the narratives of most persons interviewed. Related to the issue of the structuring power of content upon faith, these cultural features were found as individual faith qualities as well, binding the social with the personal.

Building upon the social aspect of faith and the relationship of faith to culture, the seventh feature concerns the *varieties of relationships* which bear significance upon the faith of individuals. Those interviewed revealed their faith to be inarticulate without the voices and influence of family members, peers, and mentors. These relationships of intense risk and involvement are qualitative factors in the formation, nurturance, and, perhaps, structuring of central values and images of power. The prevalence and power of the mentor in the faith journey of those interviewed raises the problem of the interpretation of tradition, which is related to the issue of language and the communication of faith. For the participants of this study, a reliance upon English-speaking teachers was necessary, given the lack of readily available materials in translation. The style of faith sustained within this norm is predictably relational and less rational, more subjective than objective.

The eighth feature concerns the issue of what constitutes faith-knowledge. This involves the *relationship of faith-knowing to action*. The data point to the binding link between the knowing and the doing of that which is called faith, suggested in the vocations of most of the interviewed. In these people, there was an intent to activate their intellectual knowledge of their faith through their present commitments. This effort contrasts with the conventionality of work in stage 3. If faith-knowledge is to be perceived as more than creedal content, then a definition of work and of value would need to undergird the faith framework.

The ninth feature involves the *relationship of content to structure*. Related to the critical impact of history and to cultural forms, the data introduce such concepts as *nembutsu* [prayer] and *shinjin* [faith] as religious realities, expressed within the particular sociohistorical context of Hawaii. Both intellectually-creedally and historically-socially, the content of the faith of those interviewed is indeed the substance from which the images, motivations, and actions of faith are drawn upon.

The tenth and final feature involves an assessment of the *faith development research method*. As established earlier, Fowler's semi-clinical, open-ended interview method was employed throughout this project. An interview guide was followed, and each interview lasted approximately two-three hours. The responses were recorded, and transcribed for analysis. These are the basic features of a faith interview process. In assessing this research method, the setting, intersubjectivity, and content of the interview are considered.

In this study, the setting and location of interviews were dependent upon availability and accessibility. Most of the interviews were conducted in the homes of the participants. Speaking in a familiar environment was a desirable feature of the home interviews. But more importantly and unpredictably, the home environment became for many an opportunity for more personal connections with their art, religious symbols, gardens, literature, and pictures. These elements were part of their total faith stories, and without such extensions of their lives, their responses would not have been as poignant and textually rich. Choice of setting is not a trivial feature of the interview setup, but a critical feature of the interview itself.

Second, the intersubjective feature of the interview involves the relationship between the interviewee and interviewer. The particular dynamics of this relationship have significant bearing upon the interview responses, often involving cultural norms. Specifically, in this study, the interviewer was aware of the particular Asian behavior of not looking directly into the eyes of the respondent when asking questions. This would have been regarded as intimidating, rude, and aggressive. Instead, care was taken to look slightly downward, away from direct eye contact. Ironically, this gives the interviewee a sense of privacy and intimacy in sharing, rather than distance. Another cultural norm involves the length of stay in someone's home. This is related to the setting of the interview, noted above. An invitation to someone's home, especially among the older *nisei*, is an act of friendship and trust. One can easily violate the delicate nature of this gesture by over-extending the interview and remaining longer than expected. During this project, the interview at times could have been extended for another hour or two, but the decision to end at the proposed time was honored.

And third, the content of the interview involves the questions and responses of the interview itself. The interview guide includes questions which were found to be powerfully disclosive as well as disappointingly barren. The questions involving the retelling of family histories were especially effective in evoking depth to the present faith understanding of the interviewees. Direct questions regarding their meaning of life were handled quite substantially. Inquiries concerning past experiences and people who have been influential in their lives were answered with detail and precision. Questions concerning the future, sexual stereotypes, and social reform were not as fruitful. The most difficult questions were those which called for responses to the explicitly Christian concepts of God, sin, and even 'religious.' Answers were given comparative treatment with Buddhism, and often revealed extremist notions of Christian ideas. While these responses were revealing in themselves, the intent of these questions did little to allow the structuring of the interviewee's own faith images to occur.

In light of the previous interview observations and this composite summary, the projected claim of universality for faith development theory can be partially substantiated. It is possible to schematize portions of the research data within the present stage and aspect framework and find appropriate stage locations for all twelve project participants. There remain, however, significant and critical areas of faith as revealed in the data, expanded in the observation analysis, and featured in this composite summary, which would need further exploration and examination. The ten issues and concerns raised here speak emphatically of the complexity of the phenomenon called faith. Finally, they should serve as research ideas toward further work in the cross-cultural realm of faith development theory.

Notes
1. James W. Fowler, 'Stages in faith: the structural-developmental approach,' in Thomas C. Hennessy (ed.), *Values and Moral Development*, New York, Paulist Press, 1976, pp. 175–176, 190.
2. James W. Fowler, *Stages of Faith*, San Francisco, Harper and Row, 1981, p. 317.
3. *Ibid.*, p. 315.
4. *Ibid.*, p. 298.
5. James W. Fowler and A. Vergote (eds), *Toward Moral and Religious Maturity*, Morristown, New Jersey, Silver Burdett, 1980, p. 63.
6. *Ibid.*, pp. 61–62.

5.5 Personal religious belief development: the 'articulate authoritarian' type

Susan Kwilecki

Introduction

Religious sensibility, like muscular coordination or visual acuity, comes in varying degrees of strength and sophistication. Like Mark Spitz in a swimming pool or Cezanne at a canvas, some individuals, in responding to the sacred, exhibit extraordinary vigor and refinement. In what forms and for what reasons does religion become motivating and complex in a personality? Focusing on one type of personal spiritual development, this paper describes the growth, in some lives, of clear, elaborate, and functional religious beliefs. It executes a scientific approach I proposed elsewhere (Kwilecki, 1988), the essential details of which I now summarize.

Some theories of religious development, such as James Fowler's (1981) 'stages of faith', purport to represent the spiritual paths of people everywhere in a single stage sequence. Criticizing these for failing to portray the variety and cultural relativity of individual religious striving, I suggest a pluralistic, culturally sensitive approach. I define 'religious development' as the unfolding in a life of a sensibility to divine reality, an awareness of a sacred dimension, that becomes increasingly (a) complex or differentiated; (b) independently directive or functional; (c) integrated in its parts, coherent; and/or (d) defined, clear, unambiguous.

In summary, developed religion functions versatilely and pervasively in a life, motivating, chiding, explaining, and comforting across areas of concern. The forms of its expression are correspondingly nuanced, i.e. tailored to the landscape of profane reality. An undeveloped sense of the sacred, by contrast, is limited in range and subtlety. My conception of development is broad enough to accommodate the various ways humans relate to the divine (ritually, experientially, ethically, and intellectually) and the assorted spiritual ideals traditions teach.

So defined, personal religious development occurs through a generative 'fit', a creative intersection, between particular collective religious forms, on the one hand, and specific personal aptitudes and susceptibilities, on the other. It is a slow, highly complicated, and variable process that, in any life, reflects the interaction of countless cultural and individual factors, sequenced and weighted in unique ways. Theoretical formulations should, accordingly, be

221

limited in scope only to some lives in some cultures. We might, I have suggested, seek developmental patterns consisting of an outcome – a recurring form of cultivated spirituality – and one or two personal and/or collective conditions significant, in some instances, to its evolution.

These patterns may be discovered through biographical case studies organized around a global dimension of religious behaviour (ritual, ethics, experience, belief). Here I investigate development in the belief dimension: why some individuals have an unusually strong and intricate *conceptual* grasp of the sacred. In the next section, I review data from two counties in Georgia and describe an 'articulate authoritarian' style of complex and functional belief.

Rural protestant thinkers: articulate authoritarians

Intermittently for over a decade, I have collected religious testimonies and biographies of men and women in two adjacent counties in the south-west corner of Georgia, referred to here as Bellamy and Dover.[1] Together these counties cover around 1100 square miles and host a population of about 46,000. Despite dramatic social and economic changes in recent decades, traditional rural values survive, with religion figuring prominently in both personal and community life. I focus here on the Protestant groups to which the majority belong, congregations whose doctrinal stances range from liberal (Episcopal, United Methodist, African Methodist Episcopal, African Baptist) to moderately conservative (Southern Baptist, Missionary Baptist, Presbyterian, U.S.) to highly orthodox and sectarian (Mormons, Jehovah's Witnesses, Presbyterian Church in America, various Bible and Pentecostal fellowships).

All traditions contain intellectual expressions of some sort – myths, proverbs, doctrines, creeds, systematic theologies, etc. (Wach, 1958, pp. 89–96). The intellectual or belief dimension of religion taps the human capacities to use language to conceptualize from experience, and reason to draw conclusions about reality. While these conceptual-verbal abilities are species-wide, in rural Georgia and elsewhere, some churches and some individuals are more disposed than others to exploit them spiritually.

In gauging belief development in my subjects (the extent to which an individual used cognitive powers to approach the divine), I looked for religious intellectual *sensitivity* and *achievement*. The former I assessed in the degree to which an individual took seriously 'ultimate questions'; reacted to differences in doctrinal perspectives; spent time reading about and discussing spiritual topics; and considered it important to communicate veridical propositions about the sacred. Reflecting the aforementioned developmental criteria, I recognized religious-intellectual accomplishment (as opposed to mere interest or sensitivity) in the expression of personal beliefs that were relatively complex, coherent, clear, and functional in life.

In the two counties, which people, by these standards, are the most developed or cultivated (i.e. intellectually sensitive and accomplished) believers? Interviews with around 150 black and white church members yielded a decisive answer: the most cultivated believers are the fundamentalists. Almost without exception, the subjects most sensitive to religious-intellectual issues and most capable of articulating coherent and complex religious ideas, regarded the bible as inerrant, as absolutely and exclusively authoritative. From scripture, they claimed to know unequivocal religious truths.

This finding conflicts with studies of belief that implicitly or explicitly portray dogmatic conviction as unintelligent and immature. For example, in Fowler's (1981) developmental sequence, which essentially traces the evolution of personal belief, recognition of the truth in all faiths marks the final stages and defensive loyalty to one's own confession, the earlier ones. Likewise, in the committed/consensual typology of religious-cognitive styles, the committed believer – whose beliefs are implicitly the more sophisticated, being described as complex, clear, and abstract – holds an open, flexible attitude towards other faiths. By contrast, the consensual – whose convictions are said to be literalistic, undifferentiated, and vague, suggesting unreflectiveness – tends to restrict religious diversity and reject alien beliefs (Allen and Spilka, 1967). 'The religion of maturity', wrote Allport (1950, pp. 78, 83), 'makes the affirmation "God is", but only the religion of immaturity will insist, "God is precisely what I say He is"'. 'Mature' believers act on probabilities, not certainties and, with the agnostic, 'may concede that the nature of Being cannot be known'.

My data suggest that this association of doubt and tolerance with theological sophistication, and of dogmatism with religious unthoughtfulness, is too simplistic. Among my subjects, uncertainty and tolerance usually coincided with theological indifference, with an essentially anti-intellectual orientation to the divine. Likewise, some individuals stated beliefs that, while highly dogmatic, were also carefully reasoned, complicated, coherent, clear, and functional. That the most thoughtful and articulate subjects belonged to fundamentalist churches suggests that the provision of absolute spiritual authority can be a stimulant rather than an obstacle to religious thinking.

The highly uncultivated status of belief among members of local liberal churches supports this hypothesis. Liberal denominations, such as the United Methodist and African Methodist Episcopal, have increasingly abdicated the task of promulgating religious truth, defining Christian piety instead in terms of responsible social conduct and personal fulfillment. For example, the minister of the First United Methodist Church in Dover County and his assistant told me, in essence, that members might believe what they liked as long as they felt complete and drawn to others in a loving manner. Subjects from this congregation either (a) held relatively intricate and clear biblical beliefs acquired as members of more conservative churches; (b) were unable to formulate clear, coherent beliefs, considered theology a divisive waste of time, and were tolerant of virtually any doctrinal stance; or (c) were sensitive to religious-intellectual problems but unable to address them effectively.

The second position – theological disinterest – was typical. Patsy, an introspective high-school science teacher, illustrates the last category. She seemed to take seriously the religious issues I raised during the interview and was dismayed at her own theological stumbling. Belief in the bible was essential for salvation, she claimed – for her at least. In a subsequent discussion of the bible, however, she said it was a human creation fraught with errors; other than the Golden Rule, she could recall little it taught. Likewise, Anne, a school teacher and lifetime member of a Dover Country AME Church, affirmed and then denied one doctrine after another. 'So many people have different ideas about the bible and everything else', she explained, 'you're left out on a limb sometimes because you don't know exactly what to say about things'. While we may sympathize, we should not mistake this doubt and confusion for belief. Indeed, it represents an opposite condition – an inability to grasp the divine conceptually. Without theological encouragement or guidance, liberals tended to neglect or fail in religious-intellectual endeavors.

By contrast, fundamentalist churches stimulated religious thinking in several ways. First, by clearly identifying a source of revelation, they 'primed the pump' of religious conceptualization, i.e. they provided a starting point from or against which personal beliefs might be generated. Second, fundamentalist churches taught that humans meet the divine through a set of writings – an intrinsically conceptual-verbal liaison. Further, they claimed that correct belief was required for salvation; how one conceptualized the sacred had eternal consequences. Certainly not every fundamentalist I interviewed had developed beliefs; when asked what their convictions were, many merely repeated biblical quotations in a disjointed, uncomprehending way, and were no more inclined than liberals to ponder religious questions. Accepting biblical authority encouraged, but did not guarantee, personal belief development.

Among my subjects, then, the most cultivated believers, the individuals who most extensively used their intellects in approaching the divine, were those who *thoughtfully but absolutely* relied on the bible for spiritual direction. Their beliefs were complex, clear, coherent, functional *and* dogmatic. These subjects, I think, represent a more general type I call the 'articulate authoritarian'.

In some lives, I am suggesting, belief development occurs through the coincidence of, on the one hand, the acceptance of an absolute spiritual authority, and, on the other, analytic tendencies and skills. Religious sensibility is expressed in beliefs that are dogmatic and inflexibly grounded in some particular revelation, but that nevertheless exhibit the conceptual refinement characteristic of sustained intellectual endeavor.

Let me discuss one at a time the authoritarian and analytical elements that together define the type. By 'acceptance of an absolute religious authority' I mean a deliberate, self-conscious recognition that some particular thing – a specific text, person, institution (or some combination of these) – constitutes a final, unequivocal, exclusive, comprehensive source of information about the divine. As exemplars of the type illustrate, believers may defend and apply a revelation thus considered in intellectually intricate ways without compromising their loyalty to it. Indeed, as we will see, incontrovertible devotion may set certain intellectual tasks.

Why some people submit to authority absolutely has been extensively investigated. The religious type I have in mind calls for the diversified understanding of authoritarian tendencies suggested by some research. Fromm (1941), Adorno *et al.* (1950), and other researchers identified an 'authoritarian' personality type characterized by the tendency to submit completely and without question to a powerful controlling figure or force. Authoritarians might be recognized by their sweeping and rigid prejudices, their classification of others as 'good' or 'bad' on the basis of an authorized set of rules. Unresolved conflicts with parents caused authoritarians to feel threatened by ambiguous, unstructured situations, and recognizing an immutable, appointed order in the world eased their anxieties.

Refining these concepts, Rokeach (1960) distinguished between 'open' and 'closed' belief systems. All belief systems, he argued, answer two needs: the cognitive need 'to know and to understand and the need to ward off threatening aspects of reality' (p. 67). Insofar as the first need prevailed, information from the outside world could be objectively processed, resulting in an open belief system – one with finely differentiated disbeliefs and well-integrated beliefs, that assumes the world is friendly and authority not absolute. To the extent that defensive needs reigned, cognitive discrimination was blocked, resulting in a closed system – one in which disbeliefs were poorly distinguished, beliefs conceptually isolated, and the world considered unfriendly and authority absolute.

This research informed many studies of religious belief. Citing nearly a dozen sources, Dittes (1969, p. 639) summarizes: 'From various kinds of data, a generally consistent correlation has been reported between orthodox religious commitment and a relatively defensive, constricted personality. . . . The label authoritarianism has become the most popular term to describe these characteristics.'

Some scholars (e.g. Stewart and Hoult, 1959; Photiadis and Schweiker, 1970; Ethridge and Feagin, 1979), however, have demonstrated the complex and variable nature of authoritarianism – spiritual and otherwise – and its psychological sources. Monaghan (1967) discovered three types of 'true-believers' in a midwestern fundamentalist church: authority-seekers, comfort-seekers, and social participators. Likewise, Ammerman (1987, pp. 190–93) noted the diversity of needs and conflicts fundamentalism resolved for members of a northeastern congregation. Many of her subjects, she speculates (p. 218), would probably score high on measures of authoritarianism. However, and this is pertinent here, for those who have always belonged to a fundamentalist church, absolute submission to scripture 'is at least as much a cultural trait as a personal one'.

In the lives of two of the rural fundamentalists we will consider, anxiety of different sorts conditioned the acceptance of scriptural authority. Authoritarian faith in a third reflects a strict fundamentalist upbringing; in the fourth, an idiosyncratic combination of circumstances we might label 'social opportunism'. In addition to their psychological diversity, I want to underscore that none of these authoritarian dynamics – not even those related to anxiety – blocked cognitive activity. Each subject testified that accepting and applying biblical authority entailed intellectual exercise, and the relative complexity and coherence of their beliefs support this. The authoritarian faith I have in mind, then, springs from a variety of personal factors, including, but not limited to, anxiety. As a cognitive system, it occupies a middle ground between Rokeach's closed and open types, resembling the first in its attitude toward authority, but the second in its form, i.e. in its degree of conceptual differentiation and integration.

Like the authoritarian tendency, the analytic component of the type should be construed pluralistically. Psychologists have broadly identified two basic cognitive styles: active, discriminating, and analytical, as opposed to passive, global, and uncritical (Wallach, 1962). Exemplars of articulate authoritarianism, indeed of belief development of any type, would exhibit the former. However, at the higher level of personality organization visible in the case studies, the analytic tendencies of the subjects appear in conjunction with a range of other traits and experiences, such as introversion or training in accounting.

Culture, of course, conditions the expression of individual cognitive aptitude. Attaching little importance to cerebral achievement, rural Southern society does not expose or invite the average citizen to sustained scholarly endeavor. The analytically inclined must make do with the intellectual opportunities and forms that are available, one of which, we shall see, is fundamentalism. A comprehensive treatment of belief must be sensitive to different societies' appraisals of intellectualism, and the various forms (mythical, juristic, philo-sophical, etc.) and tasks (e.g. defensive, practical, speculative) of religious thinking across cultures.

Thus, despite statistical evidence (Dittes, 1969, p. 637) that intel-ligence and conservative religious belief are negatively correlated, in some lives spiritual authoritarianism coincides with analytical ability. This combination, I am suggesting, augurs well for personal belief development, the first trait providing a basis and motivation for religious reflection, and the second an aptitude for it. Four of the most cultivated believers in my sample of lay persons will illustrate the type.

Cases

Emma

Emma Mitchell (1913−) is an elderly black Jehovah's Witness. Members of the Watchtower Society are required to preach door-to-door complicated doctrines derived from long chains of scriptural references and historical facts. The Society's pronouncements are rationally presented and justified, but are treated as revelations and not subject to debate.

Virtually everything I observed about Emma reflected the Wit-nesses' serious, self-controlled, bourgeois style. At the edge of a Bellamy County town called Stonewall, in a rundown black neighborhood, she occupies an island of respectability − a small, freshly-painted white house on a patch of lawn neatly outlined with flower-beds. Small-boned and plump, Emma speaks and moves cautiously. From dawn to dusk, she busies herself with Bible reading, house and yard work, and proselytizing, she said. Occasionally she watches television, but only educational shows like *Nova* or *Phil Donahue*. The soul of Watchtower pedantry, she wielded the sect's complex doctrines with sincerity and finesse.

Emma was the only child of the upwardly-mobile Ben and Vera Dennard. A farmhand in a neighboring county, Ben taught himself carpentry and moved his family, when Emma was around 7, to Tuscalossa, then to Cleveland, where major construction projects provided work. In 1925, the Dennards settled permanently in Stonewall. Emma led a sequestered childhood. Due to a recurring illness, her parents educated her at home until she was 9, instilling habits that would boost her into the middle class: instinctual and emotional restraint, an aversion to idleness and levity, a respect for learning.

She joined a classroom first in Cleveland where, Emma says, she received an education far superior to that of her peers back in Georgia. Later, in Bellamy County schools, she was several grades ahead of even the best students, which was socially a disadvantage. Adolescent pain resurfaced as Emma told how 'the students felt that I thought I was superior because I would answer questions better and everything.... Of course, it made me want to feel, you know, a little, um, depressed because of that, you see. But finally I outlived it ... I had a better education than most of them.'

Other students teased her, she said, not only because she was 'always kind of keen on the brains', but because she was plump and spoke with a slight Northern accent. Only after several years back in the South did she 'get down to earth' and talk like the locals. Never did she stoop to say '"dis"' or '"dat"'. To make matters worse, her parents forbade her to go to the movies or 'walk the road' on Sunday afternoons with the other girls, insisting instead that she entertain herself productively, with reading, cooking, or needlepoint. Describing herself as 'kind of a loner', Emma says she prefers religious 'study and research' to company. 'Not that I think I'm better than people', she said, tipping her hand, 'but I never have been a very big visitor.'

The Dennards belonged to an AME church in Stonewall, but were not very devout. Emma received no religious instruction at home, and in Cleveland the family did not attend church at all. To meet the membership requirements of her parents' church in Stonewall, the adolescent Emma had to connive with cousins in the composition of a fictitious conversion testimony!

In 1931, Emma graduated class valedictorian. Too poor for college, she wed Fred Mitchell, an illiterate farmhand; four children were born in rapid succession. They survived the Depression on cast-off food and clothing from Mrs Dennard's white employers. Without money for Sunday clothes or congregational dues, Emma was placed on the 'dead' list at the AME church. For years, Emma said, she was too preoccupied with survival to think about religion. Still, she managed to read magazines such as *Time* and *Post* discarded by her mother's employers. Likewise, a white woman for whom Emma worked as a maid recalled her surprise when Emma borrowed and read a book on nutrition.

By 1950, Emma and Fred had saved enough to purchase a lot and build their current home. In the years following, Emma advanced from maid to hotel cook to insurance collector. A midlife quest for religious truth began when, in 1951, under peer pressure, Fred decided to join the Baptist church in their new neighbourhood. For the sake of family unity, Emma moved her letter. Familiar tensions arose as she joined first the usher board and then the choir in a futile effort to belong. 'I didn't like the way they operated', Emma said, criticizing the members' competitiveness over food, clothes, and extramarital lovers. Bad feelings festered at potluck suppers when Emma refused to eat with the other women; she had had her fill, she explained, of free hotel food before she arrived – much better food, she added, than was brought to the church.

Although socially a disaster, renewed church activity piqued Emma's curiosity about religion. At midlife, she explained, many people become 'religious-minded' and 'want to look in on their lives in some way'. Thus she 'put in to study and learn a little bit about [God]'. Before long she discovered Herbert W. Armstrong, radio prophet of the Worldwide Church of God. Like the Witnesses, Armstrong foretells the coming of a world theocracy, reasoning from scripture and world events 'with an urbane professionalism that moves all but the well-informed and the very sophisticated' (Morris, 1973, p. 321). 'He has a college', Emma told me enthusiastically. 'He's educated; he's very intelligent.'

In particular, she appreciated Armstrong's clear definition of the Kingdom of God (as a world theocracy), a concept she had not previously understood. Asked its meaning, Baptists gave vague, contradictory answers. She passed the Ambassador College Bible Correspondence Course with flying colors, and her commitment grew until 1956, when she heard Armstrong say that Negroes were unintelligent. This, Emma noted, directly contradicted Genesis, which said that all humans descended from Adam and Eve and hence were equal. If Armstrong could err on such an obvious point, was he reliable in general?

Fortunately, just at that time, Witnesses began to drop by. They not only confirmed her position on race, but, with an exegetical sophistication she admired taught her to distinguish 'what was literal in the bible, what was symbolic, and what was figurative'. Working carefully through the scriptural references outlined in Watchtower publications, Emma discovered new religious facts, e.g. that Jesus and Jehovah were not the same person. She liked the way Witnesses answered her questions 'so clear, and then used the scripture so clear', without contradicting each other. In 1958, after a year's bible study, she joined the small group of black Witnesses in Bellamy County that, thanks to her efforts, has prospered.

Although untutored, Emma is a thinker; against considerable cultural discouragement, she persistently reads and analyzes. Her religious biography is the story of an upwardly mobile black introvert making the best of things in rural Southern society. Introversion, according to Jung (1971), is the tendency to focus psychic energy and attention on inner, mental realities, more than the external, empirical world. It entails conceptual or imaginative acuities and awkwardness in the realm of real people and affairs – both of which Emma exhibited. Grooming her for a higher station, her parents furthered her inward orientation, intellectualism, and social alienation.

In her midlife religious quest, Emma immediately embraced Armstrong's studious, pompous approach to the sacred, filtering in by radio from the outside world. Equally pedantic and bourgeois, the Witnesses additionally offered fellowship with nearby thinking, self-restrained blacks. As a lower-class, rural black woman, Emma has a social-psychological profile repeatedly correlated with authoritarianism (Stewart and Hoult, 1959). Certainly the absolutism of these sects may have appealed to her, but I believe that their middle-class, rational style was the more important attraction.

In this case, the evolution of articulate authoritarianism pivoted on a cultural restriction of intellectual and social opportunities. During Emma's prime, for poor blacks in the rural South, occasions for mental exercise and middle-class affiliation were limited virtually to the rational-authoritarian sects she joined. Had there been secular outlets for her ambitions and talents, it seems likely, given her lengthy period of religious indifference, that Emma would have taken them. A parallel dynamic appears in the life of another highly articulate, local black Jehovah's Witness. Born not only poor but illegitimate, by joining the army this man transcended origins that profoundly shamed him. After earning a college degree, he came home to teach high school science. For him, as for Emma, the Witnesses uniquely provided a respectable, intellectual approach to religion that boosted his sense of enlightened superiority to the black mainstream.

Henry

Henry Pitman (1921–) is a member of the Church of Christ in Bellamy County. The conservative wing of the 19th century Christian movement, the Churches of Christ uphold the old slogan: 'Where the scriptures speak, we speak; where the scriptures are silent, we are silent'. Henry, a white, 62-year-old, retired USDA auditor, spent his days pursuing family business interests and VFW and church activities. His ungentle determination to inform Baptists, especially his mother, of 'true' religion contributed to his local reputation as a hothead. During an interview, I glimpsed Henry's intemperate side as, talking on the telephone within my hearing, he reacted explosively to a business problem. Henry himself told me that, although a founder of his congregation, he is not an elder because he lacks the biblically required patience.

An extreme striving for rationality matches this combustibility – a struggle for control that sets the stage for Henry's articulate authoritarianism. His religion was of the head, not the heart, he told me. Trained as an auditor, he saw things 'from the standpoint of facts, not', he said contemptuously, 'from the standpoint of dreams'. Unverifiable or blind faith was 'just what it says it is – blind'. While he argued with precise logic, Henry's voice and gestures were tense with emotion, often aggressive.

His parents were local farmers, devout Baptists and diligent

bible readers. Henry accepted the family faith, including a profound respect for scripture. An outstanding student in math and
accounting, he earned a scholarship to a business college in north
Georgia, but completed only a year before being drafted in 1942.
After the war, Henry finished school in Kentucky and became
an auditor for businesses in the south-east and, eventually, the
government. In the early 1960s, he moved his family back to
Bellamy County.

The religious quest that ended in articulate authoritarianism began
when Henry, as a serviceman, heard preachers from different
denominations and detected a troubling doctrinal inconsistency.
'I've always said, you tell me a black truck went by, someone
else tells me a blue one, I know one of you lied, ignorantly or
otherwise', he explained. 'I've always been a fundamentalist, if
that's a fundamentalist. I believe there's only one truth. Well,
in religion, I knew there couldn't be two truths, three or four.
So I began to search.' Stationed in New Guinea with little to do
but read, he purchased a Bible at the PX in order to arbitrate
with scripture controversies over how one is saved, the meaning
of baptism, and other issues.

Citing an interview he saw on television with Wernher von Braun,
Henry justified his reliance on scripture for religious truth. Centuries
ahead of science, he said, the bible had correctly explained rainfall,
given sound nutritional advice, anticipated theories of microbiology
and astronomy. Except for divine inspiration, how could the scientific accuracy of the bible be explained? He was willing to consider
other religions only 'if they've got something that is proven to be
accurate'. With a limited graps of world religions, Henry dismissed
Islam and Buddhism as the patently foolish reverence of men (their
founders) known to be dead. Yet, suspecting there might be more
to these faiths than that, he said he wanted to 'sit down and talk'
over with me the foreign religions I had studied. In the meantime,
he concluded that if God was not revealed in the bible, there was
nowhere else to turn.

Henry's exposure to Christian diversity, then, catalyzed a precision-
demanding fundamentalism. Bible in hand, he 'corner[ed]' various
chaplains, censuring their departures from scripture. Home from
the war, he doggedly pursued the one true church mentioned in
Ephesians 4, a church whose teachings exactly conformed to the
bible. Marriage to a woman who belonged to the Church of Christ
occasioned inspection of that denomination. Immediately impressed
by the minister's use of scripture to support every point in the
sermon, Henry took notes and later verified the biblical references.
By 1947, he had, Henry said, 'studied myself straight into the
Church of Christ'. Thus, he obtained correct views on salvation, the
sacraments, Judgment Day, etc., that he later preached door-to-door
in an effort to save the lost of Bellamy County.

More than the other three subjects, Henry aggressively insisted on the exclusive correctness of his views – contrary positions were absolutely and dangerously wrong. This dogmatism was proportionate to Henry's desire for salvation, which he believed required uncompromising obedience. This life, he explained, was 'to prepare yourself [for] where you're going to live for eternity'; only a fool would not be afraid of ending up in hell. Religion, he said, plunging eagerly into a syllogism, was 'either man-made or God-made'. Either the bible revealed God's will or it did not; if it did (as he had earlier established), it had to be obeyed absolutely. He would happily immerse in vinegar, Henry jested, if scripture so dictated! Thus, when he converted it was as if, he offered the analogy, someone who had always wanted to play golf suddenly learned how. He had always wanted to please God but had to discover through scripture exactly what to do.

Henry's articulate authoritarianism evolved from a disturbed reaction to religious pluralism. Concern for his soul made it unsettling, for conscious and rational reasons, to hear divergent prescriptions for salvation. This religious anxiety, however, may have had unconscious sources as well. The lifelong requirement of one and only one truth Henry mentioned as his 'fundamentalism', corresponds to what psychologists label an intolerance of ambiguity – the tendencies to simplify conflicting or ambiguous data in absolute beliefs, to reach judgments prematurely or impulsively. An intolerance of ambiguity has been linked with threatened self-esteem (Dittes, 1959) and with the larger authoritarian syndrome (Frenkel-Brunswik, 1954).

The story of his driven search for religious truth, and his aggressive behaviour in the interviews, suggest that Henry's beliefs harness powerful irrational impulses of some sort. To identify these precisely would require data I do not have. Speculating, however, we may note his conformity, in many respects, to the authoritarian profile. Spontaneously he discoursed on female inferiority, admitted a racial prejudice he recognized as unchristian, and, as said, stated an intolerance for ambiguity. His way of arguing in syllogisms, with 'either-or' dichotomies, his denial, contrary to appearances, of emotional motivations, and his hostility towards his mother, also suit the type. While many of his authoritarian views are cultural conventions, Henry's highly charged delivery suggests they function defensively for him.

Of course, beliefs of all kinds serve emotional ends, but depending on the rest of the personality, I want to argue, this need not prevent intellectual refinement. In Henry's case, the emotional function of beliefs and their intellectual cogency seem to be reciprocal. For him, it seems to be precisely the clarity, coherence, and logicalness of beliefs that empower them to function defensively. While emotionally turbulent, his response to conflicting religious teachings also entailed several years of careful reflection. In this case, where the believer was logical as well as anxious, an irrational need for structure precipitated authoritarian religious thinking – specifically, an analytic endeavour to discover the unequivocal requirements of salvation. In the next case, we see an analogous pattern.

Mike

The youngest of the four subjects, and, unlike the others, not a native of the area, Mike Barnes (1953–) exuded neo-evangelical poise. Sporting a fashionable haircut and moustache, the white 34 year old confessed fundamentalist faith with the idiom, intonation, and gestures of a network news correspondent. Mike, his wife, Judy, and their three small children live in a new residential section of Felthurst, Dover's county seat. Mike conducts forestry research for a large paper company with local pine reserves. He spoke with the precision and dispassion of a scientist, carefully choosing every word. This was not only in the interest of accuracy, I sensed, but in order to shield from me his emotional, private self.

Mike grew up outside the South, mainly in St Louis. Although not zealous Christians, his parents took their children to church regularly. During high school, Mike became extremely active in a Presbyterian congregation, and, at the time, considered himself an informed, loyal believer. President of his youth group during his senior year, one Sunday when the teens had charge of the worship service, Mike acted as pastor and preached a sermon from a verse of scripture.

The following summer, just before he began college at the University of Missouri, a friend pointed out to Mike how prophecies in the Old Testament had come true in the life of Christ and how New Testament prophecies, in turn, were being fulfilled today. For the first time, said Mike, it occurred to him that scripture might be relevant to life. Then, in September, at the end of a dorm-floor meeting – held, ironically to Mike, to plan a beer-party – announcement was made of a bible study to be led by a campus evangelical organization. Already curious about scripture, Mike attended. He learned that Jesus was the expiation for human sin, and being Christian meant obeying, as Christ had, the will of God.

Of course, he had heard this before as a child in confirmation class. Off at school, however, responsible for himself, the gospel confronted him as a personal choice. The more he studied, said Mike, 'the more turmoil there was inside me'. The 'gospel of grace' had been presented him, and God seemed to be calling continually, '"Will you come? ... Will you come to me through my Son?"' It was a proposition to which he had to respond one way or the other, Mike explained, either 'flatly deny it' or agree, 'yes this is true. The bible is revealing something about Jesus Christ that I need to live by and regard as an authority in my life.'

The choice Mike faced seems to have been between strict Christian morality and mild hedonism, liberal beer-drinking and sexuality. He was not affected by the contemporary youth trend of experimentation in Asian faiths – although he said he did try unsuccessfully to appreciate *Siddhartha*. Groups like the Krishnas were 'too way out', said Judy, to have attracted Mike. Thus from September to December he wrestled with the biblical deity. At last, under the strain of final exams, he gave in, promising to take the bible as 'words of life that should guide what I should do, who I should be, what I should say'.

Obeying scripture in life, Mike said, entails a thought process that is intuitive as well as rational. He prays, he explained, vocalizing his need for guidance, and 'the words [God] has written in the pages of scripture [are] what I respond to as his words back to me'. After receiving the Holy Spirit in conversion, Mike could immediately discern commandments throughout the bible relevant to his daily life. Scripture told him first that he had to end a love affair. Next, observing that the lyrics to rock music stimulated unholy thoughts, and garnering the bible's policy on 'possessions displeasing to God', he destroyed his large and valuable album collection.

Through a campus religious group, Mike met Judy and their common fundamentalist faith led to marriage. In 1978, after two years of graduate study in industrial forest research, Mike took his current job and moved to Dover County, where, despite location in the bible belt, he 'found no spiritual life'. The Yankee couple discovered that while the bible was read in some churches, it was rarely applied. The door-to-door evangelism he and Judy later undertook revealed, Mike estimated, that some 95% of the citizens of Felthurst were ignorant of the scriptural doctrine of salvation!

Eventually the Barneses settled in a mainline congregation they planned to evangelize. With others of like mind, they began a bible study that grew into Trinity, a Presbyterian Church in America congregation. Trinity has attracted dissatisfied conservatives, some quite wealthy, from many local churches. Teaching the adult Sunday School class, Mike reviews scriptural commandments relative to a variety of everyday concerns and obligations, such as child-rearing or charity. 'Anything you're going to touch in life', he said, 'there's probably some reference or comment [in the bible] of what God thinks about this, what others have attempted to do, and whether they've succeeded or failed.' By carefully noting the circumstances, actions, and fates of biblical characters who interacted with God, he explained, one could learn God's nature and behave accordingly – a theological method both practical and systematic.

Some doctrines, he said, were crucial to salvation and

unequivocally expressed in scripture, e.g. that redemption occurred exclusively through Christ's sacrificial death. However, Mike had pieced together enough texts to know that to many questions, scripture gave ambivalent answers, e.g. on whether or not to drink alcohol, or if charismatic gifts were genuine. The truth, he ventured, lies at some 'balance point' in between extremes, and one must rely on the guidance of fellow believers and the Holy Spirit. I observed him lead a Sunday School discussion in which he presented, without reconciling or selecting one, conflicting scriptural injunctions relative to charity.

While not as self-revealing as I would have liked, Mike's testimony does shed light on the evolution of our type. The developmental dynamic here resembles that in Henry's case: articulate authoritarianism emerges from an uneasy response to ideological or religious pluralism. In Mike's case, the intolerance of ambiguity seems to have been situational rather than characteristic. He expressed none of the prejudices Henry did and, as said, was content with undecidedness on a number of religious issues. Making independent career and moral decisions for the first time, finding one's place on a large university campus, would generate some anxiety in most people. For reasons unclear from my data, this typical youthful search for identity disturbed Mike enough to call for an absolute and somewhat hurried resolution.

He apparently experimented only briefly before the Christian training of his high-school years became a source of censure, on the one hand, and of potential security, certain identity, on the other. His troubled reaction to the gospel, the pressure to respond yes or no, suggests both guilt and agonized unsureness. Taken for armor in the struggle towards adulthood, adolescent Christian identity became iron-clad. While relieving an emotional crisis, however, here again, authoritarian faith did not extinguish the intellect: rather, it set certain tasks for it, viz., the on-going process of synthesis and interpretation required for living by a religious text. A final case illustrates the evolution of our type from early socialization into an authoritarian faith.

Betty

A white woman in her early fifties, Betty Frazer (1936–) was raised a Baptist fundamentalist. With the quiet confidence of a lifetime believer, she enumerated unequivocal truths – unshakeable convictions that, in recent years, have led her into politics. At the same time, as an experienced voteseeker, she made an obvious effort to present her views in a congenial, noncoercive manner. Proud of her public venturesomeness, the petite redhead repeatedly emphasized her capacity for independent judgment and action. That her pastor had recommended her for the interview pleased but did not surprise her. Betty lives with her mother and her husband, a retired air-force pilot, in her family home in an old residential section of Felthurst.

Her parents moved to Felthurst from nearby when Betty was 9. She did well in school and as a senior was chosen president of an academic honor society. After graduation, she briefly tried college but gave it up to marry. Even without formal schooling, Betty stressed, she has kept her mind alive by constant reading. 'I read all the time. I love to read!' she said, gesturing at the stacks of books displaced in the remodeling of their house. During the interview she cited from and recommended a number of books on spiritual topics.

Four children were born as the Frazers moved from one air base to another, living in Texas, Massachusetts, California, Alaska, and, finally, Florida. In 1986, Betty and her husband, retired by then, returned to Felthurst to stay. Coming home has meant renewed membership in the independent Baptist congregation Betty loved as a girl. On both maternal and paternal sides, Betty descends from prominent rural Baptists. Her mother was a Missionary Baptist, her father a Primitive – each stubbornly loyal to the views of salvation, etc., that distinguish these denominations. In Felthurst, the family affiliated with Evangel Baptist, an independent fundamentalist congregation pastored at that time by the colourful, charismatic Dr Samuel Melton.

Still under Dr Melton during my own youth in Dover County, Evangel Baptist had a reputation for religious excess and moral severity; my classmates who belonged wore unfashionable clothes and were forbidden certain entertainments. Dr Melton, now dead, drove an automobile with 'Sin-fighter' painted on the side, and in daily radio broadcasts, abandoned himself to frenzied castigations of the wicked. Ideologically unchanged, today Evangel Baptist sustains a flourishing Christian academy and an up-to-date recreational facility.

At about the age of 13, Betty answered Dr Melton's altar call. Her religious ideas have been essentially the same all her life, she said, listing as major items of faith: belief in the Trinity, in salvation by grace, in baptism as an act of obedience following salvation, in the rapture, and in the bible as God's revelation. 'Not that it contains it', she clarified the last tenet, 'but that *it is* God's revealed Word'. 'My whole philosophy of life is based on scripture', she stressed. Arguments against scriptural authority have never moved her. She studied the theory of evolution in school, e.g. but since 'they were teaching something that I knew inside was wrong', she recalled, 'I just rejected it'.

For Betty it was not the personal search for religious absolutes, but the public promotion of them, that occasioned vigorous reflection.

Lifetime fundamentalist beliefs grew more complex and functional as, in her middle years, she aggressively asserted them against the tide of liberalism sweeping the country. Betty refers to herself as a 'reluctant leader': she dislikes the pressures of leadership but will serve for a cause. She made her first foray into public politics as a Republican party official, but was unable to tow the party line. 'I guess I was born independent', she explained, 'I have an independent streak in me. You don't tell me what to believe. I have to find it myself' − a self-assessment Betty's mother cited incidents to support. Refusing to champion Republican candidates indiscriminately, Betty retired from public life until the Equal Rights Amendment called her back.

Intuitively, Betty said, she knew ERA was wrong. Soon she found herself working full-time for Women for Responsible Legislation, an evangelical activist group, and debating with feminists on television. Eventually, she would chair Florida's WRL federation. For most of her life, said Betty, she had simply accepted her beliefs; entering public debate, however, she was expected to prove them. 'Through this battle [against ERA], I have grown stronger in my beliefs. I won't try to ram my beliefs down you, but I can tell you why I believe the way I do − and it all goes back to scripture.' From biblical texts justifying masculine authority, Betty reasoned more broadly on women's issues. Feminism, she said, was a spurious solution to a real problem − the abuse some women suffered from men. In both evangelical and feminist camps were women psychologically conditioned to be 'doormats'. This was hardly scriptural and these individuals needed help − not ERA but self-acceptance. 'You have to feel comfortable with yourself', she continued. 'And I do. I know myself and I'm comfortable with that.'

After the defeat of ERA, Betty ran unsuccessfully for a seat in the Florida House of Representatives. She entered the race, she said, because she felt government would improve if administered by people like herself who voted their convictions and could not be bought. Her civic goals are more conservative than Christian, e.g. abolishing social security. Religion inspires some of her current political efforts, such as her opposition to humanistic text-books; while other projects, such as her Eagle Forum leadership, serve secular conservative causes. As a politician, Betty has had to reconcile herself to American religious diversity and translate her principles from King James rhetoric into the pop-psychological vernacular. Public life, she said, had taught her to 'agree to disagree' with other Christians about theology, and even to communicate with feminists.

None of this, however, compromised her own loyalty to scripture. Betty insisted, e.g. that belief in the atoning power of Christ's bloodshed was absolutely the only way anyone could reach God. Getting along with non-believers was one thing, whether or not they were saved was another. The New Age movement, because it compromised with Asian religions, particularly disturbed her. She had gotten a headache one day simply by looking at its symbol, and speculated that it may be the 'world church' mentioned in prophecies of the tribulation.

Betty's faith in scriptural authority resembles in some ways what Rokeach (1960, pp. 40–2) called 'primitive beliefs' – premises about reality which an individual forms early in life 'the validity of which he does not question and, in the ordinary course of events, is not prepared to question'. Migrating far from home in an increasingly secular society, Betty – inner-directed – trusted and nurtured these intuitive convictions. The rising evangelical right presented the chance to defend them and to satisfy frustrated leadership ambitions. Politics set before her the practical intellectual assignment of translating ancient spiritual truth into operational modern social policy, the conceptual tasks of justifying her beliefs in terms of their pragmatic implications, expressing them in contemporary idiom, and tempering them with tactical tolerance.

Articulate authoritarians in other cultures

As generic personality traits, the qualities that define our type – authoritarianism and analytic capacity – could, in principle, appear in lives anywhere in reality, some cultures and traditions will favor the expression of these variables more than others. Space limits me to brief accounts of only two articulate authoritarians from settings outside rural Protestantism.

Nichiren

The first is a medieval Oriental figure, Nichiren (1222–82), founder of the Japanese Buddhist school of that name. Born to the troubled Kamakura period, Nichiren undertook the quest for Buddhahood at the early age of 11. The plurality of Buddhist sects and prescriptions for salvation proved a disturbing obstacle. '[A] country has only one king', he reasoned (Rodd, 1980, p. 6). 'Is not the Buddhist scripture the same? Which sutra should one believe? Which is the king of all sutras?' For 20 years, Nichiren investigated various schools and disciplines, concluding, he later wrote (Anesaki, 1916, p. 14), that 'the truth of Buddhism must be one in essence'.

Trained largely in Tendai, he discovered this essential revelation in the Lotus Sutra – the only scripture, he came to believe, that could save humanity in his own degenerate age. His public condemnations of other sects, and efforts to have them outlawed, brought him physical assault and exile. Rather than eliciting moderation, however, persecution led Nichiren to see himself as the messiah-figure prophesied in the Lotus Sutra – a solitary Champion of Truth in the Last Days who, despite rejection by the world, the text said, would persevere in the effort to save humanity. Determined to fulfill this cosmic role, Nichiren met resistance with heightened obstinacy.

Like the fundamentalism of Henry Pitman and Mike Barnes, Nichiren's spiritual authoritarianism seems to have surfaced with an intolerant response to ambiguity. Confronted with a range of religious options, Nichiren, very much like Henry, resolved to discover which was correct. It was a reasonable quest for any devout Buddhist, but one that Nichiren, like Henry, pursued with a peculiar vengeance, an emotional intensity that suggests an unconscious defensive need. Unfortunately, the data do not indicate clearly any causes of personal distress beyond the urgent demand for redemption Nichiren openly professed.

Nichiren, it seems, was typically melancholic and agitated. So strained was his youthful quest for Nirvana that he suffered a seizure of some kind (Anesaki, 1916, p. 13). Admonishing followers, he turned Buddhist clichés on the uncertainty of life into urgent statements of fact. Indeed, a poignant sense of loss and foreboding suffuses his writings. For example, given a type of seaweed he enjoyed as a child, the aging prophet responded: 'Its colour, appearance, and taste are unchanged, yet my parents both are gone. My regrets bring tears to my eyes' (Rodd, 1980: 143). This dysphoria may have stemmed from personal disposition, early training in a Buddhist monastery, a lifetime in a disaster-prone society, or all three.

In any event, here again, although anxiety related, spiritual absolutism was not intellectually paralyzing. The need for certain salvation did not prevent Nichiren from studying various spiritual teachings for 20 years (10 at Mt Hiei, the national center of Buddhist learning). His humble birth makes it unlikely that he received personal instruction from famous teachers of the day. However, years of independent scholarship are evident, according to his biographer (Anesaki, 1916, p. 14), 'not only in the erudition of his later writings, but in the comprehensive breadth of his doctrine'. Nichiren explicated his teachings for widely ranging audiences in sermons, personal advisory and instructional letters, government memorials, and technical treatises shared with fellow monks (Rodd, 1980, pp. 5, 49).

Newman

John Henry Cardinal Newman (1801–90) represents articulate authoritarianism in modern, Roman Catholic guise. Newman was born in London, to the middle class. He studied at Oxford, where he later served as a tutor. An adolescent religious awakening inclined him to a stern evangelicalism; however, influenced by his colleagues and studies at the university, he eventually embraced High Church

Anglicanism. He entered the priesthood and, in 1833, drew public attention as a leader of the Oxford Movement, endeavoring to curb liberal trends in the Church of England. His studies of early Christianity convinced him, gradually, that the Roman hierarchy, not the Anglican, had inherited apostolic prerogative. In 1845, he became a Catholic.

'From the age of fifteen', Newman (1964, pp. 50–51, 260) wrote in his autobiographical defense of his conversion, 'dogma has been the fundamental principle of my religion ...'. 'I was confident', he continues, 'in the truth of a certain definite religious teaching ... viz., that there was a visible Church with sacraments and rites which are the channels of invisible grace'. Having found that church in Rome, he professed his 'absolute submission' to its claim of infallibility. 'I believe', he continued, 'the whole revealed dogma taught by the Apostles, as committed by the Apostles to the church, and as declared by the Church to me'. This faith he ably explicated and defended in philosophical as well as confessional writings.

The extensive biographical data on Newman show in fine detail the complexities of a personality in which intellectual gifts coexisted with authoritarian longings. Biographers repeatedly note his powerful imagination, his capacity for independent and creative thought, on the one hand, and, on the other, his 'instinctive need for authority', his 'compulsive drive to religious certainty' (Robbins, 1966, p. 119). While unmistakable, Newman's authoritarian leaning was virtually always offset by countervailing intellectual and behavioral tendencies. Confessions of unequivocal loyalty to the church, like the one cited above, for example, must be read in light of his subtle and flexible understanding of ecclesiastical authority and the fact that he found himself rather constantly in conflict with Anglican and Catholic superiors. Newman's thought, Yearley (1978) argues, has both an 'authoritative' and a 'liberal' face; dogmatic tendencies are tempered by a sense of divine mystery and historical complexity. In a psychoanalytic study, Capps (1970) designates as part of Newman's larger 'anal' personality profile, a characteristic ambivalence towards authority. Newman's case underscores the difficulty, repeatedly confronted above, of precisely determining the roots of authoritarian conviction; and the need, in any event, to consider it within the context of the entire personality.

Conclusion

Experts in various traditions could surely extend my list of cross-cultural exemplars. Candidates must qualify, let me stress, on the basis of biographical data, not confessional labels. More than a conservative point of view, articulate authoritarianism designates a path or style of personal religious development in the belief dimension. It points to a conjunction of analytic ability and spiritual absolutism that fosters the use of the intellect in approaching the sacred. As a developmental type, it provides one answer to the question: How do spiritual ideas or beliefs become complex, coherent, and motivating in personalities? In at least some cases, the religious intellect develops as cognitive aptitudes are made to serve authoritarian loyalties and needs.

More specifically, the biographies of exemplars suggest that a range of circumstances and motivations may underlie the acceptance of absolute spiritual authority. In Emma's case, we observed a culturally specific dynamic in which participation in rational-authoritarian sects offered status mobility. In another life, dogmatic convictions were acquired through socialization into a fundamentalist church. In three cases, authoritarian belief was associated with a troubled reaction to pluralism; this intolerance of ambiguity was in each apparently anxiety related, but the exact and deeper sources of personal stress were unclear from available data. Whatever its derivation, religious absolutism did not block intellectual activity. All subjects had analytic gifts or training that made their faith articulate as well as authoritarian.

An active mind, the tendency to reflect about religion or anything else, seems to be rooted in broad personal traits and/or conditioning. Beyond capacity or aptitude, however, actual intellectual exercise requires motivation – a reason for reflecting – and a reference point – a set of ideas or problems to start from. Authoritarian faith can provide both, stimulating the analytically disposed to undertake any of a range of religious-conceptual tasks: the search for and defense of unequivocal religious requirements; the practical application of absolute principles; and the interpretation of authoritative texts.

Articulate authoritarianism is, of course, only one style of functional, complex religious belief. In the theoretical model I used, various cultural forms and individual factors come together, dictating particular intellectual tasks and styles. Depending on the available conceptual tools and pressing personal needs, one religious thinker doubts and revises tradition, while another seeks and applies absolutes. Both approach the sacred intellectually. Together with thinkers of still other dispositions, they begin to represent the versatility of the human mind conceptualizing the sacred.

Notes

1. I was born and grew up in Dover County and lived from 1983–84 in Bellamy County, home of my maternal kin. The interviews considered here were conducted between 1976 and 1987. Usually I recruited subjects through pastors, asking for church members who could 'tell me about their faith' as a contribution to a study that, eventually, I would try to publish. I conducted most of the interviews in Bellamy County while I worked as a reporter for the community newspaper and wrote a series of feature articles on various local churches. Expecting publicity of one sort or another, ministers usually put me in touch with their most dedicated and informed members. Although I present here only interviews with laypersons, among the pastors I interviewed,

despite the greater formal theological training of liberals, the correlation of belief development with fundamentalism generally holds.

When possible, I interviewed subjects more than once. Emma Mitchell kindly submitted to four lengthy taped interviews, and I collected impressions and information about her from her employers and friends. Henry Pitman I interviewed twice, at length. Betty Frazer and Mike Barnes were each interviewed once, for several hours. Subjects were promised anonymity, and, to guarantee it, I have used pseudonyms for local counties, towns, congregations, and persons.

References

Adorno, T. W., *et al.* (1950) *The Authoritarian Personality*, New York, W. W. Norton.
Allen, R. O. and Spilka, B. (1967) 'Committed and consensual religion: a specification of religious prejudice relationships', *Journal for the Scientific Study of Religion*, vol. 6, pp. 191–206.
Allport, G. W. (1950) *The Individual and His Religion*, New York, Macmillan.
Ammerman, N. T. (1987) *Bible Believers: fundamentalists in the modern world*, New Brunswick, Rutgers University Press.
Anesaki, M. (1916) *Nichiren, the Buddhist Prophet*, Cambridge, Mass., Harvard University Press.
Capps. D. (1970) 'John Henry Newman: a study in religious leadership', unpublished Ph.D, dissertation, University of Chicago Divinity School.
Dittes, J. E. (1959) 'Effect of changes in self-esteem upon impulsiveness and deliberation in making judgements', *Journal of Abnormal and Social Psychology*, vol. 58, pp. 348–56.
Dittes, J. E. (1969) 'Psychology of religion', in Gardner Lindzey, G. and Aronson, E. (eds), *The Handbook of Social Psychology*, Reading, Mass., Addison-Wesley, vol 5, pp. 602–659.
Etheridge, F. M. and Feagin, J. R. (1979) 'Varieties of fundamentalism: a conceptual and empirical analysis of two protestant denominations', *Sociological Quarterly*, vol. 20, pp. 37–48.
Fowler, J. W. (1981) *Stages of Faith*, San Francisco, Harper and Row.
Frenkel-Brunswik, E. (1954) 'Further explorations by a contributor to *The Authoritarian Personality*', in Christie, R. and Jahoda, A. (eds), *Studies in the Scope and Method of 'The Authoritarian Personality'*, Glencoe, Ill., Free Press, pp. 226–275.
Fromm, E. (1941) *Escape from Freedom*, New York, Farrar and Rinehart.
Jung, C. G. (1971) *Psychological Types* (*Collected Works*, vol. 6), Princeton, Princeton University Press.
Kwilecki, S. (1988) 'A scientific approach to religious development: proposals and a case study', *Journal for the Scientific Study of Religion*, vol. 27, no. 3, pp. 307–325.
Monaghan, R. R. (1967) 'Three faces of the true believer: motivations for attending a fundamentalist church', *Journal for the Scientific Study of Religion*, vol. 6, pp. 236–245.
Morris, J. (1973) *The Preachers*, New York, St Martin's Press.
Newman, J. H. (1964) *Apologia Pro Vita Sua*, London, Oxford University Press.
Photiadis, J. D. and Schweiker, W. (1970) 'Attitudes toward joining authoritarian organizations and sectarian churches', *Journal for the Scientific Study of Religion*, vol. 9, pp. 227–234.
Robbins, W. (1966) *The Newman Brothers: an essay in comparative intellectual biography*, London, Heinemann.
Rodd, L. (1980) *Nichiren: selected writings*, Honolulu, University Press of Hawaii.
Rokeach, M. (1960) *The Open and Closed Mind*, New York, Basic Books.
Stewart, D. and Hoult, T. (1959) 'The social-psychological theory of the authoritarian personality', *American Journal of Sociology*, vol. 65, pp. 274–79.
Wach, J. (1958) *The Comparative Study of Religions*, New York, Columbia University Press.
Wallach, M. A. (1962) 'Commentary: active-analytical *vs.* passive-global cognitive functioning, in Messick, S. and Ross, J. (eds), *Measurement in Personality and Cognition*, New York, Wiley, pp 199–215.
Yearley, L. (1978) *The Ideas of Newman: Christianity and human religiosity*, University Park, Pennsylvania State University Press.

6. Questionnaire data and faith development

Two papers from the *Review of Religious Research*, both published in 1989, illustrate attempts to utilize questionnaire studies for faith development research.

'The formulation of a Fowler scale: an empirical assessment among Catholics', first published in *Review of Religious Research*, vol. 30, no. 4, pp. 412–420, is a proposal by Michael Barnes, Dennis Doyle and Byron Johnson to provide a short-cut for students of the phenomenon of faith. The paper compares Fowler's account of faith-styles with those provided elsewhere in the literature on the psychology of religion. The authors then develop a scale 'that could identify different elements of each of the stages of faith development as defined by Fowler' using nine faith-style items, each comprising a set of paired statements between which a choice has to be made, together with questions designed to distinguish those who express their beliefs in a literal fashion from those who interpret them symbolically. From the 579 questionnaires returned the authors claim that this research instrument distinguishes faith-styles with good consistency, and that these faith-styles are good predictors of literal/symbolic styles of belief (no conclusions are drawn as to whether these represent developmental 'stages'). They offer this study as a contribution towards validating Fowler's theory, since 'characteristics which he assigned to each stage do cluster together in the responses'.

The second paper, by Charles Green and Cindy Hoffman, entitled 'Stages of faith and perceptions of similar and dissimilar others' was first published in *Review of Religious Research*, vol. 30, no. 3, pp. 246–254. It attempts to test the hypothesis that a person's faith stage position should show a significant positive correlation with his or her strategy of social categorization and evaluation of other people. A questionnaire was designed in which respondents (who were students themselves) had to rate prospective college students on the basis of application forms which indicated their religious positions. The respondents were then asked 'to select from a list of statements the one that most closely corresponded to their own views about their religious faith and the one that was next closest to their own beliefs'. These statements were drawn from Fowler's faith stage descriptions. Finally the respondents had to indicate what sort of authority they relied on to resolve their own religious concerns. The authors claim that the results support the hypothesis proposed, with respondents at earlier stages being more likely than those at stages 4 and 5 to discriminate in favour of candidates who had a similar religious background. The paper concludes that 'stage was an excellent predictor of the way respondents reacted to members of ingroups and outgroups'. The authors suggest that their study provides evidence for the validity of Fowler's broad theory, while recognizing the silence of their data with regard to his account of the *development* of faith.

6.1 The formulation of a Fowler scale: an empirical assessment among Catholics

Michael Barnes, Dennis Doyle and Byron Johnson

The process of empirically investigating religiousness as well as its relation to other aspects of life has turned out to be extremely difficult, partly because it is rather difficult to define what religiousness is. Cornwall, Albrecht, Cunningham, and Pitcher (1986), reviewing numerous studies on religiosity, identify three components of religion: cognitive, affective, and behavioral, and note various ways in which each of these three has been measured. King and Hunt demonstrate the multidimensional nature of religiousness as it appears in various studies (King, 1967; King and Hunt, 1972, 1975). Hilty, Morgan, and Burns (1984) add a number of specific recommendations for further adjustments in the techniques and forms of measurement of the religious variable.

A useful analysis of major aspects of religiosity has been Gordon Allport's (1950, 1967) categorization of religion into 'extrinsic' (E) and 'intrinsic' (I). This has been extended by Batson and Ventis (1982) who add a third category, 'quest' (Q). They marshall a substantial range of empirical evidence, though Hood and Morris (1985) dispute aspects of it. This three-fold categorization has partial overlap with the LAM scales developed by Richard Hunt (1972) which divides approaches to religious belief into an uncritical 'literal' (L) acceptance, an 'anti-literal' (A) rejection of belief, and a 'mythical' (M) or symbolic acceptance of belief. The LAM scale loosely parallels Wiebe's (1984) more theoretical analysis of religion into traditional (literal), modern (disbelief), and critical (symbolic) types.

In *Stages of Faith* James Fowler (1981) summarized the work of several years of interviews and analysis on types of faith, though he has not provided the data that would make it possible to assess the validity and reliability of his results. His summary nonetheless has some face plausibility because it is built on the empirical work of Jean Piaget and Lawrence Kohlberg and others (1981, pp. 41–88, 244–245). If his theory is basically sound it holds promise of bringing additional specificity, order, and integration to the many ways of measuring religiousness.

Fowler's theory describes six stages of faith development, each with its affective, cognitive, moral, and interpersonal dimension. The first, called the intuitive-projective, is that of a very young child and is not pertinent to this study. The second, the mythic-literal includes an uncritical and literal acceptance of traditional stories. The third, called synthetic-conventional, has a more explicit dependence on group allegiance and lives by a more complex narrative. The fourth, the individuative-reflective, uses a more abstract and universalizing style of thought. The fifth, the conjunctive, has a critical recognition of the symbolic nature of truth claims. There are analogous differences among the stages concerning moral reasoning, social relations, and so forth.

Fowler claims that these stages develop in sequence in a person's life, with the last of the ones considered here, stage 5, appearing only after the age of thirty and in only some adults. But Fowler's finding is that stages 3, 4, and 5 are each the faith-style of some adults. Any group of adults may have subsets representing at least these three different faith-styles, and possibly a fourth style if stage 2 style of faith is also characteristic of some adults. These four, each with its complex of characteristics, together comprise a larger theoretical framework for interpreting the Batson and Ventis three-fold division of religiousness. Chirban (1981) has already shown that the E and I dimensions correlate significantly with early and later stages of Fowler's theory. This theory may also be a good means to interpret and extend the use of the LAM scales as well as Wiebe's work, in that the stages which Fowler describes parallel, to some extent, a movement from literal to 'mythical' styles of thought from 'traditional' to 'critical' in Wiebe's frame-work.

Both the LAM scale and Wiebe's theory, however, propose only two major types of belief, along with a type of unbelief, whereas the E-I-Q division provides three types and Fowler's scale provides as many as four for adults. The extrinsic style of faith as described by Batson and Ventis (1982 pp. 234−235) sounds rather like the stage 2 sort of faith in Fowler's descriptions, one in which religion or faith is important only as one of the facts of the environment that must be dealt with in order to satisfy one's own needs. The intrinsic dimension as described by Batson and Ventis (1982, pp. 235−236) seems to include aspects of Fowler's stage 3, such as concern for conformity and the greater organization and unification of life that comes through having a more complex narrative. It is also compatible with stage 4 concern for greater coherence and greater confidence in one's own analysis and judgment. The quest dimension (1982, pp. 236−237) has the kind of open-mindedness and flexibility characteristic of Fowler's stage 5. If this correspondence between the two theories can be substantiated better through studies on either or both of them, Fowler's analysis will have added an extra dimension to the 'intrinsic' category, thereby helping to define more precisely the religious variable.

Our purpose was to devise a scale that could identify different elements of each of the stages of faith development as defined by Fowler. Two predictions could be made on the basis of Fowler's claims as ways of testing them. First, statements devised to reflect different aspects of the same stage of faith development ought to be selected by the same respondents a high percentage of the time. Secondly, Fowler's theory would also predict not that people would have different beliefs, though they might, but that they would have a different way of holding these beliefs, ranging from a quite literal to a somewhat more sophisticated to a highly symbolic style. As part of a survey on current Catholic beliefs[1] we were administering such a literal-to-symbolic scale, so that we were able to compare responses to these items to responses to the Fowler scale.

For reasons of time and cost we did not try to test Fowler's claim that these styles of faith are really 'stages,' appearing sequentially in the life of an individual, as that would require either a longitudinal study or a much larger survey of different age groups. We call each 'stage' of faith, therefore, a faith-style except where referring more directly to Fowler's own work and using his language.

Methods

Survey groups

In the Fall of 1985 we surveyed the College Theology Society (CTS), a largely Catholic group of college teachers of theology or religious studies, and the members of a Catholic parish in Dayton, Ohio, to find out how literal-traditional or how symbolic-liberal they were in their beliefs. For the basis of comparison with the Fowler scale it was not important whether they represented typical American Catholic theologians or parishioners nor how large a percentage responded. It was only important that there was a sufficient number of responses over a wide enough range to allow us to match the results of the survey on belief items with the responses meant to identify the different Fowler styles of faith. Both teachers and parishioners were sufficiently diverse in their responses, and the parishioners were distributed fairly well as to age, income, and education. The parish members also included a good number of respondents (about 60) who belonged to either a charismatic movement or a special Tuesday morning prayer group whose members were mainly the charismatics. We received 275 usable responses from the CTS (a response rate of 36%) and 304 from the parishioners (a response rate of 28%).

Scale to identify styles of faith

Fowler's theory claims that there are up to six stages of faith, ranging from the unthought basic trust of the infant up through a hypothetical stage 6 faith of unusual persons such as Mahatma Ghandi. For surveying a limited number of adults it was more practical to attempt to measure only stages 2 through 5 (treating them as faith-styles), with the main emphasis on stages 3 through 5 as the styles most typical of adults, according to Fowler. There were nine faith-style items in all, each a set of paired statements. The respondents were asked to chose between the two statements of each pair by using a Likert-type scale: A a ? b B. Those who chose 'A' or 'a' were scored as agreeing with the first statement, and those who chose a 'b' or 'B' as agreeing with the second statement. In each case the respondent was being given a choice between statements designed to represent two different styles of faith.

The statements were devised to represent three aspects of each style, as a way of testing for the internal coherence of each style. Following Fowler's descriptions we characterized the style 2 person as one who finds relatively little coherent logic to larger sequences of life's events, who equates power with authority, and who sees interpersonal relations as a series of deals made between people. As characteristics of style 3 we used concern for loyalty to a leader, concern for conformity to group standards, and a fairly literal story-telling way of understanding doctrines. For style 4 we selected a universalist outlook (an interest in relating all aspects of reality together), a related concern for overall coherence of beliefs in a fairly logical way, and a sense of adherence to objectively valid norms rather than just to one's group standards. For style 5 we chose belief in the tentativeness of all standards, a related openness and flexibility of belief and tolerance of differences, and a concern for general human well-being over all other standards. The statements were attempts to capture some of these characteristics in ways that could be understood by both theologians and parishioners.

According to Fowler's findings few adults would consistently choose style 2 statements, so we included only three style 2 items, just to identify and control for those who would select responses for other styles at random when no style 2 option was given. There were five statements each for styles 3, 4, and 5. In each case a statement representing one style was paired with a statement representing another style. (See appendix for the paired faith-style statements.)

Survey on beliefs

Mixed in with the faith-style items were a larger set of questions about ten issues of Catholic belief: life after death, church authority, God, exclusiveness vs inclusiveness, eucharist, divinity of Christ, the resurrection, founding of the Catholic Church, Jesus' self-identity, and the miracles of Jesus. For each of the ten issues the respondent was presented with two pairs of statements. The first pair offered a choice between a literal or a symbolic way of expressing the belief. The second pair offered a choice between a somewhat literal and a very symbolic, highly liberal way of expressing the belief. Those who chose the literal statements on a given issue both times were classified as Literal (L); those choosing the symbolic both times were classified as Symbolic (S); and those who chose first the symbolic statement but then chose the somewhat literal over the highly symbolic were classified as Nuanced (N). Extremely few chose first the literal and then the highly symbolic; these we classified as Inconsistent.

Findings

The findings show that in response to the items based on Fowler's theory of faith development the respondents fall into distinct faith-style groups with good consistency. On the basis of the faith-style groups it is further possible to predict how the respondent will answer on the issues of belief items, and even as to whether the style of belief will fall into one of the three distinct categories: very literal (L), nuanced (N), or highly symbolic (S). It is also possible to predict to some extent, on the basis of the relation between faith-style responses and belief responses, whether the respondent is more likely to be a theologian, a regular parishioner or a prayer-group member. (For the CTS members this may be a result of their theological education.)

Description of responses

Table 1 summarizes the responses of the theologians (CTS members) and parishioners on each of the nine pairs of statements. The theologians tend to chose a higher response (3 over 2, 5 over 4, etc.) on eight of the nine items. The parishioners are more mixed in their preferences. Neither group favors the stage 2 answers, though there is a somewhat higher proportion of parishioners choosing these statements.

Faith-style groups and their relation to the issues of belief

Faith-style groups (F-groups) were formed of those respondents who had chosen any given category of answer (3, 4, or 5) at least four times out of the five possible (or two times out of three for faith-style 2). On this basis, of the 579 respondents there were 25 in the F-2 group; 66 in the F-3; 125 in the F-4; and 162 in the F-5 group. Altogether 378 out of the 579 had selected statements belonging to a single faith-style with a high degree of regularity, meaning that about 65% of the respondents showed great consistency in their choices, indicating that the faith-style items were fairly successful in identifying different styles of belief. There were 167, 29% of the total, who had spread their responses across the options, with most clustering them around two contiguous categories, as would

Table 1: Frequency distribution of theologians and parishioners on the nine pairs of faith development statements

Faith development statements	Statement preference	Theologians %	Parishioners %	Total %
stage 2 versus	stage 2	8	8	8
stage 3	uncertain	26	14	20
	stage 3	66	78	72
stage 2 versus	stage 2	11	32	22
stage 4	uncertain	17	20	19
	stage 4	72	48	59
stage 2 versus	stage 2	5	14	10
stage 5	uncertain	6	8	7
	stage 5	89	78	83
stage 3 versus	stage 3	29	50	40
stage 4	uncertain	19	8	13
	stage 4	52	42	47
stage 3 versus	stage 3	12	31	21
stage 4	uncertain	11	12	12
(second set)	stage 4	77	57	67
stage 3 versus	stage 3	48	48	48
stage 5	uncertain	25	7	16
	stage 5	27	45	36
stage 3 versus	stage 3	4	26	16
stage 5	uncertain	13	11	12
(second set)	stage 5	83	63	67
stage 4 versus	stage 4	41	70	56
stage 5	uncertain	15	5	10
	stage 5	44	26	24
stage 4 versus	stage 4	26	59	43
stage 5	uncertain	20	12	16
(second set)	stage 5	54	28	41
	(N)	(277)	(301)	(578)

be consistent with Fowler's developmental theory. There were also 34 respondents, 6% of the total, who had chosen the question mark (indicating no preference between the two statements) at least five of the nine times possible.

Faith-style groups correlated with responses on the issues

The F-groups results were correlated with the simplest responses on the issues – Literal or Symbolic – on each of the pairs of belief statements. Table 2 shows the responses on the first ten pairs of belief statements, which were each a flatly literal statement combined with a general symbolic statement, and on the second ten pairs, which were each a vaguely literal statement combined with a highly symbolic (and highly liberal) statement of belief. Responses on the first ten show the clearest differences among F-groups. The F-2 groups are most literal, the F-5 groups most symbolic. This is true also on the second ten pairs of statements but less strongly so, as many found a mildly literal statement preferable to a statement that was, presumably, excessively symbolic or liberal for them.

A more significant set of relationships appeared when the respondents were divided into three population subgroups: the theologians (CTS members), the regular parishioners, and the prayer group (our name for the parishioners who were part of the special, largely charismatic, prayer group). Among the theologians the F-group membership allows us to correctly classify whether the respondent chooses literal or symbolic statements 81% of the time by discriminant analysis.[2] Presumably the theologians use religious language with a certain consistency and precision and were more consistent in their interpretation of the meaning of the statements. The comparable figure for the regular parishioners, a group more likely to read variable meanings into the statements, is 61%. For the prayer group members the discriminant analysis figure is 94%. They consistently chose the more literal statements.

When the responses on the issues are classified more carefully as Literal, Nuanced, or Symbolic a similar pattern of relation to F-group membership appears. Those who are most literal are also concentrated in the F-2 and F-3 groups. The F-4 is more nuanced and partly symbolic and the F-5 most symbolic (though as often nuanced) in their choices.

Controlling for education we found that having a Ph.D. or M.A. in religious studies or theology, which was the case with all of the CTS members, made it very unlikely that a person would fall into an F-2 or F-3 group (only 9% combined), and twice as likely to be in an F-5 group (60%) than an F-4 (31%). Among parishioners, whose educational backgrounds were more varied, those with a high school education or less were spread out most widely across the F-groups. Of those falling into some group 11% were in the

Table 2: Distributions for stages of faith development by the twenty pairs of statements of religious belief*

Religious issues	Preference on issues	First ten pairs of statements				Second ten pairs of statements			
		Faith development stages				Faith development stages			
		2	3	4	5	2	3	4	5
belief	L	57%	57%	48%	18%	60%	65%	54%	55%
in	?	0	5	1	4	8	9	6	9
afterlife	S	33	39	51	78	32	26	41	36
authority	L	54	55	26	9	83	99	94	73
of the	?	4	12	7	0	4	2	2	12
church	S	42	32	67	91	13	0	4	15
founding	L	50	76	34	9	92	99	98	83
of the	?	4	5	10	9	8	2	1	6
church	S	46	20	56	82	0	0	2	11
miracles	L	92	96	80	86	96	96	94	71
of Jesus	?	4	2	3	7	0	2	2	14
	S	4	3	17	56	4	3	5	16
inclusivity	L	46	79	49	7	65	82	74	50
exclusivity	?	4	3	6	7	9	12	7	10
	S	50	18	46	85	26	6	19	40
Jesus'	L	88	89	63	32	48	64	74	44
self-	?	0	0	6	12	9	20	7	12
identity	S	13	11	31	56	44	17	18	44
divinity	L	88	91	78	31	92	89	94	71
of Christ	?	4	2	6	8	4	2	1	7
	S	8	8	16	61	4	9	5	22
resurrec-	L	88	83	73	30	75	85	74	40
tion of	?	0	3	2	8	0	6	10	20
Christ	S	12	14	26	62	25	9	17	40
interpreta-	L	68	79	69	36	88	91	94	62
tion of the	?	0	2	4	6	0	0	0	9
eucharist	S	32	20	27	58	12	9	5	29
belief in	L	92	95	82	41	83	96	89	58
God	?	0	0	3	8	8	2	2	12
	**S	8	5	14	51	8	3	9	30
	(N)	(24)	(65)	(124)	(161)	(25)	(66)	(125)	(161)

* Cross tabs produce significant Chi Square values (p < .01) throughout.

** L = Literal   ? = Uncertain   S = Symbolic

F-2, 28% in F-3, 39% in F-4, and 21% in F-5. Parishioners with a college degree or beyond fell between the theologians and the other parishioners, tending towards the F-4 and F-5 groups but less so than the theologians. For reasons unknown to us those with only a basic college degree were more likely to be in the F-5 group than were those with a graduate degree. (In this parish those with a graduate degree were somewhat older than those with only a B.A.).

Discussion

This survey of beliefs and of faith-style characteristics is a beginning in the work of devising ways to test Fowler's theory for inner consistency and for validity. Although much more needs to be done these current results add to the plausibility of Fowler's claims. Characteristics which he assigned to each stage do cluster together in the responses; and each style of faith does correlate fairly well with at least some measure of how literally or symbolically a person interprets religious beliefs. While an advanced education, in theology especially, is related to the faith-style of the person, even among those with no more than a high school degree there are distinct faith-styles and corresponding styles of belief ranging from literal to nuanced to symbolic.

Fowler's work, already an integration of the work of Piaget, Kohlberg, and others, provides a thorough description of aspects of religiousness, integrating those aspects into coherent patterns. It can provide an interpretive framework for understanding the many aspects to the patterns of religiousness, and should generate new productive lines of investigation. In general the major result we hope from this study is to promote interest in the continuation of empirical research and development on Fowler's theory, particularly through methods that are easier to administer than interviews.

Appendix: paired faith-style statements

Note: the number in parentheses indicates the Fowler stage ('style' here) which the statement is intended to identify. The respondents were asked to express a preference for one of the two statements on each of the nine items.

(2) 1.   A.   Those who do what God wants are given special rewards.
(3)   B.   God grants comfort and strength to those who are loyal and faithful.
(2) 2.   A.   God can do whatever God wants without any particular reason.
(4)   B.   It is important to try to make sense out of how God acts and why.
(2) 3.   A.   A good way to relate to God is to do what God wants, so that God will help you in return.

(5)   B. It is best to think of God as utterly and freely giving.

(3) 4. A. Following Christ with loving devotion is more important than having a thorough and correct understanding of true doctrine.

(4)   B. It is important to reflect on one's beliefs to make them reasonable and logically coherent.

. (3) 5. A. True followers of Christ will often find themselves rejected by the world.

(5)   B. Most people in the world are doing their best to live decent lives.

(4) 6. A. God's revealed truth is meant for all people everywhere.

(5)   B. No set of religious beliefs is the whole and final truth for everyone.

(3) 7. A. It is important to follow the leaders to whom God has entrusted his church.

(4)   B. Religious leaders must respect the need for reasonableness, consistency, and coherence in their interpretation of doctrines.

(3) 8. A. It is often hard to understand why people are disloyal to their family and religion.

(5)   B. People have to make their own best choices about religion, even if it means following new ways.

(4) 9. A. The moral teachings of the church are objectively valid for all people, even though many do not realize this.

(5)   B. Love of neighbor requires being open to new ideas and values.

Notes
1. A report on this appears in *Sociological Analysis*, vol. 49, 1989, pp. 430–439.
2. Discriminant analysis is a statistical technique by which variables can be used to distinguish between groups and predict into which group a case will fall based on the value of these variables. See Tatsuoka (1970) for a fuller explanation.

References
Allport, Gordon W. (1950) *The Individual and His Religion*, New York, Macmillan.
Allport, Gordon W. and Ross, J. M. (1967) 'Personal religious orientation and prejudice,' *Journal of Personality and Social Psychology*, vol. 5, pp. 432–443.
Batson, C. Daniel, and Ventis, W. Lawrence (1982) *The Religious Experience: a social-psychological perspective*, New York, Oxford University Press.
Chirban, John T. (1981) *Human Growth and Faith: intrinsic and extrinsic motivation in human development*, Washington, D. C., University Press of America.
Cornwall, Marie, Stan L. Albrecht, Perry H. Cunningham, and Brian L. Pitcher (1986) 'The dimensions of religiosity: a conceptual model with an empirical test,' *Review of Religious Research*, vol. 27, pp. 226–244.
Fowler, James W. (1981) *Stages of Faith*, San Francisco, Harper and Row.
Hilty, Dale M., Morgan, Rick L., and Burns, Joan E. (1984) 'King and Hunt revisited: dimensions of religious involvement,' *Journal for the Scientific Study of Religion*, vol. 23, pp. 252–262.
Hood, Ralph W. and Morris, Ronald J. (1985) 'Conceptualization of quest: a critical rejoinder to Batson,' *Review of Religious Research*, vol. 26, pp. 391–397.

Hunt, Richard H. (1972) 'Mythological-symbolic religious commitment: the LAM scales,' *Journal for the Scientific Study of Religion*, vol. 11, pp. 42–52.

King, Morton B., and Hunt, Richard A. (1967) 'Measuring the religious variable: nine proposed dimensions,' *Journal for the Scientific Study of Religion*, vol. 6, pp. 173–190.

King, Morton B., and Hunt, Richard A. (1969) 'Measuring the religious variable: amended findings,' *Journal for the Scientific Study of Religion*, vol. 8, pp. 321–323.

King, Morton B., and Hunt, Richard A. (1975) 'Measuring the religious variable: national replication,' *Journal for the Scientific Study of Religion*, vol. 14, pp. 13–22.

Rest, James R. (1979) *Development in Judging Moral Issues*, Minneapolis, University of Minnesota Press.

Tatsuoka, Maurice M. (1970) *Discriminant Analysis: the study of group differences*, Champaign, Ill., Instrument for Personality and Ability Testing.

Wiebe, Paul (1984) *The Architecture of Religion*, San Antonio, Trinity University Press.

6.2 Stages of faith and perceptions of similar and dissimilar others[1]

Charles W. Green and Cindy L. Hoffman

James Fowler's recent book, *Stages of Faith* (1981), outlines his psycho-social theory of the development of personal faith across the life span. He defines faith, broadly, as the primary motivation of one's life. Faith, in this sense, does not depend upon religious supports or assent to credal statements. However, because religious groups exist in part to help give answers to life's ultimate questions, faith and religion often are intertwined and the faith of many people is grounded in religious beliefs and behaviours. Fowler's goal for a decade has been to chart faith development throughout the life span, characterizing common faith stages and the transitions that separate them (Fowler and Keen, 1976; Fowler, 1980, 1981). We have examined the implications of the faith stages for an important and related variable, perceptions of members of various outgroups. The faith development of college students was measured, and their faith stage was used to understand their attitudes toward similar and dissimilar others.

Fowler's stages of faith

Fowler believes that the stages he has outlined are descriptive of the universal and unvarying pattern of faith development. Individual differences exist principally in the number of stages through which people pass, and in the rate at which they pass through them. In addition to a 'pre-stage' during infancy, Fowler proposes six stages of faith development.

Stage 1, intuitive-projective faith. This stage is typical of Jean Piaget's pre-operational child, ages three through seven. Stories and visual impressions are especially important in influencing the child's thoughts and feelings. These childhood images and reactions likely will be re-examined later in life. Transition from this stage into the next occurs with the movement into concrete operational thinking.

Stage 2, mythic-literal faith. Stage 2 faith is more logical and reality oriented than the faith of stage 1, due to the increasing cognitive abilities of the child. The myths and beliefs of the child's community begin to be internalized. These stories are interpreted literally, and are understood only at their most superficial level. Some adults remain in this level of faith development.

Stage 3, synthetic-conventional faith. This is the stage that typifies

256

the adolescent's approach to faith, though a significant number of adults stay at this level. It develops initially in response to the emergence of formal operational thinking. Stage 3 is essentially a group-oriented stage, for the beliefs and norms of significant others are more influential at this time than at any other, though they are not subjected to serious scrutiny. Authority figures are especially revered. Relationships with important others who share one's beliefs provide the foundation for stage 3 faith.

Stage 4, individuative-reflective faith. Stage 4 most often begins to emerge during young adulthood, though for a significant number of people it occurs during mid-life or may never occur at all. Stage 4 is an individualistic stage, with a heavy emphasis upon the development of a rational and self-conscious 'world view.' Fowler calls this a 'demythologizing stage,' because symbols and stories are analyzed objectively for the first time.

Stage 5, conjunctive faith. The transition to stage 5 begins when one becomes dissatisfied with the relative sterility of the fourth stage and its emphasis upon the rational construction of a world view. People in stage 5 have begun to appreciate paradox and the importance of experience. The contributions of people outside one's own group are accepted more readily in stage 5 than before, for there is more emphasis upon the commonality of all people than upon the unique aspects of one's own group. Fowler believes that stage 5 is rarely encountered before middle age.

Stage 6, universalizing faith. A very small percentage of people reach what Fowler describes as the sixth and last stage. These people are able not only to appreciate truth in all forms, but strive to become an 'incarnation' of that truth as well. Radical action based upon belief is an important component of the stage 6 person.

Paloutzian (1983) has mentioned the dearth of empirical work on faith development and suggested that more research be done to determine whether or not Fowler's hypotheses accurately predict the behavior of people at varying stages of faith. Chirban (1981) related Fowler's ideas about faith development to Allport's distinction between intrinsic and extrinsic religiosity (Allport, 1966; Allport and Ross, 1967). He reported that intrinsic motives were present in individuals in each of Fowler's stages, but that extrinsic motives were absent in those persons beyond stage 3. Additional empirical research would establish the relationships between faith development and related areas of research. Additionally, to the extent that those relationships are consistent with Fowler's predictions, such research would provide needed construct validity for his approach.

Faith development and perceptions of others

A social psychological perspective on faith development would focus, in part, on individuals' perceptions of their group memberships and how those perceptions change as they move from one stage to the next. Drawing boundaries to include some people as being 'like me' and exclude others as being 'not like me' is a fundamental process in our construction of the social world (Allport, 1958; Brewer, 1979; Wilder, 1981). Henry Tajfel's social identity approach to the study of intergroup relations emphasizes social categorization as the fundamental determinant of attitudes toward other people and other groups (Tajfel, 1978; Tajfel and Turner, 1979). Tajfel's research has demonstrated that placing other people into simple 'like me' and 'not like me' categories is sufficient to elicit both prejudiced attitudes and discriminatory behaviors (Tajfel, 1970, 1978). Because faith development, as conceptualized by Fowler, is fundamental to one's self-definition, persons of varying faith stages should use different rules for differentiating between similar and dissimilar others. Differing categorization strategies should reflect differing self- and other-perceptions, the extent to which ingroup-outgroup lines are drawn inclusively or exclusively, and religious and denominational prejudices and stereotypes.

Fowler's descriptions of the ideal types of each of his faith stages can be used to develop predictions as to how people in various stages would view others who were perceived as being similar to or dissimilar to themselves. For example, adults in stage 2 are said to emphasize a literal interpretation of their beliefs and traditions. Such an approach should lead to negative perceptions of those who do not share those views, especially if the group believes that it possesses the only valid interpretation of faith. Stage 3 people are said to be oriented very strongly toward the members of their ingroup. Such relationships make up the foundation of their faith. Since it is very rare that strong ingroup ties exist without negative outgroup attitudes (Dion, 1979), people in this third stage also are likely to express positive attitudes toward people in their ingroup and negative attitudes toward people in an outgroup.

The social categorization strategies of individuals in stage 4 are not as easily predicted. This is the most individualistic of all the stages. Stage 4 people are focused upon their own personal construction of a coherent world view, and they believe they are less dependent upon other people, similar or dissimilar, to help them comprehend the social world. These people therefore are much less dependent upon their ingroup than those persons in stage 3. As their ingroup shrinks to include only those persons who share their specific views about faith, the outgroup grows correspondingly. The ingroup/outgroup dichotomy should continue to be important for them, but not as important or in as many ways as for stage 3 persons. Stage 5, by contrast, is characterized by a deliberate effort to go beyond old social boundaries and learn from a variety of sources and faiths. Persons in this stage should be much less concerned with social group distinctions and should not view ingroup and outgroup members as differently as those in earlier faith stages.

We hypothesized that faith development would have implications for social categorization strategies and their concomitant evaluations of others. We predicted that persons categorized as stage 2 or stage 3 would be especially attuned to ingroup/outgroup differences and would show preferences for members of the ingroup. Stage 5 people should be much less affected by social group distinctions and should discriminate less among persons due to group memberships. Stage 4 should be a transition stage between the salience of group differences seen in stage 3 and the relative unimportance of such differences in stage 5. Stage 4 persons should make fewer distinctions among ingroup and outgroup members than persons in earlier stages, but more distinctions than those in later stages.

Method

Sample and procedure

One hundred and sixty students in a liberal arts college affiliated with a mainline Protestant denomination were mailed a survey and asked to complete and return it. The sample was selected randomly, stratified by gender and year in school.

Instruments

Applicant evaluations. Each respondent was asked to rate five hypothetical prospective college students on the basis of their applications. Each applicant was described as an unmarried, Caucasian transfer from a state university. The gender of the applicant was not indicated. The questions on the application form that pertained to religious affiliation and campus involvements were used to create five persons who varied in their religious orientations. One student was described as a devout and active Protestant who wanted to transfer in order to associate with other Christian students. Another student was a practicing Roman Catholic who wanted to come to a liberal arts college in order to attend a less impersonal institution. A third student was described as a Christian with no particular denominational preference who stated, 'I am comfortable being in a religious setting, but I don't want it forced on me by anyone else.' Another student was a self-described agnostic who wanted to come to this college because of its size, location, and academic standards. The fifth student was an active atheist who claimed to be interested in attending this college because of its reputation and because 'I think it would be interesting to be at a church-related college so that I can explore why so many people have a need to believe in God.'

These applications were presented in a random order that varied from respondent to respondent. After reading each application, the respondents were asked to indicate their agreement or disagreement with five questions on a five-point scale, ranging from strongly agree to strongly disagree with a neutral midpoint. These questions were:

a.   this is the kind of person I would like to see at this college;
b.   this person has a lot to contribute to this college;
c.   this person shares many of my personal beliefs;
d.   I would like for this person to live with or near me at college;
e.   I would like to be friends with this person.

The final question asked, 'Compared with other students here, do you think this person is generally good or generally bad?' The response options ranged from very good to very bad, again on a five-point scale.

Faith stage questions. After the respondents answered the questions about the college applicants, they were asked to select from a list of statements the one that most closely corresponded to their own views about their religious faith and the one that was next closest to their own beliefs. These statements were designed to enable us to categorize the faith stage of the respondents. Each statement was based upon Fowler's (1981) descriptions of the most important features of each stage and reflected the defining characteristics of each stage. Those statements (presented in a random order and without the stage labels) were as follows.

a.   God tells us what he wants from us (for instance, through the bible and people in important positions) and we are to follow his will obediently (stage 2).
b.   I learn much from parents, Christian teachings, Christian peers, and/ or my home church and similar groups and have found deep satisfaction in internalizing the biblical tradition through my relationships with them (stage 3).
c.   Ultimately I must decide religious issues for myself even though I value the input of others. Sometimes there are fundamental conflicts between my beliefs and traditional Christian teachings. Those teachings must be subjected to reasoned reflection so that my faith can provide me with a logical and coherent view of life (stage 4).
d.   Both traditional Christian teachings and my own rational approach to faith are too simplistic to comprehend adequately all religious truth. I have found that faith is inherently both paradoxical and relative and that both reason and intuition are important in a personal faith (stage 5).

Each student then was asked to answer the following question by selecting the desired alternative. 'The last time I had a personal concern that had any religious implications or significance, I depended upon _____ the most for helping me to decide what to do.' The response options were:

    a. the bible or a church authority (stage 2);
    b. 'fellow believers' – those in my church or in an informal group who are important to me (stage 3);
    c. my own judgment as informed by Christian teachings, logic and reason (stage 4);
    d. my judgment based on my experience, intuition, and reflection on many sources of human wisdom, those in and out of the Christian tradition (stage 5).

Respondents then were asked to indicate their age, gender, year in school, major in college, and denominational or religious affiliation.

Results

Of the 71 completed surveys, only the Protestants were used in the analyses because of the relatively small number of Roman Catholics and other groups represented. Because only two of the Protestants selected the stage 2 response to the first question, we examined only those persons who selected stage 3, 4, or 5 statements as best representing their views. This left a sample of 45 Protestants used in the analyses. Some demographic characteristics of those who returned a survey were compared with the distribution of those characteristics in the population (Smith, 1983). The distribution of gender, year in school, and denominational preference of the respondents was very similar to that of the student body as a whole. Particularly striking was the nearly identical pattern of preferences for a dozen different denominations. Although the response rate was relatively low, the similarities between the final sample and the population provide some evidence of the representativeness of the respondents. Preliminary analyses indicated that there were no gender, year, or age differences in faith stage.

A categorization scheme which took into account both the first and second choices for both of the faith stage questions was devised. The scheme was based on the assumption that the greatest cleavage between two adjacent stage levels occurs between stages 3 and 4 because stage 4 is the first genuinely reflective stage. Each student selected a first and second choice for each of the two faith questions; their responses were categorized as being either in stages 2 or 3 or in stages 4 or 5 (recall, however, that the two respondents who selected the stage 2 option for the first question as best representing their views were excluded from the analyses). The number of stage 4 or 5 responses was counted for each student. Those with either zero or one stage 4 or 5 response were placed into the first category. Those with two stage 4 or 5 responses were placed into the second category. Those with three stage 4 or 5 responses were placed into the third category, and those with four stage 4 or 5 responses were placed into the fourth category. This created a categorization variable with four levels with approximately the same number of respondents in each level.

Six 4 (faith stage) × 5 (religious category of person rated) analyses of variance were performed with the responses to the six questions concerning each applicant as the dependent measures. Faith stage was a between groups variable and religious type was a within subjects measure. The stage × religious type interaction effect was significant for two of the dependent measures and nearly significant for a third ('Like to see at college,' $p<.063$; 'Shares my beliefs,' $p<.003$; and 'Like to live with,' $p<.001$). Simple main effects tests showed that the first stage group, those with zero or one stage 4 or 5 responses, rated the Protestant most favorably, followed by the Catholic and the nondenominational Christian, and, finally, the agnostic and the atheist ('Like to see at college,' $<p.001$; 'Shares my beliefs,' $p<.001$; and 'Like to live with,' $p<.001$; see table 1 for means). The second stage group, those with two stage 4 or 5 responses, exhibited basically the same pattern ('Like to see at college,' $p<.01$; 'Shares my beliefs,' $p<.001$; and 'Like to live with,' $p<.003$). The same was true of the third stage group, those with three stage 4 or 5 responses ('Like to see at college,' $<p.022$; 'Shares my beliefs,' $p<.001$; and 'Like to live with,' $p<.023$). Those students who responded to the faith stage questions entirely with either stage 4 or stage 5 options, however, did not differentiate among the applicants on the basis of their religious preferences. This would seem to indicate a threshold effect in the ratings of the applicants between those persons who were stage 4 or 5 in all of their responses, who did not discriminate among the persons they rated, and all other respondents, who did discriminate among the persons they rated.

The main effect for stage was significant for two of the dependent measures not involved in the stage × religious type interaction ('Has a lot to contribute,' $p<.025$ and 'Like to be friends,' $p<.006$). Follow-up tests, however, did not find differences between any pair of means, and the pattern of the means was not systematic. The effects of religious type for the three variables with the insignificant stage × religious type interactions were examined. The pattern of the means shows that, regardless of the faith stage of the raters, the Protestant was consistently rated most positively, followed by the Catholic and the non-denominational

Table 1: Ratings of applicants by composite stage of respondent

| *Number of Stage 4 or Stage 5 Responses Selected by the Respondents* | | *Religious preference of the applicant* | | | | |
| | | | | *Christian* | | |
		Protestant	*Catholic*	*Nondenom*	*Agnostic*	*Atheist*
	see at college	1.31_a	2.00_b	1.92_b	2.77_c	3.00_c
0 – 1	shares beliefs	1.46_a	3.00_b	2.85_b	4.54_c	4.31_c
	live with	2.00_a	2.46_a	2.46_a	3.46_b	3.54_b
	see at college	1.20_a	1.70_{ab}	1.80_{ab}	2.30_b	2.40_b
2	shares beliefs	1.70_a	2.90_{bc}	2.60_b	3.50_{cd}	4.10_d
	live with	1.90_a	2.50_b	2.60_b	2.70_b	2.90_b
	see at college	1.90_a	2.10_{ab}	2.80_{bc}	3.00_c	2.80_{bc}
3	shares beliefs	2.10_a	2.80_a	2.70_a	3.80_b	3.90_b
	live with	2.50_a	2.70_{ab}	3.20_{bc}	3.10_{abc}	3.40_c
	see at college	2.11_a	1.89_a	2.44_a	2.22_a	2.11_a
4	shares beliefs	2.78_a	2.78_a	2.67_a	3.22_a	3.44_a
	live with	2.89_a	2.56_a	2.44_a	2.67_a	2.44_a

Note   Smaller numbers indicate greater agreement with the items. Means within a row without common subscripts are significantly different from each other, $p < .05$ (Duncan's test).

Table 2: Ratings of applicants by all respondents

| | *Religious preference of the applicant* | | | | |
	Protestant	*Catholic*	*Nondenom Christian*	*Agnostic*	*Atheist*
has a lot to contribute	1.88_a	2.02_a	2.38_b	2.55_{bc}	2.79_c
like to be friends	2.10_a	2.19_{ab}	2.43_{bc}	2.57_c	2.57_c
generally good or bad	1.98_a	2.24_b	2.33_{bc}	2.48_{cd}	2.62_d

Note   Smaller numbers indicate greater agreement with the items. Means within a row without common subscripts are significantly different from each other, $p < .05$ (Duncan's test).

Christian, followed by the agnostic and the atheist (see table 2).

Discussion

The results supported the hypothesis that one's faith stage affects one's evaluations of members of ingroups and outgroups. Respondents who selected statement options from earlier stages reacted differently in some ways to similar and dissimilar others than did respondents who were in later faith stages. In response to three of the questions, those in the earlier stages rated a fellow Protestant more favorably than non-Protestant Christians, who, in turn, were rated more positively than non-religious applicants. Those respondents who selected all stage 4 or stage 5 options did not make such distinctions; their ratings of the applicants did not differ. This threshold is quite clear, and may be related to the greater self-awareness inherent in stage 4 and beyond. However, three of the measures were significant only for the main effect of religious type. For these variables, no differences among the various stages were found; the Protestant was rated most positively and the atheist least positively by all respondents.

The hypothesis that stage 4 would be a transition period in terms of one's perceptions of ingroup and outgroup members received only partial support. There did not appear to be gradual changes occurring between the third and fifth stages; rather, abrupt differences existed between those respondents with three stage 4 and stage 5 responses and those respondents with four stage 4 and stage 5 responses. This 'transition' versus 'threshold' question should be explored further.

In a broader sense, these data support the contention of Fowler and others that one's faith stage has an important impact upon other aspects of one's behavior. Stage was an excellent predictor of the way respondents reacted to members of ingroups and outgroups. This relationship provides evidence for the construct validity of Fowler's theory. It is important to note, however, that a cross-sectional study such as this cannot provide support for Fowler's contention that he has identified stages of faith and not types of faith. Our data do not speak to the issue of development. Perhaps, like Pargament *et al.* (1984), we have measured different types of faith, not different stages of faith.

It also should be noted that Fowler believes that most people are not likely to enter stage 5 before middle age. A significant number of our youthful respondents were categorized as stage 5, however. Perhaps stage 5 does occur earlier for more people than has been believed. Alternatively, there may be some college students who are attracted by stage 5 sentiments, and therefore say they agree with them, who are not actually living by stage 5 ideals.

The small size of the final sample used in the analyses is problematic. Clearly, replication utilizing additional samples from different populations is needed to confirm the utility of this approach to studying faith development. However, to the extent that this technique is successful in measuring faith development, additional research will be more feasible and more reliable. As a result, more will be learned about Fowler's faith stages and their relationships with other important variables.

Notes
1. We would like to thank Cheryl Torsky and Martha Vermeulen for their assistance in data collection and Jane Dickie, Lars Granberg, and John Shaughnessy for their helpful comments on an earlier draft of this manuscript.

References
Allport, Gordon W. (1966) 'The religious context of prejudice,' *Journal for the Scientific Study of Religion*, Vol. 5, pp. 447–457.
Allport, Gordon W. (1958) *The Nature of Prejudice*, Reading, Mass., Addison-Wesley.
Allport, Gordon W., and J. Michael Ross (1967) 'Personal religious orientation and prejudice,' *Journal of Personality and Social Psychology*, vol. 5, pp. 432–443.
Brewer, Marilyn B. (1979) 'In-group bias in the minimal intergroup situation: a cognitive-motivational analysis,' *Psychological Bulletin*, vol. 86, pp. 307–324.
Chirban, John T. (1981) *Human Growth and Faith*, Washington, D. C., University Press of America.
Dion, Kenneth L. (1979) 'Intergroup conflict and intragroup cohesiveness,' in William G. Austin and Stephen Worchel (eds), *The Social Psychology of Intergroup Relations*, Monterey, California, Brooks/Cole Publishing Company, pp. 205–224.
Fowler, James W. (1980) 'Moral stages and the development of faith,' in Brenda Munsey (ed.), *Moral Development, Moral Education, and Kohlberg*, Birmingham, Alabama, Religious Education Press, pp. 130–160.
Fowler, James W. (1981) *Stages of Faith*, San Francisco, Harper and Row.
Fowler, James W. and Sam Keen (1978) *Life-Maps: conversations on the journey of faith*, Waco, Texas, Word Books.
Paloutzian, Raymond F. (1983) *Invitation to the Psychology of Religion*, Glenview, Illinois, Scott, Foresman and Company.
Pargament, Kenneth I., Ruben J. Echemendia, Steven M. Johnsons, Cheryl A. McGath, Vaughn Maatman, and William Baxter (1984) 'Assessing the religious needs of college students: action-oriented research in the religious context,' *Review of Religious Research*, vol. 25, pp. 265–282.
Smith, Tom W. (1983) 'The hidden 25 percent: an analysis of nonresponse on the 1980 General Social Survey,' *Public Opinion Quarterly*, vol. 47, pp. 386–404.
Tajfel, Henri (1970) 'Experiments in intergroup discrimination,' *Scientific American*, vol. 223, pp. 96–102.
Tajfel, Henri (1978) *Differentiation Between Social Groups*, London, Academic Press.
Tajfel, H., and John Turner (1979) 'An integrative theory of intergroup conflict,' in William G. Austin and Stephen Worchel (eds), *The Social Psychology of Intergroup Relations*, Monterey, California, Brooks/Cole Publishing Company, pp. 33–47.
Wilder, David A. (1981) 'Perceiving persons as a group: categorization and intergroup relations,' in David L. Hamilton (ed.), *Cognitive Processes in Stereotyping and Intergroup Behaviour*, Hillsdale, New Jersey, Lawrence Erlbaum Associates, pp. 213–257.

7. Pastoral care and faith development

These last two sections deal with the possible practical implications of faith development theory. Some of these papers inevitably take a positive view of Fowler's work, building on it rather than critically evaluating it. They are therefore in a different category from many of the other essays in this volume. Two species of 'practitioner' have found value in the faith development framework: pastors and educators. In section 7 we have drawn together some work that indicates its possible relevance for those involved in the ministry of pastoral care.

Thomas Droege has written widely on religious development and its practical implications.[1] In 'Pastoral counseling and faith development' he rehearses the similarities and differences of concern and content between these two areas. Each is concerned with diagnosis, but from different perspectives ('pathology' and 'growth'), utilizing different categories. It is claimed that faith development has something to learn here from more Freudian interpretations. Both pastoral counselling and faith development theory are interested in the nurture of the whole person and the ways in which this can be facilitated, but with different emphases ('healing' and 'guiding'). Here again faith development theory may need supplementing by insights from depth psychology. Each area also focuses on a different set of transitions (psychosocial transitions in the case of counselling theory, and structural transitions in the case of faith development). The author claims that a dialogue between the two areas is instructive. The paper was first published in *Journal of Psychology and Christianity*, vol. 3, no. 4, 1984, pp. 37–47.

The following two papers are both from *The Journal of Pastoral Care*. The first, by Steven Ivy, provides an assessment model for pastoral diagnosis that is drawn both from Fowler's work and from the ego development studies of Robert Kegan. In 'A faith development/self-development model for pastoral assessment', *The Journal of Pastoral Care*, vol. 41, no. 4, pp. 329–340, Ivy writes of our 'styles of consciousness' ('discernable patterns to the ways in which persons make life meaning') which may be discerned through the pastor's diagnostic 'structures for pastoral assessment'. A taxonomy of eight styles of consciousness ('literalizing consciousness', 'reflective consciousness', etc.) is provided, and the diagnostic structures of 'style of symbolic communication' and 'style of community' described in detail. A range of style-specific responses of pastoral care is also outlined. The paper concludes with a case illustration.

Dennis Schurter's article, from *The Journal of Pastoral Care*, vol. 41, no. 3, pp. 234–240, reflects on 'Fowler's faith stages as a guide for ministry to the mentally retarded'. Shurter inevitably deals mainly with stages 0, 1 and 2 of Fowler's faith development scheme, applying the stage descriptions to the mentally retarded and making some practical suggestions for ministry in this context.

Richard Shulik's 'Faith development in older adults' was published in *Educational Gerontology*, vol. 14, 1988, pp. 291–301. After summarizing Fowler's work and some of the criticisms that have been made of it, Shulik outlines his own findings from faith development interviews that he administered (along with other measures) to forty subjects aged sixty or over. Various hypotheses from gerontology were tested against the data derived from this study, and some other findings emerged in the course of it. These include Shulik's proposed variable *agesense*: 'the degree to which the older person was subjectively aware of changes in general, as he or she advanced' in age. Subjects at a more mature faith development stage were far more likely to be aware of changes associated with ageing than other subjects. Shulik also claims that subjects who are at intermediate stages of faith development are much less likely to be depressed than those assessed either at a 'lower' or at a 'higher' faith stage.[2]

Notes

1. See his *Self-Realization and Faith: beginning and becoming in relation to God*, River Forest, Ill., Lutheran Education Association, 1978; and *Faith Passages and Patterns*, Philadelphia, Fortress, 1983.

2. Other examples of the use that has been made of Fowler's work by those who reflect on the ministry of pastoral care include: Gary L. Chamberlain, *Fostering Faith: a minister's guide to faith development*, New York, Paulist Press, 1988; Michael Jacobs, *Towards the Fullness of Christ: pastoral care and Christian maturity*, London, Darton, Longman and Todd, 1988; K. Brynolf Lyon and Don S. Browning, 'Faith development and the requirements of care', and Carl D. Schneider, 'Faith development and pastoral diagnosis', in Craig Dykstra and Sharon Parks (eds), *Faith Development and Fowler*, Birmingham, Alabama, Religious Education Press, 1986, pp. 205–220 and 221–250; and Kenneth Stokes, *Faith is a Verb*, Mystic, Connecticut, Twenty-Third Publications, 1990.

7.1 Pastoral counseling and faith development
Thomas A. Droege

There have been relatively few attempts to relate pastoral counseling and faith development. Pastoral counseling has been linked historically to pastoral care. Faith development, fast becoming a separate discipline in theology, is generally linked to Christian education. Those alliances have been natural and appropriate, but it is time to bring these two unique theological perspectives into conversation with each other.

There are obvious similarities between pastoral counseling and faith development theory. Both are stepchildren of psychology and are suspect within some theological circles. They are step-children because their core concepts come from psychology; they are suspect because the language of both is more psychological than theological. Our discussion will show that some of the major differences between pastoral counseling and faith development have to do with psychological rather than theological issues. That is not to minimize the differences but only to point to a more fundamental problem which confronts both perspectives, namely, the justification of their theological identity.

Perhaps the most striking similarity between pastoral counseling and faith development theory is the importance of development to each. That is more obvious with the latter since development is at the very heart of its theory, but pastoral counseling has drawn heavily on Sigmund Freud and Erik H. Erikson's theories of development along with Carl R. Rogers' growth metaphors. It makes almost no use of the structural theory of development of Jean Piaget, Lawrence Kohlberg, and James W. Fowler, while faith development makes only limited use of the life cycle theory of Erikson and Daniel J. Levinson, and virtually no use of Freud. This means that counselors often use development to define pathologies or sin, while faith development theory uses it to define healthy growth or sanctification. Evidence of this difference will be apparent in what follows.

There are three areas in which a dialogue between faith development theory and pastoral counseling seems most natural and appropriate: diagnosis, faith nurture, and transitions. First, both pastoral counseling and faith development theory have elaborate and sophisticated methods of diagnosis, though one probes pathology and the other growth. Diagnosis used to be a bad word among pastoral counselors, especially Rogerians, but Paul Pruyser and others have reclaimed the term for use within the perspective of pastoral care. Second, both pastoral counseling and faith development theory are concerned with the nurture of the whole person and ways in which that can be facilitated. Faith development theory focuses more specifically on the nurture of faith, a focus often lacking in pastoral counseling. Finally, there are resources in each theory for dealing with transitions and the crises which inevitably accompany transitions. Each focuses on a different set of transitions, one psychosocial and the other structural, but a dialogue on the similarities and differences can be productive.

I assume that I do not need to introduce readers to counseling theory. I think a word of introduction to the other dialogue partner, faith developmental theory, may be helpful. The reader does not need a detailed knowledge of faith development theory, but it is important to understand some of the basic assumptions and goals of its method in order to understand how faith development relates to pastoral counseling.

The theory of faith development

Developmental psychology has made great advances since the turn of the century, and the church has made direct use of its findings, especially in the area of educational methods and curriculum planning.

There are two broad traditions of developmental theory which have relevance for understanding faith. Life cycle theory, identified almost exclusively with Erikson for many years, provided an impetus to think about the life of Christians, including their faith, from cradle to grave. Recent studies in adult development have made life cycle theory an even richer resource for reflections on Christian life and faith. The other stream of developmental theory originated with the insights of Immanuel Kant regarding the *a priori* structures of the mind. It was Piaget who translated this philosophical insight into a developmental psychology of genetic epistemology. He describes a sequential series of increasingly complex structural stages in cognitive development. Kohlberg discerns a similar structural development in terms of moral judgments. Fowler (1981) uses a modified form of the same schema in distinguishing developmental stages of faith.

These two approaches to understanding the developmental dimension of faith are complementary, the first psychosocial and the second cognitive. The life cycle approach identifies the existential issues of faith that are likely to be dominant at a particular stage of life; the cognitive approach shows how such faith seeks understanding through the capacities of knowing and valuing which develop in an orderly manner through a sequential progression of stages.

Developmental insights from the theories of Erikson and Piaget have only recently been applied to an understanding of faith. For centuries faith was described almost exclusively as an adult experience. The classical description of faith, dating back to Peter Lombard, is knowledge, assent, and trust. These three aspects of faith are ordered sequentially. Knowledge comes first, because it is necessary to know what is being promised or commanded before one can respond. Assent is the next step. It is considered an act of the will by which one affirms what one has heard and come to know as true. The final step is trust by which one clings to what has been promised. This classical description of faith makes sense for adults but not for children, especially those in the first years of life. One of the most divisive controversies in the early period of Reformation history was over infant baptism, which was really a controversy about whether children were capable of faith at an early age. On the basis of the classical definition of faith, they surely were not.

A developmental approach opens up a whole new way of understanding faith. For example, if trust is the foundation of faith as it is of the personality, as Erikson's theory would suggest, then it makes sense to hold up a little child, as Jesus did, as a shining example of faith. Then the educational task of parents and Sunday school teachers is not to get some kind of content into children's heads, e.g. Jesus died for our sins, but to foster a felt sense of trust in the nurturing support of a holding environment.

Fowler has done more than anyone else to develop a systematic theory of faith development. Following the lead of Piaget and Kohlberg, he provides us with a schema of what I would call faith-knowing or faith seeking understanding. In 'faith as knowing,' the mind is actively engaged in forming the content of faith in patterns or mental structures. These patterns can and do change in predictable, developmental stages. On the basis of the empirical evidence of faith interviews, Fowler has been able to distinguish consistent patterns or stages of faith. Each of these stages has its place within a sequential order. The sequence of stages never varies. Furthermore, each new stage builds and incorporates into its more elaborate pattern the operations of the previous stage. This means that development from one stage to the next is always in the direction of greater complexity and flexibility.

Growth from one stage to the next is not automatic and not as directly related to age as are the stages in the life cycle theory. Biological maturation, chronological age, psychological development, and mental growth are all factors that affect the readiness to make a stage transition. Transitions occur when the stability of a given stage is weakened by crises, new disclosures, and challenges that stretch the person's present pattern of faith knowing.

The transitions between stages are critical junctures (crises) at which a person's life of faith can be severely threatened. A stage transition means a painful ending as well as a new beginning. It means giving up a total way of making sense of things. It frequently entails confusion, doubt, uncertainty, and what may appear to be a loss of faith.

Thus it is not surprising that people cling to one way of thinking even when this proves to be constricting and distorted. Fowler's research indicates that many people remain at the stage of conventional faith for an entire lifetime. It is important to remember that a particular pattern of thinking determines the stage of knowing in faith and not the content of the person's faith. People with widely different theological positions may share a common stage of knowing. At the same time two people who make the same biblical or doctrinal affirmation may employ two different ways of thinking about it.

Though the above sketch of faith development theory is condensed and says nothing about individual stages of development, it should suffice as background for the dialogue that we wish now to pursue.

Diagnosis in pastoral counseling and faith development

One of the most obvious links between pastoral counseling and faith development theory is that each is concerned with diagnosis and each offers a conceptual apparatus for making a diagnosis. How important diagnosis is for pastoral counseling is a matter of continuing debate. Many pastoral counselors dislike the term diagnosis because they do not want to put labels on people, but in the broad sense of determining the nature of the problem, diagnosis has always been a part of counseling, including a part of the church's counseling. Faith stages are the diagnostic categories used in faith development theory. The Center for Faith Development Studies, which Fowler heads, has developed a rather sophisticated method of scoring faith interviews to determine the faith stage of particular individuals. There are two fundamental issues that need to be raised in relation to the diagnostic function of both pastoral counseling and faith development theory. The first has to do with the nature of the diagnostic categories: are they theological, psychological, or a combination of both? The second issue has to do with the use of diagnosis in pastoral ministry.

In pastoral counseling the problem is primarily the fact that psychological rather than theological categories are used. As Paul Pruyser observes in *The Minister as Diagnostician* (1976), it is thought that the pastor's perspective should be theological just as the psychotherapist's perspective should be psychological.

The same critique can be made of faith development theory, which is heavily dependent on the developmental psychology of Piaget, Kohlberg, and Erikson. Fowler (1981, p. 99) attempts to avoid that critique by making a sharp distinction between structure and content in his analysis of faith. He maintains that the diagnostic categories which are used to discern faith stages show how faith works and not what faith says. Psychology helps us understand the structure of faith, and theology helps understand its content. It is not obvious, however, that structure and content can be that cleanly differentiated. To say that a person is in stage 2 rather than in stage 5 is to say something about the quality of his or her relationship to God and others, and not just something about the level of his or her psychological development.

As one who is trained in pastoral counseling, both AAPC and CPE, and who is immersed in faith development theory, I would like to offer a preliminary observation relative to this issue. I think that both pastoral counseling and faith development theory need to heed the warning of Pruyser. Pruyser's warning is not a fundamentalist call to ignore the insights of contemporary psychology but rather an insistence that the pastoral perspective on counseling and human development be unique and true to the faith of the church. I think Fowler heeds this warning more than the leading theorists of the pastoral counseling movement. He keeps the focus on faith and carefully distinguishes faith from other patterns of human development: cognitive, moral, life cycle. As Pruyser (1976) notes, pastoral counseling has not made a similar effort to differentiate a faith perspective. He suggests the following categories in his own effort to distinguish a pastoral perspective: awareness of the Holy, providence, grace, repentance, communion, and vocation. These categories may not be the best ones to define the pastoral perspective of faith, but I believe that such a perspective is needed in pastoral counseling.

Though Fowler is right in keeping the focus on faith, he defines faith so broadly as a human universal that the unique Christian meaning of the term is lost. The only place in his theory where a Christian emphasis shapes his description of the faith stages is in his use of the image of the kingdom of God to describe stage 6. Most of Fowler's critics argue that this is too much of a Christian focus. I think it is too little. A pastoral perspective needs a focus on faith that is uniquely Christian if it is to aid in a ministry to persons in their process of development. Let me cite one obvious example. A biblical study of faith reveals the centrality of trust for a Christian understanding of faith. In Fowler's theory trust is mentioned only in his description of undifferentiated faith, a description that is not even included in *Life Maps* (1978) and appears only as a pre-stage in *Stages of Faith* (1981). If pastors were to use Fowler's faith stages, their understanding of how faith works and of the kind of nurture it calls for would be deficient and their pastoral care and counseling would suffer.

I think that Pruyser is right when he says that the discipline of psychology can be used for theological purposes only after you have defined a *pastoral* perspective that is true to the Christian faith. My own constructive attempt to use developmental theory as an aid in understanding faith follows that methodology (Droege, 1972, 1978). I use Erikson's life cycle theory as an aid in ordering the various elements or aspects of faith, such as trust, obedience, and commitment. I do not think it is advisable or even possible to make a sharp distinction between the content and structure of faith, as does Fowler, getting the content of faith from theology and the structure of faith from psychology. Scripture talks about the how as well as the what of faith when it refers to specific elements of faith like trust, obedience, commitment, and knowledge. A pastoral perspective on human development needs to be faithful to a biblical understanding of both the structure and the content of faith. A developmental theory can be used *within* such a perspective to aid in a ministry which is done *from* that perspective.

The second issue relative to diagnosis is a more technical one. It concerns the diagnostic categories used by both pastoral counseling and faith development theories. Generally speaking, pastoral counselors use psychodynamic categories and faith development theorists use structural categories in making a diagnosis. The difference this makes for case analysis is brought out clearly by Carl D. Schneider (1986) in an essay on 'Faith development theory and pastoral diagnosis.' His essay was delivered originally to an annual meeting of the Institute for Faith Development sponsored by the Center for Faith Development Studies at Emory University. Schneider reports on a study which he and colleagues at the Pastoral Psychotherapy Institute did on a faith interview which Fowler included in *Stages of Faith*. This report is the only critique of faith development theory from the perspective of pastoral counseling of which I am aware. It is a valuable study, because it critiques Fowler's theory from within, i.e., the way it interprets case material with the aid of the diagnostic categories of stage theory. Schneider writes that:

> Fowler has the apparatus for a major advance in pastoral diagnosis. But his actual use of his instrument in this case is more a reversal of the classical Freudian position than an advance upon it. That is, the classical Freudian interpretation of religious material was skewed toward a pathological interpretation, construed mainly in terms of its defensive function. Ego psychology has attempted to improve upon this formulation by reminding that an adequate formulation would have to include both defensive and adaptive function. *But Fowler often seems to see only the adaptive function, and neglects the defensive.*

Schneider's thesis is that the structural categories of stage theory lend themselves to idealized and intellectualized interpretations. According to Schneider, Fowler's interpretation needs to be corrected by a psychodynamic perspective that is more sensitive to the defensive reactions of distortion and denial. Schneider uses Ricoeur's phrase 'a hermeneutic of suspicion' in order to analyze Mary's Pilgrimage, the extended case study in *Stages of Faith*. While Fowler classifies Mary as stage 3, Schneider suggests that she is stage 2 or at best is in transition between stages 2 and 3.

Though it is not feasible to report the details of his analysis, I find Schneider's critique convincing. He employs a different set of diagnostic categories, psychodynamic rather than structural, to interpret a deeper level of ego functioning that is more defensive than adaptive. Schneider does not argue for one level of interpretation and against another, but rather suggests that they can and should be complementary. His essay represents the kind of responsible conversation which needs to go on between pastoral counseling and faith development theorists. Though I do not know of anyone who has tried it, a structural theorist could make a similar critique of a psychodynamic interpretation of case material by highlighting the adaptive as over against the defensive function.

It is noteworthy, that Schneider's critique is made from a psychological rather than a theological perspective. It is basically a difference between a Freudian and Piagetian point of view, though Schneider's ego psychology and Fowler's faith development theory have moved far beyond the founders of these two theoretical schemas of interpretation. The point to be highlighted is that the difference of interpretation between Fowler and Schneider is psychological and not theological. That does not make the difference trivial, but it does serve as one more example of what Pruyser has warned us about – that the pastoral perspective easily gets lost in a debate about different psychological opinions.

The nurture of faith

The diagnostic categories of pastoral counseling and faith development theory are useful only to the degree that they contribute to the nurture of faith. Both pastoral counseling and faith development theory are concerned about the nurture of faith. However, each has a unique emphasis which becomes sharper when compared to the emphasis of the other. Using the traditional categories to differentiate aspects of pastoral care (healing, guiding, sustaining, reconciling), the emphasis in pastoral counseling falls on healing and the emphasis in faith development falls on guiding. This difference is similar to the one that is made in relation to faith diagnosis where pastoral counseling stresses cure and faith development stresses growth.

Seward Hiltner (1958, p. 90) defines healing as 'the restoration of functional wholeness that has been impaired as to direction and/or schedule.' For the most part, pastors as counselors will see themselves as healers. When making a sick call at the hospital they may see their role differently, for the physician is seen as a healer and the minister as a sustainer. That role differentiation matches the soul-body split which until recently has been the accepted way of distinguishing between the functions of physician and pastor. But if pastoral counseling falls into the realm of the spiritual, then the pastor should function as a healer, and the role of healer is shared with mental health professionals who have helped to define the nature of healing and wholeness.

Pastoral counseling begins with the assumption that there is an impairment, some problem to be resolved, some deficit to be removed. The function of diagnosis is to determine the nature of the predicament, but even if the predicament is not defined explicitly, both counselor and counselee have some sense of the functional wholeness that is the goal of the process. Counseling is a means of moving from the predicament to the goal.

This model of healing corresponds to the classic model of salvation. In the latter model, sin is the predicament, salvation is the goal, and being saved is the process of moving from one to the other. The healing model of pastoral counseling is at least analogous to the salvation model of theology. I would say that the former is a dimension of the latter, a part of the larger whole. This relationship has prompted Protestant ministers to be leaders in the pastoral counseling movement, including in the Clinical Pastoral Education movement.

'What saves?' is a question that has always fascinated Protestants. The question assumes that the individual is in need of rescue, understood as some form of sinfulness. The saving power of grace, received through faith, enables the person to move toward the normative state of salvation or redemption. Theorists of pastoral counseling have changed the language: estrangement for sin, acceptance for grace, fully functioning for salvation; but the model is the same and healing/saving is the dominant concern.

Given this framework of understanding, it is not surprising that pastoral counseling theorists are critical of faith development theory for its failure to pay sufficient attention to pathology (sin). Again, Schneider's essay is an example. He contrasts Fowler's theory with Erikson's schema of psychosocial development, noting that Erikson identifies not only the task to be mastered at each stage: trust, autonomy, initiative; but also the result of failing to master the task: distrust, shame, doubt, guilt. Schneider writes that:

> Such polarities are absent from Fowler's theory. John McDargh, speaking of this tendency, suggests it may result from the influence on Fowler of the structural-developmental mode 'with its characteristic avoidance of depth psychology's preoccupation with pathology....
> This reluctance to describe faith in terms of a life trauma or inquiry that must be mastered seems to be the influence of the more ameliorative bent of structural developmental thought.'

*The language of developmental fixation, immaturity, or repression
is never evoked because of its presumed invidious connotations.*
This is indeed a blind spot in Fowler's theory. When he turns to
the difference between psychoanalytic and structural-developmental
theories, the discussion tends to focus around the issue of the
inability to *regress* stages in structural-developmental formulations.
But even that comparison is the most innocuous one possible. One
talks merely of going forward or backward, not of the possibilities
of being warped, bent, misshapen. Theologically we are talking
about an *inadequate doctrine of evil and sin in Fowler's theory.*
That judgment is accurate when made from a pastoral perspective
that is informed by the salvation model which sees healing as the
dominant function of pastoral care.

'What saves?' is not the only, or always the most important,
question to be addressed by those who are charged with the responsibility for nurturing faith. Faith is not only on the receiving end of
a rescue operation, but it grows and matures as an active expression
of what it means to be a Christian. 'Justification by grace through
faith' may be the central core of a Protestant confession of faith,
but a doctrine of sanctification is necessary to describe the shape
of the Christian life both within the community of the faithful
and in active involvement in the life of the world. One of the
major ecumenical contributions of the Methodist tradition, under
the influence of John Wesley, has been to remind Protestantism
of the importance of sanctification and the perfection of faith.
Faith development theory belongs in the center of that tradition.
It should not surprise us that Fowler is a Methodist and that the
Center for Faith Development Studies is located at Emory's Candler
School of Theology, a highly regarded center of theological studies
within the Methodist tradition.

The first thing one must say about faith is that it is the gift which
is rooted in and nourished by the forgiveness of sins. Having said
that, faith development theory becomes a marvelous resource for
discerning and facilitating the growth of faith to the point of its
full maturity.

Guiding is the pastoral care function which best describes what
will emerge as central from a pastoral perspective shaped by faith
development theory. Diagnosing the faith stage of an individual is
useful if it will aid in facilitating the growth of faith from one stage
to another. It is for this reason that Christian educators (Groome,
1980; Moran, 1983; Westerhoff, 1976) have been much more
responsive to faith development theory than pastoral counselors.
The identification of structural stages of faith contributes directly
to an understanding of the concepts of intellectual growth and
readiness for learning which have always been at the heart of
educational theory.

If pastoral counseling puts the emphasis on being saved, then faith development theory puts the emphasis on the state or 'way' of salvation. The stages of faith are clearly prescriptive as well as descriptive. Fowler (1981, p. 199) acknowledges that 'it has become clear that we are trying to do both descriptive and normative work.' Each stage builds on and incorporates into its more elaborate pattern the operations of the previous stage. This means that development from one stage to the next is always in the direction of greater complexity and flexibility. It is for this reason that the more developed stages can be considered more adequate than the less developed stages. The structure of stage 5 is better than that of stage 3, though that does not mean that a stage 5 person is better than a stage 3 person or believes something different as far as content is concerned.

Can one be prescriptive about faith and the process of its development? That question points to what is most unique and also most problematic about faith development theory and about what it can tell us regarding the nurture of faith. Fowler is aware of the issue when he says:

> Perhaps most important among the developmentalists' contributions, and among the most controversial, are the visions they offer us of optimal human development. While claiming to be descriptive of human experience generally, developmental theories, overtly or covertly, point toward an end-point or fulfillment of the pilgrimage of growth, that represents a normative vision of the human calling and possibility.... The growing edge, in constituting developmental approaches to religious education, lies in the direction of reclaiming, in education and ethics, normative images of human excellence. These naturalistic accounts of human moral and faith development must be engaged by the necessity for conversion of the heart and will. Theology and developmental research are needed which can clarify for us the permanent modifications of the path of human development that result from conversion or justification, and from the resulting unfolding *synergy* of divine and human love. This means a renewal of attention to the process my theological forebear, John Wesley, called *sanctification*.

In these words Fowler expresses the unique contribution of faith development theory, its emphasis on sanctification and optimal faith development, and its relationship to the process of justification by faith. Therein lies the difference between the two contexts within which pastoral counseling and faith development can and should be interpreted theologically. 'What saves?' is the question that pastoral counselors ask. If taken seriously, it places one squarely into the doctrinal domain of justification. 'How does faith grow?' is the question that developmentalists ask. If this question is taken seriously, then one is placed squarely in the doctrinal domain of sanctification.

Ideally, the doctrines of justification and sanctification should be complementary. Practically, the tensions created by the different emphasis within each have been the cause of heated controversies. Is faith primarily a passive reception of a gift that comes from beyond the self or an active power within the individual which energizes and shapes the Christian life? Is faith primarily a mystery known only to God, or is it an empirical reality which can be measured and charted? Is faith a gift or an achievement? Is faith a human capacity and skill which can be strengthened and perfected or is it the power of God at work within us to do what we are not capable of doing? Are we to approach people with a hermeneutic of suspicion, never underestimating their capacity for deception and destruction, or do we look for constructive ways in which faith is working in the lives of people and attempt to nurture its growth?

The tensions between pastoral counseling and faith development theory may not appear in the form stated in the above paragraph, but I think the questions reflect the difference in theological orientation between them. The tension is a healthy one as long as these two ways of looking at faith are recognized as complementary. Each perspective is a partner in the dialogue about faith as a whole. The tension becomes destructive only when justification and sanctification become either/or alternatives for understanding and nurturing faith.

Periods of transition

Both pastoral counseling and faith development theory have emphasized the importance of transitions. Pastoral counseling emphasizes the transitions related to situational crises such as divorce, bereavement, loss of job, and illness; faith development emphasizes the transitions related to the move from one stage to the next. Though there are differences between situational and developmental transitions, I want to focus on the characteristics which both have in common in order to highlight the fact that they are times of high vulnerability and great potential for growth.

What is involved in transitions? First, they represent an ending. Most of us try to ignore endings by acting as if we can go through a transition without coming to terms with what is left behind. We focus on the challenges of the next stage, the next job, the next marriage. In teaching on a college campus, I witness each year the transition that every graduating senior must experience. I have sat through many commencement addresses but have never heard one that mentioned ending, much less one that used it as a theme. Yet for college graduates there are many treasured relationships that come to an end – parting with friends with whom one has shared many intimacies, leaving mentors who have modeled a life of faith and hope, and departing from a community in which one's identity was shaped.

The second characteristic of transitions is that they carry people into a wilderness period, a time when nothing is firmly in place, a time when the pervasive feeling is a sense of loss. Persons are no longer who they were, and they are not yet who they will be. They are not sure who they are. Though this confusion is a normal and necessary part of a transition, it can be very unsettling, especially when there are no culturally established rituals to facilitate the movement between what was and what will be.

Only after we have attended to the first two characteristics dare we make the observation that transitions lead to a new beginning. Things fall into place, and the way into the future becomes clear. This does not happen all at once, and more often than not the new beginning is something that happens to a person rather than something the person chooses. Awareness of the new beginning may come as we realize that there is more order than chaos, more power to act than feelings of helplessness, more acceptance of self and world than self-doubt and self-contempt. As this happens, a surge of energy fortifies the person in transition for the new opportunities that make each new period of life and each new stage of faith exciting and challenging.

A transition is a painfully dislocating process of letting go and rebuilding. It means the dissolution of a way of being and knowing that was fairly stable and comfortable. It means living with ambiguity and a sense of uncertainty, often for a considerable period of time. It is no wonder that there is so much resistance to transitions, even when present modes of being and thinking prove constrictive and stunting.

In periods of situational or developmental crisis, then, there is often a need to go back to the roots of faith, back to trust as the sure foundation of faith. Both pastoral counseling and faith development literature describe the threat of chaos and the feelings of powerlessness that come to persons in transition. During such periods people often feel diminished and impoverished because there is so little to nourish a sense of self-worth and competence. The experience of people in transition is often like going back to the beginning of life in order to find a supporting environment and a solid foundation on which to build a future.

It was Erik Erikson who reminded us that trust is the foundation for both a healthy personality and faith. Or as he put it, religion supplies the systematic undergirding of basic trust for all of life. There is ample biblical support in both the Old and the New Testament for that insight. The supreme symbol of trust sustaining faith through a period of transition is the cross. All other transitions pale by comparison. Jesus was facing death, the most difficult of transitions, and the new beginning was not at all obvious. The crisis was magnified by Jesus' awareness of the importance of this event for the coming of the Kingdom of God. He felt the awful pain of dislocation and abandonment in the wilderness experience. He was forsaken by almost all who had supported his mission, which now seemed a total failure. He even felt forsaken by God. Nevertheless, he called out, 'My God, My God.' In this call is the trust of faith in spite of a sense of being abandoned. It was this trust that sustained him in the midst of chaos, loss of meaning, and powerlessness as he approached a death that threatened darkness for all the earth.

It is this kind of trust that pastors need to nourish in persons who are going through periods of transition. A careful reading of the pastoral care and faith development literature will sensitize pastors to such periods of transition and help them to identify the kind of transition that the person is experiencing. To recognize trust as the need of faith in such periods of transition can lead to an appropriate judgment about the kind of pastoral care that should be provided. At times the care may be nothing more than an attentive presence. At other times it might mean exploring values and beliefs. At yet other times it might be simply meeting material needs. Whatever form it takes, pastoral care makes real and concrete the promise of the Gospel to which faith clings all of the time. Hopefully, this is especially true in periods of crisis like transitions.

Pastoral care has always responded in some form to the needs of persons in transitions, but for the most part it has been an intuitive rather than an informed response. As a result, many transitions are understood poorly, or they are even resisted, by well-meaning pastors. It is a temptation for pastors to reinforce what Fowler calls a stage 3 level of faith, a conventional faith that believes what the church believes. A transition to a more independent, critical stage 4 level of faith is often painful. It is accompanied by doubts and often leaves the person isolated from the more conventional believer. For the pastor, it takes an act of courage to provide a supportive environment to a person engaged in such a transition, partly because the person may become a restless and disruptive influence in the community of faith. Nevertheless, the transition is vital to the person's life and to the life of the community of faith. Both pastoral counseling and faith development theory can provide us with reliable tools for facilitating this painful but productive process.

References

Droege, Thomas A. (1974) 'A developmental view of faith,' *Journal of Religion and Health*, vol. 3, pp. 313–329.

Droege, Thomas A. (1978) *Self-Realization and Faith*, River Forest, Ill., Lutheran Education Association.

Fowler, James W. and Keen, S. (1978) *Life Maps: conversations on the journey of faith*, Waco, Texas, Word Books.

Fowler, James W. (1981) *Stages of Faith*, San Francisco, Harper and Row.

Fowler, James W. (1982) 'Renaissance in religious education,' unpublished George H. Colliver Lecture, University of the Pacific.

Groome, Thomas (1980) *Christian Religious Education*, New York, Harper.

Hiltner, Seward (1958) *Preface to Pastoral Theology*, New York, Abingdon.

Moran, Gabriel (1983) *Religious Education Development*, Minneapolis, Winston.

Pruyser, Paul W. (1976) *The Minister as Diagnostician: personal problems in pastoral perspective*, Philadelphia, Westminster.

Schneider, Carl D. (1986) 'Faith developmental theory and pastoral diagnosis,' in Craig Dykstra and Sharon Parks (eds) *Faith Development and Fowler*, Birmingham, Alabama, Religious Education Press, pp. 221–250.

Westerhoff, John (1976) *Will our Children have Faith*? New York, Seabury Press.

7.2 A faith development/self-development model for pastoral assessment
Steven S. Ivy

One point of conflict, confusion, and promise for pastoral caregivers focuses on the task of pastoral assessment. Pastors (both parish and clinical) constantly evaluate situations, persons, and needs. We seek to hear and understand the life concerns and stories of our parishioners so that we can enable healthier, more whole, relationships to self, others, and God. The models which inform our evaluative processes include psychiatric, psychological, sociological, and theological resources. Pastoral persons may well use any and all of these models. However, our central need is for a model which focuses upon the sense of life purpose, the ultimate concerns and the meaning-making processes of those to whom we minister.

Persons develop meaning through relationships and projects which give coherence and continuity to life. Persons' ways of making sense of life develop through time. Pastors enable persons to develop life meaning. Pastors need to develop a sense of others' life meaning if we are to respond with accurate pastoral care. These issues are the overt concerns of constructive-developmental theory.[1] This article will demonstrate ways in which 'developing meaning' can inform pastoral evaluation processes. Stated more directly, this paper describes a model of pastoral assessment based upon constructive-developmental theory.[2]

'Assessment' refers to the activity of interpreting persons' life stories and experiences. Synonyms include diagnosis, discernment, and appraisal.[3] While these terms can be distinguished technically and practically, they each point to the act of interpreting. 'Pastoral' locates this act within the ministry of the church. Pastoral assessment is the art of understanding the concerns, perspectives, and life story of another person within the context of the ministry of the church.[4] Pastoral assessment examines persons' life fabrics so as to appreciate their sense of purpose, identity, and meaning. The broader theological foundations of pastoral assessment can be appreciated by reviewing the importance of 'theological hermeneutics' in contemporary pastoral dialogue.[5] The essential connection is that every pastoral act involves interpretation. Thus, it is incumbent upon the pastor to clearly recognize and consistently utilize the interpretative canons appropriate to the interpretative task at hand. In pastoral care and counseling, we have relied most heavily on psychological and psychiatric principles. The model proposed in this article utilizes the integrative research of constructive-developmental theory to indicate ways for the pastor to gather key information, perceive patterns in that information, and take action indicated by those patterns.

Key theoretical foundations

James Fowler's pioneering and integrative research into faith development has received much attention from religious educators. It has not yet found ready inroads into parish and clinical pastoral practice. Robert Kegan was a colleague of Fowler when he taught at Harvard. His integration of object relations theory and constructive-developmental theory provides a natural bridge to pastoral care and counseling concerns which has not been developed. The pastoral assessment model proposed here is based upon their theories and research.

Faith development theory is dependent upon the constructive-developmental school of psychology for its theoretical foundations. The chief advocate of this perspective was Jean Piaget, while Lawrence Kohlberg has extended the perspective into moral development issues. Several assumptions provide the foundation for this perspective. First, faith development theory assumes that persons construct their worlds. We cannot take for granted that each of us thinks and feels in relation to the same world. As pastors we need to understand the world-view which our parishioners create. Second, persons construct their worlds through clearly defined patterns. These patterns consist of such structures as forms of logic, stages of moral judgment, relationships to authority, and inclusion-independence cycles in relationships. Pastoral assessment need not utilize all of these patterns, but they do provide useful points of focus in examining the fabric of life. Third, persons develop. Each of us changes how we experience and structure life in clearly discernable stage (or stage-like) processes. Thus, pastoral assessment will utilize stages as a basic component. There has been significant criticism of the implied hierarchal structures of stage theory. Thus, I prefer to think in terms of styles or patterns of meaning-making. Fourth, the rhythms of meaning and faith define who we are as persons and communities. We live through narratives which shape our lives in clear and direct ways.[6]

Kegan has stressed that the stages or styles of world-construction are not the essential concern for those called upon to help others. Rather, the transitions between stages are frequently the occasion for pain, struggle, and hope. Transitional experiences call upon the person to give up a former way of experiencing the world and risk movement to another world-view which is not yet visible. He argues therefore that accurate appraisal of the person's transitional experience is essential if the helper is to provide accurate care. For example, some transitions demand that the person give up a dependent perspective and develop a more autonomous stance while others require the opposite. It is then incumbent upon the pastor to realize whether the parishioner is moving toward a more dependent or independent perspective so that appropriate interventions can be instituted.

I believe that the use of constructive-developmental theory in pastoral assessment will deepen the pastor's appreciation of and care for those whom we are called to help. This developmental model enables the pastor to focus on how life meaning is made. The pastor may then assess the quality and viability of the parishioner's world construction. This model also attends to religious ideas and rituals as ways of expressing life meaning. Finally, this model allows pastors to attend to transformation during life transitions. During transitions the tension between falling forward and falling backward may be a source of pain. Moral concerns, religious concerns, and relational concerns all find a way of being heard and understood through this particular framework.

A pastoral assessment model

Pastoral assessment begins in good pastoral conversation which enables persons to tell their stories in their own words and at their own pace. The skills of active listening and accurate interpretation are crucial to this task. Pastoral assessment can then proceed on the basis of two principles. First, there are discernable patterns to the ways in which persons make life meaning. We are more alike than otherwise. I refer to these patterns as 'styles of consciousness.' Second, these patterns may be perceived through diagnostic lens. These lens provide windows on the inner life of persons. These lens are the 'structures' for pastoral assessment.

Styles of consciousness.

Style of consciousness describes a coherent pattern of meaning-making, action, and relationship. These styles provide frames for the person's experience of on-going issues and times of transition. The following summaries highlight key descriptive elements in persons' styles. It is important to remember that 'more mature' styles are never pure and thus may contain elements from previous styles. This pastoral perspective emphasizes how each style forms an interpretative framework fo consciousness and spirituality. The descriptions enable the pastor to trace patterns of increasing integration, life frameworks of shaped meaning, and transformations of those frameworks. While the developmental levels are the focus of this discussion, the experiences of transition from one style to another are crucial.[7]

Pleasure consciousness describes the foundational period of

composing one's story. The typical age for this period is birth to two years. It involves preconscious psycho-physiological drive satisfaction and regulation. Physical reflexes and their satisfaction by a nurture giver provide seeds which later bear fruit in one's affective-cognitive experiences of hope and trust. Thus, the affective foundations of trust and hope grow through relational dependence and an emerging capacity for differentiation. While children are not able to express verbally their spiritual world-view, the seeds are sown which may significantly influence later experiences.

Magical consciousness describes the next period which usually develops during two to six years of age. This style involves a deep affective response to stories with little capacity to reflect on that story. There is also little capacity to tell one's own story. Fantasy, intuition, and perception are the focus of this person's experience. For the developing child, play and language are the tools for gaining control of one's psycho-physiological reflexes. This period is marked by affective lability and a growing awareness of causality so that self and world are differentiated. One's family of origin provides the dominant context for this developmental era.

Literalizing consciousness is typical of the six to twelve year old child. This person attends to order and dependability so that impulses are controlled. One's own needs and wishes become prominent so that personal autonomy becomes increasingly important. Literalness in relation to self and others is a key hallmark. Cultures which influence one's sense of self-esteem are of primary importance. Story telling and role oriented behavior is primary. Abstract notions of justice have no appeal for this person nor do characters who have no concrete reality. The focus is on tradition and literal interpretation.

Interpersonal consciousness is usually not seen prior to age twelve. One's allegiance is to a primary reference group and its values. Other norms and perspectives tend to be uncritically synthesized with those of the primary group. Authority and values are often entrusted to a powerful other. This opens the possibility for conflict when differing contexts have differing authorities and norms. But as long as there is a consensus of authority, this perspective may be stable throughout life. Interpersonal consciousness allows the person to step outside the flow of life and to reflect on the various patterns and meanings of life. Further, there is a capacity to see self as do others and to hunger for acceptance of that self by peers, authorities, and God. Identity is thereby formed in the mirror of how others respond to attempts at self-authorship. This style of meaning-making becomes the stable, life-long perspective for many adults.

Idealizing consciousness is a transitional period frequently evolving between ages eighteen and twenty-four. This person lives out of ideology and joins with those whose ways of thinking are the same. Personal identity is derived from authorities, although these authorities are personally chosen. The emotive power of symbols is transferred to thought patterns in this severe demythologizing period. Commitment to a task, an idea, or a group with a purpose is the central theme. Consciousness is fused with the dominating myth of one's chosen culture.

Reflective consciousness is usually not seen prior to age twenty-nine and is likely to remain stable at least to forty-five. This person cognitively and emotionally accepts responsibility for making choices of authority, ideology, values, and relationships. The prior impetus toward demythologization forces awareness of individual uniqueness. Institutions which support expressions of identity and self-authorship in light of differing points of view nurture this form of consciousness. Identity formation is the drive of this person. A need for explicit doctrine rather than mystery and for living deed rather than rich symbol characterize this person. The struggle for self-authorship may leave a sense of relational emptiness and sterility. In addition, experiences which break the molds of explicit paradigms may open reflective consciousness to further development.

Integrative consciousness seldom emerges prior to age forty-five and is quite rare, at least according to Fowler's research. This person values the life of unification and feeling. Rather than focusing on explicit systems, this person experiences the reality which the many systems represent. Intimacy with the conflicts of self as well as intimacy with relational conflicts become the hallmark of this era. Myths and images emerge out of the person's depths. Participation with the divine rather than description of the divine is the goal. Openness to self-change as well as support for others' changes is possible. This person's confidence in self opens the way for intimacy with others and with the Other.

Unitive consciousness is seldom experienced prior to age fifty. This person is concerned with universals and essences. Unitive consciousness no longer maintains the boundaries of partial visions but incarnates the vision of unity in life and the negation of self. While the on-going fulfillment of unity may elude this person in external life, the internal life no longer maintains self boundaries. Rather, this person embodies with imperfection the highest values and stories of their ultimate commitments.

A few qualifying notes are needed when using styles of consciousness to organize pastoral assessment. First, these eight styles of meaning-making are relatively coherent and stable. Transition from one style to another may be generated by either internal development or external crisis. Transitional experiences are painful, yet ultimately satisfying times of change. Second, regression is potential in each transition and crisis. That is, there is no assurance that the next style of consciousness will emerge from a particular crisis. Crisis experiences may lead one to function at an earlier level of consciousness than might be expected by development. Finally, there is evidence that we can function with differing styles of consciousness in different spheres of life. For example, when functioning in her profession, one may exhibit one style and when participating in religious activities, she may exhibit another style.[8]

Diagnostic structures.

If we are to attune ourselves to another's style of meaning-making, specific structures for assessment must be considered. These structures provide lens, listening posts, or windows through which the pastor can focus attention on values and meaning systems. These structures are style of symbolic communication and style of community.

Style of symbolic communication focuses our attention on the person's use of symbols and expressions of conceptual meaning.[9] The self joins cognition and affect, 'the rational and passional,' in language, metaphor, story, and ritual. These expressions represent the person's mediation of ultimate convictions. Symbolic communication attends to the ways in which symbols and faith stories enhance the stability of the person's present level of consciousness and aid movement between levels. Because symbolic communication attends both to the content of the person's story and to the emotional intensity of those contents, it is a key integrative theme. Symbolic communication expresses the person's sense of identity and transcendence.

While listening to and encouraging the telling of another's story, the pastor will listen for answers to the following questions, along with the implied 'Why?' which accompanies each.

a. What beliefs, values, symbols, or rituals are important to you?
b. What purpose or plan is there for your life?
c. What place does sin or evil have in the world?
d. What does being a religious person mean to you?
e. What spiritual disciplines or actions are important to you?

Reflective questions through which the pastor evaluates the person's responses to the above questions include the following.

a. What symbols, metaphors, and images are used in referring to what is ultimate for the person?
b. Are references to meaning, symbols, and metaphors literal or metaphorical, one-dimensional or multi-dimensional?
c. What level of reflection constitutes the person's sense of meaning and the ultimate? Are consistency and comprehensiveness important elements of reflection? How are pain and ecstasy dealt with in the person's sense of meaning?

Table 1: *Diagnostic criteria for symbolic communication*

Spiritual consciousness	Characteristic criteria
Pleasure	Affective communication dominates. No narrative experience. Embedded in world of affect and image.
Magical	Magic, fantasy, and non-reflective affect. Little narrative capacity. Consistency is irrelevant.
Literalizing	Non-reflective orthodoxy. Dramatic narratives in which identification with heroic images is primary. Literal consciousness with rigid requirements for consistency.
Interpersonal Symbols	Embedded in conventional, tacitly held systems. Authoritative narratives communicate existential values through limited abstraction and critical reflection. Conventional, multi-dimensional, consistent consciousness.
Idealizing	Ideal translation of symbols to thought with powerful affective content. Narratives are measured by explicit values which are 'over-against' the previous, tacit values. Idealizing, differentiated consciousness with focus on consistency with the ideal.
Reflective	Pragmatism within explicit ideological systems. Symbols are reduced to their ideational content. Narratives are critically measured by explicit, self-conscious experiences and values. Dialectical, multi-dimensional consciousness with focus on consistency.
Integrative	Paradoxical joining of opposites (affect-cognition, symbol-idea). Narratives maintain tensions of self, groups, and the ultimate. Paradoxical cconsciousness in which symbols evoke deeper reality of self and world. Comprehensiveness valued more than consistency.
Unitive	Unity within paradox joins symbols, self, and ultimate reality into a complex system. Narratives hold the unity between mundane and ultimate realities. Direct awareness of and participation in 'Oneness' transcends consistency and comprehensiveness.

Table 1 provides a summary of the diagnostic criteria relevant to each style of symbolic communication.

Recently I was privileged to sit with the young adult children of a man who was dying. When I entered the room it was as if I had entered a tomb. After introductions and joining in their silence for a few minutes, I began to inquire into the situation and some of their history. They appeared relieved to talk. At one point I asked, 'Is your father a religious man?' The son responded: 'Well, he was thoughtful toward his friends and family and he prayed.' Chaplain: 'So he believes in God?' Son: 'Oh yes, although I don't know much about that. We just never talked about such things.' Chaplain: 'Does church mean anything to him?' Son: 'He was baptized and when he was trying to stop drinking he went with us and he always made us go.' Chaplain: 'What is important to your father?' Daughter: 'He wants us to be happy and not be burdened with him.'

This conversation suggests a literalizing style which is concrete and non-reflective. There is little room for them to transcend their pain. The very concrete symbols of church, prayer, and happiness inform their perspective but provide no interpersonal support.

In summary, symbolic communication is that aspect of the person's meaning-making which channels choice, self-awareness, and commitment through a system of values, representations, and stories. Key elements in this assessment process include the interaction of cognition and affect, the use of narratives, and the level of consciousness reflected by focal concerns.

A second diagnostic structure is style of community (table 2). This category focuses upon the nature of community which the person experiences.[10] Since ultimacy is conveyed and expressed within the individual's construction of community, pastoral assessment of a person's sense of community is of crucial importance.

The pastor can attend to persons' style of community by considering their stories with the following questions in mind, along with the implied 'Why?' which accompanies each.

a. Does independence or inclusion (autonomy or relationship) appeal most to you?
b. Who is most important to you now?
c. To whom do you look for advice when you have a difficult problem?
d. What values, commitments, and relationships are significant to you?

In considering the person's story the following reflective questions enable clear evaluation.

a. Is this person striving more for independence or for inclusion? Are autonomy needs or attachment needs most closely related to the pain or joy of this person?
b. What persons, groups, and classes are included and excluded as decisions are made and meaning is formed?
c. Who are significant others with whom the person maintains a sense of identity and meaning? What questions and criticisms do these significant others raise for the person?
d. How does the individual experience the community's tasks of holding on, letting go, and staying put? How are pain and ecstasy experienced by the individual within the community?

A seminarian came to my office on referral of a professor who said, 'I think she has fallen out with her boyfriend and can't get

Table 2: Diagnostic criteria for style of community

Spiritual consciousness	Characteristic criteria
Pleasure	Mothering culture. Attachment with little differentiation. Affective embeddedness within family.
Magical	Parenting and family culture. Attachment with growing sense of will. Unreflective identity with visible signs of power and family; e.g., sex, ethnic, size, impulses.
Literalizing	Peer culture; those like me. Autonomy, role differentiation, and competence. Cooperation, and stereotypical images. Traditional meanings.
Interpersonal	Mutual, interpersonal, tacitly valued groups and persons. Attachment and belonging with those who are experienced as similar. A derived identity of shared experiences and feelings. Leads to compartmentalizing of values.
Idealizing	Mutual, interpersonal, explicitly valued groups and persons. Attachment and belonging based on similar commitments. An identity of shared ideals in which authoritative leaders are validated by the individual.
Reflective	Self-authorship and self-selected culture. Autonomous yet shares intimacy with those who share norms. Internalized identity and authority with encouragement for achievement and choice that is self-congruent.
Integrative	Intimacy within interdependent and complex cultures. Attachment and autonomy dialectically joined for inter-dependent self-definition. Paradoxical quality which joins personal experience and reflection on others' experiences in search for love and justice.
Unitive	Intimacy with universal community of persons and Being. Attachment and autonomy transcended for sense of at-one-ness. Compassionate identification with universal principles linked through purified ego and disciplined intuition with ultimate ground of being.

over it.' Her initial complaints were that she was crying but had no feeling, that she was isolated, and that she had no friends who truly understood her. At the end of our first conversation I interpreted to her my understanding that she was in the midst of changing her relational and emotional values and offered to walk with her in exploring her changes. This resonated with her and was comforting. During our second conversation I asked her what was really significant to her right now. She gave a long explanation of how her dating change was a result of theological disagreements with the young man, with wanting more freedom to be herself, and with feeling stifled emotionally by their group of friends. This young woman was caught in a painful transition between idealizing and reflective styles of consciousness. She was moving from an interpersonal to an autonomous style of making meaning.

In summary, style of community is that aspect of meaning-making through which the person experiences community and relationship. Key dynamics for pastoral assessment purposes include the persons who make up the significant community, the nature of relatedness to these persons, and the shaping power of this community on the individual's framework of meaning.

Pastoral interventions

Pastoral assessment is an important step in pastoral care-giving. Indeed, pastoral interventions must flow from the assessment if assessment is to have more than intellectual value. How does this model contribute to pastoral practice? What suggestions and insights into persons are crucial to this diagnostic perspective which generate accurate empathy and clear directions for care?

First, the emphasis of this assessment model is on the inner perspective of the person. The open, semi-structured method gives persons an opportunity to put their pilgrimage into words. While the inner experience of the person is of primary interest, other aspects (such as behavior, affect, relationships, and environment) are considered within the model. This encourages the pastor to listen for the inner meaning of the person's story and pilgrimage. Yet valuing the uniqueness of each person does not obscure the importance of the normative image which lies at the heart of the method. This normative image offers possibilities for both hope and judgment in pastoral care.

Second, this diagnostic model empathetically considers the plight of each individual since the same processes of development and change form the ground of us all. The sensitive pastor is aware of both quiet and transition in his or her own experience. Thus, whether the present shape of the person's life is quiet or transition, the pastor can find a point of compassion. Further, this allows the same assessment paradigm to be used for both prevention and intervention, both educative work and remedial work. Educative work focuses on current life tasks while remedial work integrates earlier tasks into the present life situation. In this light, there is attention to the fundamental stories and the elements of character through which the person is known. There is also sensitive account taken of the community environment.

This model of pastoral assessment offers a clear way for the pastor to hear patterns of order and meaning. Further, the developmental model itself encourages the pastor to focus on growth and anticipate crises. The pastor is helped to focus attention on the pain and costs involved in growth. Since dialogue is at the heart of the structural method, the pastor will be able to avoid objectifying and analyzing the person apart from significant relationship. The normative image of this perspective is theological in that its imagery attends to the meaning inherent in life narrative and story. The strengths and weaknesses of persons' life positions are evaluated in light of their style of symbolic communication and style of community. The pastor can then care for and empathize with persons' senses of wholeness at their place along life's way.

The thrust of this model for pastoral assessment clarifies the underlying structures which shape a person's world-view. It offers a care-full way of being with people suffering pain and joy. Tables 1 and 2 illustrated adaptive religious capacities through symbolic communication and community. We may hypothesize that the failure to develop these capacities may lead to maladaptive, or at least less than optimal, religious capacities.

These diagnostic possibilities may be further considered in light of adaptive responses on the part of the pastoral care-giver as outlined in Table 3. This table suggests style-specific directions for pastoral care. As an illustrative summary it is intended to provide approximations of important developmental considerations for pastoral care. This summary provides possibilities for both educational and therapeutic pastoral care. Pastoral assessment does make a difference with how we respond to people. We may intervene in order to comfort another. At other times the pastor may take a position slightly ahead of the other in order to spur growth. That is, appropriate interventions may be gleaned for both crisis ministry and nurturing ministry. Hence, the model offers guidance for pastoral care.

An illustrative case

I met Mary as her clinical supervisor when she was 26 years old. She and her husband were in a time of determining their life directions. She entered clinical training in order to test both personal growth and professional direction. Her style of symbolic communication was most evident in her reflections on her spiritual disciplines which included meditation and interpretative dance. She wrote that:

> Prayer is, at least for me, intensely personal and intimate.... My prayers come out of personal encounter and are related to specific experience, person, and place.... Dance and movement are often my meditation. I return more centered and more aware of a loving Other. God seems nearer in love in these times than in times of formal meditation.

The reflective, self-conscious ways in which Mary met her world are well illustrated in this quote. She was open to varied levels of meaning and was willing to make claims on the basis of her own experience.

Mary's style of community was most evident in relation to her parents. Initially she struggled to free herself from her lack of freedom. 'I think I have tended to idolize my father as my perfect model for a professional person.' Later she began to focus more on her own power and direction.

Table 3: Suggestions for style-specific pastoral care

Spiritual consciousness	Adaptive pastoral care
Pleasure	Support and encourage investment and dedication on part of parents. Provide comfort and pleasurable involvement when in presence. Gospel as nurture.
Magical	Support and encourage family to provide tolerant yet firm boundaries for autonomy. Provide symbols and fantasy experiences which help organize action and feeling in light of limits. Gospel as concern for fear and trust.
Literalizing	Support assertiveness and competence. Tell dramatic stories in which heroes demonstrate difference between good and evil. Expect traditional responses, nurture sense of fairness, and provide emotional intimacy. Gospel as a trustable promise.
Interpersonal	Support engagement in peer groups and attachment with those who are similar. Provide authoritative perspective with affirmation of tacit values. Do not expect independent answers. Watch for dichotomizing between authorities. Gospel as acceptance and guide.
Idealizing	Support development of self-identity. Engage in critical consideration of previous tacit values. Attend to dynamics of marital and vocational choices. Challenge easy acceptance of dominant myths. Gospel as ideal call.
Reflective	Support explicit self-conscious reflection on values and self in relation to self-authority and ulitmate meaning. Balance ideal and pragmatic in support of self-definition. Evaluate direction of marriage and vocation. Gospel as self-evaluated truth.
Integrative	Support both coping with inner needs and toleration of needs of others. Evaluate and interpret previous ideology. Examine deeper and more holistic ways of knowing. Encourage search for love and justice through self-surrender. Gospel as celebrated depth.
Unitive	Support mediation between master myths and present fulfillment. Nurture dreaming and prospective symbols which give the future living meaning. Allow relativization of ideology and support universal compassion. Gospel as embodied dream.

> My constriction and tendency to freeze up in ministry may just be because I was expecting to be a 'female (father).' Somewhere emerging out of my cocoon is Mary. I feel much more hopeful and alive and energized in that happening than ever before.

Mary was looking to her own power and authority in seeking to resolve her problems. Her pain and frustration were out of her mixed need for both attachment and authority.

I assessed that Mary was experiencing a transition from idealizing to reflective consciousness. In this transition she was making a critical self-evaluation of her God-images, was seeking a nurturing community which would give her autonomy more support, and was seeking to embody more dancer than thinker styles. I sought to support her moves to reflective consciousness by helping her connect with some of the diverse communities she wished to experience, by offering a safe place for reflection to counter her feeling of being uncared for and uncaring as she made the transition, and by maintaining a pragmatic base to counter her flights back into idealism. My pastoral assessment enabled me to offer accurate empathy and care to support Mary through a painful experience.

Conclusion

Pastoral assessment is a way of caring for the person through structured attention to their pain and hopes. The diagnostic process involves hearing persons' perspectives in the context of their life stories, using the styles of meaning-making as ways to structure the information, and evaluating their story in light of clear diagnostic criteria. Accurate pastoral responses may then follow. Through this process, the pastor can move from intuitive to informed pastoral care. Then the depths of care can be fully experienced thereby embodying God's love in our mutual stories.

Notes

1. The most comprehensive pastoral statement of this research is in James W. Fowler, *Stages of Faith: the psychology of human development and the quest for meaning*, New York, Harper and Row, 1981, and *Becoming Adult, Becoming Christian: adult development and Christian faith*, New York, Harper and Row, 1984. Other literature which informs this article includes Robert G. Kegan, *The Evolving Self: problem and process in human development*, Cambridge, Mass., Harvard University Press, 1982, and 'There the dance is: religious dimensions of a developmental framework,' in Christiane Brusselmans (ed.), *Toward Moral and Religious Maturity*, Morristown, N. J., Silver Burdett Co., 1980. An important feminist critique is Carol Gilligan, *In a Different Voice: psychological theory and women's development*, Cambridge, Mass., Harvard University Press, 1982.
2. This article is based on the author's Ph.D. dissertation, 'The structural-developmental theories of James Fowler and Robert Kegan as resources for pastoral assessment, The Southern Baptist Theological Seminary, 1985; Edward E. Thornton, committee chair.
3. Paul Pruyser, *The Minister as Diagnostician*, Philadelphia, Westminster, 1976; Seward Hiltner, 'Judgement and appraisal in pastoral care,' *Pastoral Psychology*, 1965, vol. 16, pp 41–47; Wayne Oates, *The Christian Pastor* (3rd. rev. ed.), Philadelphia, Westminster, 1982, pp. 167–189.
4. For clarity this article will utilize individual language and examples. However, diagnostic models focused on families and groups are also important. The model proposed here does offer unarticulated possibilities for family and group assessment.
5. Charles Gerkin, *The Living Human Document*, Nashville, Abingdon, Press, 1984; Donald Capps, *Pastoral Care and Hermeneutics*, Philadelphia, Fortress, 1984.
6. James William McClendon, *Ethics: systematic theology*, vol. 1, Nashville, Abingdon Press, 1986.
7. The names given to these styles are the author's. They are influenced by the stage theories of Fowler and Kegan but emphasize slightly different concerns. They should be used descriptively rather than nominatively.
8. Ronnie Lesser and Marilyn Paisner, 'Magical thinking in formal operational adults,' *Human Development*, 1985, vol. 28, pp. 57–70.
9. Style of symbolic communication is primarily founded on Fowler's structures of symbolic functioning and world coherence. Fowler, *Stages of Faith*, pp. 243–252.
10. Style of community is primarily founded on Fowler's structures of locus of authority and bounds of social awareness and on Kegan's autonomy-attachment needs and functions of embeddedness cultures. Fowler, *Stages of Faith*, pp. 241–249; Kegan, *The Evolving Self*, pp. 107–110, 115–132.

7.3 Fowler's faith stages as a guide for ministry to the mentally retarded

Dennis D. Schurter

When Kyle, my fourteen-year-old, returned from his six day camping trip with the Boy Scouts last summer, he was delighted to find that Nana, his grandmother, had come for a visit. Kyle immediately launched into tales of his 'super-campout' in the Guadalupe Mountains of west Texas. Nana was confused. She didn't know where he had been or where the Guadalupe Mountains were. Patiently Kyle had to get out a map and show Nana where he had been and what the trip was about before he could continue his exciting tales of high adventure.

A road map is often helpful in showing others where one has been or giving directions on where one is going. Those of us who minister to persons who are mentally retarded would be glad for a road map that would give direction as we guide these people on their faith journey. In recent studies I have found the research of James Fowler to be that kind of helpful road map as I have walked with people who are retarded on their spiritual pilgrimage.

Fowler's developmental model

In James Fowler's *Stages of Faith*, he sees faith in the same dynamic way that the bible does; that is, not simply as a belief concerning certain ideas, but rather as a dynamic commitment, loyalty, and trust toward something or someone. To have faith is 'to get one's heart on' that something or someone. Unlike the scriptures, however, Fowler says that every person has a faith, not only the person who places his or her trust in God. Each person's faith is the 'generic consequence of the universal human burden of finding and making meaning.'[1] Faith is built on a relational triad involving self, others, and a 'shared center of value and power.'[2] In the Christian's faith, that shared center of value and power is God in Christ.

Fowler adopts a structuralist's developmental model in defining the stages of faith development in a person's life. He follows in the footsteps of other developmental researchers such as Piaget in cognitive development, Kohlberg in moral development, and Erikson in psychosocial development. Fowler proposes six stages of faith development based on his interviews with over 350 persons of all ages in this country. The six stages form a theoretical road map of the faith pilgrimage from age two through adulthood. These stages are sequential; that is, one cannot jump from stage 2 to stage 4 without going through stage 3. They are also not meant to be an achievement scale that one must climb in order to have a 'successful' faith. Nor is it necessary for a person to go through all stages. For example, many adults remain comfortably in stage 3 most of their lives after going through stages 1 and 2.

Fowler's pre-stage and faith in people who are retarded

Our purpose in looking at Fowler's stages of faith development is that we might use his theory as a road map of the mentally retarded adult's faith journey. With this in mind we will be looking only at stages 1 and 2 plus what Fowler calls the 'pre-stage' of the infant. As we shall see, movement through these stages and into stage 3 is predicated on normal intellectual development. Therefore, stages 1 and 2 are where we find people who are retarded.

The pre-stage is the period of undifferentiated faith for the child from infancy to one and a half or two years of age. It is the time prior to language development and, thus, is beyond the kind of research that Fowler has done. This pre-stage is important because it is during this time that 'the seeds of trust, courage, hope and love are fused in an undifferentiated way' and 'underlie all that comes later in faith development.'[3]

In his discussion Fowler quickly moves on to stage 1, but we need to look at the pre-stage more carefully, for it is here that we find people who are profoundly retarded. Those of us who are chaplains to people who are mentally retarded may give the least attention to those who are profoundly retarded because of their very limited response. They seem to respond as infants in adult bodies. In visiting with those who care for these people, we are aware of the tedium of the daily care they require, the endless rounds of feeding, bathing, and diaper changing.

Fowler's description of the stage of undifferentiated faith can remind us that the profoundly retarded adult has spiritual needs just as a very young child does. These needs include love and trust, which can be demonstrated through consistent care, mutuality of eye and voice contact with others, aid in controlling and using an adult body with an infant's mind — all of which help combat a person's fear of insecurity and abandonment. When the chaplain recognizes the critical role of the retarded person's family members and other care givers in meeting these needs, he or she can provide support for them in these tasks. The chaplain can help these significant others to know that they are addressing spiritual needs as they accomplish their daily routine duties with the person who is profoundly retarded.

Roy's description of Mary, who resides at the facility where I serve as chaplain, is a case in point. During his six months as an aide on her dormitory, Roy had grown close to Mary. She was a thirty-year-old woman in a severely under-developed body and was unable to speak or to do anything for herself. Nevertheless, Roy enjoyed giving her special attention. He worked to interpret her non-verbal communications and to understand when she was happy, was hurting, or had had enough to eat. She responded with smiles, eye contact, and other signs of increasing trust and affection. In this process Roy was nurturing an undifferentiated (as far as we can tell) faith in Mary, which can only be nurtured through the personal relationship with another caring person.

Fowler's stage 1 and people who are severely retarded

Fowler calls stage 1 the time of intuitive-projective faith. For the normal child it develops between the ages of two and six. The transition from undifferentiated faith to intuitive-projective faith is generated by the convergence of thought and language. It is during this period that preoperational thinking develops, according to Jean Piaget; *i.e.*, the child thinks and expresses herself in language but cannot do cognitive operations such as discerning cause and effect relationships or reversing logical thought.

Some other characteristics of the person in stage 1 include fluid and magical thinking, not logical thought. The person is characterized by egocentrism and cannot see another's perspective, only his or her own. This person's locus of authority is external. His or her perceptions of reality are made up of clusters of images, not yet logical associations or narratives. He or she can listen to stories but cannot retell them.

Fowler notes the dominant faith development issues in this stage are awakening to consciousness and memory; awakening to reality beyond everyday experience (*e.g.*, death and God); differentiation of self from others; and introductory learning of language and gestures, which opens the way for learning the rituals of faith.

Adults who are severely or moderately retarded will have a stage 1 faith all of their lives because they will not be able to move beyond Piaget's preoperational thinking. Recognizing the characteristics of stage 1 faith can aid the minister or chaplain in guiding these men and women in their faith journey.

One of the most important points on the road map is that persons in stage 1 organize their perception of reality through clusters of mental images, not necessarily causally connected or in logical order. For the normal child these images are the building blocks for further growth as the blocks are put together in later years through concrete operational thought. Fowler points out that education 'has a tremendous responsibility for the quality of images and stories we provide as gifts and guides for our children's fertile imaginations'.[4]

For the mentally retarded adult in stage 1, however, the issue is more critical. For them their images shape all of life and are the mainstay of their way of relating to the world. Tommy, a thirty-year-old man, is an example. Nine years ago I had my first meeting with Tommy in order to tell him that his father had died. He smiled, did not understand, but seemed appreciative of the special attention he received from me that day. From that time until his death last year, whenever Tommy came to the chapel or saw me on campus, he would smile and say, 'Daddy died.' I had planted an image in our first meeting which he responded to whenever we met. Although we had other experiences together, he never moved beyond that mental image in his relationship with me.

As clergy we are in the business of creating images for these persons in stage 1 of faith development. The quality of those images can affect their lives and their relationships with God and others. When those images convey qualities such as graciousness, security, affirmation, and caring, we are helping those persons in stage 1 to develop a faith that can support them in the future.

The worship service is an important setting for creating images. The adult who is severely retarded may spend a lifetime learning the language, gestures, and rituals of the faith community, but it is important to persevere. The atmosphere of the service, the stories told, the songs that are sung, the actions shared – all these can serve to help establish positive images concerning the church building, the community, the minister, and God.

Retarded adults with a stage 1 faith can experience symbols as important objects in the worship setting but may not attach other meaning to them. Someone may gain a positive image of the cross and associate it with the church but could not tell the story behind it or why it is important. Nonetheless, the central symbols of the faith (such as a specific cross or bible) should be shared so that they can become part of the images associated with religious practice.

At Denton State School a small group of women came to chapel service each week. During the Lenten season I spent five or ten minutes each week taking an eighteen inch wooden cross to each person, asking them to handle it and tell me what it was. I asked each one, 'Who died on the cross for you?' If they could not answer, I repeated the words, 'Jesus died on the cross for you.' Through this ritual I hoped to familiarize them with this important symbol of the faith and to help them associate the cross with Jesus, the chapel, and the chaplain. As we went through the six weeks of Lent together in this manner, they became more comfortable with the ritual and began to anticipate handling the cross each week.[5]

Fowler's stage 2 and people who are mildly retarded

Fowler calls stage 2 that of mythic-literal faith, the stage that organizes reality into narrative form (mythic) but without discerning meaning in the narrative (literal). This stage is primarily from age seven through twelve. The transition from stage 1 to stage 2 begins with the emergence of what Piaget calls concrete operational thinking; that is, thinking logically and recognizing cause and effect relationships, applying these thought processes to life experiences in a concrete way but not in abstractions.

Other characteristics of the mythic-literal faith stage include the ability to narratize one's experience, giving the images of stage 1 unity and value. The person in stage 2 still uses imagination but within the realm of logical scrutiny. Stories become the medium for organizing reality, yet a person cannot examine a story for its meaning. ('Story' in this usage does not mean fictional material but refers to narrative as a way of organizing reality.) This person has only a one-dimensional use of symbols. He or she can begin taking the perspective of the other person. This opens the way for an ethics of reciprocity and a basic concept of fairness.

Fowler describes the dominant faith development issues in this stage as affiliation, belonging, being cherished; differentiation of self and one's group from others; learning the lore, legends and language of the religious group; sorting out fact and fantasy, the real and the 'made up.'

The person with moderate retardation may acquire some of the characteristics of a stage 2 faith. The person who is mildly retarded is more likely to have a more fully developed mythic-literal faith because of more adequate cognitive development. Numerous implications for ministry with retarded adults grow out of Fowler's insights.

One of the most important insights concerns the ability to organize reality in narrative form, which is the outgrowth of the ability to think logically and to organize the images of stage 1 into sequence and order. Obviously, this point is important for religious education and preaching because stories are a major medium for imparting biblical material and the faith of the community. More importantly, shared stories are a way of building community. In this stage a person has great interest in belonging to a group and in distinguishing one's own group from others. A primary way of doing that is to learn the stories, language, and rituals of one's group.

This is a critical concern for adults who are retarded. They will very likely spend their lives in stage 2 and must depend on stories as a way of expressing and organizing reality and as a way of being a part of the community of faith. This fact does not mean that their faith is of less value or importance than the faith of people in stage 3 or 4. It simply means that what for most people is a developmental stage to be passed through is for the retarded adult a lifelong task.

A sense of belonging is so important for persons who are retarded because they have experienced rejection in so many ways. Therefore, the narratives and rituals of the faith community that instill a sense of belonging need to be repeated many times over. Although the interpretation of the stories may not be recalled, nevertheless the stories themselves bind the person to the community.

A person's participation in the community's periodic celebration of the Lord's supper is this kind of experience. While there are various interpretations of the meaning of the eucharistic celebration, at a basic level it summons each member of the community to recall Jesus' death and resurrection and to share in the benefits of that sacrifice and victory. The person who is retarded and has a stage 2 faith can learn the story, share meaningfully in the celebration, and know that he or she belongs to the community that gathers at the Lord's table.

At Denton State School the presentation of the Christmas pageant has become an annual tradition. Rehearsals begin early in October, and over ninety residents take part in the cast and choirs that present the Christmas story in December. During the past ten years hundreds of different people have participated in the story. Many look forward to doing so again and again. Their ritualized participation in the Nativity story not only helps them learn the story, but also enhances their sense of belonging to the faith community that celebrates faith in Jesus throughout the year. Their participation in the story binds them to the community.

It is also helpful when the individual's story can intertwine with that of the community. One example of this would be when a person who is handicapped shares his or her testimony. Then that person's experience becomes part of the faith community's experience, and their stories merge. At one church in Denton, which has a bible class for adults who are mentally retarded, the class members periodically share a brief 'concert' in the Sunday evening service. Their musical presentation not only builds their sense of belonging but also enhances the unity of those class members with the entire congregation.

The mildly retarded adult's ability to take the perspective of another person has implications for ministry. First, an ethic of reciprocity becomes possible. As one becomes able to look at things from another's point of view, one also is more able to discern a basic fairness in relationships. It helps for the chaplain to know what ground he or she can stand on when talking with someone about right and wrong behaviour. Second, this kind of perspective taking opens the door for an anthropomorphic image of God. Someone who can construct another person's position, can also construct God's position, thus seeing God as another person. The way in which a chaplain may want to deal with this ability of the person in stage 2 may vary with the pastoral goal in mind. Nevertheless, it is important to note that this person will probably not develop a more abstract or spiritual image of God.

The person in stage 2 has a one dimensional, literal view of symbols. The person cannot discern the meaning in the symbol, but that does not mean that the symbol is of no value. There can be great value even though that person's relationship to the symbol is concrete and literal. For example, when a retarded adult receives instruction for participation in baptism, the importance and value of the sacramental act can be imparted through story, both the biblical story and the faith community's story. The act of using water can also be related to daily events which are part of the person's experience, such as bathing. After the person's participation, he or she can be encouraged to tell and retell his or her own story and reinforce the importance of the act.

Summary

For ministers, chaplains, and educators who are seeking to minister to people who are retarded, James Fowler's theory of faith development offers one kind of road map to give guidance to that ministry. The characteristics of Fowler's stage 2 faith are generally applicable to people who are moderately and mildly retarded. We can apply Fowler's description of stage 1 faith to persons who are severely retarded. Even his brief discussion of undifferentiated faith can point us in some directions with those who are profoundly retarded.

Yet no road map can describe all aspects of the terrain. Fowler does not claim that his is the definitive statement on faith development or the faith journey. His is only one perspective, admittedly a structuralist, humanistic perspective, based on a developmental model. He does not try to deal with other ways in which one's faith can grow, such as the bible discusses under the topic of the fruit of the Spirit. He does not purport to measure the depth of a person's commitment, love, or capacity for joy and peace within. These also may be important aspects of our ministry with people who are mentally retarded. Nevertheless, Fowler's theory provides us with one kind of road map for the pilgrimage of faith, a road map that can assist us in being spiritual guides to people who are mentally retarded.

Notes
1. James W. Fowler, *Stages of Faith: the psychology of human development and the quest for meaning*, San Francisco, Harper and Row, 1981, p. 33
2. *Ibid.*, p. 17

3. *Ibid.*, p. 121
4. *Ibid.*, p. 132
5. For further implications for ministry growing out of stage 1, see the excellent study of preaching for children by Revd James Carr which appears in the 1983 issue of *Perkins Journal*, published by Southern Methodist Unviersity, Dallas, Texas.

7.4 Faith development in older adults

Richard N. Shulik

This paper addresses two streams of research that have enjoyed increasing popularity in recent years: gerontology and the paradigm of faith development. In writing for a journal such as this, I will assume that my readers have more familiarity with the field of gerontology, in general, than with the field of faith development research. Accordingly, I will organize this paper around the following two questions. First, what is the paradigm of faith development? Second, can the faith development paradigm make a contribution to the field of gerontological research? Can it teach us anything about the aging process that we do not already know?

Faith development paradigm

I will begin by providing a brief history of the paradigm of faith development research. This paradigm was first developed during the 1970s by James Fowler (1981). As an ordained minister in the United Church of Christ, and as a faculty member of the Harvard Divinity School, Fowler worked with students who were in the process of preparing for careers in various facets of religious work. Some hoped to become members of the clergy, and others were preparing for academic careers. Fowler involved his students in training experiences in which he asked them to perform some of the following exercises. First, he asked them to define their sense of religious faith. This process involved such questions as: What is my faith? What are the bases or foundations of my faith? and What worldly commitments are required by my faith? Fowler then asked them to trace the history or development of their faith, as they recalled it. This process involved such questions as: Have I always believed as I do now? Can I recall a time when my faith was not as developed, or not as complete? What were some of the significant influences (including individuals and life experiences) that changed the nature of my faith? How do I feel that my faith is more complete at present, than it was before? and In fact, do I feel as if my faith is continuing to evolve? Thereafter, Fowler pursued his discussions with his pupils along different lines. He asked more specific questions, including: How has your faith helped you with specific ethical dilemmas? How has it impinged upon your most intimate relationships? Has it influenced your grasp of political and social change? How do you view relationships among different faiths or religions? and How do you construe the meaning of *community*?

This pattern of questioning his students did not emerge spontaneously, in a highly systematic form. Rather, it emerged over a period of years. It was unstructured at first, but eventually it became more structured. Within several years, Fowler began to sense that his students' responses to these 'faith questions' exhibited recurring patterns. Some of these patterns included the following. Students frequently described earlier phases or stages of development, in which their faith seemed to be less comprehensive or less mature. Moreover, many students described similar influences (e.g., a significant mentor, a cross-cultural experience) which they associated with an expansion of their faith. Fowler began to immerse himself in the research literature of developmental psychology as a means of understanding more clearly some of the patterns that he perceived in his students' interviews and reports. Specifically, he turned to the structural-developmental paradigm of Jean Piaget (1972), which some investigators had already applied to the study of facets of religious belief. (For example, David Elkind [1961, 1962, 1963, 1964] had studied the ways in which children's concepts of God seem to evolve in a stagewise sequence; similarly, Maria Nagy [1948] had studied the ways in which children progress in their grasp of death and dying, along a sequence of stages.) Fowler also explored the research of Lawrence Kohlberg, (1969, 1973) who had shown that children and adolescents conform to Piagetian stages in the development of their faculties of moral reasoning and moral judgment. Fowler then formulated several basic hypotheses, as follows. First, he hypothesized that the phenomenon which we call religious or spiritual faith can be viewed as a *system*. He also hypothesized that that 'faith system' could be viewed as an entity which develops gradually, over the course of a lifetime. And he hypothesized that the faith system would be found to progress through a stagewise sequence of growth processes, closely resembling the stages described by Kohlberg and Piaget.

A thorough review of Piagetian theory is well beyond the scope of this paper. However, Piaget's basic principles of development are reviewed in his book, *Principles of Genetic Epistemology* (1972) and in Kohlberg (1969). Briefly, these principles may be summarized as follows.

a.   Processes of psychological development are conceptualized in terms of stages.
b.   A stage may be characterized as a stable, consistent mode of functioning.
c.   Each stage represents a state of equilibrium between the individual and his or her environment.

d. Progress from lower to higher developmental stages is fostered by interaction with the environment.

e. Stages of development differ from one another qualitatively but not necessarily quantitatively. (E.g., intellectual growth is not merely a matter of his knowing more facts but rather a matter of his structuring knowledge in qualitatively different ways.)

f. Processes of psychological development that are of greatest interest are those that occur universally.

g. These are processes of development which occur in universal sequence. (E.g., each person progresses through the program of stages in the same sequence.)

h. Development may be arrested at any point along the sequence or continuum of growth. (E.g., for whatever reason, a given person may not reach the final developmental stage.)

A major thrust of Fowler's early work was an ecumenical spirit. His divinity school students represented many different religious backgrounds, even including some students who practised oriental faiths. In focusing upon stages of development, Fowler wanted to examine ways in which his students' 'faith journeys' were similar or alike, despite the fact that they came from different cultural traditions.

Within a short time, Fowler transcended even the spirit of an ecumenical perspective. He experienced an important 'leap of faith' (if a very bad pun may be tolerated) as follows. His earliest research had been limited to a highly specialized sampling of subjects (divinity school students). It then occurred to him that he might study the faith systems of people whose lives are entirely outside the sphere of traditional, organized religious institutions. Fowler contemplated some of the questions that he had posed to divinity students (e.g., What are your bases or rationales for believing, or not believing, in God? How do you understand the significance or the meaning of your life in this universe? What are the moral or ethical implications of your system of belief?). He understood that he could pose such questions to people who were not members of institutional or organized religious bodies. Moreover, he hypothesized that nonreligious subjects would reveal 'faith journeys' that closely paralleled those of some of his religious subjects. For example, imagine that we may interview the following hypothetical subjects:

a. a person who practices some religion, even to the point of attending his congregation but who openly admits that spiritual and religious concerns do not play a central role in his life;

b. an agnostic who attends meetings of the Ethical Culture society;

    c.   a self-proclaimed atheist who disavows the need for congregations or communities of any kind;

    d.   a person who is devoted to a secular pursuit (e.g., a career or the arts) who claims never to have addressed spiritual or religious questions;

    e.   a Soviet citizen whose 'faith,' or method of constructing the world and the community, has always been guided by Marxist-Leninist teachings.

Fowler hypothesized that such individuals could provide meaningful faith development interviews, and he also hypothesized that their interviews could serve as the basis for an assessment of their level or stage of faith development. In fact, it was at this point that Fowler formally named his research paradigm the study of *faith development*, as distinguished from *religious* or *spiritual* development. He also resisted suggestions that his paradigm be called *belief system* research or the paradigm of the *system of personal philosophy*, for he recognized that the word *faith* had spiritual connotations, and he wanted to acknowledge the importance of spiritual experiences for those subjects who would have been so inclined.

Having broadened his scope of research in this manner, Fowler now began the second phase of his research. He and his students began to interview subjects of many ethnic, educational, and socio-economic backgrounds, including people who had religious identifications and affiliations, and people who had none. This was a major undertaking that lasted for many years. Moreover, at this time, he also began the difficult task of refining his formulation of the stages of faith development. Again, a thorough review of Fowler's stages of faith development is beyond the scope of this paper. However, in brief, his six stages of faith development may be described as follows.

Faith stages

Stage 1: intuitive-projective faith This is the faith of the very young child, who is preverbal or in the early stages of verbal development. He or she is responsive to feelings or moods associated with family gatherings and congregations but is not aware of subtler issues of faith or belief.

Stage 2: mythic-literal faith At this stage, the young child is fascinated by myths and stories. He or she enjoys congregations or gatherings and may also respond to physical faith-symbols (e.g., altars, crucifix). But scriptures, parables, and religious concepts are taken literally and not endowed with abstract meaning.

Stage 3: synthetic-conventional faith This is a stage of older childhood which represents terminal development for some adults. Faith is seen primarily as a means of bringing people together, fostering a sense of unity in family or community, or a sense of 'belongingness.' Differences among faiths are not truly acknowledged or are treated as not really existing. This stage may also be characterized by naive egocentrism in which one believes that his or her faith is 'best' or is the only possible faith.

Stage 4: individuating-reflective faith This faith may occur in adolescence. Faith is seen as something that one must develop within oneself, not so much for the purpose of achieving a sense of union with family or community, but more for the purpose of making sense of oneself and one's place in life. The need to establish a personal foundation of faith or belief is paramount, even for those who stay within the scope of organized religion.

Stage 5: conjuctive faith At this stage, one acknowledges certain paradoxes inherent in the 'faith journey,' which perplex and challenge all systems of faith (e.g., all people strive for meaning and achievement in life, and yet all are 'leveled' in the end by death). Alternatively, there are things that some seekers hunger to know, and yet these things often seem to be unknowable. At this point, faith 'tests itself' by addressing some of these universal paradoxes. There is also a deepening of appreciation for the complex issues associated with faith, and also a deepening of empathy for people who are at other stages in their faith journeys.

Stage 6: universalizing faith This is not so much a distinct stage but rather a category of individuals (e.g., Mohandas Gandhi, Martin Luther King, Jr.) whose faith was so refined that they served as moral or spiritual exemplars for their communities. They had profound effects upon the faith of others around them.

Evaluation

Fowler's paradigm of faith development has enjoyed increasing popularity in recent years. It has attracted the attention of religious educators, who see in it a framework for understanding the processes of religious growth and development more clearly. Moreover, those who are interested in the religious/spiritual education of adults have also found Fowler's work to be very exciting (Stokes, 1981). Fowler's perspective has had other practical applications as well. Some clinical psychologists (including this writer) have used Fowler's perspective as a means of formulating some clinical syndromes that may not be adequately described according to existing diagnostic frameworks (cf. Shulik, 1981). Moreover, Fowler's framework is extremely appealing as a means of studying individual lives.

Fowler's paradigm has generated its share of controversy. Many objections and criticisms evoked by Fowler's work parallel those generated by the work of Kohlberg in the area of moral development and moral education, including the following:

First, the phenomena described by the words *faith, belief,* and *spirituality* are not clearly distinguished. Some critics charge that the entity whose growth Fowler proposes to examine is too poorly defined.

Second, even if faith development is accepted as something that may be defined, some critics resist the notion that it conforms to structural-developmental principles of growth. Some protest that it does not develop along the lines of a stage-continuum at all. Others allow that it may manifest stages of development, but they protest that Fowler has not correctly described these stages, or that the stages may not form a 'universal sequence.'

Third, most significantly, some critics have charged that there is a subtle form of elitism inherent in Fowler's work. This criticism holds that there is a subtle but inescapable tendency for readers to place a higher value upon the higher stages of development. In other words, those who reach the higher stages must somehow be 'better' or 'more adequate' than those whose growth was arrested at earlier stages. Fowler himself has been concerned with this criticism and has strictly urged his readers to avoid using his theory as a means of valuing some people more highly than others. Moreover, he has not endorsed any curricula of religious education that are intended to foster growth or change in the students' levels of faith development. (Curiously Kohlberg was somewhat bolder in response to such criticism. He did endorse some training programs that were meant to foster moral development in children and adults, and he did openly acknowledge that he regarded higher levels of moral development as being more adequate.)

In brief, Fowler's work has emerged gradually and has evolved into a research paradigm of wide-ranging interest. It has intrigued theologians, educators, and clinicians alike and has shown great promise in many academic and applied fields.

Faith development and gerontology

Let us now consider the second major question of this paper. What does Fowler's paradigm offer to the field of gerontology? Does Fowler's perspective reveal aspects of the aging process which we have not yet observed?

I became interested in the application of Fowler's work to gerontology in the late 1970s. In 1977, I began to attend Fowler's informal seminars at Harvard Divinity School, in which he met with faculty and students for the purpose of exploring his theory of faith development. I became interested in the practical task of helping Fowler enlarge his data base. At that time, Fowler had compiled nearly 400 complete faith development interviews. He generously offered to share his interview files with me. He and I noted with interest that only four of his subjects were over 60 years of age. I noted the lack of older subjects in his data base. Fowler accounted for this deficiency by noting that most of the interviewees had been selected by his own students, who usually favored younger subjects. He had not tried to use random sampling or scientific selection techniques. I proposed to compensate for the deficiency in his data base by finding 40 new subjects – 20 women and 20 men – who were at least 60 years of age.[1] I incorporated this research endeavor into my doctoral dissertation proposal.[2] In turn, Fowler agreed to serve as an unofficial member of my dissertation committee, despite the fact that I was attending a different university.

Hypotheses

In seeking older subjects, I was largely motivated by pure curiosity. Apart from expectations or research hypotheses, I merely wanted to see what I would find. But I was also aware of several hypotheses that had been popular among gerontologists in recent years, which had stimulated empirical research. Some of these were as follows:

a. the 'disengagement' hypothesis (Cummings and Henry, 1961), which held that old age is a time in which it is normal or appropriate for people to begin to withdraw from many spheres of life in which they were much more active in earlier years;

b. the 'life review' hypothesis (Erikson, 1950; Butler, 1963), which held that old age is a time in which one deliberates upon one's history or past experiences in order to render one's life a coherent or meaningful totality;

c. the 'preparation for death' hypothesis (Hinton, 1967; Kübler-Ross, 1969) which held that old age is a time when many people normally begin to prepare for the approaching end of life;

d. the 'philosophical development' hypothesis (Kohlberg, 1976) which held that there are certain philosophical insights and perspectives that can only be achieved in old age, that are inaccessible to the young.

I felt that these and several other hypotheses that purported to describe the normal experience of aging could be tested by means of Fowler's empirical methodology. In addition to asking questions that were derived from these hypotheses, I also administered to my 40 subjects a host of psychological tests and measures. These included basic projective techniques (the Rorschach and Thematic Apperception tests), the Jane Loevinger Ego Development questionnaire (Loevinger, 1970) and two Kohlberg moral judgment interviews.

Findings

First I found that older individuals made excellent subjects for faith development research. It was indeed possible to administer the Fowler interview virtually to every subject who had agreed to join the research endeavor. The faith development interview is a 'semi-clinical' technique, which is structured in a rather loose manner. The subject is encouraged at first to present a brief life sketch highlighting some of the basic features of his or her life story. The first questions are highly objective, focusing upon demographic material (e.g., familial, residential, educational, and career histories). Thereafter, the focus moves gradually toward more subjective questions (e.g., questions about experiences and influences which have been most central or significant in the subject's life). Still later, the examiner encourages the subject to address questions of faith, belief, and world view. Again Fowler and his associates had developed this interview technique in the process of working with much younger subjects. It was gratifying to find that older subjects could be engaged in such an interview process in a meaningful, revealing manner. In fact most of my older subjects enjoyed their interviews.

I did not succeed in finding any broad based support for any of the above-mentioned hypotheses concerning the nature of the 'normal' aging process. For example, two or three of my subjects had begun deliberate, self-conscious processes of reviewing their lives, but the vast majority of them had not done so. Moreover, most of my subjects could not reveal any philosophical perspectives that they regarded as being unique to old age. Relatively few of my subjects were preoccupied with the issues of death and dying. Similarly, hardly any of them considered themselves to be 'disengaging' or 'disengaged' from most spheres of life. Several reported to me that they were busier than they had been prior to retirement. Their activities and interests had changed since middle life, but they were every bit as much involved in their families and communities as they had been in earlier times. In brief, I failed to find support for several broad hypotheses which had been offered by psychologists and gerontologists over a period of years. (Actually, this finding was neither original nor surprising. For example, the disengagement hypothesis of Cummings and Henry had provoked much research over a period of years, but generally the hypothesis had not found much empirical support.)

However, some positive findings emerged. Early in the course of my research, I created a variable which I called 'agesense.' I defined it as the degree to which the older person was subjectively aware of changes in general, as he or she advanced through the periods of late middle age and old age.[3] Interestingly, the subjects' *agesense* ratings were very closely related to their levels of faith development. Subjects who had achieved more mature levels of faith development were far more likely to be subjectively aware of changes associated with aging processes. Those whose faith development was less mature tended to have little or no subjective sense of changing as they grew older.

Other findings had implications that exceeded the sphere of gerontology. There was the question of the relationships between faith development and other psychological variables. I was especially interested in the relationships among Fowler's faith development stages and the Kohlberg and Loevinger (1973; 1976) measures of moral and ego-development. I found very high correlations among all three of these structural-developmental variables. In other words, subjects who revealed advanced stages of development within Fowler's framework were also likely to reveal mature development within other structural-developmental frameworks. This finding raised the interesting question of whether there is some central process of development which all structural-developmental theorists are viewing from different perspectives.

My findings also suggest, unexpectedly, that subjects who have achieved *intermediate* stages of faith development are much less likely to be depressed than subjects whose developmental stages are low or high. This finding seemed to have clinical implications, but in the context of my research, I left this avenue unexplored. As my research effort came to an end, I also regretted having omitted measures of intelligence and life satisfaction among my variables. My interviews suggested that subjects at higher stages of faith development were generally more satisfied with their lives, although there were exceptions to this general trend. I also sensed that there was a relationship between intelligence and faith development, but again the relationship would not necessarily be a linear one, in that superior intelligence would not necessarily guarantee that a subject achieve a mature level of faith development.

Generally, the faith development paradigm seemed to be readily adaptable to research in the field of gerontology. In the context of my limited research experience, I felt that Fowler's paradigm revealed some interesting and unexpected aspects of the aging process. My hope is that Fowler's perspective may be embraced by other gerontologists and that it can help us achieve a clearer, more detailed picture of the processes associated with normal aging.

Conclusion

This paper has served two purposes: to introduce and review James Fowler's faith development paradigm and to review one endeavor in which that paradigm has been applied to gerontological research. The faith development paradigm can indeed make a meaningful contribution to many fields of psychological research; gerontology is one of those fields. Fowler's paradigm of research is extremely appealing, both in its theoretical underpinnings and in its empirical techniques. Again Fowler's paradigm is controversial, inasmuch as many of the criticisms which have been leveled against the research of Kohlberg may also be directed toward the work of Fowler. Be that as it may, Fowler's work, like Kohlberg's before it, appeals to those who prefer holistic perspectives. Fowler seeks ways of drawing together many different aspects of the individual's life in order to establish a sense of unity or wholeness. Fowler's work also appeals to existentialists, who like to discern trends of meaning in the course of a life, and it surely appeals to those who prefer the developmental life-span perspective. This writer also hopes that Fowler's work will increasingly appeal to gerontologists and to social scientists who are interested in rigorous, well-grounded empirical resarch.

Notes
1. My subjects consisted of nearly equal numbers of Catholic, Protestant, and Jewish subjects, and they also represented a wide range of educational, vocational, and economic backgrounds. Moreover, the sample included no subjects who were chronically ill. Three of the forty subjects had been involved briefly in psychotherapy, but none suffered chronic mental illness.
2. In the process of conducting my interviews, I spent between 6 and 10 hours with each subject. The transcripts of my interviews, and most of the additional raw data, are on file at the Henry A. Murrey Research Center of Radcliffe College, Cambridge, Massachusetts.
3. Subjects were rated in agesense on the basis of responses to such questions as: Do you feel as if you have changed in any significant way as you have grown older, especially in your most recent years? Do you feel the changes that you have experienced have been important? In what areas of life have you changed? How would you describe these changes? Subjects received a rating of 1 if they stated that they had not changed in any significant way, of 2 if they said that changes had occurred, but that the changes had been primarily physical (e.g., decreased stamina or endurance) or health-related (e.g., greater vulnerability to illnesses, or weaker recuperative powers); and of 3 if they responded in terms of changes in their emotional, philosophical, or psychological characteristics.

References
Butler, R. (1963) 'The life review: an interpretation of reminiscence,' *Psychiatry*, vol. 26, pp.65–76.
Elkind, D. (1961) 'The child's concept of his religious denomination: I, the Jewish child,' *Journal of Genetic Psychology*, vol. 99, pp.209–225.
Elkind, D. (1962) 'The child's concept of his religious denomination: II, the Catholic child,' *Journal of Genetic Psychology*, vol. 101, pp.185–193.
Elkind, D. (1963) 'The child's concept of his religious denomination: III, the Protestant child,' *Journal of Genetic Psychology*, vol. 103, pp.291–304.
Elkind, D. (1964) 'Piaget's semi-clinical interview and the study of spontaneous religion,' *Journal for the Scientific Study of Religion*, vol. 4, pp.40–46.
Erikson, E. (1950) *Childhood and Society*, New York, Norton.
Fowler, J. (1981) *Stages of Faith*, New York, Harper and Row.
Hinton, J. (1967) *Dying*, Harmondsworth, Penguin.
Kohlberg, L. (1969) 'Stage and sequence: the cognitive-developmental approach to socialization,' in D. Goslin (ed.), *Handbook of Socialization Theory and Research*, Chicago, Rand-McNally.
Kohlberg, L. (1973) 'Stages and ageing in moral development: some speculations,' *Gerontologist*, vol. 13, pp.497–502.
Kübler-Ross, E. (1970) *On Death and Dying*, London, Tavistock.
Loevinger, J. and Wessler, R. (1970) *Measuring Ego Development*, San Francisco, Jossey-Bass.
Loevinger, J. (1976) *Ego Development*, San Francisco, Jossey-Bass.
Nagy, M. (1948) 'The child's view of death,' *Journal of Genetic Psychology*, vol. 73, pp.3–27.
Piaget, J. (1972) *The Principles of Genetic Epistemology*, New York, Basic Books.
Shulik, R. (1979) 'Faith development, moral development, and old age: an assessment

of Fowler's faith development paradigm,' unpublished doctoral dissertation, University of Chicago.

Shulik, R. (1981) 'Faith development and clinical psychology,' in K. Stokes (ed.), *Faith Development and the Adult Life Cycle*, New York, Grolier.

Stokes, K. (1981) 'A germ of an idea,' in K. Stokes (ed.), *Faith Development and the Adult Life Cycle*, New York, Grolier.

8. Christian education and faith development

Religious educators took up Fowler's faith development thinking before those whose primary interest was in pastoral care. Most serious discussions of religious formation or socialization make some reference to Fowler, as do many of those concerned with more 'critical' forms of education in religion or with Christian approaches to general education.[1] In this section we have drawn together five papers from the journals, two of them from the pen of Fowler himself. They discuss the relevance of the faith development perspective in the context of the family, the school, the university and the Christian congregation.

Fowler's 'Perspectives on the family from the standpoint of faith development theory' is an early essay, first published in the *Perkins Journal*, vol. 33, no. 1, 1979, pp. 1-19. It provides an extended account of the 'ontic needs' ('needs intrinsically related to human being and well-being') of the family for communion and place, agency and autonomy, rituals of shared meaning, and sustenance, shelter and sexual identification. Through a sample of 'vignettes of faith' Fowler then gives an account of his understanding of faith and its different stages, before using faith development theory as a way of looking at family units as 'ecologies of faith consciousness'. The problems and possibilities of Christian nurture and life within families, where people of different faith stages live together, are then reviewed in an illuminating way. Particular stress is placed on the fact that 'the modal level found in a majority of Christian families and congregations can best be characterized in terms of the synthetic-conventional stage of faith development'.[2]

Gary Chamberlain's paper on 'Faith development and

campus ministry' is also early, having been published in
Religious Education, vol. 74, no. 3, 1979, pp. 314–324.
Here Chamberlain applies Fowler's work to the 'high
school campus' of school-aged adolescents and their
'campus ministers' (who serve as 'models of faith' and
'carriers of faith histories and visions'). He also discusses
the applicability of the concept of church as community
within a schooling context. The paper requests schools to
examine their 'faith atmosphere' and how it operates in
developing and nourishing faith. Particular attention is
paid to the application of faith development theory to
the school setting in three areas: (i) the movement from
literalism to symbolic thought, (ii) the pupil's growing
ability to take the perspectives of others, and (iii) the
community's 'sense of belonging in which each individual
can find meaning'.

Mark Rutledge's 'Faith development: bridging theory
and practice', first published in *New Directions for Student
Services*, no. 46, 1989, pp. 17–32, attempts to relate
the faith development reflections of Fowler, Parks and
Gribbon to the problem of ministry to college-age students.
Eight particular implications are noted for the practice of
'campus religious professionals', with illustrations from
the experience of the author and others in universities in
the United States.

Fowler's second essay, from *Moral Education Forum*,
vol. 12, no. 1, 1987, pp. 4–14 and 36, centres on 'Religious
congregations: varieties of presence in stages of faith'.
Fowler contends that 'any time a pastor, priest or rabbi
greets a congregation of any real size gathered for worship,
he/she addresses persons whose range of stages of faith
and selfhood includes at least three or four stages'. The
congregation is thus also 'an ecology of multiple stages of
faith and selfhood'. Each of these different faith stages is
analysed by Fowler with particular reference to the
implications of the stage for strategies of both pastoral
care and Christian nurture. Here, as in other papers in this
section, the intimate interrelation between care and
education is clearly revealed, and Christian formation is
shown to be a species of pastoral ministry.[3]

William Avery's paper, 'Enhancing supervision using Fowler's developmental theory', first published in *Journal of Supervision and Training in Ministry*, vol. 10, 1988, pp. 3–18, applies Fowler's notion of the 'modal developmental level' of a congregation to the problems of placing and supervising students and probationary ministers in congregations. Avery claims that such 'interns' must 'learn to work with the parish at whatever modal level it has attained', and advocates the use of a shortened form of Fowler's interview as a useful tool to aid this learning.

Notes
1. See, for example, Thomas H. Groome, *Christian Religious Education: sharing our story and vision*, New York, Harper and Row, 1980, ch. 4; John M. Hull, *What Prevents Christian Adults from Learning?*, London, SCM, 1985, ch. 4; Craig Dykstra, 'Faith development and religious education', in Craig Dykstra and Sharon Parks (eds), *Faith Development and Fowler*, Birmingham, Alabama, Religious Education Press, 1986, pp. 251–271; Richard Robert Osmer, *A Teachable Spirit: recovering the teaching office of the church*, Louisville, Kentucky, Westminster, 1990, ch. 10; Jeff Astley *et al.*, *How Faith Grows: faith development and Christian education*, London, National Society, 1991, ch. 4.
2. See also James W. Fowler, 'Faith development through the family life cycle', *Network Paper*, no. 31 (Rochelle, N.Y., Don Bosco Multimedia, 1990).
3. The issues of conversion and development, and their relevance to Christian education, are taken up with reference to Fowler's work in Gabriel Moran, *Religious Education Development*, Minneapolis, Minnesota, Winston Press, 1983, especially ch. 6, Gabriel Moran, 'Alternative developmental images', in James W. Fowler, Karl Ernst Nipkow and Friedrich Schweitzer (eds), *Stages of Faith and Religious Development: implications for church, education and society*, London, SCM, 1992, pp. 149–161 and Walter Conn, *Christian Conversion: a developmental interpretation of autonomy and surrender*, New York, Paulist Press, 1986. For reflections on the socio-political dimensions of developmental theories see the essays by John M. Hall and Gloria Durka in Fowler, Nipkow and Schweitzer (eds), *op. cit*, pp. 209–223, 224–237.

8.1 Perspectives on the family from the standpoint of faith development theory
James W. Fowler

The family and ontic needs

The family, in some form, is a universal feature of all societies. Though the forms vary, and the gender role assignments differ, all societies recognize some form of stable, publicly sanctioned relationship between men and women, legitimating sexual relations and providing for their offspring. All societies include some form of incest taboo in these provisions, and all designate informal or formal patterns of the division of labour based on gender.[1]

For our present purposes we need not tackle the knotty question of definition of the family.[2] Contemporary efforts to make the concept 'family' inclusive of the pluralism of communal, common law, merged, or single parent groups represent important recognitions that the family does not connote only the two-parent, nuclear, two-generational unit frequently taken as proto-typical.

Our focus on the family and faith development should begin with some reflection on the remarkable fact of this pervasive presence of family structures in societies. The evolution of this institution in all human groups suggests compellingly that our species has a set of predictable, recurring needs which the family uniquely and indispensably tries to meet. Needs of this sort, if we can identify them, may be called 'ontic' needs, needs, that is to say, which are essential to *being* and *well-being*. We cannot address the question of the relations between families and faith development without trying to clarify the character of these ontic needs of our species. Insofar as we succeed in grasping this set of needs we will have a purchase on such universal functional requirements for the family as may be identified. Recognizing that our analysis will inevitably show cultural biases and distortions, let us, nonetheless, take the risk of trying to name the several universal ontic needs that give rise in human societies to the family in its myriad forms.

Four clusters of such ontic needs – needs intrinsically related to human being and well-being – suggest themselves.

    a.   The members of our species need primal experiences of *communion* and *valued 'place.'*

b. Our kind require a quality of protective restraint and sup-
    portive leeway for the development of *agency* and *responsible
    autonomy.*
c. From birth we require *assurance* of *meaning* and participation
    in *rituals* of *shared meaning and orientation.* We need *bodily
    sustenance, shelter,* and *sexual identification.*

These needs are not absolute. Human children survive and develop
with deprivations and lacks in any or all these dimensions. But
severe lack in one or more of these dimensions inevitably wounds
the individual child and weakens him or her as a link in the ongoing
cycle of the generations. Let us consider each of these clusters of
ontic need more fully.[3]

Experiences of communion and valued 'place'

As the fetus takes form in the womb there is a profound experience of
place and communion. Insofar as the forming fetus 'knows' anything
it is a knowing born of profound symbiotic mutuality. Birth must,
therefore, be an equally profound experience of displacement and
interrupted mutuality. It would be a mistake to suggest that our
human hunger for mutuality and relational 'place' can be reduced
to a never-forgotten nostalgia for the womb. But we can say that
this initial dis-placement gives rise to a powerful dis-ease with our
apartness if the displacement is not balanced with a few relationships
in which we know ourselves to be *irreplaceable.* The tendency toward
anxiety that comes with being displaced and dependent centers
of potential consciousness requires a knowing and being known
marked by mutual regard and cherishing. To be irreplaceable means
to have place. It means to be welcomed, to be 'at home.' To be
cherished, for the infant, means to receive – through the tangible
media of consistent care, sensitivity fitted to his/her needs – the
unmistakable taste and feel of being 'in place.'

Biologists and psychologists have documented what sensitive
observers have known for a long time. The neonate brings to
the initial encounter with the caring one pre-patterned reflexes for
searching and sucking, and for behaviors which recruit the love and
tenderness of the carer. Recent research in endocrinology clarifies
some of the remarkable shifts in hormonal levels which women
experience during pregnancy and immediately after childbirth.
These shifts, it is claimed, create powerful propensities in the new
mother *to be recruited* into the child's nurture.[4] This mutuality of
need, and of need to be needed, gives rise to the most primal
experience of communion and place we experience. Because it comes
first, and because it responds to our most profound situation of
separation and lack, it inevitably assumes, for the individual and
for the species, a paradigmatic power. Whatever the quality of
its mutuality, this primal relationship of new-born child with the

one (or ones) providing the first tangible gifts of care and regard, leaves a charged residue of sedimented 'sense' about one's value and about one's place. The seeds of self-hood take first and most lasting root in that charged relational sediment. Into it also drop the potent seeds of the child's pre-images of 'how it is here.'

While we have gravitated toward infancy in our discussion of the ontic need for communion and place, it should be clear that we do not outgrow this cluster of needs. If the mother-child relationship (or its surrogate) constitutes the paradigmatic instance of primal intimacy, the family as a whole provides a pivotal arena for forms of reciprocal knowing and regard which meet this ontic need for communion and 'home' over a longer span of time.

In this and later sections we must resist the temptation to idealize the family. The family can be and has evolved to be a matrix of inter-generational and connubial intimacy. We must remember, however, that intimacy includes conflict and strife; powerful experiences of closeness and 'place' – precisely because of our ontic need for such relations – may have crippling and distorting, as well as strengthening, impacts on the child or sibling, parent or spouse.

Experiences of agency and responsible autonomy

Birth *is* a separation. While the infant ontically craves communion and 'place' there seems also to be, from the outset, a movement toward separateness. When the baby has been held and fed, soon there is the squirm for release – for freedom to move the limbs, to move the head and eyes freely, to explore the environment visually and tactually. From the fourth to the eighth month the baby begins to be able to construct and maintain a mental image of removed objects or persons.[5] Here lie the seeds of the child's recognition that she/he is separate from other persons and from objects. Here sprouts the roots of the eventual ability to stand apart – and if necessary – alone.

The nerve to separate depends on the assured return to communion. Practice in the dangerous business of standing alone or walking away requires benevolent protection against the dangers of going too far. There must be supporting encouragement which makes it safe to fail and prevents failure from resulting in the overwhelming loss of face. The family (or family surrogate) provides the first context for experiments in autonomy. With the family's support and encouragement, as well as its restraint, the child tests how far she/he can go. In face of the family's neglect of restraint the child goes too far, endangering self or others. Or the child bites off more than it can chew – a precocious grasp for responsibility – which results in failure and risking the threat of shame.

The adult's patterns of autonomy and responsibility are not

determined by the kind and quality of childhood experiences. But we can scarcely overestimate the extent to which earliest experiences with autonomy and willfulness, and the responses they elicited, set the horizons and provide the reservoir of confidence for the adult's initiatives. The theater of action and interaction widens beyond the family as we move through the life cycle. But the verve and responsibility with which we play owe a good bit to the audience participation we elicited in our first childish enactments. 'Who first slapped you back into your little corner?' Carlyle Marney used to ask inhibited and withdrawing participants at Interpreters' House. Benevolent memory screens and a child's need to have a parent he could honor prevent his remembering. 'But in the group, under pressure,' says Marney, 'he assumes the posture the little child first found tolerable in face of the parental threat to autonomy and worth.'[6]

With each stage of life we re-negotiate the quality of our autonomy and responsibility. The intimate relationships of love and mutuality, which help us sustain identity and meaning, necessarily exert a powerful influence on our sense of agency. Particularly in a time when sex role images are changing markedly, attitudes and adaptability of a spouse or a parent can make a tremendous difference in the leeway a person can take in re-defining patterns of agency and responsible autonomy in those relations and in other dimensions of life.

Provision of shared meanings and ritualizations

Human beings are the primates burdened with the necessity of creating systems of meaning and orientation. Distinct from our near and distant relatives in the animal kingdom, we lack genetically programmed instinctual guidance systems which determine our needs, goals and satisfactions. *Homo Poeta*, Ernest Becker calls us.[7] We can not live by bread, or sex, or instinct alone. We are creatures who require meaning.

The first 'social construction of reality' in which we participate is that mediated by the family or family surrogate. The *fact* that the parenting ones participate in realms of meaning – if not the content of those meanings – finds communication in and through the quality of care they provide their infants. Writers such as Harry Stack Sullivan and Erik Erikson tell us that the assurance of meaning communicates itself in almost somatic, bodily, mediation.

> The amount of trust derived from earliest infantile experience does not seem to depend on absolute quantities of food or demonstrations of love, but rather on the quality of the maternal relationship. Mothers create a sense of trust in their children by that kind of administration which in its quality combines sensitive care of the baby's individual needs and a firm sense of personal trustworthiness within the trusted

framework of their culture's life-style.... Parents must not only have certain ways of guiding by prohibition and permission; they must also be able to represent to the child a deep, almost somatic conviction that there is a meaning to what they are doing. Ultimately, children become neurotic not from frustrations, but from the lack or loss of societal meaning in these frustrations.[8]

Some very powerful awakenings on the horizon of meaning happen before children start school. Between twelve and twenty months one of the most dramatic events in all human development occurs. During this period thought and language, which previously have distinct root systems during the sensory motor stage of infancy, begin to converge. Thought, or intelligence, has been, until this period, primarily a matter of the coordination of reflexes and actions. The young infant 'knows' his or her environment by moving about in it and by learning to coordinate space and time so as to move purposefully. He/she learns to coordinate movements of eye, hand, arm and neck so as to grasp and manipulate a world of permanent objects. Language, during the first few months, consists primarily in the enjoyable production of random sounds and rhythms. Through the responsive reinforcement of some of the sounds the infant learns to repeat them and to appreciate the attention and investment they evoke from primal persons. But around the end of the first year a kind of Copernican revolution occurs. The child begins to construct the exhilarating insight that *sounds* and *words refer to objects* – that things have names, and that names stand for things. This brings the child to the dawn of symbols: the capacity to represent one thing by another; the power to name and communicate about objects without having to point; the power to grasp and claim without physical possession. *Here arise the first shared representations of meaning.*[9]

With the birth of symbolic representation comes the beginning of the capacity for meaningful participation in ritual activities. Ritual, in simple terms, may be thought of as repeated patterns of action, shared by two or more persons, in which their actions represent actual or potential relations of the participants to personally significant centers of transcendent value and/or power. Parent-child rituals may consist in repeated gestures and verbalizations in which the 'significant center of transcendent value or power' they relate to is the hoped-for potential of the child, which in effect becomes a shared myth between them. But there are other kinds of ritual. In one family a three-year-old generated a verbal 'blessing' which she insisted on repeating each morning before her father left for work. The blessing took the form of admonitions. 'Be careful on your motorcycle; watch for strangers; don't leave the sunshine; and please don't miss your party!' The roots of this ritual in the family's history are somewhat obscure. It appears that the little girl, who had moved into a new and strange territory less than a year before, and whose mother was lonely and unhappy in the new place, felt a special need to try to protect the father – who had bought a small motorcycle to commute to work – from harm during the day. The father, preoccupied by the demands of a new job, had recently created a domestic explosion by forgetting the family's celebration of their younger child's first birthday. In what had to be a traumatic experience for the three-year-old, the mother and father had come to terms with the fact that their present patterns of life and work had to change. They had planned to move again. In this context, the priestly blessing of the three-year-old – which became a morning family ritual at her insistence – was a powerful daily evocation of protection for them in the service of the transcendent values of family unity and peace.

Through the language, gestures and rituals initiated by the adults in their environments children 'participate' their ways into shared loyalty to a family's ethos of valued meanings. Language and ritual of this sort awaken the child's imagination. They give it material to work with, incentives and direction. The resulting images – fusing 'information' with sentiment and feeling – for better or worse become powerful sources of orientation for the child. It seems likely that many of the convictions adults hold can be traced to imaginal roots which have their origins in the years prior to six, and in the context of their powerful affective relations with primal adults.[10]

Provision of bodily sustenance, shelter and sexual identification

In many discussions of ontic needs 'survival needs' are typically treated first and as first level affairs. Certainly the unequilibrated neediness of the human neonate makes the provision, by others, of food, shelter, clothes and cleansing a critical matter. Our present discussion treats this dimension of our ontic neediness last in order to indicate that the strategy of placing these ontic needs in a hierarchial arrangement is a mistake. As the preceding sections suggest, the human provision for communion and place, for experiences of agency and autonomy, and for meaning and ritual, are met in significant part *through the provisions for bodily sustenance and shelter*. The provision of care of this basic sort therefore takes on something of a sacramental character. (For St. Augustine a sacrament means 'the visible form of invisible grace.'[11]) Through the media of personal caring in family or family-like relations the 'invisible grace' of conferred worth, supported agency, and shared meaning become tangible for the recipients. We should not overlook the way in which the child's feelings of absolute dependence upon the providing parent(s) play a crucial role in binding the child to the authority and example of the parent figure(s).

This brings us to the question of sexual identification. Here we cannot review the rich literature on the formation of sexual identification.[12] Nor can we provide an incisive perspective for understanding these complex matters. But we should note that the process of achieving a sense of congruence between the sexual characteristics of one's body, and a unified set of accepted cultural meanings of those physical characteristics, cannot easily be achieved apart from the child's having intimate, sustained interaction with other persons of the same and opposite sex. Family patterns, as varied as they are from culture to culture, have evolved as the most reliable contexts in which this vital aspect of personal identity can get underway.

Faith

A woman in her mid twenties tells her story. 'The years from 17–22 were my lost years, the years I searched and tried everything, but accomplished nothing. I tried sex, illicit drugs, Eastern religions, the occult, everything. I filled myself with vain knowledge, but gained nothing as far as my real spiritual hunger was concerned.' At twenty-two, eight months after 'an extraordinary experience on L.S.D.,' and after having two persons close to her witness to the Lordship of Jesus Christ, she accepted him as her Lord. Her story of the next five years resembles those of many of her generation: movement from one new Christian, true church movement to another, submission to the often conflicting authority of self-appointed Christian elders and to the disciplines of neo-Christian group life. She suffered the psychological violence inflicted by newly converted folk who, in radically denying their own pasts and affirming their new beings, in Christ, projected much of the horror and guilt of what they denied in themselves onto others. Her odyssey carried her through at least four such groups before she found one led by mature Christians. At the encouragement of one ill-prepared leader she had married a man she hardly knew, and for two years 'submitted' to horrendous marital anarchy and degradation. Through it all, she affirms, 'The Lord never left me bereft. He was leading me, teaching me, shaping me.' Though raw and hurting, her faith in the Lord more than ever occupies the center of her efforts to discern what she should do next and to know how to think of herself. 'I just pray that the Lord will show me the ministry he has for me.'

A small-town merchant pours six long days a week into the management of his clothing store. A kind man with a friendly and helpful attitude, his business flourishes. He belongs to a local church and contributes generously. He belongs to a local civic association and gives modestly of his time to its projects. He is a respected member of the town's Chamber of Commerce, and is admired as a progressive force in the refurbishing of Main Street.

One day his son, intending it as a joke, gives the attentive observer a frightening clue. 'Daddy,' he says, 'doesn't have a thing except Mama that he wouldn't sell if the price were right!' And this was true. It would be too extreme to speak of money in his case as a *fetish*,[13] but clearly his son had named the center of the father's value system. And the other involvements and extensions of self – even to the extent of caring financially for an alcoholic brother – served this central devotion to enlarging his 'estate.'

The fourth of ten children born to an Irish-Italian marriage, Jack grew up in 'the Projects.' 'There were so many of us boys that people never knew our first names. They just called us "Seely". My voice sounded so much like my brothers that sometimes even I got confused.' Under the influence of the Sisters in parochial school he became, during his late childhood and early adolescence, a faithful churchgoer. 'One year,' he said, 'I made mass every day and did two Novenas, which was hard. I got up early every day and went over there; I never sat on the bench, but always stayed on my knees. I felt like I was one of Jesus's special kids. I liked it, and I kind of made a bargain that I would do all this for him if he would sort of straighten my dad's drinking out a little bit. He would go out on Friday, Saturday and Sunday nights and come back drunk. Sometimes he beat mother when they argued.' At the end of his seventh grade year Sister called him up to the front of the room and publicly recognized him as the only boy who had been faithful in attending mass daily throughout the spring. 'She shouldn'a done that,' he said. 'They got me then, the bullies. They gave me a hard time for the next two years. I quit going to church. But I guess it was just as well. The old man didn't ease up on the drinking. In fact, he started going out on Thursday nights too!' Today, near thirty, still out of church, he lives in a nice but confining low-cost private housing project. Every thirty seconds during most of the day the large jets taking off or landing at the nearby airport shake the windows in their apartment. He and his wife lead the Tenants Association in its struggle against rent gouging landlords. They have helped organize tenant groups all over their part of the city, and, for their troubles, have two separate one million dollar suits against them initiated by landlord associations. His $12,000 per year job and her nightly work as a waitress keep them both very busy. 'Blacks and poor white people need to get together here. We've been pitted against each other, to *their* advantage, for too long. I don't know much theory; I can't talk about Hegel and philosophy, and I don't know Marx too good. But I do know my class and I know we're getting stepped on. Me and my wife want to give everything we got to giving poor folks a break. And while we do it, we gotta remember that there are people under us too, people worse off. We may be in the alley fighting, but down below in the cellar somewhere they are fighting for a chance to breathe too. We gotta be careful not to step on them.'

These are vignettes on faith: windows into the organizing images and value patterns by which people live. The stories let us in on their life wagers. They give us access to the ways three persons are pouring out their life energies − spending and being spent in the service of valued projects, in light of which their own value and worth as persons seek confirmation.

In this way of thinking faith need not be approached as necessarily a religious matter. Nor need it be thought of as doctrinal belief or assent. Rather, faith becomes the designation for a way of leaning into life. It points to a way of making sense of one's existence. It denotes a way giving order and coherence to the force field of life. It speaks of the investment of life grounding trust and of life-orienting commitment.

Now let's look at these matters a little more systematically. This way of approaching faith means to imply that this phenomenon is a human universal. That is to say, as members of a species burdened with consciousness, and with self-consciousness, and with freedom to name and organize the phenomenal world, we nowhere can escape the task of forming tacit or explicit coherent images of our action-worlds. We are born into fields of forces impinging upon us from all sides. The development of perception means a profound limiting and selection of the *sense* to which we can consciously or unconsciously attend. The development of cognition − understood here in its broadest sense − means the construction of operations of thought and valuing in accordance with which the *sensa* to which we attend are organized and formed. Composition and interpretation of meanings, then, are the inescapable burdens of our species. Consciously or unconsciously, in this process, we invest trust in powerful images which unify our experience, and which order it in accordance with interpretations that serve our acknowledgement of centers of value and power.

We encounter this force-field of life in the presence of others. From the beginning others *mediate* in our interaction with the conditions of our existence. Somatic contact, gestures, words, rituals from other persons − all serve to link us with aspects of the surrounding environment. And before we can think with words or symbols, primitive images or pre-images of felt 'sense' begin to form in us. Therefore we must think of even our earliest steps toward interpretation and meaning as shared, as social.

Reflection on this social character of even our earliest moves toward constructions of meanings points to another important feature of faith. Our investment of reliance upon or trust in interpretative images does not occur apart from our investment of reliance upon or trust in the significant others who are companions or mediators in our acts of meaning construction. Faith involves, from the beginning, our participation in what we may call tacit covenantal fiduciary relationships. Put another way, our interpretations of and responses to events which disclose the conditions of our existence are formed in the company of co-interpreters and co-respondents whom we trust and to whom we are loyal. Faith is a relational matter. As we relate to the conditions of our existence with acts of interpretative commitment we do so as persons also related to and co-involved with companions whom we trust and to whom we are loyal. This means that the interpretative images by which we make sense of the conditions of our lives inevitably implicate our companions. It also means, reciprocally, that our experiences with these companions in interpretation have decisive impact on the forming and reforming of our interpretative images and for the values and powers they serve.

Let us designate those images by which we holistically grasp the conditions of our existence with the name *images of the Ultimate Environment*. And let us point out that such images of the Ultimate Environment derive their unity and their principle of coherence from a center (or centers) of value and power to which persons of faith are attracted with conviction. Faith then, is a matter of composing an image of the Ultimate Environment, through the commitment of self to a center (or centers) of value and power giving it coherence. We do this in interaction with communities of cointerpreters and co-commitants. And our commitments so made, with the interpretative impacts they carry, become occasions for the re-ordering of our loves and the redirecting of our spending and being spent.

We have intended in these paragraphs on faith to present it as a dynamic phenomenon. Faith is an ongoing process. It is a way of being and of leaning into life. Crises, disclosure-events, the fulfillment or failure of hopes, betrayals and experiences of fidelity in the force field of life continually impact a person's image of the Ultimate Environment and his or her commitment to the value-or-power-center(s) sustaining it. Conversion or re-conversion in small or large ways can be precipitated without conscious desire or intent. Confusion, doubt, and the conflicts of double or multiple pulls to commitment represent inherent dynamics of faith. And for most of us our controlling image of the Ultimate Environment is likely to be as much an aspiration to worthy and true faith as it is an accomplishment and integrated reality of faith. Competing master images for the Ultimate Environment contend for loyalty in societies and cultures, and within individual human breasts.

In English the term belief and the verb 'to believe' are frequently used as synonymous with faith. Hopefully our discussion of faith has put us in position to make some clarifying distinctions between faith and belief or believing. Wilfrid Cantwell Smith, the historian of religion, has helped us to understand the process by which terms for faith in the classical languages (*pistuein* in Greek, and *credo* in Latin) have fallen, in the modern West, into an unfortunate confusion with our post-enlightenment understandings of belief. Originally both these classical words (both of which have verb forms, as English does not) carried connotations of trust, commitment, of 'resting one's heart' upon a person or a reality. In both cases faith clearly meant a total disposition of oneself to trust in and rely upon the trustworthiness of another. In both Greek and Latin this usage implied *belief*, but not belief, in the distinctly modern sense of assent to a proposition stating an opinion of dubious verifiability. *credo* could never properly be reduced merely to the 'I believe' as used in some such statement as, 'I believe in the existence of God.' Properly understood, to use *credo* in relation to God, *assumes* the existence of God: that is not in question. Rather, what is being brought to language is a declaration of allegiance, a pledge of fealty and fidelity, the designation of person's commitment to an encompassing and powerfully orienting image of the Ultimate Environment.[14]

Let us try to bring this introductory characterization of faith into summary focus. Faith, we may say, is:

- a disposition of the total self toward the Ultimate Environment
- in which trust and loyalty are invested in a center or centers of value and power
- which order and give coherence to the force field of life, *and*
- which support and sustain (or qualify and relativize) our mundane or everyday commitments and trusts
- combining to give orientation, courage, meaning and hope to our lives, and
- to unite us into communities of shared interpretation, loyalty and trust.[15]

Stages in faith development

We are going to examine here stages of faith development as we have identified them in the course of seven years of research. A few explanatory points of orientation may be helpful. Detailed accounts of our research procedures, our sample, and of the stages themselves have been or are being published. These should be consulted for the elaboration and background of what we are presenting here.[14] Though we now count nearly 380 interviews in our sample, we have only a limited number of longitudinal studies. We have not conducted cross-cultural investigations. Therefore the stage description we offer here must still be considered as provisional. We ask you to help us avoid several traps of misunderstanding to which stage theories are susceptible. First, please do not think of the stages as pigeon-holes in which to stuff persons. They are heuristic models or lenses through which to see and identify *some* aspects of persons' attitudes, beliefs, values and actions. Second, do not think of the stage sequence as an achievement scale against which to 'grade' persons or to use in creating acceleration educational courses. A person best described by one of the more developed stages is not a 'better' person than one characterized by a less developed stage. They are different, and they do go about the business of making sense of their world and of making their commitments and shaping their actions in different ways. Third, remember that a 'stage' is a kind of still photograph of what in life is a very dynamic phenomenon. A stage description is a kind of 'ideal type' or model against which to compare the features of a person's way of being in faith. Real people, while exhibiting features dominantly associated with one stage, almost always show, in addition, some features characteristic of either or both the previous or the next stage. Fourth, stages are not 'there' like a set of stair-steps to climb up. To make a transition from one stage to another is to undergo the often painful process of giving up one's familiar and comfortable ways of making meaning and sustaining commitment. It means a kind of coming apart as well as a new construction. Periods of transition can be protracted over several years.

Now with all these warnings in hand, what do we mean by this term 'stage'? In contemporary usage this word has a lot of meanings. Here we shall mean by it the following: *one of a sequence of formally describable 'styles' of composing an Ultimate Environment, of committing the self to centers of value and power, of symbolizing and expressing those commitments, and of relating them to the valued perspectives of others.* We speak of stages rather than types because we believe that the stage sequence we have identified is invariant. That is, we believe the stages come in the order presented here and that persons do not skip over a stage. Please notice that we say 'formally describable.' This means that a stage is not defined by a particular *content* of belief or valuing. Rather a stage is a particular *way* of organizing, rather than on the *what* or the content of faith. Though we are not prepared to claim universality for these stages, we do believe that they are capable of characterizing persons' *ways* of being in faith despite great differences in the variety of religious and non-religious content traditions in which they may stand.

Finally, we must make one other potentially confusing matter clear. Many stage theories, such as Erikson's 'Eight ages of the life cycle,'[17] tie the movement from one stage to another directly to chronological age and biological maturation. Particularly in the earlier stages which, for Erikson, are most directly psycho-sexual stages, maturation sets the pace and precipitates the movement from one stage to another. Our stages are dependent upon age and maturation in that these factors provide some of the *necessary* conditions for stage transition. But they are not *sufficient* conditions. Other factors, such as the richness and stimulation of the environment, the availability of models of the next 'place,' and the person's encounter with crises or dilemmas which shake up his or her faith outlook, play significant roles in determining the rate and timing of stage changes. To show what this means, it is not too unusual to find normal persons who are chronologically and biologically adult, whose patterns of faith can best be described by our stage 2. This is a stage that typically arises during the years from seven to eleven. We are suggesting that 'normal' persons may equilibrate or arrest in faith growth at any of these stages from the second on. Certain factors in maturation must occur before the school child is ready for transition to stage 3, but maturation and age, by themselves, do not guarantee readiness for the next stage.

Now we are ready to examine an overview of this sequence of stages. The description of each stage will include a general characterization. This will be followed by a somewhat more detailed elaboration. Then briefly we will suggest some of the signs of transition to the next stage.[18]

Undifferentiated faith

The pre-conceptual, largely pre-linguistic stage in which the infant unconsciously forms a disposition toward its world.

> Trust, courage, hope and love are fused in an undifferentiated way and contend with sensed threats of abandonment, inconsistencies and deprivations in its environment. Though really a pre-stage, and largely inaccessible to empirical inquiry of the kind we pursue, the quality of mutuality and the strength of trust, autonomy, hope and courage (or their opposites) developed in this phase, underlie or undermine all that comes later in faith development.

Transition to stage 1 begins with the convergence of thought and language, opening up of symbols in speech and ritual-play.

Stage 1: intuitive-projective faith

The fantasy-filled, imitative phase in which the child can be powerfully and permanently influenced by the examples, moods, actions and language of the visible faith of primal adults.

> The stage most typical of the child of three to seven, it is marked by a relative fluidity of thought patterns. The child is continually encountering novelties for which no stable operations of knowing have been formed. The imaginative processes underlying fantasy are unrestricted and uninhibited by logical thought. In league with forms of knowing dominated by perception, imagination in this stage is

extremely productive of long-lasting images and feelings (positive and negative) which later, more stable and self-reflective valuing and thinking will have to order and sort out. This is the stage of first self-awareness. The 'self-aware' child is egocentric as regards the perspectives of others. Here we find first awareness of death and sex, and of the strong taboos by which cultures and families insulate those powerful areas.

The emergence of concrete operational thinking underlies the transition to stage 2. Affectively, the resolution of Oedipal issues or their submersion in latency are important accompanying factors. At the heart of the transition is the child's growing concern to *know* how things are and to clarify for him/herself the bases of distinction between what is real and what only seems to be.

Stage 2: mythic-literal faith

The stage in which the person begins to take on for him/herself the stories, beliefs and observances which symbolize belonging to his/her community. Beliefs are appropriated with literal interpretations, as are moral rules and attitudes. Symbols are taken as one-dimensional and literal in meaning.

> In this stage the rise of concrete operations leads to the curbing and ordering of the previous stage's imaginative composing of the world. The episodic quality of intuitive-projective faith gives way to a more linear, narrative construction of coherence and meaning. Story becomes the major way of giving unity and value to experience. This is the faith stage of the school child (though we sometimes find its structures dominant in adolescents and in adults). Marked by increased accuracy in taking the perspective of other persons, stage 2 composes a world based on reciprocal fairness and an immanent justice based on reciprocity. The actors in its comic stories are full-fledged anthropomorphic 'personalities.' It can be affected deeply and powerfully by symbolic and dramatic materials, and can describe in endlessly detailed narrative what has occurred. Stage 2 does not, however, step back from the flow of its stories to formulate reflective, conceptual meanings. For this stage the meaning is both carried and 'trapped' in the narrative.

The implicit clash or contradictions of stories leads to reflection on meanings. The transition to formal operational thought makes such reflection possible and necessary. Previous literalism breaks down; new 'cognitive conceit' (Elkind) leads to disillusionment with precious teachers and teachings. Conflicts between authoritative stories (i.e. Genesis on creation versus evolutionary theory) must be faced. The emergence of mutual interpersonal perspective-taking ('I see you seeing me; I see me as you see me; I see you seeing me seeing you.') creates the need for a more personal relationship with the unifying power of the Ultimate Environment.

Stage 3: synthetic-conventional faith

The person's experience of the world now extends beyond the family. A number of spheres demand attention: family, school or work, peers, street society and media, and perhaps religion. Faith must provide a coherent orientation in the midst of that more complex and diverse range of involvements. Faith must synthesize values and information; it must provide a basis for identity and outlook.

> Stage 3 typically has its rise and ascendency in adolescence, but for many adults it becomes a permanent equilibration. It structures the Ultimate Environment in interpersonal terms. Its images of unifying value and power derive from the extension of qualities experienced in personal relationships. It is a 'conformist' stage in the sense that it is acutely tuned to the expectations and judgments of significant others, and as yet does not have a sure enough grasp on its own identity and autonomous judgment to construct and maintain an independent perspective. While beliefs and values are deeply felt, they typically are tacitly held – the person 'dwells' in them and the meaning world they mediate. But there has not been occasion to reflectively step outside them to examine them explicitly or systematically. At stage 3 a person has an 'ideology', a more or less consistent clustering of values and beliefs, but he/she has not objectified it for examination, and in a sense is unaware of having it. Differences of outlook with others are experienced as differences in 'kind' of person. Authority is located in the incumbents of traditional authority-roles (if perceived as personally worthy) or in the consensus of a valued, face to face group.

Factors contributing to the breakdown of stage 3 and to readiness for transition may include any one or more of the following: serious clashes or contradictions between valued authority sources; marked changes, by officially sanctioned leaders, of policies or practices previously deemed sacred and unbreakable (i.e., in the Catholic Church changing the mass from Latin to the vernacular, or no longer requiring abstinence from meat on Friday); the encounter with experiences or perspectives that lead to critical reflection on how one's beliefs and values have formed and changed, and on how 'relative' they are to one's particular group or background.

Stage 4: individuative-reflective faith

The movement from stage 3 to stage 4 is particularly critical for it is in this transition that the late adolescent or adult must begin to take seriously the burden of responsibility for his/her own commitments, life-style, beliefs and attitudes. Where genuine movement toward stage 4 is underway the person must face certain unavoidable tensions: individuality versus being defined by a group or group membership; subjectivity and the power of one's strongly felt but unexamined feelings versus objectivity and the requirement of critical reflection; self-fulfillment or self-actualization as a primary concern versus service to and being for others; the question of being committed to the relative versus struggle with the possibility of an absolute.

> This stage most appropriately takes form in young adulthood (but let us remember that many adults do *not* construct it and that for a significant group it emerges only in the mid-thirties or forties). It is marked by a double development. The self, previously sustained in its identity and faith compositions by an interpersonal circle of significant others, now claims an identity no longer defined by the composite of one's roles or meanings to others. To sustain that new identity it composes a meaning frame conscious of its own boundaries and inner-connections, and aware of its self as a 'world-view'. Self (identity) and outlook (worldview) are differentiated from those of others, and become acknowledged factors in the reactions, interpretations and judgments one makes on the actions of the self and others. It expresses its intuitions of coherence in an ultimate environment in terms of an explicit system of meanings. Stage 4 typically translates symbols into conceptual meanings. This is a 'demythologizing' stage. It is likely to attend minimally to unconscious factors influencing its judgments and behavior.

Restless with the self-images and outlook maintained by stage 4, the person ready for transition finds him/herself attending to what may feel like anarchic and disturbing inner voices. Elements from a childish past, images and energies from a deeper self, a gnawing sense of the sterility and flatness of the meanings one serves – any or all of those may signal readiness for something new. Stories, symbols, myths, paradoxes from one's own or other traditions may insist on breaking in upon the neatness of the previous faith. Disillusionment with one's compromises, and recognition that life is more complex than stage 4's logic of clear distinctions and abstract concepts can comprehend, press one toward a more dialectical and multileveled approach to life-truth.

Stage 5: paradoxical-consolidative faith

This stage involves the integration into self and outlook of much that was suppressed or evaded in the interest of stage 4's self-certainty and conscious cognitive and affective adaptation to reality. This stage develops a 'second naivete' (Ricoeur) in which symbolic power is reunited with conceptual meanings. Here there must also be a new reclaiming and reworking of one's past. There must be an opening to the voices of one's 'deeper self.' Importantly, this involves a critical recognition of one's *social* unconscious – the myths, ideal images and prejudice built deeply into the self-system by virtue of one's nurture within a particular social class, religious tradition, ethnic group or the like.

Unusual before midlife, stage 5 knows the sacrament of defeat and the reality of irrevocable commitments and acts. What the previous stage struggled to clarify, in terms of the boundaries of self and outlook, this stage now makes porous and permeable. Alive to paradox and the truth in apparent contradictions, this stage strives to unify opposites in mind and experience. It generates and maintains vulnerability to the strange truths of those who are 'other'. Ready for closeness to that which is different and threatening to self and outlook (including new depths of experience in spirituality and religious revelation), this stage's commitment to justice is freed from the confines of tribe, class, religious community or nation. And with the seriousness that can arise when life is more than half over, this stage is ready to spend and be spent for the cause of conserving and cultivating the possibility of others' generating identity and meaning.

Stage 5 can appreciate symbols, myths and rituals (its own and others') because it has been grasped, in some measure, by the depth of reality to which they refer. It also sees the divisions of the human family vividly because it has been apprehended by the possibility (and imperative) of an inclusive community of being. But this stage remains divided. It lives and acts between an untransformed world and a transforming vision and loyalties. In some few cases this division yields to the call of the radical actualization that we call stage 6.

Stage 6: universalizing faith

This stage is exceedingly rare. The persons best described by this stage have generated faith compositions in which their felt sense of an Ultimate Environment is inclusive of all being. They become incarnators and actualizers of the spirit of a fulfilled community.

They are 'contagious' in the sense that they create zones of liberation from the social, political, economic and ideological shackles we place and endure on human futurity. Living with felt participation in a power that unifies and transforms the world, universalizers are often experienced as subversive of the structures (including religious structures) by which we sustain our individual and corporate survival, security, and significance. Many persons in this stage die at the hands of those whom they hope to change. Universalizers are often more honored and revered after death than during their lives. The rare persons who may be described by this stage have a special grace that makes them seem more lucid, more simple, and yet somehow more fully human than the rest of us. Their community is universal in extent. Particularities are cherished because they are vessels of the universal, and are thereby valuable apart from any utilitarian considerations. Life is both loved and held too loosely. Such persons are ready for fellowship with persons at any of the other stages and from any other faith tradition.

The family as an ecology of Christian consciousness

The faith development theory suggests a way of looking at family units that may prove fruitful. Families may be thought of as *ecologies of faith consciousness*. In using the term ecology here we mean to suggest the interplay, across age and stage differences, of family members' individual and joint constructions of meaning and value. Minimally a family involves the long-term interaction of representatives of at least two generations. Frequently three generations or even four may be represented. The ecology of consciousness arising from their respective stage-specific ways of contributing to and appropriating from the family's shared meanings will necessarily be quite complex. Our purpose now allows us merely to point out that family members co-exist and interlive across age and stage differences precisely because they generate and maintain shared images, values and life-styles which give meaning to their struggles with and for each other. Families live by implicit and explicit covenants to meaning and values which serve to 'educate' the ties of matrimony and of blood-kinship.

But let us turn from the family more generally to consideration of the Christian family. What is a Christian family? Within this frame of reference we may suggest the following. *A Christian family is an ecology of consciousness whose principle of coherence and meaning centers on God as disclosed in Jesus Christ.* We must avoid any misunderstanding that would give an excessively idealist interpretation to this definition. 'Consciousness' as used here includes life-style and patterns of action as well as the images, beliefs and values which inform and arise from them.

The stages of faith development examined in the previous section intend to focus primarily on patterns of imaging, valuing and action-response characteristic of individual persons. Hopefully, however, our explanations made clear how *social* a matter faith in the ongoing process of formation and transformation must be. Our shift in this section to the family as an ecology of consciousness encourages an extension of the stage descriptions to the family as a collectivity. Can these characterizations of a sequence of 'ways' of composing and committing in faith help us make sense of the way different types of families sponsor (or block) their members in faith development?

We must note in passing that to bring the stage theory to bear on faith development in Christian families begs several questions of considerable theological importance. Is Christian faith inherently developmental in tendency? If so, is the inherent developmental tendency in Christian faith compatible with that described in the faith development theory? We can only acknowledge these questions here. Our claim would be that both questions may be answered 'yes.' But definitive answers would require systematic inquiry and argument beyond the scope of what is possible in this context. Our present purposes will be best served if we provisionally assume affirmative answers to both questions. To do so will allow us to test the conceptual framework provided by the faith development theory for its usefulness in helping us understand some of the dynamics of faith in families.

Let it be acknowledged from the outset that we are entering a terribly complicated and mysterious area of reflection. Christians rely heavily on the categories of revelation, grace and the work of the Holy Spirit in trying to account for the birth in persons of faith in God through Christ. These categories, which suggest divine initiative beyond human control or explanation, are appropriate to the phenomenon. In our efforts to conceptualize families as ecologies of Christian faith consciousness we dare not obscure this essential and fundamental domain of mystery.

But let it also be noted that the theory of faith development does provide a frame of reference in which some of the mysteries of the mundane or humanward side of faith's genesis and growth can at least be accounted for, if not specifically predicted and controlled. Mark Twain's oft quoted adage about adolescents' surprise at the learning their parents undergo by the time the youths reach young adulthood has its parallels in earlier stages of faith in childhood. Children compose meaning and invest faith through the images and insights *they* construct. Efforts by parents and other significant adults to 'teach' faith doubtlessly provide usable material – and constitute guidelines – for the child's constructions. But the child's 'inventions' of meaning and coherence, particularly in infancy and the intuitive-projective stage, may use the materials so provided in ways quite unforeseen by the providers.

These disclaimers notwithstanding, it will repay our efforts to think together for a bit about some different family styles of the communication and nurture of faith. Based on preliminary research by Hunt,[19] and upon our own observations, we believe it may be fruitful to characterize different family styles by reference to faith stages. Methods and approaches to the nurture of faith in children and young persons consciously and unconsciously reflect the nurturers' operative image of Christian adulthood. Any consistent approach to the teaching of faith envisions some end point, some cluster of capacities or a style of being which the nurturers value as right, appropriate or true.[20] Therefore, assuming that nurturing adults will construe Christian maturity within the frame of reference of their operative stages of faith development, it makes sense to ask whether there are stage-specific styles of nurturing Christian faith in families.

Helfaer's research on socialization into certain types of Protestant fundamentalist and pentecostalist faith illustrates family patterns of faith nurture within a framework dominantly characterized by the mythic-literal stage.[21] Employing vivid and concrete imagery, these stage 2 versions of Christian faith characterize God as bound by laws of reciprocity to punish the sins of his erring children. Our only hope for escaping the searing fires of hell lies in God's atoning sacrifice of Jesus Christ, through whose blood we are set right with God. Conversion, usually occurring in the years from seven to ten, constitutes the public transaction in which the child accepts Jesus Christ and is 'saved.' In this mode of faith nurture salvation is pre-personal and almost mechanical. It is the prerequisite for relationship to God *and* for real acceptance into family and church. Helfaer's study documents how the 'precocious identity formation,' which this kind of socialization brings about, makes truly personal relations of faith and intimacy problematic in the persons' later lives.

In our own research we are led to suspect that the most common familial pattern of Christian faith nurture still may be a style characterized by stage 3, synthetic-conventional faith. Its informing vision of adult faith is conformist. To be a Christian adult means to live up to the expectations of significant authority figures, including the holding of certain beliefs, and to live in peace and harmony with one's neighbours. (Neighbours tend to be operationally defined as those persons with whom one is in face to face relationships at work, in social organizations – including church – and occasional strangers.) In the synthetic-conventional style of Christian socialization greater emphasis is placed upon sincerity and genuine feeling in one's faith commitments than upon intellectual or critical clarity about the contents, meaning or warrants for them. This style relies, at least implicitly, on hierarchical understandings of authority. Others, authorized by training and/or institutional sanctions, or by personally impressive charismatic qualities, are trusted to 'know' for lay Christians. Christian community, in this stage's style, is organic; it is made up of 'our kind' of people – people who believe and feel and value as we do. Loyalty and fidelity to Christ manifest themselves in loyalty to the visible church. The implications of this stage's understandings of Christian faith for sponsorship in the family seem obvious.

Patterns of faith nurture that envision stage 4, individuative-reflective faith in adulthood are less common in families, though we suspect they are increasing. Where parents and other nurturing adults have struggled to critical and self-reflective decisions about their own faith commitments they are likely to encourage their children to discuss, question, clarify and evaluate with regard to beliefs and values from an early age. When sensitive to children's needs for visible and tangible images and rituals of faith the sponsorship of stage four families can be imaginative and creative in that regard. Frequently, however, parents in this stage mistake the child's need for *leeway* in constructing his/her versions of the family's faith ethos, with a specious sense that the child should be left free to choose religiously when he/she is ready. In any case, Christian nurture in stage 4 families will see the church as an intentional community of persons who belong because belonging expresses a self-conscious commitment to God in Christ. Theological formulations of conviction are likely to be valued, and attention will be given to biblical or other warrants for holding them. Understandings of authority, in this context, are likely to be more egalitarian than hierarchial, and to see authority as a function of personal preparation and informed reflection. While sincerity and genuineness are to be respected, stage 4 Christians are more likely to encourage their children towards authenticity, consistency and clarity in their commitments. Stage 4 patterns of nurture will aim toward the recognition that persons – 'neighbours' – are shaped by their institutional contexts and by the 'world views' they form. Therefore, the Christian imperative to love the neighbour will need to include social forms of love (justice) for persons whom one may never know personally.

Our research suggests that most parents of young children will not have developed beyond stage 4. Stage 5, which develops only near mid-life, if at all, may be the stage best suited for adults as they attempt to relate to their children as the latter move toward the transition (in late adolescence or young adulthood) from stage 3 to stage 4. Paradoxical-consolidative faith intuitively knows as felt truth that God is bigger than our names for God, and that the absoluteness of Jesus Christ is more profound than the Christian community's absolutes about him. Stage 5 faith has begun to sort out the idolatries and ambitious distortions it packed in its stage 4 knapsack of consciously committed Christian faith. It has begun to learn to re-mythologize; to let conceptual clarity and doctrinal orthodoxy be ventilated and regrounded in story and myth. It may have begun to learn about prayer as contemplative listening and the renewal of images. If their adolescent or near adult children cannot, for the present, use stage 5's new found playfulness in faith, his/her grandchildren – or other children, youth or younger adults in the community of faith – will soon take it seriously as liberating and welcome sponsorship. In fact, stage 5 patterns of nurture really ought to characterize the larger ecology of Christian consciousness that is the church, taken as a whole. Only from such a perspective can there genuinely be provided space, leeway, and the range of 'meat' and models required to nurture Christian faith development in persons at each of the earlier stages.

This examination of stage-specific styles of Christian nurture in families has suggested four major patterns. Of these, the pattern of stage 2 nurture really does not envision faith development beyond that stage. The synthetic-conventional approach represents a significant advance. While it does not provide for development in faith beyond stage 3, it nonetheless is inevitably more open-ended. The tragedy of synthetic-conventional patterns of nurture, however, is that in order to develop beyond that version of Christian faith persons so frequently find themselves required to leave family, church, and Christian faith as living contexts and communities of faith. This results from the fact that Christian faith, in their experience of it, is incompatible with critical self-reflection and autonomous responsibility, as well as with serious intellectual and moral enquiry. It is also because there are so few viable churches whose faith ethos are characterized by either stage 4 or stage 5 ways of being in Christian faith.

It is hard to avoid the conclusion that any proper grasp of the intentionality of Christian faith negates the possibility of its being 'contained' in stage 3 patterns. Whatever else it represented, Jesus' proclamation of the sovereignty of God and of the coming Kingdom of God was a call to decision about where one would place his or her trust. Each person was called to decide for him/herself in an individuating choice. The traditional institutions of family and temple were not negated by this radical call for decision. But they were radically dis-established as determinative contexts for the shaping and containment of faith. Patterns of ascriptive and hierarchical authority were broken: 'You heard it said by men of old, but I say unto you. . . .' A quality of radical commitment to personal discipleship constituted the basis for joining the church.

Christian faith involves a call to adult, individuated commitment and to an ongoing process of *metanoia* (repentance and new commitment).[22] Adulthood, in Christian terms means pilgrimage toward the absolute standard represented in Jesus Christ (Ephesians 4:13). Relative to that standard we are all incomplete, unfinished, on the way. Christian adulthood includes women as well as men, and has ongoing continuities with childhood. In all these respects it resists interpretation in hierarchical terms.[23]

Because Christian adulthood calls for individuated commitment, the act of joining the church – even for those socialized from childhood into Christian faith in the church – needs to be a post-adolescent event. Jürgen Moltmann in his lectures at Emory in January 1978, suggested that church membership should mark the time when a person, of individuated commitment to Christ, publicly commits his/her vocation as a Christian to be part of the ministry of the church.[24]

From these perspectives the family – surely part of the Divine orders of creation, governance and redemption – must, nonetheless, be clearly recognized, Christianly speaking, as a sub-unit of the church. That is to say, the family as an ecology of Christian consciousness cannot be confused with or substituted for the more comprehensive ecology of the church. This is not just a tidy theological distinction. Rather, it is a necessary correlate of the claim that Christian adulthood requires individuated commitment to God in Christ. Families, Christianly speaking, are formed of adult Christian men and women, sacramentally united in and by the community of faith. Christian marriages, baptisms, confirmations and funerals – as well as the eucharist – are symbols of that understanding. Children do not belong to their parents in *exclusive* ownership or responsibility. Nor do one's biological children have exclusive claim on the parent or parents. Each adult bears some responsibility for the nurture of all the children and youth – as well as their fellow adults – in the *ecclesia*.

Karl Barth was right in refusing to use the term family (*familia*) in his discussion of the Christian-ethical understanding of the relation of parents and children in *Church Dogmatics*. The term family, he points out, is of pre-Christian, classical pagan rootage, and as such defines the boundaries of the retinue of a ruler, lord or military leader. The tragedy of too many contemporary churches lies in the way we organize and perpetuate ourselves as extended traditional families. Christian identity is confused with membership in the loose-knit clan, and the nerve of the call to individuated choice and commitment is lost. Many who are hungry for challenge and sponsorship for individuative reflective Christian faith, leave, on principle, and search elsewhere. Others stay, and with a sense of loneliness – or worse, of guilt and 'bad faith' – conform for the sake of the children, to the inter-personal niceness and pious warmth of the church community.

Some concluding speculations

The kind of analysis given in the last section does not translate immediately and optimistically into programs to correct 'the problems.' Faith development theory, and the examination of families and congregations as ecologies of faith consciousness, if anything leads to great soberness about the possibility of any rapid and pervasive transformations in people's patterns of faith. Though we have not dwelt on it, congregations – and perhaps families – have *modal levels* of faith development. A faith community's modal level is that stage of faith development socially expected of adults in the community.[25] Lawrence Kohlberg means something similar when he speaks of the controlling stage level of moral decision-making in a prison or school as its 'moral atmosphere.'[26] There is a social coerciveness in the modal level. Adults who develop beyond it are deviant; those who fail to develop to it are deviant. Patterns of socialization and methods of sponsorship in the community are geared to encourage adult development *to* the mode, but not beyond it. Effective intervention on behalf of faith development in a congregation – and perhaps in a family – involve both a neutralizing of the power of the modal level, in the short run, and an effort to revise the modal level upward in the longer run.

We have suggested that the modal level found in a majority of Christian families and congregations can be best characterized in terms of the synthetic-conventional stage of faith development. The difficulties of overcoming the inertia of a modal level in institutions notwithstanding, there may be significant reason for believing that conditions are right for – and already moving toward – a broad transition in modal faith levels toward the individuative-reflective stage. Mobility, higher education levels and a wide-spread familiarity with and use of conceptual models in business, industry and the professions, are all pushing people into new forms of self-aware, critical reflection. The increasing flow of self-help psychology and social science 'populars' are giving rise to metapsychological reflection by lay persons about their own needs, perceptions and behaviour patterns. Professionals in every field feel growing pressure to provide models by which their clients can understand and participate in the course of their own treatment, cases or therapies. Add to all this the explosion into general awareness among literate adults of theories of ongoing development in adulthood, and you see just how impoverished our pre-critical, vestigially hierarchical appeals to institutional conventionalities really are.

In all this ferment people have profound hungers for images and beliefs which reliably inform their relatedness to true centers of value and power. They long for images which can give unity to their frighteningly fragmented experiences of the force-fields of life. They ache for communities in which they are known in more comprehensive identities than of consumer, producer, donor, expert, boss, employee, student, teacher, parent or air traffic controller. And those who live in families are hungry for more comprehensive communities in which the little nuclear ecology of faith consciousness can find real support and ongoing nurture.

Christian churches are under pressure to respond to the voids people carry – within and without the communities that gather in their walls. Faith development theory may give us a framework which will prove useful as a rich model to use in helping our 'clients' name their needs and hunger. It may help to guide and goad a synthetic-conventional church in the process of submitting today to Jesus' radical call for individuating, adult commitment and discipleship. And it might provide some help toward a new theological method in which the Story that is the Christian Gospel can be released to make contact with, lift up and transform, the stories of folk who search for home.

Notes

1. Kathleen Gough, 'The origin of the family', in A. Skolnick and J. Skolnick, (eds), *Intimacy, Family and Society*, Boston, Little, Brown and Company, 1974, pp. 41–60.
2. Donald W. Ball, 'The "Family" as a sociological problem,' in A. Skolnick and

J. Skolnick, (eds), *Intimacy, Family and Society*, Boston, Little, Brown and Company, 1974, pp. 25–40.

3. For a more complete discussion of these ontic needs see my paper entitled 'Alienation as a human experience', in Francis A. Eigo, (ed.), *From Alienation to At-One-ness*, Villanova, Pennsylvania, Villanova University Press, 1977, pp. 1–18.

4. See the fascinating article by Alice S. Rossi, 'A biosocial perspective on parenting', *Daedalus*, Spring, 1977; *The Family*, vol. 106, no. 2, pp. 1–31.

5. See Jean Piaget and Bärbel Inhelder, *The Psychology of the Child*, New York, Basic Books, 1969, pp. 14–15.

6. Carlyle Marney, 'How to be a human being,' taped lecture, published at Nashville, Tennessee, Broadman Press, 1976.

7. Ernest Becker, *The Structure of Evil*, New York, Macmillan, 1968, p. 210.

8. Erik Erikson, *Childhood and Society* (2nd ed.), New York, W. W. Norton, 1963, pp. 249–50.

9. J. Piaget and B. Inhelder, *op. cit.*, pp. 84–91; also, Jean Piaget, *Six Psychological Studies*, New York, Vintage Books, 1967, pp. 17ff.

10. For examples see the life-studies contained in James W. Fowler and Robin W. Lovin, *et al.*, *Trajectories in Faith*, Nashville, Tenn., Abingdon Press, 1979.

11. Quoted in 'Sacraments' in S. G. F. Brandon, (ed.), *Dictionary of Comparative Religion*, New York, Charles Scribner's Sons, 1970, p. 544.

12. See particularly Eleanor Maccoby and Carol Jacklin, *The Psychology of Sex Differences*, Stanford, Calif., Stanford University Press, 1974.

13. See Ernest Becker's use of the idea of 'fetishization', in 'The pawnbroker,' part of *Angel in Armor*, New York, George Braziler, 1969.

14. W. C. Smith, *Belief and History*, Charlottesville, Virginia, The University Press of Virginia, 1977.

15. For more extensive treatments of the character of faith see Fowler, 'Faith, liberation and human development,' lecture I, in *Foundations*, Gammon Theological Seminary, Atlanta, GA, vol. 69, 1974; and Jim Fowler and Sam Keen, *Life Maps: conversations on the journey of faith*, Waco, Texas, Word Books, 1978, pp. 14–25.

16. See Fowler and Keen, *op cit.*, pp. 25–101. In addition, see Fowler, 'Stages in faith: the structural-developmental approach,' in Thomas Hennessy, (ed.), *Values and Moral Education*, New York, Paulist Press, 1976, pp. 273–311.

17. Erik Erikson, *op. cit.*, ch. 7.

18. These descriptions build on and supplement those given in the previously noted articles by Fowler. Longer and more articulated descriptions are to be found in Fowler and Keen, *op. cit.* and Fowler in Hennessey, *op. cit.*

19. Linda C. Hunt, 'The impact of family dynamics on adult faith development', unpublished MA dissertation, Whitworth College, Spokane, Washington, 1978.

20. See James W. Fowler, 'Faith development theory and the aims of religious socialization,' in G. Durka and J. Smith, (eds), *Emerging Issues in Religious Education*, New York, Paulist Press, 1976, pp. 187–211.

21. Richard Helfaer, *The Psychology of Religious Doubt*, Boston, Massachusetts, Beacon Press, 1972.

22. H. Richard Niebuhr's influence will be apparent here. See especially *The Meaning of Revelation*, New York, Macmillan, 1941; and *Radical Monotheism and Western Culture*, New York, Harper and Row, 1960.

23. William J. Bouwsma, 'Christian adulthood,' in Erik H. Erikson, (ed.), *Adulthood*, New York, W. W. Norton, 1978.

24. Jürgen Moltmann, 'The diaconal church,' in Theodore Runyon (trans), *Hope for the Church*, Nashville, Tenn., Abingdon Press, 1979.

25. This concept is adapted from Kenneth Keniston in his 'Psychological development and historical change,' in R. J. Lifton, (ed.), *Explorations in Psychohistory*, New York, Simon and Schuster, 1974, pp. 149–164.

26. Lawrence Kohlberg, 'The moral atmosphere of the school,' in N. Overly, (ed.), *The Unstudied Curriculum*, Monograph of the Association for Supervision and Curriculum Development, Washington, D.C, 1970.

8.2 Faith development and campus ministry

Gary L. Chamberlain

Tutoring younger students ... counseling peers ... planning liturgies ... building a retreat program ... visiting a nursing home ... exploring common beliefs. All these activities reflect one of the most exciting recent developments in Christian education – the emergence of the high school campus ministry program. For years 'ministry' at the parochial or private Christian high school was viewed as an adjunct of the religion department or an extra-curricular affair. Today, while campus ministry takes a variety of forms in the high school setting, the movement has established itself as a core contribution to the intellectual and moral as well as spiritual development of students.

In this study I will examine the implications for campus ministry in the faith development theory of Dr James W. Fowler. Fowler's theory provides an important and challenging set of formal criteria with which to evaluate high school campus ministry as it extends to the entire school. Before I discuss the implications of the theory for campus ministry, I will highlight those features of Fowler's theory which are of particular importance to the high school experience.[1]

In Fowler's use of the word, 'faith' is neither cognitive belief nor necessarily religious faith. Rather faith is viewed as a universal phenomenon, an active way in which every individual, regardless of any particular religious affiliation, understands and relates himself or herself to a sense of self, others, the surrounding world, and the Transcendent. In addition, Fowler emphasizes faith as a way of knowing or understanding in which the individual construes and interprets experience through interaction with the world. Finally, an important dimension in our discussion is Fowler's emphasis upon faith as an interpersonal pattern of valuing and committing, related intimately to the development of a sense of self and of community. It is precisely in his or her faithful relationships that the individual is 'discovered' by himself or herself. Others care for and provide the individual with reflections of the self, and gradually through this interaction the individual begins to form and construe reliable images of the self, the community which supports the self, and the Transcendent. By means of these imaginings and symbols the 'faithing' person construes an idea or image of a God which in turn shapes and interprets our everyday experience.

Adolescence and faith

In terms of the faith development stages elaborated by Fowler, faith development from the concrete literalism of stage 2 'narratizing' faith through the interpersonal relationships and dependence upon conventional understandings of faith as seen in stage 3 and on to the beginning of independent faithing of stage 4. As we know from the work of Erik Erikson and others, the adolescent during these years is searching for a sense of selfhood that can hold together the new ideas, feelings, ideals, loyalties and commitments which emerge from self-conscious awareness of what others think and feel about that 'self.' In search of an answer to the questions of 'Who am I?' and 'What will I become?' the adolescent tries on different roles to see how well they fit, how comfortable they are, how free and yet secure they make him or her feel. The roles which the adolescent explores are worn by adults who both prove themselves trustworthy and lovable to the adolescent and at the same time confirm that the adolescent is a trustworthy and lovable person. In Erikson's words the adolescent is one who 'looks most fervently for men (and women) and ideas to have faith in, which also means men (and women) and ideas in whose service it would seem worthwhile to prove oneself trustworthy.'[2] The search for identity involves a careful and crucial search for models who exemplify faith in the form of fidelity, a trusting commitment of self to another.

If faith in the early high school years is emerging from the narrative, 'heroic,' literal form of stage 2 and searching for an embodiment in real adult models, then every adult in the high school, whether teacher, administrator, or staff person, becomes a faith model, of 'bad faith,' as well as 'good faith,' whether realized or not. It seems obvious to say that if the adults in the high school are models of faith, then 'faithing' must be evident in action and words. If faith is a way of trusting in and remaining loyal to an ultimate reality, then the models who mediate that reality must be seen as worthy of trust and loyalty of the adolescent as well as visibly trusting in and loyal to the ultimate.

Just as importantly, the various 'campus ministers' as models of faith are carriers of faith histories and visions. Yet how seldom are those histories and visions shared with one another, let alone with students. If we accept the findings of a recent study of faith development that biographies served as an important element in the development of faith, especially in the movement toward stage 4,[3] then we can understand how the examples of people who had a sense of their own identity and who were faithful to their visions provided powerful faith models for others. By sharing faith histories and visions, the campus ministers become not only models *in* faithing but models *of* the varieties of faith expressions. Thus it would be important for the adults of the high school community to share such histories and visions among themselves and with students. In addition, younger students could benefit from hearing the faith stories of the older students who are themselves models. Such sharings would provide confirmation of faithfulness in a variety of ways and would stimulate the challenge to an individual's faith perspective which is necessary for any development.

The school as community

A note of cautious realism creeps in at this point. For a fundamental question the campus ministry program faces is what are the operative concepts of church and of a faithing person which inform the school. If the primary image is that of church as embodiment of rules and regulations which foster loyalty to the institution, then the faithful person is one who conforms to those rules. Violation of the rules and disloyalty to the institution constitute 'unfaithfulness.' The painful and difficult transition from stage 3 to stage 4 will not find nourishment in such a conforming environment. Adolescents may continue to develop but without the realization that there is room within the structures of the church for the kind of individual expressions of faith seen in stage 4. The individual will not find confirmation of his or her own 'faithing.' All too often rebellion, even 'a-theism,' is a healthy movement of independent 'faithing' against conventional ('theistic' = dogmatic) constructions of reality which serve as constrictions of faith.

If we turn to the model of church as community, a different process for 'faithing' is possible. Church in this sense would mean the web of relationships which confirm the individual in his or her 'faithing,' which challenge the adolescent and nourish a movement from a stage 2 mode of 'faithing' to stage 3. At this level adult models become the embodiment of faith in sharing a common tradition and a consensus of faith. At the same time the community can provide for the older adolescent a home and support for the kind of individual challengings of the conventional 'faith' world which leads to the grasp of an independent 'faithing' in young adulthood. The very process of questioning can receive validation and encouragement. Thus the church as embodied community within the school can be seen as supportive of rather than challenged by those individual expressions of faith which question the conventional consensus.

Such a conception of church within the school rests upon a value judgment that a stage 4 expression of faith is somehow 'better' than a stage 3 expression. A complete response to that assumption or to the related question of *why* or *when* to intervene in the development of faith go beyond the scope of this discussion. At the moment I would reply that each stage is a graced whole which provides the expression of faith appropriate to each individual at a particular point in the life-cycle. However, the call of the Gospel is toward a gift of oneself to the Lord and an understanding of reality as God understands it. As long as my sense of self as a faithful person rests upon formulations outside myself, upon conventions, I am unable to make such a gift of 'myself' in response to the Lord. And as long as my understanding of reality, of others, of God, is limited to any one group's understanding, the revelation of the world in all its complexities and yet its fundamental oneness remains hidden.

In the school setting the concept of the church as community leaves us with some broad implications. If the adolescent is searching for faithful models who have faith in him or her, then students must be trusted to make decisions governing their own relationships. Most student governments, for example, are only advisory at best, and the students in realizing their lack of real power over their lives feel the lack of trust in them as persons. Using a model of moral development with high school students, Dr Lawrence Kohlberg of Harvard University's Center for Moral Education has demonstrated the possibilities and promise in allowing students to develop their own governing patterns and concepts of justice.[4] The faith development model demands an even greater context of trust and 'faithing' on the part of faculty members and administrators.

Secondly, inasmuch as faith development in community calls for the articulation of personal beliefs, attitudes and values and the opportunity to hear those of others, faith sharing ought to be an important dimension of the school as community. Here I am not speaking only of sharing common beliefs but of sharing faith journeys, the stories of how each individual came to be a faithing person. This kind of sharing could permeate the classroom, school retreats, liturgies, and decision-making processes. In an extended sense, hiring new faculty members might be based not upon membership in any particular institutional church but upon the faculty member's attention to his or her own development in faith. Especially for juniors and seniors the presence of faithful models of other religious traditions could provide a vivid sense of the multi-colored world of faith while the students are still within a context in which such different perspectives can be used to support and confirm a 'faithing' within their own tradition. Within the community the pluralisms of 'faithing' should be embraced and lived with: the variety of traditions within and beyond Christianity as well as the variety of 'faithing' styles within any one Christian tradition. Once again the modeling function of all adult 'ministers' on the campus is important here. For these 'ministers' must have their own sense of an individuative faith in the midst of such pluralisms.

In summarizing this portion of the discussion, I am asking that the school examine the faith atmosphere on campus in view of the realization that 'faithing' people are shaped by their environment, particularly in the adolescent years. The understanding of faith as interpersonal and communal at stage 3, the operative stage of most adolescents, calls into question the structure and functions of the high school. Clearly some structures and functions are more suitable for developing and nourishing faith than others. And the question is whether a bureaucratic, rule-dominated, hierarchical organization in which 'ministry' is relegated to the functions of one person or department promotes development as well as a participatory, organic, interpersonal structure based upon a sharing community and a shared sense of ministering.

Applications

In this final section I would like to outline areas in which the theory of faith development has particular application to the high school setting. These include the movement from literalism to symbols important in the transition from stage 2 to stage 3, the ability to take the perspective of other individuals and groups, and the sense of involvement and participation in community which supports the emerging sense of identity and fidelity at stage 3.

From literalism to symbols

A provocative study of high school students by Dr Margaret Gorman, Boston College, found that a functional literalism served as a hindrance to later stages of faith development.[5] In particular such literalism centred around the perceived opposition between religion and science and the literal understanding of Biblical materials. What seemed to help in this transition were courses involving and understanding of myth and symbolism. While we might include other courses such as an understanding of evolution and religion, the strictly cognitive dimensions could be supplemented by retreat experiences, exposure to older students whose faithing has developed to stage three and beyond, and powerful experiences of liturgy in which such symbols as light, water, bread, wine, incense are explored. Without such challenges and experiences the symbolic realities of Word and Sacrament will be locked in a confining literalism.

Perspective-taking

If a conscious, reflective faith is ever to develop, the 'faithing' person must develop the capacity to step outside his or her own perspective and work to understand the world as others understand it. This begins even for the infant who soon learns that the parental figure does not always respond to cries for food or diaper changes. But such development emerges powerfully in the adolescent years when the young person yearns for someone to understand his or her feelings and is overwhelmed by the force of powerful ideas and ideals recently encountered. The critical factor for development at this point is the way in which the individual begins to incorporate or reject systems of thinking different from his or her own.

Since cognitive conflict is one of the most important tools enabling an individual to take the perspective of another, courses such as comparative or world religions serve as a way of exposing students to different understandings of faith questions within the context of other traditions. In addition, the Gorman study underscored the feeling of teenagers that their faith questions were not being addressed when submerged in courses involving doctrine or belief with no reference to adolescent development. Dr Gorman noted that in many cases students responded to her interview questions on death, suffering, injustice and values by stating: 'Nobody ever asked me about these questions before.' Certainly a fundamental dimension of faith development from adolescence on is the opportunity and encouragement to articulate one's own understandings and constructions of reality. The correlative factor is the chance to hear the 'faithing' of others without the necessity to make judgments.

In this context we can offer some concrete suggestions. As I mentioned earlier, the 'faithing' community should offer all participants the opportunity to articulate their faith journeys while listening to those of other community members. Biographies of committed individuals who demonstrate their faith in their own lives can be utilized. Finally, students could be encouraged to write a statement of faith throughout their high school career.[6] In conjunction with individual faculty advisors each student would explore his or her faith at the end of each semester or year in school. Then in senior year students could be encouraged to share their faith statements with one another in a seminar, in liturgies, on retreats in a testimony and witness to their own growth and faith.

A final aspect of perspective-taking involves the creation of a trusting environment in which such sharing and conflict as described above can take place. In particular that involves the legitimation of conflict and disagreement and the exploration of skills to articulate those disagreements as well as to resolve them. The entire context demands a growing sense of responsibility for one's own ideas and feelings and a care for the ideas and feelings of others.

Sense of participation

If the concept of community is to serve as the basis for developing faith, then it must minimally involve a sharing of resources, prayers and praise, decision-making and selves. The community must involve a sense of belonging in which each individual can find meaning, a sense of self-identity and a context for developing relationships with peers and models. We have discussed several of these factors earlier. Thus, I will cover only two important dimensions here.

In the first place campus ministry in the broad sense should involve students in the planning and administration of each program as much as possible. Students will feel 'faithed' in, trusted, and thus trusting, when they *experience* being trusted with responsibilities. Such involvement is obvious in such an area as the liturgy in which students can choose the readings, prepare the music and carry out much of the service. But students should likewise be encouraged to assume responsibilities in governing the school, preparing classes, teaching fellow students, and so forth. This kind of community recognition and support strengthens the emerging self-identity and fidelity necessary to the independent faith stance (stage 4) of the mature, committed believer.

A second dimension of participation involves the growing practice of involving students, particularly seniors, in programs of community service. From the point of view of faith development such programs are particularly important inasmuch as they expose students to perspectives and life-styles different than their own, stimulate cognitive conflict, and/or provide confirmation for personal faith. Furthermore, such programs involve the students in a sense of justice on a level at which they can understand the meaning of justice best, that is, in terms of fairness in interpersonal relations. The more abstract, analytic sense of justice which involves a criticism of social systems will be all the more powerful as it emerges from the context of personal contact with the deprived, the aged, and other victims of injustice, ignorance, suffering and failure in society.

Another important factor in faith development which such programs facilitate is the sense of responsibility for others which students gain from the experience. The teenager's overriding concern with self is expanded to include the problems of others and the problems of the world at large. Such experiential challenges ground the cognitive conflicts encountered in the classroom or in discussions with those of differing 'faithings.'

However, service alone is not enough. If the experience is to serve as a factor in faith development, it must be incorporated in reflective study through a seminar or some other form of discussion. The seminar would serve as the basis for support in the students' own form of ministry and service, for analysis of the success and failure of individual efforts at service, for incorporation into a larger framework of Christian living, and for a critical understanding of the ways in which those whom the students serve are not being served by the larger society. The seminar can provide the students with a place to integrate their individual experiences with those of others in the group and with their personal and corporate faith.

While seniors might be involved in such programs throughout the year, other classes could be involved in developmental stages. Thus sophomores might serve as apprentices to the seniors with less time involvement but with some exposure to the seniors as older models living out their experiences of faith. Since the seniors are in some ways much more realistic models than adults for younger students, the seniors provide a concrete embodiment of service. In view of the expanded notion of campus ministry and community I outlined earlier, 'community service' could and should also include service within the high school of older students to younger students and peers to peers.

Conclusion

Although there are certainly several other implications and applications of faith development theory to the high school setting, I hope that this discussion has provided some basis for further discussion and analysis. The Christian parochial or private high school provides a unique setting in which the richness of the *content* of the Christian faith (the cumulative tradition) can interact with the stages of 'faithing' appropriate to adolescents. For too long, 'faith development' has been identified with religion classes, and those students were considered to be 'faithing' Christians who knew well the doctrinal, moral and historical aspects of Christianity.

Throughout this discussion I have stressed a different perspective. In the first place, 'faithing' has been described as a dynamic *process* involving the appropriation and interpretation of the content of the faith tradition according to the developmental structures of the individual. Secondly, only when the high school is seen as a total environment which informs, supports, challenges or perhaps contradicts the faith of individual students will the content of the Christian tradition provide nourishment and growth for the individual Christian. As a corollary of this second point, I have emphasized the roles of all adults on the campus as models of 'faithing.'

Finally faith development theory must not be confused with the content of the Christian faith. Rather faith development refers to how we understand and *re*-interpret that content. And 'faithing' always involves 'faithing' about some content. Nor should faith development be considered as a new *program* or *technique* in Christian education. However, faith development does offer formal, evaluative criteria which any religious education program must meet if it takes the developmental perspective seriously. At the very least, programs which inhibit development, restrict growth to accommodate the particular needs of the church would be inconsistent with the words of Jesus: 'I have come that they may have life and have it to the full.'[7] On a more positive note, religious education based upon faith development must provide a variety of models in faith, roletaking opportunities, re-interpretations of symbols, cognitive challenges, honest appraisals of other religious traditions and supporting structures for movement beyond the comfortable, conventional 'faithing' of stage 3. Because of the crucial period of adolescence in the life-cycle and because of the formative influence which the high school setting plays in shaping values, attitudes and beliefs, the theory of faith development can provide an important new look at every dimension of the Christian high school in the continuing development of 'faithing' people and in the task of building a community which incorporates a vision of the coming Kingdom.

Notes
1. For a discussion of Fowler's theory, cf. James W. Fowler, 'Toward a developmental perspective on faith,' *Religious Education*, vol. 69, 1974, pp. 207–219; 'Faith, liberation, and human development,' *Foundation* (Gammon Theological Seminary), vol. 79, 1974, pp. 1–29; and 'Stages of faith,' in Thomas Hennessy (ed.), *Values and Moral Education*, New York, Paulist Press, 1976.
2. Erik Erikson, *Identity, Youth and Crisis*, New York, W.W. Norton and Co., 1968, pp. 128–29; my addition in brackets.
3. Eugene J. Mischey, 'Faith development and its relationship to moral reasoning and identity status in young adults', unpublished Ph.D. dissertation, University of Torronto, 1976.
4. Cf. Elsa Wasserman, 'Implementing Kohlberg's "Just Community" concept in an alternative high school,' *Social Education*, April 1976.
5. Margaret Gorman, 'Moral and faith development in 17 year old students,' *Religious Education*, vol. 72, 1977, pp. 491–504.
6. The concepts of the faith statement and the community service seminar are developed by Paula Symes, 'Faith and faith community in the Catholic high school,' unpublished paper, Webster College, 1977.
7. John 10:10b, *The Jerusalem Bible*.

8.3 Faith development: bridging theory and practice
Mark Rutledge

Student services professionals will readily recognize names such as Piaget (1950), Kohlberg (1971), Erikson (1963), Perry (1970), Keniston (1971), and Gilligan (1982). The works of these and other scholars have provided theoretical bases for the profession of student services for many years (Delworth, Hanson, and Associates, 1980). What is less known is that these same developmental theorists also provide the base for an emerging body of research and literature on faith development. Acknowledging his debt to Kohlberg and other developmental theorists, Fowler (1981) has developed a theory of faith development that is used extensively by religious professionals. Parks (1986), a colleague of Fowler's, focuses on the search for faith by students and details the unique contributions that higher education makes in that developmental process.

Faith defined

Fowler (1981, p. 33) considers faith a human phenomenon, a consequence of 'the universal human burden of finding or making meaning'. He describes faith as 'triadic,' in that faith is a felt sense of relation between (1) the self and (2) others as conditioned by loyalty to (3) a center of power and value. This relational character of faith includes the necessity of composing a sense of the whole — of self, world, and God. All human action could be said to occur within a felt sense of 'how life really is or ought to be and what has ultimate value' (Parks, 1986, p. 17).

In the dynamic activity of composing the meaning of life, the pattern persons ultimately depend on for their existence functions as God for them. Whatever serves as the centering, unifying linchpin of their pattern of meaning — that center functions as God. Both Fowler and Parks cite theologian H. Richard Niebuhr's understanding of faith: 'To deny the reality of a supernatural being called God is one thing; to live without confidence in some center of value and without loyalty to a cause is another' (Niebuhr, 1941, p. 24).

Other elements in faith as a human activity include faith as imagination, faith as truth and trust, faith as act, and faith as suffering. Faith as imagination forms a way of life in relation to holistic images of reality in what Fowler (1981, p. 29) calls a person's 'ultimate environment'. Through symbols, metaphors, and concepts, life is unified or given character in this ultimate environment. Truth and trust are at stake in the composing of faith. Faith must stand up under the test of the truth of lived experience. Persons must not only compose a sense of what they take to be ultimately true but also depend on or trust in that ultimate center of value and power. Faith also is related to doing. Persons act in accordance with what they really trust, in contrast to what they may only proclaim. They act according to their actual, most powerful centers of trust and meaning. Finally, faith includes suffering. The experience of betrayal tests the real force of faith. Faith includes the suffering of doubt, of being overwhelmed, of drifting, of struggle, of yearning, and of despair – all of which may be significant dimensions of a student's faith experience (Parks, 1986).

Stages in faith development

Following Piaget (1950) and Kohlberg's (1971) stage theories, Fowler likewise argued that faith develops through recognizable and sequential stages. Thus, a child's faith differs from an adult's not just in its content but also in the inner patterned structure of operations by which the child has faith. Fowler's research indicates that six distinctive stages can be recognized in the developing capacity for faith activity. Each stage is its own structural whole, but the stages are related to each other hierarchically and sequentially; they develop in an ascending order, and each stage incorporates, while adding to, the previous stage. The transition from one to another can be protracted and painful. A new stage emerges when a person becomes consciously aware of the limitations of the present stage and seeks to move beyond it. Fowler insists, however, that each stage has its own integrity. Stage 4, for example, is not 'more faithful' than stage 3; rather, it is merely a more developed or mature expression of faith than stage 3 (Groome, 1980). Each stage includes components of logic, roles, authorities, social religion, moral judgments, and symbols. The following brief overview of the six stages is based upon Groome's (1980) helpful summary.

Stage 1 is intuitive or projective faith. This is the faith of the person (generally four to eight years old) in which meaning is made and trust established intuitively and by imitation of the moods, example, and action of significant others, primarily parents. Feelings dominate; knowing and feeling are fused. In stage 1, fact and fantasy are not yet differentiated, symbols are taken literally, and God is thought of in anthropomorphic, magical terms. There is an awakening of memory and self-consciousness, and the capacity to take the role of another (empathy) is beginning, but only in a rudimentary form.

Stage 2 is the mythic or literal stage. This is an affiliative stage that occurs approximately between the ages of seven or eight and eleven or twelve years. Persons in stage 2 come more consciously to join and belong to their immediate group or faith community. They now come, with some enthusiasm, to learn the 'lore, the language, and the legends' of their particular community and to appropriate these as their own. This can happen because there is now a greater awareness of the differences between the self and the collective of immediate others.

The way of making meaning is now more linear and narrative than episodic as in stage 1. The child's ultimate environment is conceptualized in stories and myths that are taken literally. Life is as it appears to be. Reasoning and thought beyond intuition are now possible, but thinking is still in concrete, sensory terms, with little abstraction possible. The child is beginning to differentiate the natural from the supernatural, but God continues to be understood largely as a being who has human characteristics and patterns.

At this stage, faith is a joining faith. The person consciously joins the immediate social group; takes on its stories, symbols, myths, and doctrines; and interprets them literally. The word of significant elders dominates over that of peers.

Stage 3 is the synthetic or conventional stage. It usually begins when a child is eleven or twelve years old as personal experience is extended beyond the family and primary social group. It can last long into adulthood, and for some it becomes a permanent home. A person in this stage interprets, relates to, and makes meaning out of life according to the directions and criteria of what 'they say' — in other words, according to popular convention. It is a conventional or conformist stage in that the person is anxious to respond faithfully to the expectations and judgments of significant others. Persons in this stage lack a sufficient grasp of their own identity to make autonomous judgments from an independent perspective.

Stage 3 is an advance beyond stage 2 in that a person consciously experiences a division of life into different segments or theaters of action. Now there are many 'theys' impinging on the person's way of knowing and relating to the world: family, school, work, church, peers, leisure ethos, and the like. Each of these segments of life is likely to provide a variety of different perspectives, expectations, and ways of making meaning. They inevitably come into conflict. How then does the person in stage 3, who is dependent on authority in each theater of action, reach equilibrium and synthesis? Fowler claims that synthesis is reached either by subordinating the different authorities under what the person perceives to be the one highest authority, or by compartmentalization. The latter occurs when a person tends to make meaning and interpret the world differently depending on the group the person is with. On specifically religious questions, there is a strong tendency to rely on institutional authority.

Faith is still not self-chosen; it continues to be conventional, with the confirming authority localized outside the person. A synthesis occurs, but it is not a personal autonomous synthesis. Rather it is a choosing and a balancing of the various conventional expectations of the person's various worlds (thus the title synthetic or conventional).

Stage 4 is the individuating or reflexive stage. It does not usually begin before age seventeen or eighteen. For a significant number, it emerges only in the midthirties and forties, and many adults never achieve it. The transition from stage 3 to stage 4 is particularly crucial for the continuation of the faith journey. Here the conventional synthesis of stage 3 begins to collapse because of a lack of congruence between the self and the various conventional expectations of the person's different groups. The transition to stage 4 comes when persons can no longer tolerate being 'different' when they are with different groups, or when they realize that they cannot hand the making of their meaning over to even the highest authority. Now the responsibility for synthesis and making meaning shifts from relying on conventional authority or authorities to taking personal responsibility for commitments, life-style, beliefs, and attitudes. As a result, there is now a qualitatively different degree of autonomy, beyond stage 3. An individual's ways of knowing and relating to the world – identity and world view – are more personally chosen and self-consciously differentiated from the attitudes and expectations of others. In fact, they become acknowledged factors in the person's way of interpreting, judging, and reacting to experience.

Even as a person achieves a more autonomous faith, stage 4 brings a newfound awareness of the paradoxes and polarities of life. Decisions about life's ambiguities and polar tensions can no longer be avoided as they were at stage 3. Fowler (1981) lists some of those polar tensions as individual versus community; particular versus universal; relative versus absolute; self-fulfillment versus service to others; autonomy versus heteronomy; feeling versus thinking; subjectivity versus objectivity. A person's faith activity now attempts to handle these tensions and maintain equilibrium between them. However, the tendency at stage 4, particularly in its early formulation, is to collapse the tension to favour either side. The person is likely to take an either/or approach to such questions and paradoxes.

It is not unusual for a stage 4 person to join a strong ideologically grounded community that offers ready-made answers to the ambiguities and paradoxes of life. However, the joining is based on a more self-chosen commitment. Stage 4, then, is a new ability to stand alone, and a person's class or group is chosen reflectively rather than simply accepted or received, as at stage 3 (thus the name, individuating or reflexive).

Stage 5 is the conjunctive stage. In this stage, which usually does not occur before midlife, the paradoxes that were previously dealt with by some strategy of tension reduction are now embraced and affirmed, and the tension is incorporated into the person's way of 'being in faith.' Life is no longer seen in terms of either/or: there is a willingness to live with ambiguities. This is not a relativism but a recognition that a person's own position is not the final fullness of truth. This requires a genuine openness to others and a willingness to enter into dialogue with them even at the risk of changing a person's own way of making meaning and relating to the world.

Stage 5 faith involves a reappropriation of past patterns of commitment and ways of making meaning. This is not a regressing; it is, instead, a reclaiming of old truths in a new way. If stage 3 was dependent, and stage 4 self-dependent, then stage 5 is interdependent. The person is capable of depending on others without losing independence. Now there is empathy with and active concern for all peoples and groups – for the whole human family, not just for the person's own immediate community.

Stage 6 is the universalizing stage. When Fowler speaks about stage 6, his language becomes somewhat poetic. This seems to be inevitable, as stage 6 is difficult to name with the concrete language of everyday speech. He likes to point to examples of it, rare as they are, and he frequently cites Mother Teresa of Calcutta. The self as the centering reference point is replaced by the ultimate. The person has an ongoing experience of immediate participation in the ultimate and makes encounter with the ultimate available to others. The stage 6 person dwells in the world as a transforming presence, 'spending and being spent in order to transform present reality in the direction of a transcendent reality' (Fowler and Keen, 1978, p. 88).

A much simpler developmental theory (Gribbon, 1977) uses four styles of faith to describe the developmental process. Experienced faith is dominant in childhood, as the person learns through touch and experience to trust parental figures, the world, and God. Affiliative faith takes precedence during the school years when persons learn the story of their nurturning community. They depend on and derive identity from affiliation with the community. Searching faith is a period of questioning, experimentation, acting against the community, and forming commitments to various ideologies. This style often occurs in the late teenage years. Owned faith, emerging from the previous styles, makes commitments and choices that strengthen the community in a mutually beneficial dynamic.

Connections with theories informing student development

Student affairs staff members who have studied psychosocial and cognitive theories of student development will recognize parallels with faith development theory. For example, the process of moving from affiliative to searching to owned faith (Gribbon, 1977) is parallel to the movement from dependence to independence to inter-dependence in establishing a sense of autonomy (Chickering, 1969). The psychosocial task of establishing a personal sense of identity (Erikson, 1963) is parallel to the transition to the individuating or reflexive stage of faith (Fowler, 1981). Fowler's description of conjunctive faith, in which a person makes commitments while simultaneously remaining open to truths in others' positions, is similar to the cognitive theory of Perry (1970), which speaks of students making tentative commitments within a general framework of relativism. Carol Gilligan (1982), a colleague of Kohlberg, speaks of human development in relational rather than in more individualistic terms and in so doing parallels Fowler, who defined faith in relational terms of self, other, and ultimate center of power and value. The concept of the moratorium used by Erikson (1963) to describe a psychosocial stage between childhood and adulthood parallels Gribbon's searching style of faith. The moratorium is a time for students to step apart from the culture, to question previously held beliefs, to experiment with new identities and roles, and to suspend previously learned behaviors. This corresponds to the questioning and experimentation that Gribbon says is characteristic of young adult faith. Kenneth Keniston (1971) has developed a theory positing a new postadolescent stage of development, in which many students cannot be adequately described as either adolescent or adult, and Parks (1986) uses this observation in her argument for a distinct new stage between Fowler's third and fourth stages.

There are many echoes of the developmental theories used by student affairs staff in the dynamics of faith development – maturation, making sense, composing meaning, ordering relations, and 'an activity that transforms being, knowing, and doing' (Parks, 1986, p. 39). Faith development theorists hold in common that faith cannot be reduced to psychological and sociological processes. Faith is something different; it is an activity of composing and being composed by ultimate meanings.

Faith in college students

Parks's new stage between Fowler's third and fourth stages describes processes of faith development in young adulthood and the college-age years. This new stage includes four processes: form of cognition, form of dependence, form of community, and role of imagination. These may be understood as strands or aspects of the total developmental process. Attention is focused on how these issues are presented in the transition from synthetic or conventional faith to individuating or reflexive faith, which are so critical for young adult students between the ages of eighteen and thirty.

Form of cognition refers to the ways in which young adults

'know' about themselves, the world, and God through four stages: authority-bound and dualistic, unqualified relativism, probing commitment, and tested commitment. In the first form of knowing, what a student trusts, knows, and believes is based on some external authority, such as a person, group, or models from popular culture. These authorities are confirmed by the 'various stories, myths, and symbols that hold the meaning of a people and their institutions' (Parks, 1986, p. 45). This form of knowing is dualistic in that it makes clear divisions between what is true and untrue, right and wrong, we and they – there is no tolerance for ambiguity. This stage of intellectual development begins to break down when students see that professors differ from one another and that it is not easy to reconcile these differences into simple right and wrong categories.

The student now acknowledges that the human mind acts on its world to compose it, rather than simply receiving it 'as it is,' and that knowledge is relative – that is, 'conditioned by the particularity of the relation or context in which it is composed' (Parks, 1986, p. 47). This requires the student to recognize that the most trusted adults and the most revered academic disciplines, including the sciences, all must compose reality in a pluralistic and relativized world. This is a universe in which 'every perception leads to a different "truth"; therefore every opinion and judgment may be as worthy as another' (Parks, 1986, p. 47). The certainties of the student's conventional world collapse, and during experiences of failure of intimate relationships or in the class room, where authority-bound beliefs are criticized, the student suffers not only the obvious loss but also a sense of the unraveling of self, world, and God. These can be painful times for many students. Yet, it is hard to maintain a position of unqualified relativism forever. Students discover that there are glaring differences between opinions that matter and that some opinions are better than others.

Certainty may not be possible, but students also discover that choices must be made that have consequences both for the students themselves and for the persons they love. Especially in relation to moral issues, students may look for a place to stand, a way of composing truth that is more adequate to their lives than other possibilities are. Here, students take self-responsibility for their own knowing while, at the same time, remaining aware of the finite nature of all judgments. This emerging commitment first takes the form of a tentative, or what Parks (1986, p. 82) calls 'probing,' commitment. The student explores possible forms of truth and their fittingness to the student's experience of self and world. At this stage, even deeply felt affirmations have a tenuous, exploratory, and divided quality.

Cognitive, intellectual development does not take place apart from the affective dimension of life. The student is struggling to reorder the meanings inherent in feelings and relationships at the same time. Thus, forms of dependence are a crucial affective strand of development in the weaving of mature faith. It has to do with the locus of authority, in the shift of authority out there to a critically aware sense of authority within. Parks (1986) identifies four aspects of dependence: dependence or counterdependence, fragile inner-dependence, confident inner-dependence, and interdependence.

Counterdependence is a move in opposition to authority, in which the person pushes against previously held conventional patterns but is not yet able to create new ones. The person remains dependent on the relationship with the authority with whom there is contention. The motion of inner-dependence occurs when 'one is able to self-consciously include the self within the arena of authority' (Parks, 1986 p. 57). Other sources of authority may still hold power, but the person now recognizes and values also the authority of the self. Persons begin to listen within and trust the inner life as they compose the meaning of life in faith. Parks distinguishes between a fragile inner-dependence of the young adult student and a more confident inner-dependence of the adult. For both, the relationship with a mentor is important. The young adult student can be described as 'subject to the emerging self that is yet dependent upon authority "out there" to beckon and confirm its integrity . . . the self depends upon mentors not so much for its integrity as for its expression, confirmation, and fulfillment' (Parks, 1986, p. 88). Adults, in contrast, are less dependent on others for the ordering of their own sense of value and become strong enough to let the mentor be other — even to have feet of clay; 'the mentor becomes peer' (Parks, 1986, p. 88).

True interdependence is a movement that usually does not appear until the mature adult years. The young adult, having grown to trust the limitations and strengths of the self, can grow to be more at home with the truths embedded in the strengths and limitations of others. The locus of authority and trust is not solely in the assumed authority of others, nor only in the courageously claimed authority of the inner self. Rather, trust is now centered in 'the meeting of self and other, recognizing the strength and finitude of each and the promise of truth that emerges in relation' (Parks, 1986, p. 59).

For the young adult, the learning era finds its most powerful form in a 'mentoring community' (Parks, 1986, p. 89). The student develops within one or more social communities. Faith is embodied, not in the individual alone, but in the social fabric of life. Persons never outgrow their need for others, but 'what others mean for us undergoes transformation' (Parks, 1986, p. 63). In the student years, much transformation occurs in the forms and roles of community, particularly in the tension to become independent and the longing to be connected in a 'network of belonging and communion.' Parks identifies five movements: conventional community, diffuse community, ideologically compatible groupings (mentoring), self-selected class or group, and community open to others.

The first two movements are typical of the years before young adulthood as Parks identifies it. Conventional community is composed of groupings that conform to class norms and interests, and a person is born into them. The person is only aware, socially, of those 'like us.' But when knowing becomes more relative, the sense of community may become more diffuse. When one truth is as good as another, then any sort of relationship may be as good as another. The person may experience simultaneously the freedom to explore new relationships and a new vulnerability to the potential power of those relationships.

In the student years, the young adult develops a new relation to community that corresponds to the commitment within the relativism movement in cognitive development. Parks (1986, p. 89) notes that it is the combination of the emerging truth of the young adult with the example and encouragement of the mentor, grounded in the experience of an ideologically compatible social group, that 'generates the transforming power of the young adult era'. Because of the fragility of the self emerging into inner-dependence and probing commitment, the young adult depends on and responds to those persons and groups 'who express patterns of meaning resonant with the experience and new awareness of the fragile, emerging self' (Parks, 1986, p. 89). Thus, young adults are extremely receptive to any group or community that promises a place of nurture for the potential self in faith. This form of community is described as ideologically compatible. The last two forms of community generally occur beyond the young adult years.

A strength of the young adult student is the capacity to respond to visions of the world as it might become. This is the time in every generation for renewal of the human vision. In young adulthood, the primal force of promise is again recomposed. In the language of Jewish and Christian religious traditions, this developmental moment includes a particular readiness to envision and experience the presence of God. Parks (1986, p. 96) argues that this should not be dismissed as mere 'youthful idealism, for young adulthood is the birthplace of adult vision'.

A central task for the young adult student is the formation of a dream (Parks, 1986). In this regard, the role of imagination is a critical human power or capacity. Imagination is the power by which faith is composed. It is the human ability that gives rise to images and symbols that unify and make meaningful all that had seemed to be 'unreconcilably disparate and complex.' Sometimes in moments of insight an image comes to a person that incorporates the elements of previous conflicts into a single, unified whole, thereby 'repatterning' it (Parks, 1986, p. 122). Images, as metaphors for what is happening in inner life, use pictures, objects, persons, and events from the external world to stand for meanings that the person makes, or that 'grasp' the person. Persons give form to their ultimate meanings with images and symbols.

In the process of imagination, the moment of insight or image is, in religious terms, the moment of revelation. It is that part of the inner experience of a person or group that 'illuminates the rest of it' (Parks, 1986, p. 125). Revelation is the event that provides an integrative, unifying image of meaning. Niebuhr (1941) likens such revelatory images to a luminous sentence in a difficult book from which the reader can go backward and forward and so attain some understanding of the whole.

Imagination is a key to many of the change processes that take place in the dynamics of faith development. Parks (1986) has identified five movements that seem to be universally applicable to persons in this process. These are:

a. a period of conscious conflict that describes the person who is aware of conflicting tensions and is uncomfortable in the present situation;
b. a period of pause when a person is aware of inner stress but unable to resolve it;
c. a period of achieving a new image that resolves the conflict and establishes a uniquely new perspective;
d. a period during which various aspects of life are repatterned;
e. a period when the person interprets, celebrates, and acts out a new understanding by sharing personal experience with others in some form of acknowledgment and celebration (Yeaney, 1983).

Thus, the power of human imagination is critical for the development of faith in students. It bears the capacity to negotiate the painful and slippery transitions from one form of faith to another. It is a new image or insight that enables persons to do and to see the whole of life in ways that previously eluded them. Parks (1986, p. 125) asserts that occasions of just such revelatory insight are the motivating purpose of all truly liberal education and that it is 'this moment in which the purposes of higher education and the journey of faith are most inextricably linked'.

Calling higher education a potential community of imagination, Parks points to the many ways that images of meaning are present both in and out of the classroom and to how education may either cooperate with or impede the change processes of faith development in students. All of campus life is a context for mediating the images by which students will recompose their sense of the meaning of themselves, the world, and God.

The hidden curriculum of the academy — those out-of-classroom experiences of students 'embedded in the institution as a whole' —

is a powerful bearer of images. For example, Parks argues that the academy teaches, through its 'prevailing ethos' that professional competence in a person's field, verified by institutional certification, will enable students to avoid tragedy and to ensure economic success and social recognition. She goes on to argue that such images are simply untrue and that they fail to touch and engage the deepest yearnings of the human spirit: 'They do not lead out toward an adequate human future' (1986, p. 157).

The kinds of communities, both curricular and extracurricular, that are available to students on campus are critically determinative of how faith development occurs. As old meanings dissolve under the impact of relativism, and new images and commitments emerge in the transitions to more adequate forms of faith, students are vulnerable and need to be held in communities that confirm and challenge their new insights and affirm that the journey is worthwhile. Yet, many within the academy have only a minimal sense of community, as many factors lead to fragmentation, competition, and lack of identification with campus life. At the same time, Parks (1986, p. 61) insists, attention to the quality of the total campus environment is 'not an expendable luxury.' Rather, every classroom, residence hall, department, faculty meeting, athletic facility, student union, task force, campus religious center, college, professional school, and student services program is a setting in which 'a mentoring community of imagination may be formed.'

Bridges to practice

Although no theory is completely adequate to describe the real-life students with whom student services professionals work daily, there are nevertheless some implications for these professionals' practice in the faith development theories explored in this chapter. The implications presented here reflect a commitment toward inclusiveness in faith development programming. These implications include the following eight.

First, because students are at different stages of development and depend on supportive communities for successfully responding to challenges in life and growing in an expanding faith, campus religious programs should be intentional about providing nurturing and challenging groups and fellowships for students at different and appropriate stages. Thad Holcomb, director of United University Ministries at the University of Oklahoma, designs activities and programming for students that correspond to Fowler's stages of faith development. Programs are developed to reflect a diversity of 'entry points' for students, depending on where the students are in their particular stage of development. The ministry seeks to nurture an atmosphere for a sense of community in which students feel open to share and reflect on their faith journeys.

Second, because students grow through the transitions appropriate to more and more adequately structured faith by encounters with persons who are different, campus religious programs should provide opportunities for those relationships to occur. The United University Ministries at the University of Oklahoma has developed a cross-cultural/cross-racial conversations program that brings together students in a group composed of black, Asian-American, Hispanic, Native-American, and Anglo-American students for conversation on how personal identity is influenced by the ethnicity and cultural influences represented in the group. These programs are based on several goals, including the fostering of a process of growth, change, and quest for meaning for life.

Third, because opportunities for active engagement in the real world can enrich students' experience and provide an impetus for growth through exposure to different situations, campus religious programs should facilitate student involvement in volunteer service to others, and in positive action designed to address contemporary social problems. Holcomb's United University Ministries at the University of Oklahoma also has developed a service learning project in which students volunteer with community agencies and then meet in small reflection groups to process their experiences.

Fourth, because mentors are so important in student development, programs should be provided for enabling one-to-one interaction between students and older adults; faculty can thereby share their deeply held values, as well as serve as spiritual guides and cotravelers on the journeys of faith. When Ross Miller was director of the United Christian Fellowship at Bowling Green State University in Ohio in 1981, he developed a model for a faculty/student mentoring program designed to enable students' development in faith. He identified faculty members who were willing to engage in an ongoing relationship and dialogue with students who were in a searching stage of faith. He and his colleagues provided training to faculty members in small groups where information about student and faith development was shared. Each faculty member was assigned one student to develop a mentoring relationship with, and they made a one-year commitment to meet regularly for open-ended dialogue. In addition, the faculty members met with one another in small support groups to share insights and ideas as they went along. Faith concerns grew naturally out of the relationships that were established will students, and a spin-off was that the faculty members were challenged to grow in their own faith development. Recruitment of both faculty and students, as well as training in faith development theory and practical skills for dialogue, were conducted

by the campus ministry in cooperation with college and depart-
mental advisors, resident life personnel, and the staff of the
counseling center.

I developed a program that brought students together on an
individual basis once a semester for two years with an adult
mentor from within one of the faith traditions involved in United
Campus Ministry at the University of New Mexico. The mentors,
all volunteers, would invite students to explore questions and
issues the students were experiencing on their faith journeys.
Each mentor was assigned five students and guided each student
personally through a series of conversations structured on the
basis of questions from Fowler's work. The mentors were trained
with workshop material based on Gribbon's faith development
approach, and they continued to meet regularly for support and
mutual sharing.

Fifth, because all of campus life is potentially an educating
force for shaping the meanings that students make, and because
it represents many alternative centers of value, campus religious
programs should work to enhance the center of campus life
and provide opportunities for student leadership development,
as well as encourage students to take personal responsibility for
their own lives and faith. Nancy Moffatt, director of United
Ministries in Higher Education at the University of Wisconsin
at Stevens Point, is working as part of the student affairs team
to provide a spiritual dimension of a holistic wellness project
that addresses the total student. She makes herself available to
student affairs staff members and counselors to address matters
of spiritual awareness as these matters arise in the lives of individual students. She also works cooperatively with these campus
personnel to plan spiritual awareness programs for groups on a
campus-wide basis. She works with staff members in the student
activities office as they help students see the relationship between
volunteering and skill building that can help students develop as
well-rounded individuals. She serves as a volunteer on a campus-
wide retention committee and works closely with its mentoring
subcommittee.

Sixth, because of the inevitable vulnerability and anxiety that
accompanies the experience of transition from one stage to another,
students should be provided supportive counseling that helps them
bear that discomfort and stay with the journey. Darrell Yeaney,
director of United Ministries in Higher Education at the University of Iowa, has worked with Sharon Parks's five movements
in the change processes of faith development. When he was
campus minister at the University of California at Santa Cruz
(UCSC), he worked together with the UCSC Counseling Center
to cosponsor a group called the Spiral Journey, which offered
students opportunities to discover, explore, and enrich their personal

spiritual and life journeys. The groups focused on responses to six questions:

a. what conflict initiated the change or transition?
b. how long did you experience this conflict before a new awareness came to you?
c. what event or experience brought you to a new awareness of your situation?
d. what action did you take based on this new awareness that integrated your life and brought you relief?
e. how did you celebrate that change?
f. was there a religious experience associated with the change?

Seventh, because students need images adequate to express the deeper meanings of their spiritual lives, they should have opportunities to hear the stories of the various faith traditions, in which those deep images, symbols, and events are related to the students' changing faith understandings. Holcombs' ministry, described previously, provides a Tuesday lunch where students meet and talk with others; several discussion groups facilitated by the ministry that meet after university-sponsored lectures given by distinguished scholars, in which participants share differences about what was 'heard'; weekly meetings of students who interact through bible study, discussion, prayer, and personal sharing; and a freshman support group, facilitated by upper-class students that meets weekly to assist students to survive creatively in the university.

Eighth, because students need ideologically compatible communities at a certain stage of their development, campus religious programs should provide many small groups and opportunities to put faith into social action that are built around religious world views and practical solutions to global problems. At the same time, students need to remain open to others, recognizing a degree of relativity that remains within commitment. Each of the religious programs described in these implications and many other ministries in higher education provide public presentations as well as opportunities for short-term task groups or long-term commitments on the diversity of issues facing the society (hunger, homelessness, capital punishment, revolution and the search for freedom, multicultural relationships, and so forth).

Summary

Throughout this chapter, many points of contact between campus religious and student affairs professionals have been explored in several areas of theory and practice. It is clear that administrators in both groups can acknowledge that the faith development of students is important to the groups' respective missions. Many fruitful partnerships can be built among colleagues from the respective professions.

Many of the faith development theories described in this chapter are concerned with the formal processes by which students know, make meaning, develop in psychosocial dimensions, and change through the dynamics of imagination. These are all fairly neutral in relation to the content of faith, in that they have to do with operations and structures and universal human abilities. They are the how as opposed to the what of faith. In saying this, campus religious professionals affirm that the distinctions between students spiritual lives and all other aspects of their lives are not absolute and clear. Faith is the way persons make ultimate meaning out of *all* of their life. Put another way, there are multiple centers of value and meaning around which students integrate their meaning, multiple images that inform the students' dreams. Not all of them are ultimate.

Persons who represent faith traditions cannot be neutral in regard to the ultimate images of power and meaning that inform their faith. They cannot remain silent when confronted by images or centers of value that lead to evil consequences, are simply inadequate for a mature form of faith, or are less than ultimate. They respect the pluralism of campus life and affirm an inclusive approach to faith out of their own spiritual perspectives, but an understanding of student development in merely structural, neutral terms is only part of what they seek. Yet, even in this responsibility, they can find common ground with colleagues in student affairs. They can jointly encourage one another and the students with whom they work to understand, reflect critically on, change, and confess the various faiths. In so doing, they become part of an interdependent community of imagination and embody a maturing faith, precisely because of their differences.

References

Chickering, A. W. (1969) *Education and Identity*, San Francisco, Jossey-Bass.

Delworth, U., Hanson, G. R., and Associates (1980) *Student Services: a handbook for the profession*, San Francisco, Jossey-Bass.

Erikson, E. (1963) *Childhood and Society*, New York, Norton.

Fowler, J. (1981) *Stages of Faith: the psychology of human development and the quest for meaning*, New York, Harper and Row.

Fowler, J., and Keen, S. (1978) *Life Maps: conversations on the journey of faith*, Waco, Texas, Word Books.

Gilligan, C. (1982) *In a Different Voice*, Cambridge, Mass., Harvard University Press.

Gribbon, R. (1977) *The Problem of Faith Development in Young Adults*, Washington, D. C., Alban Institute.

Groome, T. (1980) *Christian Religious Education*, New York, Harper and Row.

Keniston, K. (1971) *Youth and Dissent: the rise of a new opposition*, San Diego, Calif., Harcourt Brace Jovanovich.

Kohlberg, L. (1971) 'Stages of moral development,' in C. M. Beck, B. S. Crittenden, and E. V. Sullivan (eds), *Moral Education*, Toronto, University of Toronto Press.

Niebuhr, H. R. (1941) *The Meaning of Revelation*, New York, Macmillan.

Parks, S. (1986) *The Critical Years: the young adult search for a faith to live by*, New York, Harper and Row.

Perry, W. G. (1970) *Forms of Intellectual and Ethical Development in the College Years: a scheme*, New York, Holt, Rinehart and Winston.

Piaget, J. (1950) *The Psychology of Intelligence*, San Diego, Calif., Harcourt Brace Jovanovich.

Yeaney, D. (1983) *Practical Implications for Ministry of Faith Development*, Santa Cruz, Calif., United Campus Ministry.

8.4 Religious congregations: varieties of presence in stages of faith

James W. Fowler

In presenting my theory of the stages of faith to groups which include pastors, rabbis, educators and clinicians, I have found repeatedly that I am not presenting something totally new to them. Most savvy practitioners of ministry have already constructed, as part of what Michael Polanyi has called their 'tacit knowing', something resembling a developmental theory of faith and selfhood. Experience and reflection have led them to recognize differences in the ways persons compose and express their meanings. Their teaching and living with the sources of faith in scripture and tradition have also led them to form more or less determinate images of maturity or fullness in faith and selfhood. For these reasons I recognize that faith development theory and its elaboration in practical theology is neither alien nor necessarily new for persons in ministry. Instead, it offers an opportunity for practitioners to make their own observations and insights more explicit, and to bring to more specific and conscious awareness the elements of their own practical theologies of pastoral care and nurture in faith.

It is a paramount concern of mine that the stages of faith and selfhood never be used for purposes of nefarious comparison or the devaluing of persons. Properly used, the stage theories should facilitate our understanding of persons whose ways of being in faith may differ significantly from our own. The theories should provide frameworks for seeing persons and their differences more clearly and less judgmentally or defensively. It is important that religious leaders understand that there is no sense in which a person must have constructed a given stage of development in faith or selfhood in order to be 'saved.' It is possible to point to persons of serenity, courage and genuine faith commitment who would be described, even as adults, in terms of any stage from intuitive projective to universalizing, inclusively. It is not necessarily the goal of pastoral care or counseling employing developmental perspectives to try to propel or impel persons from one stage to another. Of course there is a normativity to the developmental theories we have introduced. Other things being equal, persons should be supported and encouraged to continue to engage the issues of their lives and vocations in such ways that development will likely be a result. Pastoral care will seek to involve them in disciplines and action, in struggles and reflection, that will keep their faith and vocations responsive to the ongoing call of God. But we must remember that developmental stage transition is a complex and often protracted affair. Transitions cannot and should not be rushed. Development takes time. Much of our concern in pastoral care has to do with helping persons extend the operations of a given stage to the full range of their experiences and interactions. Integration and reconfiguration of memories, beliefs and relationships in the light of the operations which a new stage makes possible are every bit as important as supporting, encouraging and pacing persons in the move from one stage to another.

My interest in developing a theory of faith development has been exceedingly practical: how can a thoughtful pastor or educator discern the underlying structure of a parishioner's faith and world view? How do we recognize a transitional person dealing with the movement from one stage to another? Alongside questions of recognition and identification we must give attention to what these stage characteristics imply for preaching, counseling, teaching, spiritual direction, or doing organizational work with persons of different and transitional places. Finally, there are questions that derive from trying to understand and relate to groups in which persons of several stages may be interacting. How does 'cross-stage static' manifest itself in the tensions and struggles of group life? Do congregations or sub-congregations have *modal developmental levels*; i.e., average expectable levels of development for adults? If so, how do the presence and pressures of this modal level affect the common life, decision making, and pastoral care of a congregation?

Varieties of congregational presence

Any time a pastor, priest, or rabbi greets a congregation of any real size gathered for worship, he/she addresses persons whose range of stages of faith and selfhood[1] includes at least three or four stages. In addition to being an ecology of care and vocation, the congregation is an ecology of multiple stages of faith and selfhood. In a typical service of worship the clergy leads the congregation in one liturgy, with one sequence of prayers, one set of scripture readings, and one sermon or homily. But because the congregation represents a pluralism of stages of faith and selfhood, that experience is subject to constructive interpretation in at least four or five distinctively different modes. From young to old, participants literally make sense of what is going on in that service in a variety of systematically different ways. Preachers and leaders of congregations know this from the conments people make after their sermons: sometimes one recognizes what a listener names as having been so helpful to them from the sermon; at other times one does not. The listener constructs the meanings in accordance with the particular set of experiences, needs, hopes and beliefs which he/she brings to the service, to be sure. But the listener also constructs meanings from and within the service in accordance with the structuring patterns characteristic of her/his stage of selfhood and faith. These structuring patterns constitute basic elements in the person's *hermeneutics* – the procedures of knowing, valuing, experiencing and reasoning, by which personal meanings are constructed and appropriated. Let us consider some of the typical patterns of interest and interpretation we can anticipate in congregations.

Intuitive-projective and impulsive presence

The intuitive-projective and impulsive presence in congregations is most obvious among children of pre-school age. They bring the community their curiosity, their energy, their imaginations, and their special quality of living liminally. By living liminally I mean that children in this stage move freely back and forth across boundaries that they only later will sort out as fantasy and reality. They also bring their impulsiveness, and their need for a relational environment with a set of stories and symbols that can provide experiences and templates for the ordering of their souls.

Our challenge in pastoral care with this stage is to provide for our childrens' forming faith and selfhood what Horace Bushnell called 'gifts to the imagination.' We must share biblical narrative with our children in ways that are open-ended, and which avoid tying the intriguing suggestiveness of story and parable too quickly to a moral or moralistic meanings. As Jerome Berryman once put it, both we and they will be refreshed and informed by sharing biblical narratives in a way in which we 'wonder together' about their meanings and implications.

Intuitive-projective children are fascinated by the metaphysics and stories of a God introduced to them as invisible and living in an inaccessible realm, and who is at the same time everywhere as a loving God.[2] Care requires that we listen carefully to what they do with these stories in their own constructions. We must listen for the distortions that mirror a chaotic and abusive relational environment in which a child may be caught. We must listen for the over-constricting appropriations children may make of the moralisms they have pressed upon them in church or synagogue, at home, or by their peers. We must support one-parent households in providing consistent relational access to a parent substitute of the same sex at those critical times in early childhood when children are at risk of over-inclusion with the parent of the opposite sex.[3] And we must find ways to reduce children's dependence upon the mixed bag of commercial television as a prime mediator of images of the world and reality, and as a substitute for relations with loving others and for the stories of faith. In the absence of an environment that mediates this kind of coherence with trustworthy affection, children are exposed extensively to a scrambled hodge-podge of narrative and vivid sensation which exploits, without ordering, children's fascination with violence, action, impulsive destructiveness and death.[4] Our concerns, in this regard, carry us beyond the congregation to our responsibility for the nurture toward wholeness of all the children of our common entrustment.

Before we leave this stage and its congregational presence we should note that occasionally adolescents and adults exhibit the structural features of this stage. Typically when the liminality and emotional lability characteristic of this stage are encountered in adolescents or adults we are dealing with episodes of regression or psychotic breakdown. There are, however, at the most primitive end of the fundamentalist spectrum, some kinds of congregations which seem regularly to involve persons in collective manifestations of something very like the structurings of this stage. I have in mind cults which practice extreme forms of serpent handling and the ritual drinking of acid or poisons as tests and proofs of the magical, protective powers of the spirit on behalf of the faithful. Such groups seem to provide religious sanction for the acting out of fantasies and impulses relating to violence, power, death and miracle which show the primitive structures of unrestrained and un-protected early childhood.

Mythic-literal and imperial presence

The presence in congregations of the mythic-literal and imperial stage of faith and selfhood has some unique features. When the congregational context is one of middle and upper class parishes, in the mainline Protestant, Catholic, or Reform Jewish stream, this presence consists mainly of children of elementary and middle-school age. Some adolescents in these settings will also be best described by this stage, as will a limited number of adults. In other social class settings, however, mythic-literal faith and imperial selfhood can constitute the modal developmental level for the community. Here again I have in mind certain fundamentalist and some pentecostal communities. Though the structural features of faith and selfhood at this stage are similar in these two different kinds of settings, it makes a considerable difference whether this stage is experienced in a community as a way-station on a longer journey, or as having the characteristics of a final destination.

In both its childhood and adult forms this stage enables persons to construct a stable, linear and predictable experience of the world. Cause and effect relations are understood; systems of classification and sorting have been created; simple perspective taking is a reliable acquisition. Narrative emerges as the powerful and favoured way of forming and conserving meanings and experience. This stage, however, is largely limited to the world of concrete experience and of literal interpretations of symbols and events. It does not yet rise to the level of reflective consideration of its stories and experiences in order to formulate meanings at a more generalized level.

From the standpoint of pastoral care, one of the most valuable insights developmental theories offer us about this stage is its relatively undeveloped understanding of the interiority of persons — its own, and that of others. Almost in the manner of behaviourist psychology, persons of this stage regard others — and themselves — as being rather like Skinner's characterization of the psyche as a 'black box.' By this term Skinner suggested that the structure of persons' interpretations, motivations, internal evaluations, and shaping of actions are largely inaccessible to scientific investigation and understanding. Moreover, he was also suggesting that there may be little or no reliable relation between what people say they are going to do, the motives they claim, and what they actually do. Persons best described by this stage are largely inattentive to the internal patterns that constitute their own and others' 'personality.'

In the absence of an ability to understand interiority, persons of this stage must construct some basis for discerning predictability and pattern in the behavior of God and of other persons. Consistently we find that lawfulness and order are imposed on the universe in this stage by recourse to the idea of moral reciprocity. In simple fairness the cosmos is construed as rewarding good actions and as punishing bad actions. God is seen in the analogy of a stern but just and fair parent or ruler. In effect, this is a strong and clear narrative imposition of meaning based on a concrete understanding of cause-effect relations.

In young people this construction frequently gives way during a phase we have come to call 'eleven-year-old atheism.' This phase comes when thoughtful children, whose religious and social environments have given them sufficient emotional space to question and reckon for themselves, begin to come to terms with the fact that ours is not a 'quick-payoff universe.' The good do *not* always get rewarded; the wicked are *not* always punished.

For other youths, however, where religious norms and beliefs have been enforced with rigidity and forms of emotional coercion, this construct of moral reciprocity becomes a more permanent fixture in their souls. Though they too may reject the God of the quick-payoff universe at the level of cognitive self-understanding, emotionally they get stuck in the structures of the mythic-literal stage. They move on into adolescent and eventually adult roles and relationships without the emotional freedom and capacity for intimacy which are required for mutual interpersonal perspective taking. Often they operate in the areas of relations and religion with the kind of naive manipulation which first arose as a result of the embeddedness of the mythic-literal stage in the structure of its own interests, needs, and wishes. In fact, we see a fair number of persons, usually men, who may exhibit considerable cognitive sophistication in their occupational worlds (as physicians or engineers, for example) but who, in their emotional and faith lives, are rather rigidly embedded in the structures of mythic-literal faith and imperial selfhood. To their marriages and family life they bring a rigidity, often coupled with authoritarian patterns, which inflicts psychic, and sometimes physical violence on their partners and children. It often leads them to a kind of baffled bereftness in their forties and fifties where, in the shambles of their shattered families, for the first time they may begin the painful task of learning about the interior lives of selves, starting with their own.

Whether at thirteen, when it comes much more naturally and painlessly, or at fifty-three, when it comes out of the agony of broken relationships, the movement into mutual interpersonal perspective taking opens the way for a reflective relation to the self and others which gives one access to the world of the self's interiority. It seems clear to me, after a number of years of observation, that we cannot be more intimate with others than we are ready to be with ourselves. Similarly, we cannot be more intimate with God than we are prepared to be with ourselves and others. The emergence of mutual interpersonal perspective taking prepares the way for a new structure of faith and selfhood whenever it appears.

Synthetic-conventional and interpersonal presence

A large number of persons in the congregation, if it is typical, will be best described by the synthetic-conventional stage of faith and the interpersonal stage of selfhood. With varying degrees of intensity they bring to the service the desire to be in a relationship with God and with the important persons of their lives. They care greatly about whether or not they are living up to the expectations these important others have of them. Prayers of confession and penance will be construed as occasions for asking forgiveness for failures of attitude and action, and for restoration in the love and acceptance of God. Persons best described by these stages feel that their very selfhood is constituted by their roles and their relationships. It is likely, therefore, that any sense of alienation from God they experience will be derived from, or closely related to, feelings of estrangement or tension with persons from their circle of family, lovers, friends, work associates, and acquaintances. When the sermon or prayers of petition include concern for the welfare of persons from other social classes or other nations, this group will likely envision both needs and solutions in interpersonal terms. From the sermon they hope for a sense of emotional confirmation of their personhood, and a sense of warmth and connectedness with the priest or pastor. They hunger for a sense of confirmation in the meanings they invest in the roles and relationships that constitute their selfhood. They may feel a special gladness in thinking of the congregation as an intergenerational community bound together in friendship and shared experiences. Such persons long for harmony and conflict-free living in the community of faith. Conflict and controversy are disturbing to them because these conditions seem to threaten the basis of community. The maintenance of peace and the restoration of good feelings and unity within the community frequently loom as far more important to them than dealing with issues that might cause conflict.

The underlying metaphor for religious community most commonly held by persons described here is that of the ideal or romanticized extended family. The community of faith is seen as a network of persons related through their common values and beliefs in God, Torah, or their common love for Jesus Christ. These values and beliefs do not need to be made explicit or clear; they sense that such an effort might lead to disagreements and breaches of relationships. The important thing is to provide mutual support in times of trouble or difficulty, and to maintain a supportive web of interpersonal connectedness through the community of faith.

The kind of persons we have been describing often constitute the most consistent corps of committed workers and servers in the community. Though they typically are not innovative leaders, they bring gifts of inclusion and care for each person in the community, and often their loyalty to the religious community, viewed as an extended family, can sustain them in a kind of acceptance of and loyalty to others whose faith outlook may be somewhat threatening to their own. They have limited ability to take account of the *systems* that shape, constrain and sometimes oppress persons. They have difficulty in relating their faith to social, economic and political structures. Analytic approaches to religious experience and to the central symbols of the faith may be uninteresting or threatening to such persons. In confrontation with pastoral leadership or groups who insist upon critical and analytic approaches to matters of faith, persons of the synthetic-conventional and interpersonal stage may take a stance that seems anti-intellectual, oriented to emotions and experience, and defensively conventional.

In pastoral counseling with persons in this stage there are a number of predictable sources of struggle and 'dis-ease' that derive from the structuring of synthetic-conventional faith and interpersonal selfhood. Due to the absence of third-person perspective taking, persons in this stage are over-dependent upon significant others and the community for confirmation in selfhood and faith. Adults in this stage have internalized the influence of significant others who helped to play a balancing and guiding role in their internal life.

And there is a collection of present face-to-face relations that are significant. For adults in this stage the pastor or rabbi, like other persons who have institutionally important roles in their lives, are invested with a kind of double significance or weight as regards the maintenance of a sense of selfhood and self-esteem. Crises or times of distress can arise when a person feels dissonance between him or herself and one or more of these significant others. Dissonance can also occur when two or more of the important authorities in one's life are in conflict or serious disagreement. Similarly, experiences of conflicting role expectations can be upsetting and disorienting.

In all these cases the person feels distress which he/she cannot resolve, because there is no transcending standpoint from which the issues, struggles or conflicts can be seen, evaluated, and adjudicated. Developmentally helpful counseling calls for a vicarious experience of third-person perspective taking. It requires teaching and modeling which can help persons in this stage recognize the *possibility* of a third-person perspective − its liberation and responsibility − and support in beginning to rely upon it and exercise the new quality of self-authorization it brings. In this pastoral alliance several kinds of resistance and tension can be expected. The person's recognition of dependence upon the pastor and other authorities gives rise both to feelings of gratitude and affection, but also to often unrecognized feelings of resentment of the other. This resentment, coupled with anxieties about change, anxieties about one's ability to cope with new responsibilities, and anxieties about the effects of new self-authorization on one's network of relations, can all make the person ambivalent about the course of pastoral counseling.

From a different source, persons in this stage are likely to experience a special kind of crisis at times of loss or threat to their central relationships and roles. Since identity and faith are inextricably tied up with these central roles and relationships, events such as the death of a spouse or close friend, divorce, retirement, or sudden unemployment can have devasting effects. The grief or loss takes on a special power because the role or relation, or both, which has been lost, constituted one of the fundamental elements of one's sense of self. The loss drastically diminishes the sense of selfhood and threatens its very existence. At such times, the person, deeply at risk, needs a consistent and continuing outpouring of community assurance about the worth, the value, the identity and special selfhood which the person continues to have in the eyes of those who care for him/her. Developmentally it becomes a time to face the question, 'Who am I when I am not defined by this key relation/role which has been taken from me?' It can be a time of deepening one's reliance and relation for selfhood and faith upon God and the community. It can also be a time for claiming a different kind of basis for one's faith and sense of self. In either case one needs consistent affirmation and support in reconstructing the bases of one's selfhood and outlook.

Individuative-reflective and institutional presence

In many congregations another substantial presence is constituted by that group of persons who may best be described by the individuative-reflective stage of faith and the institutional stage of selfhood. What do they bring to the congregation's service of worship? They bring an approach to faith and an experience of selfhood that contrasts in some important ways with those described previously. In the fully developed forms of this stage, persons come to worship aware of an 'I' or a sense of selfhood that has emerged to control and manage the various roles and relations that make up his/her life structure. This 'I' has had to struggle, to some significant degree, with those external authorities, both personal and institutional, that guide, constrain, and support one in growth toward adulthood. It has also dealt in some clear ways with the internalized voices of parents and other authorities from the past. From the service of worship, the prayers, the preaching and teaching, the person of this stage wants acknowledgement of and support in her/his self-authorization. Worship needs to recognize and celebrate the hard-won assumption of responsibility for choices regarding life-style and beliefs. This stage wants what it perceives to be a fully adult form of worship and faith.

At the same time, however, persons in this stage seem to seek spaces and relationships within their religious community in which the stress of consciously orchestrating and managing the self-responsible self can periodically be relaxed. Persons who perceive themselves to be rowing their own boats in competitive and multiply demanding circumstances respond to communities of others like themselves where it is safe to let down a bit. They find release in acknowledging their need for relationship and solidarity with likeminded others. Worship and other settings will make this possible if they combine a certain measure of intellectual stimulation and challenge with a quality of community fellowship that does not try to reimpose external and conventional religious expectations and authority.

The underlying metaphor for religious community, correlated with this stage is likely to be a kind of unspoken pragmatic, con-tractual individualism. One *has* roles, relationships, commitments, and intentions. One *has* a now more explicit and clear set of beliefs and values. Religious faith is valued and interpreted in accordance with the contribution it makes to supporting and extending the perspectives and commitments that express and support one's selfhood. Depending on the depth and intensity of one's com-mitments, faith can also constitute a source of accountability and normative direction for one's selfhood and goals. One's tradition can be selectively appropriated and interpreted to shape and support one's individuative orientation. In this process demythologization and conceptual restatements of central elements and symbols of the tradition are welcomed and relied upon.

Persons best described by the stage of individuative-reflective faith and institutional selfhood have an often unrecognized need for both a confessional and a wailing wall. The structuring patterns of this stage, and the pressures of our particular culture, place heavy burdens on persons of individuative faith to be what I sometimes call 'tubs that sit on their own bottoms.' They are called to be self-sufficient, self-starting, self-managing, and self-repairing units. In the absence of a trusted community of others with whom one shares central meanings and values, and with whom one can afford to disclose the self, this set of expectations can lead to privatized and sick self-dialogues. When things are going well, persons caught in this privatization are vulnerable to forms of inflation and inflated self-deception. They may identify with self-aggrandizing personal images which result from the continual pressures to over-advertise the self and to identify with the advertisements. In that state of over-inflation they can fall into the trap of allowing themselves privileges and moral leeway that later prove to be terribly destructive of work patterns, of relationships and values which they temporarily took for granted. On the other hand, the person who is too dependent upon private self-dialogue for the maintenance of a sense of self and direction, is also subject to deflation and excessive despair about the self, when things go badly. The pervasive individualism that characterizes this society – and too often our religious communities as well – makes the provision of a context of pastoral care to persons caught in these dangerous orientations difficult. It is imperative that we develop groups where persons who are susceptible to the pressures I have described can find trustworthy community with peers. We need to provide circles where the armour of their defences can be ventilated and where they can stand to submit their images of self to each other – and to the tradition's faith – for correction.

The individuative-reflective orientation responds to – and often demands – a different quality of religious leadership than the synthetic-conventional stage. It is impatient with 'mystery-mastery' approaches to religious leadership in which leaders attempt to heighten and perpetuate dependence upon them by accentuating awareness of their special training, their ordination, and the complexity and mystery of the matters of faith. Individuative-reflective types welcome being made partners in inquiry into the sources of faith. They enjoy going 'into the kitchen' with the rabbi or pastor to join in the struggle of making sense of particular texts or elements in the tradition. They have a preference for a reasoned and reasoning faith. They tend to fear obscurantism more than they fear admitting that faith may not provide all the necessary answers to ethical and religious questions. They have the capability, and often the interest, to engage in inquiry into the tradition to find new resources for the effort to relate faith to their lives and challenges in the world.

Commonly those communities which have a modal developmental level at the synthetic-conventional and interpersonal stage have found it hard to make space and welcome for the individuative types. By the same token, persons in transition to or already equilibrated in the individuative stage often find life in synthetic-conventional communities stifling and dull. Clashes or antipathies between persons in these two stages represent one common form of 'cross-stage static.' Enabling such groups to coexist and work together with integrity in a community, when it occurs, represents one of the major accomplishments of pastoral leadership and care.

Conjunctive and inter-individual presence

Generally persons best described by the conjunctive and inter-individual stage have reckoned with the paradox that God's self-revelation is always a matter of both disclosure and concealment. They have come to know in their bone marrow that the mystery we name God can only partially be represented in our best symbols and parables. They bring to church a tensive conviction that 'it is meet, right and our bounden duty' to pray, praise, and proclaim the reality and love of God. At the same time, they instinctively avoid the kind of symbolic domestication which makes of favoured formulations and doctrines idolatrous and shoddy graven images of an exceedingly elusive transcendent reality. I am trying to describe a dialectical form of faith and selfhood in which persons find it necessary to affirm perspectives which maintain polar tensions in faith. God is both transcendent and immanent; God cannot be contained in anthropocentric categories, yet there is that which is personal in our experience and testimony to God.

Most of the persons who can be identified with this stage are at mid-life or beyond. Occasionally, by virtue of early experiences of suffering and loss, or due to a kind of precocious spiritual or religious seriousness, a younger person may move into the conjunctive stage. But usually, like that brokerage firm that advertises that it 'makes money the old-fashioned way', such persons *earn* it. They earn it by having taken on irrevocable responsibilities for others or for some sector of our shared life. They earn it by having their noses rubbed in our finitude, through the sacrament of failure and through the death or loss of loved ones. They earn it by recognizing that our feelings of autonomy and self-control as a species, and our vaunted capacities for technical management of our vastly interdependent systems, are maintained at the cost of a considerable degree of self-deception and illusion. Put positively, they have come to the conviction that the principal acting units in human and divine history are the great social and economic systems of which we are a part. Individual human beings, while responsible and gifted with a measure of genuine freedom, must learn to exert that freedom effectively in the interdependence of systems.

Selfhood, at this stage, no longer focuses its concern so heavily on control and self-management, and on maintaining the boundaries of a consciously chosen set of affiliations and commitments. In this stage concern with selfhood becomes a matter of attending to deeper movements of the spirit within and working at disciplines by which to discern and integrate elements from the unconscious structuring and wisdom of the self into consciousness. The self continues to be a responsible actor and agent in her/his world. In that action and agency, however, the agenda is set less by socially determined aspirations and more by attention to the subtle but insistent impulsions of the spirit.

In this attending to the impulsions of spirit the person of conjunctive faith and inter-individual selfhood should not be understood primarily in Jungian terms. There the guiding truths and insights for one's individuation are seen as coming from one's psyche with its archetypes and symbols and its balancing responsiveness to the ordering and integrative power of the collective unconscious. In contrast, the religious person of this stage is learning to trust his or her tradition in new ways and at new depth. Its symbols, doctrines, narratives, and rituals are acknowledged as structuring means of grace. Prayer and discernment become modes of opening oneself and attending radically — that is, with both conscious attention and with a responsiveness of the deeper self — to the truth which takes form and comes to expression in the scriptures and tradition, and in the living interpretations of the community of faith.

In conjunctive faith, and in communities influenced by it, there is a taste for the stranger. Persons have begun to learn to acknowledge and live with the stranger within their own spirit and unconscious life. Having an experience of the disclosure and concealment of God in revelatory traditions, they begin to encounter the religious traditions of others as strangers which may be sources of new depths of insight, and of correction in our appropriation of our own traditions. Further, for Jews and Christians, there seems to be in this stage a coming to terms, at stirring new depths, with God as the liberating and redeeming stranger, in the biblical traditions' radical sense of solidarity with the despised or oppressed stranger. Such people have the capacity to understand and relate to persons at each of the other stages. In this sense, they can serve as sponsors and guarantors for others. At the same time, from the depth of their religious commitments they have a capacity to receive and dialogue at depth with the faith witnesses of people from other traditions.

But there are pitfalls for persons of conjunctive faith as well. In ways that are perhaps distinctive to this stage, people can feel a deep sense of cosmic aloneness or homelessness. The dark side of their awareness of God's revelation, both as disclosure and concealment, lies in a deepened appreciation of the otherness and the non-availability of God. The dark side of their receptiveness to the witness and truth of other traditions can be a subdued sense of the imperative to share and commend their own tradition. The dark side of their awareness of our being enmeshed in vast and complex systems can be a sense of paralysis and retreat into a private world of spirituality. Having had their eyes burned by all that they see and have seen, persons of conjunctive faith can fall into a kind of immobilization which cuts the nerve, if prolonged, of the call to partnership with God. In these respects persons of faith best described by the conjunctive stage – as do those of the other stages – need the gifts and the structuring orientations of persons of other stages to encounter them with correcting emphases and energies.

Diversity characterizes our world, our nation, our institutions. In my experience as a theologian, minister, and educator, experience has taught me not only the value of comprehending the structures of moral reasoning and faith development, but also the value of including them within the microcosm of a religious community.

Conclusion

In the fully developed presentation of these stages in my other writings – and in the one from which this article is taken – I write about the earliest stage of *primal* (infancy) and the most developed stage, *universalizing* faith. For purposes of exploring the variety of stages present in religious congregations, however, those stages we have dealt with here seem most important.

Crucial for further research is the question of whether congregations exhibit what I have called 'modal developmental levels,' expectable levels of development in adult faith. In ways that parallel the work by Clark Power and others on 'moral atmosphere,' in schools and other institutions, this promises to be a rewarding area of investigation, with both theoretical and practical significance.[5]

Notes
1. The references to stages of selfhood included in this paper are derived from the work of Robert G. Kegan in his *The Evolving Self*, Harvard University Press, 1982. I also acknowledge the helpfulness of the work of Steven S. Ivy, 'The structural-developmental theories of James Fowler and Robert Kegan as resources for pastoral assessment,' unpublished doctoral dissertation, Southern Baptist Theological Seminary, Luisville, Kentucky, 1985.
2. See David Heller, *The Children's God*, University of Chicago Press, 1986.
3. See Alfted Messer, M.D., 'Father hunger,' *Journal of the Medical Association of Georgia*, vol. 74, no. 12, 1985.

4. On the impact of television and other media on contemporary children see Thomas Lickona, *Raising Good Children*, Bantam Books, 1983, and David Elkind, *The Hurried Child*, Addison Wesley, 1981, pp. 71–94.
5. This article is used by permission of Fortress Press, 2900 Queen Lane, Philadelphia, PA 19129, and is taken, in edited form, from *Faith Development and Pastoral Care*, by James W. Fowler, 1987.

8.5 Enhancing supervision using Fowler's developmental theory

William O. Avery

The intern and supervisor seemed to be a perfect match. The intern, married and in his early 30's, was intelligent, resourceful, hard-working, a person of faith and conviction who was not afraid to express his faith in Jesus Christ. Only a few years older than the student, the supervisor shared many of the same characteristics and was known among his fellow pastors for his dedication to evangelism, good preaching, enthusiasm for the church, and workaholic work habits. Moreover, the chemistry between this supervisor and intern was initially positive. When the intern interviewed with the supervisor, both parties came away saying, 'This is a person with whom I want to work.' A two-day team-building workshop three months later confirmed their initial enthusiasm and enhanced their anticipation of the year they would spend together.

The supervisor's congregation of 800 baptized members consisted predominantly of blue-collar workers employed in the steel mill and other industries in the Western Pennsylvania town. The mill was still producing steel, and unemployment was low among the church members. The congregation included a few public school teachers, nurses, and clerical workers, but no doctors, dentists, lawyers, or persons at the middle or top levels of corporate management. Less than ten per cent of the congregation was college-educated. Most of the members had lived in the community all their lives and there were a number of extended families in the congregation.

The congregation had a long and stable history and, under the supervisor's five-year tenure as pastor, had experienced numerical growth from his evangelistic efforts. However, since the area around the church was not growing significantly, this growth was not perceived as a threat to the present power structure of the congregation, and growth had enhanced the self-image of this congregation as a beacon and witness for Jesus Christ.

The intern began his relationship with the congregation with great enthusiasm and anticipation. Less than four months later, I was called because of significant problems between the intern and the congregation. I began a series of painful meetings which ended with the termination of that internship five months after it had begun. What had happened? What had gone wrong? What had I failed to see which would have alerted me to potential problems in this match?

The answers to these questions are complex and involve many different elements, but one critical component of the potential problems in this match would have been apparent to me if I had possessed a thorough knowledge of what James Fowler calls 'stages of faith.'[1] Given the stages of faith development to which I now think this intern, supervisor, and congregation had attained, making such a match was inviting disaster. I would like to discuss why I have come to this conclusion.

I will show why careful attention to Fowler's developmental stages can assist in the selection of appropriate intern supervisors, can be one element in making a match between supervisor and student, can provide a warning for matches which should not be made, and, when difficulties arise in the internship setting, can provide a helpful perspective on the possible causes of difficulty. Finally, I will show that an intern can enhance his or her learning on-site by using a shortened form of Fowler's interview to discover the 'modal congregational level' of faith development at the internship site. Conducting the interview is also an excellent tool for helping the intern become acquainted with members of the parish.

Fowler's stages

Faith development, according to Fowler's research, is 'a sequence of stages by which persons shape their relatedness to a transcendent center or centers of value.'[2] There are several components to the stages Fowler has developed. First, faith, as Fowler defines it, is a human universal. It is not necessarily religious in content, but is rather a person's way of constructing their world or making sense of life. Faith is the dynamic system of images, values, and commitments that guides one's life. Faith involves a person in three different kinds of construing: a patterned knowing (belief), a patterned valuing (commitment), and a patterned construction of meaning (usually in the narrative form). This construing is partially and progressively conscious, but is in large degree unconscious.[3]

Second, Fowler identifies six developmental stages of the basic faith people live by[4]:

a. intuitive-projective faith (early childhood);
b. mythic-literal faith (school years);
c. synthetic-conventional faith (adolescence);
d. individuative-reflective faith (young adulthood);
e. conjunctive faith (mid-life and beyond);
f. universalizing faith.

The six stages occur in an invariant sequence, and all people move through the same sequence of stages. Fowler's stages are not primarily defined by the contents of faith, but rather reflect differences in styles and in the operations of knowing, valuing, and imaging. Each new stage carries forward the operations of all the previous stages.[5] Structurally, developmental change moves toward 'increasingly more complex, differentiated, and integrative patterns of making sense of one's life.'[6]

Third, most people do not complete the full sequence of stages, but remain on a plateau at some level below universalizing faith. Because it is not inevitable that people will move through all the stages, adults can be found at all the stages above primal faith.[7]

Modal developmental level

Because most people plateau at one of the developmental stages, Fowler maintains that congregations have a modal developmental level: *'the average expectable level of development for adults* in a given community.'[8] While not everybody in a congregation will be at the same level of development, the modal level operates as a magnet in religious communities. It tends to pull people up to the level of the average expectable stage, but it also imposes a limit which people find it difficult to move beyond.

Several points Fowler makes regarding the modal developmental level of a congregation have a direct impact on the appropriateness of congregations as internship sites and of the pastors as internship supervisors. First, Fowler suggests that most mainline congregations are at the synthetic-conventional modal level: 'My observations lead me to judge that the modal developmental level in most middle-class American churches and synagogues is best described in terms of synthetic-conventional faith or perhaps just beyond it.'[9] Moreover, Fowler maintains that churches at the synthetic-conventional stage find it hard to make space for and welcome people at the individuative-reflective stage. At the same time, people in transition to or already in the individuative stage usually find synthetic-conventional communities to be stifling and dull. Fowler calls clashes between people at different stages 'cross-stage static.'[10] Inasmuch as many seminary students are in transition to or already at the individuative stage, Fowler's conclusions suggest that placing students at this developmental stage in a synthetic-conventional stage congregation can be asking for trouble.

While Fowler sees strengths and weaknesses in all stages except universalizing faith, the limitations of the lower stages are greater if seen in the light of the possibilities of adulthood. Fowler is therefore caught in a dilemma. On the one hand, propelling persons from one stage to another is not considered a primary goal in his theory. Educationally speaking, the church's primary task is to be most helpful to people at whatever stage they have reached. On the other hand, because the lower stages are so limited, providing an open environment in which people have freedom to move through the stages *is* a goal.[11]

Furthermore, Fowler maintains that there is a 'stage level of aspiration' toward which church leadership, pastoral care, and adult education ought to encourage people to strive: conjunctive faith.[12] At this stage, persons have the capacity to understand and relate to Christians at each of the other stages. Such persons do not expect that everyone will believe as they do because they have experienced both God's hiddenness and otherness. They no longer think they have all the answers. The religious traditions of others may be sources of new insights and corrections in their view of their own traditions. They begin to come to terms with Jesus as the redeeming stranger and with Christ's radical sense of solidarity with the despised and oppressed stranger.[13]

When the modal congregational level is the conjunctive stage, the parish can be 'a public church' (a phrase Fowler borrows from Martin Marty). A public church is deeply and particularly Christian and committed to Jesus Christ. At the same time, the encouragement of intimacy within the church community is balanced by care about the structural domains of public life, and the church is unafraid of engagement with the ambiguities of thought and ideology in this age of ideological pluralism.[14] The public church can, should, and does 'pioneer in the creation and development of "multimodal" communities of faith.'[15] That is, the community makes allowance for the variety of stages of faith and selfhood in its congregation and nurtures and stimulates people at various points of development.

Given the enthusiasm with which Fowler advocates the conjunctive stage as the stage level of aspiration for the public church, one might conclude that internship sites are most helpful for students if they are at this stage. Such a conclusion is erroneous, however, for these same students will graduate from seminary and many will become pastors of parishes with different modal congregational levels. It is more helpful for the intern to learn to work with the parish at whatever modal level it has attained.

Developmental stages and implications for internship

The developmental stage of a parishioner is important because she or he constructs meaning from worship and other parts of congregational life in accordance with the structuring patterns characteristic of her or his stage of faith. 'These structuring patterns constitute basic elements in the person's hermeneutics: the procedures of knowing, valuing, experiencing, and reasoning by which personal meanings are constructed and appropriated.'[16]

Fowler argues that in a congregation the presence of persons at the intuitive-projective stage is most obvious among children of preschool age. But he also maintains that at the 'most primitive end of the fundamentalist spectrum' there are congregations which involve persons in collective manifestations of something of this sort: 'I have in mind cults that practice extreme forms of serpent handling and the ritual drinking of acid or poisons as tests and proofs of the magical, protective powers of the Spirit in behalf of the faithful.'[17] These groups provide religious sanction for the acting out of fantasies and impulses relating to violence, power, death, and miracles. Groups such as this may in fact exist, but I do not believe there are many, if any, mainline congregations whose modal congregational level is at the intuitive-projective stage.

In regard to the next stage, the mythic-literal, Fowler suggests that for congregations in middle- and upper-class Protestant or Catholic parishes, this stage is seen mainly in children of elementary- and middle-school age. Fowler also says that 'certain fundamentalist and some pentecostal communities' may have their modal congregational level at this stage.[18] In my opinion, congregations which serve as internship sites for mainline denominations are seldom at this stage.

However, in typical mainline Protestant or Catholic congregations, a large number of persons will be best described at the synthetic-conventional stage of faith. The modal congregational level of many internship parishes is the synthetic-conventional stage. Because of specific characteristics of persons at this stage, such a congregation may pose particular issues for the intern. Inasmuch as people at this stage feel their selfhood is constituted by their roles and their relationships, any sense of closeness to or alienation from God will be derived from or closely related to feelings of closeness to or estrangement from the family, friends, work associates, or fellow church members.

> Such persons long for harmony and conflict-free interliving in the community of faith. Conflict and controversy are disturbing to them because they seem to threaten the basis of community. The maintenance of peace and the restoration of good feelings and unity within the community frequently loom as far more important to them than dealing with issues that might cause conflict.[19]

Fowler contends that the underlying metaphor for the church constituted of people at this stage is the romanticized ideal of the extended family. People at this stage will really work for their family 'in Christ' and often constitute the most consistent corps of committed workers and servers in the church.[20]

What happens when an intern, an 'outsider,' comes and questions aspects of the life and beliefs of a congregation at the synthetic-conventional modal level?

Because no one directly involved in the situation can attain a third-person perspective, when disagreements or crises occur, the parishioners feel distress they cannot resolve 'because there is no transcending standpoint from which the issues leading to tensions, struggles, or conflicts can be seen, evaluated, and adjudicated.'[21] Such people do not understand why the intern is 'rocking the boat,' and they experience a particular threat not just to their church, but to their own sense of selfhood.

People at the individuative-reflective stage have a sense of selfhood that controls and manages the various roles and relations that make up their life structures. These people are on a journey toward self-authorization and what they want from worship, prayers, and preaching is acknowledgment and support for this journey. Their worship celebrates their hard-won assumption of responsibility for choices regarding life-style and beliefs. The underlying relationship to church correlated with this stage is 'a kind of unspoken pragmatic, and contractual individualism.'[22] Often these people want to be partners with the pastor.

At the same time, according to Fowler, people at this stage have 'an often unrecognized need for both a confessional and a wailing wall.'[23] These people feel they have to be self-sufficient, self-starting, self-managing, and self-repairing units. Without a trust community in which they can expose vulnerabilities, such self-reliance can lead to privatized and sick self-dialogues. When things go well, these people are vulnerable to inflated (and self-deceptive) egos. When things go badly, they are subject to deflation and excessive despair about the self.

Fowler notes that congregations at the synthetic-conventional level find it hard to accept the individuative types. Likewise, people in transition to or at the individuative-reflective stage find life in synthetic-conventional parishes uninteresting and suffocating.[24]

What is there about the individuative-reflective stage that often makes it so difficult for people in this stage to accept people at the synthetic-conventional stage? My suggestion is that people at the individuative-reflective stage have a special tendency to exaggerate the absoluteness, and to minimize the relativeness of the 'answers' they have discovered about life's meaning. Thus, a person at this stage might ask: What is the role of the pastor? What is 'good' worship? What does it mean to be a church member? When others seem uninterested in the positions the person has come to or the correctness of these positions, these other people are judged to be plain wrong. The issues are critical for the person at the individuative-reflective stage because their sense of identity is tied up with the answers they have obtained to such questions. They have developed an 'executive ego' and others should see things 'correctly' − as *they* do!

These observations pose particular difficulties for directors of internship. While the average age of the seminary population is increasing, the majority of students remain between twenty-two and forty years of age. Chronologically these students are at the stage where they are most likely to be in transition to or already at the individuative-reflective stage. If many internship parishes are at the synthetic-conventional modal level, then the potential for disharmony from both sides is very high. Nor does it solve the problem to say that students should not be placed in congregations at the synthetic-conventional stage, because when these same students graduate many will be placed in parishes at the synthetic-conventional modal level! Enabling these kind of matches to flourish and being able to handle the cross-stage static can be a major accomplishment of supervisors and interns.

Directors of internship may be able to help cross-stage matches to flourish in their preparation of interns and supervisors for internship. If students were trained to recognize congregations at the synthetic-conventional stage and were taught characteristics of congregations at this modal congregational level, they would have a better understanding of how disruptive they could be to the life and identity of the parish. This is not to suggest that internship parishes are never to be challenged, but that the students need to be aware of unintended threats to a parish's sense of identity.

Supervisors also could be warned of potential cross-stage static when a student at the individuative-reflective stage is placed in a congregation at the synthetic-conventional stage. With an under- standing of the cross-stage static which may occur, the supervisor can be prepared to deal creatively with this phenomenon and to defuse potentially explosive situations. In fact, internship supervisors may be the key to making such a match function as a help or a hindrance to the congregation and intern. The pastor or supervisor can serve as an effective buffer between intern and congregation to ensure that learning occurs for the intern and that explosive situations are defused. In my opinion, the intern's supervisor is able to be most helpful in this situation when she or he is at the conjunctive stage.

Why do I say this? Most people at the conjunctive stage are in mid-life or beyond and are no longer so focused on the self. They are no longer inclined to think they have the answers for their own and everyone else's lives. They live with the paradox that God's self-revelation is always a matter of both disclosure and concealment. They are learning to trust the Christian tradition in new ways and at new depths:

> Its symbols, doctrines, narratives, and rituals are acknowledged as structuring means of grace. Prayer and discernment become modes of opening oneself and attending radically . . . to the truth that takes form and comes to expression in the Scriptures and tradition and in the living interpretations of the community of faith.[25]

People at this stage are more likely to welcome strangers because they have begun to acknowledge the stranger within theselves. Most importantly for directors of internship, Fowler says these persons 'have the capacity to understand and relate to Christians of each of the other stages.'[26] In this sense they make excellent supervisors of others. From the depth of their Christian commitments, they have a capacity to receive and to dialogue with people whose faith stances are far different from their own or from that of the congregation they serve.

Matching students to pastors at the conjunctive stage does have its own particular risk. Because people at this stage often feel a deep sense of cosmic aloneness or homelessness, of 'what's the use,' there may be a quality of paralysis in their own ministry, a retreat into a private world of spirituality. Such an example of immobility communicates itself too clearly to the intern and undercuts any advantages of such an internship match. Nevertheless, pastors at this stage are best able to work creatively in situations of cross-stage static between the intern and the parish or the intern and the supervisor herself or himself. Supervising pastors at this developmental level simply are able to be more open to theologies, personalities, and leadership styles at variance with their own.

Shortened questionnaire

How might an intern make a tentative estimation of the modal developmental level of the congregation where the internship is to be served? How can she or he gain the information in a way which will also develop some personal relationships within the parish? How might she or he describe the results in a way which is not threatening to the members of the congregation or the pastor? James Fowler has developed 'Guidelines for brief faith interviews' which he has used for at least seven years with his students in courses he has taught (see appendix). While one cannot demonstrate the reliability of the short form by empirical social-scientific research, Dr Fowler has told me that, based on his use of it with students in his classes, he has confidence in the results. Unlike the longer questionnaire, which can take two to three hours to administer and many more hours to grade, the short interview is designed to last approximately one-half hour and is more quickly graded.

Using the short form, an intern can interview a random sampling of the internship congregation, evaluate the results, and make a tentative stab at identifying the modal congregational level. Depending on the size of the parish, the intern can interview every fifth or tenth name as it appears in the parish register and have a sample from which to measure the modal level. In addition, the intern may interview a representative sample of the leaders in the church and learn, by analyzing this data, whether the leadership is at a different level of modal development than much of the rest of the congregation.

There is an important side-benefit to be gained through the use of the brief faith interviews by the intern. Interviewing the parishioners is an excellent way to become acquainted with members of the parish in some depth in a relatively brief period of time. Although the questions are relatively nonthreatening, the intern would certainly want to become acquainted with the people to be interviewed before actually interviewing any parishioners. Furthermore, before a student launches enthusiastically into the process of using this instrument to decide the modal congregational level of her or his internship parish, there are several critical dangers of which she or he ought to be aware.

One obvious danger is that a student could learn the general descriptive features of each stage and be tempted to use the knowledge to caricature and label others. No student should be allowed to use and grade the interview without a thorough grounding in the seven aspects Fowler uses to define each stage and without knowing in detail the description of each aspect at each stage. Such information can be gained by use of the *Manual for Faith Development Research* prepared by Fowler and his associates.[27] Even grounding in the *Manual* is not sufficient by itself, however. Students should not use the interview until they have been trained and tested in its use by a person formally trained in Fowler's methodology.

A second source of difficulty arises from the fact that Fowler's theory articulates a hierarchical model in which each new stage incorporates and builds on each previous stage. But his definition of faith is so broad that he claims it is 'faith' that is involved in this hierarchical development. I have argued elsewhere that many Christians have a different concept of faith than Fowler's and that what he is really measuring through his research is different ways or styles of living in one's baptism.[28] In that article, I have also argued that all grace for a Christian is given in baptism, and that there is no need to add anything to baptism. It is to the sufficiency of this gift that the Christian returns again and again throughout her or his life. In my opinion, it is less threatening to speak of different styles of living in one's baptism than of different stages of faith. One person's style of living in one's baptism may be more complex and sophisticated than another's, but it is not that one person's *faith* has grown to a higher stage than another's! Therefore, I recommend that students interviewing parishioners talk about different styles of living in one's baptism rather than different stages of faith.

A third potential pitfall is that Fowler's hyphenated titles for the stages are convoluted and opaque. For interns working in mainline Protestant and Catholic parishes and interviewing adults, I would restrict the options to Fower's middle four categories and give them one-word titles as follows:

a.   lexical (mythic-literal): persons interpret experience through a literal structuring of narrative;

b.   consensual (synthetic-conventional): persons form and maintain identity on the basis of a consensus of their relationships and roles;

c.   ideological (individuative-reflective): persons develop an independent identity based on their own interpretation of reality apart from roles and relationships;

d.   dialectical (conjunctive): persons realize the paradoxical nature of much of experience which must somehow be held together.

I would furthermore downplay the significance of any hierarchy and emphasize instead that the theory represents a kind of typology in which there are four distinct and different ways to live in one's baptism. (The fact that the typology is hierarchically structured is accurate but not particularly important since baptismal grace is sufficient in and of itself.)

Once the intern has learned the modal congregational level, she or he and the supervisor have an opportunity to engage in fruitful dialogue about the implications of this finding for the exercise of pastoral leadership in the parish. The intern, in consultation with the pastor, has an opportunity to outline specific pastoral goals on the basis of the modal congregational level and then to implement these goals and see how effective they are. In this way, a thorough grounding in Fowler's theory of stages will not only aid in making appropriate internship matches but will also enhance the learning and the ministry that is experienced during internship.

In concluding, let us return to the disastrous match with which this article began. It is my judgment, based on my knowledge of the congregation, that its modal congregational level was best placed at the consensual (synthetic-conventional) stage. Furthermore, I would place both the pastor and the intern in the ideological (individuative-reflective) stage. Congregations at the consensual stage have trouble dealing with people at the ideological stage who stir up issues within the parish. By the same token, the intern, strongly in the ideological stage, had trouble understanding the tacitly held belief system of the congregation. Why, he asked, aren't the members more interested in investigating the great issues of the faith?

When the intern arrived at the church, he immediately alienated the longtime sexton by refusing to help set up tables and chairs for an evening meeting, declaring it was not 'proper' work for a pastor or intern. Informed that the pastor often helped out in this way, he responded that the pastor ought not engage in improper work. Soon the congregation scheduled a strawberry pie festival as a fund-raiser and the intern objected to 'incorrect stewardship practices for a Christian Church.' In the worship service, the intern made several suggestions to 'improve' the service. However, the straw which broke the camel's back occurred in a sermon, based on Ephesians 5, especially verses 22–23: 'Wives, be subject to your husbands, as to the Lord. For the husband is the head of the wife as Christ is the head of the church.' The intern announced, 'In my opinion and in this instance, the bible is wrong.' The only words most members heard were, 'the bible is wrong!' At this point, I was called because of the trouble the student had created.

The supervising pastor, like the intern, was at the ideological stage. How did he cope with the cross-stage static between himself and the congregation? The pastor had developed his own view of himself as a 'successful' pastor. He dealt creatively with the congregation by developing a myriad of effective programs and by placing an emphasis on evangelism. He focused many of his ideological concerns in evangelism, bringing new people into the parish and teaching them what it meant to be members of the *Lutheran* Church.

While the supervisor admitted the intern was not wrong in all of his concerns, he felt the intern lacked tact and diplomacy and did not create an environment in which the Good News of Jesus Christ could be readily heard. Conversely, the intern questioned the supervisor's integrity in living with beliefs and practices with which he did not totally agree.

As Director of Internship, I had made a bad placement. I had not been sufficiently aware of the potential disaster in placing a student at the ideological stage in a congregation at the consensual stage. This does not mean that I would not ever make such a cross-stage placement again. Since many congregations are in the consensual stage, interns at every stage need to be prepared to minister to parishes at this stage. It does mean that I would be alert to possible dangers and would attempt to prepare both intern and supervisor to anticipate such problems. A supervisor at the dialectical (conjunctive) level may be best able to deal with cross-stage static between an intern and a parish. A supervisor at this stage can be very open to the differences between the intern and the congregation and between the intern and himself or herself and can work most creatively with this situation.

My study of Fowler's stages has provided me with valuable information which will be of immense help to me as Director of Internship. I hope that this article will in turn assist supervisors and students not only in the context of internship but also in all other supervised field-education experiences.

Appendix

1. Depending on the size of the parish, select every fifth (or eighth, or tenth, etc.) person as their names appear in the parish register so that you interview 10–12 persons. Or, as an alternative, ask the secretary to compile a list of all leaders in the parish (church school teachers, committee members, church council members, worship assistants, etc.). From the alphabetized list choose every third (or fifth, or seventh) name so that you interview a total of 10–12 leaders.[29]

2. Ask each parishioner to give you about one-half hour of their time. Meet them at a place where you will have privacy and not be interrupted. Do not schedule your interviews so close together that you will be rushed if you take longer, or that you will confuse the answers given by your respondents.

3. Explain that you would like to ask them some questions pertaining to their attitudes about religion. It is important to assure them that you are not going to judge or evaluate their answers, and that you're very interested in having their true feelings and thoughts. As far as you are concerned, in this interview there are no right or wrong answers, only *their* answers. Promise them anonymity; ask permission to tape record your conversation. *Use an exterior microphone if you possibly can.*

4. Ask a sequence of questions such as those below.[30]

   a. Do you consider yourself a religious person? Why or why not?

   b. Do you have, or have you had, experiences that you might call religious experiences? Please explain.

   c. When you think of *God*, what associations, what feelings, do you have?

   d. Are there particular life-experiences or events in your past or present life that might help me understand why you feel and think about God in these ways?

   e. At present, what gives your life meaning and purpose? What makes your life feel worth living?

   f. Is there a 'growing edge' in your life now? Do you have feelings that something in your life needs to change in order to be more full or complete? Please explain.

Be sure to probe and keep questioning until you are sure you understand what they are saying. Be a 'dumb' interviewer; patiently and persistently ask 'why?' or 'can you help me understand that better?' until you've gotten what they have to give. Be sure to give them time to answer. Don't be embarrassed by silences or by their struggling for an answer. This is not the Today Show!

Notes
1. James W. Fowler, *Stages of Faith*, San Francisco, Harper and Row, 1981.
2. Romney M. Moseley, David Jarvis, and James W. Fowler, *Manual for Faith*

Development Research, Atlanta, Center for Faith Development of the Candler School of Theology, 1986, p. 1.

3. James W. Fowler in a lecture given at the Association for Clinical Pastoral Education, October 1986, in Atlanta. The lecture subsequently became a chapter in *Faith Development and Pastoral Care*, Philadelphia, Fortress Press, 1987, p. 56.

4. James W. Fowler, *Stages of Faith*, pp. 117–213; Fowler, *Becoming Adult, Becoming Christian*, San Francisco, Harper and Row, 1984, pp. 48–76; *Faith Development and Pastoral Care*, pp. 53–77; 'Stages of faith and adults' life cycles,' in Kenneth Stokes (ed.), *Faith Development in the Adult Life Cycle*, New York, W. H. Sadlier, 1982, pp. 178–207.

5. Fowler, *Stages of Faith*, pp. 52, 99–100.

6. Craig Dykstra, 'Faith development and religious education,' in Craig Dykstra and Sharon Parks (eds), *Faith Development and Fowler*, Birmingham, Alabama, Religious Education Press, 1986, p. 262.

7. Fowler, *Faith Development and Pastoral Care*, pp. 96–97.

8. Fowler, *Stages of Faith*, p. 294.

9. *Ibid.*

10. Fowler, *Faith Development and Pastoral Care*, p. 92.

11. *Stages of Faith*, p 263. Karl Ernst Nipkow makes a related point in an unpublished manuscript and address, 'Stages theories of faith development as a challenge to religious education and practical theology,' given at the International Symposium on Religious Development and Education, Blaubeuren, University of Tübingen, June 12–17, 1987.

12. Fowler, *Faith Development and Pastoral Care*, pp. 94–97 and Nipkow, pp 19–22.

13. *Ibid.*, 92–94.

14. *Ibid.*, 22–25.

15. *Ibid.*, 97.

16. *Ibid.*, 82.

17. *Ibid.*, 84.

18. *Ibid.*, 85.

19. *Ibid.*, 87–88.

20. *Ibid.*, 88–89.

21. *Ibid.*, 89.

22. *Ibid.*, 91.

23. *Ibid.*

24. *Ibid.*, 92.

25. *Ibid.*, 94.

26. *Ibid.*

27. Moseley, Jarvis, and Fowler, *Manual for Faith Development Research*.

28. William O. Avery, 'A Lutheran examines James W. Fowler,' *Religious Education*, vol. 85, 1990, pp. 69–83.

29. Dr Fowler's *Guidelines* were designed for a different context. His read: '1) Select three persons of varying ages or backgrounds.' I have substituted my own 1 to fit the internship context.

30. James W. Fowler, ©.

Select bibliography of works by James Fowler

* indicates that the piece is reprinted (in whole or part) in this volume.

James W. Fowler, 'Faith, liberation and human development', *The Foundation* (Atlanta: Gammon Theological Seminary), vol. 79, 1974, pp. 1–35.*

James W. Fowler, 'Toward a developmental perspective on faith', *Religious Education*, vol. 69, no. 2, 1974, pp. 207–219.

James W. Fowler, *To see the Kingdom: the theological vision of H. Richard Niebuhr*, Nashville, Tenn., Abingdon, 1974.

James W. Fowler, 'Faith development theory and the aims of religious socialization', in Gloria Durka and Joanmarie Smith (eds), *Emerging Issues in Religious Education*, New York, Paulist Press, 1976.

James W. Fowler, 'Stages in faith: the structural-developmental approach', in Thomas C. Hennessy (ed.), *Values and Moral Development*, New York, Paulist Press, 1976.

Jim Fowler and Sam Keen, *Life-Maps: conversations on the journey of faith*, ed. Jerome Berryman, Minneapolis, Winston Press, 1978; Waco, Texas, Word Books, 1985.

James W. Fowler, Robin W. Lovin *et al.*, *Trajectories in Faith: five life-studies*, Nashville, Tenn., Abingdon, 1979.

James W. Fowler, 'Perspectives on the family from the standpoint of faith development theory', *The Perkins Journal*, vol. 33, no. 1, 1979, pp. 1–19.*

James W. Fowler, 'Faith and the structuring of meaning', in James W. Fowler and Antoine Vergote (eds), *Toward Moral and Religious Maturity*, Morristown, N.J., Silver Burdett, 1980.

James W. Fowler, 'Moral stages and the development of faith', in Brenda Munsey (ed.), *Moral Development, Moral Education, and Kohlberg*, Birmingham, Alabama, Religious Education Press, 1980.

James W. Fowler, *Stages of Faith: the psychology of human development and the quest for meaning*, San Francisco, Harper and Row, 1981.

James W. Fowler, 'Stages of faith and adults' life cycles', in Kenneth Stokes (ed.), *Faith Development in the Adult Life Cycle*, New York, W. H. Sadlier, 1982.

James W. Fowler, 'Reflections on Loder's *The Transforming Moment*', *Religious Education*, vol. 77, no. 2, 1982, pp. 140–148.

James W. Fowler, 'Practical theology and the shaping of Christian lives', in Don S. Browning (ed.), *Practical Theology: the emerging field in theology, church, and world*, San Francisco, Harper and Row, 1983.

James W. Fowler, *Becoming Adult, Becoming Christian*, San Francisco, Harper and Row, 1984.

James W. Fowler, 'Practical theology and theological education: some models and questions', *Theology Today*, vol. 42, 1985, pp. 43–58.

James W. Fowler and Richard Osmer, 'Childhood and adolescence – a faith development perspective', in Robert J. Wicks, Richard D. Parsons and Donald Capps (eds), *Clinical Handbook of Pastoral Counseling*, New York, Paulist Press, 1985.

James W. Fowler, 'Faith and the structuring of meaning' and 'Dialogue towards a future in faith development studies', in Craig Dykstra and Sharon Parks (eds), *Faith Development and Fowler*, Birmingham, Alabama, Religious Education Press, 1986.

Romney M. Moseley, David Jarvis, and James W. Fowler, *Manual for Faith Development Research*, Center for Faith Development, Atlanta, Georgia, Emory University, 1986.*

James W. Fowler, *Faith Development and Pastoral Care*, Philadelphia, Fortress Press, 1987.

James W. Fowler, 'Religious congregations: varieties of presence in stages of faith', *Moral Education Forum*, vol. 12, no. 1, 1987, pp. 4–14.*

James W. Fowler, 'The enlightenment and faith development theory', *Journal of Empirical Theology*, vol. 1, no. 1, 1988, pp. 29–42.*

James W. Fowler, 'Strength for the journey: early childhood development in selfhood and faith' and 'The public church: ecology for faith education and advocate for children', in Doris Blazer (ed.), *Faith Development in Early Childhood*, Kansas City, Sheed and Ward, 1989.

James W. Fowler, 'Structuralism', 'Faith development research', 'Identity', 'Faith and belief', 'H. Richard Niebuhr', 'Erik H. Erikson', in Rodney J. Hunter (ed.), *Dictionary of Pastoral Care and Counseling*, New York, Abingdon, 1990.

James W. Fowler, 'Faith development through the family life cycle', *Catholic Families: growing and sharing faith* (Network Paper, no. 31), New Rochelle, N. Y., Don Bosco Multimedia, 1990.

James W. Fowler, *Weaving the New Creation: faith development and public church*, San Francisco, Harper and Row, 1991.

James W. Fowler, 'Stages in faith consciousness', in Fritz K. Oser and W. George Scarlett (eds), *Religious Development in Childhood and Adolescence* (New Directions for Child Development, no. 52), San Francisco, Jossey-Bass, 1991.

James W. Fowler, 'The vocation of faith development theory', in James W. Fowler, Karl Ernst Nipkow, and Friedrich Schweitzer (eds), *Stages of Faith and Religious Development: implications for church, education and society*, New York, Crossroads, 1991; London, SCM, 1992.

Acknowledgements

The publisher and editors would like to acknowledge the following permissions to reproduce copyright material. All possible attempts have been made to contact copyright holders and to acknowledge their copyright correctly. We are grateful to: *British Journal of Religious Education*, for D. Heywood, 'Piaget and faith development: a true marriage of minds?' 8, 72–78, 1986, for M. Smith, 'Answers to some questions about faith development,' 8, 79–83, 1986, and for D. H. Webster, 'James Fowler's theory of faith development,' 7, 14–18, 1984; *Character Potential*, for E. J. Mischey, 'Faith, identity, and morality in late adolescence,' 9, 175–185, 1981, and for J. W. Berryman, R. E. Davies and H. C. Simmons, 'Comments on article by E. J. Mischey,' 9, 186–191, 1981; *The Drew Gateway*, for S. D. Parks, 'Faith development in a changing world,' 60, 4–21, 1990; *Educational Gerontology*, for R. N. Shulik, 'Faith development in older adults,' 14, 291–301, 1988; *The Foundation*, for J. W. Fowler, 'Faith, liberation and human development,' 79, 1–10, 1974; *Journal of Empirical Theology*, for J. W. Fowler, 'The Enlightenment and faith development theory,' 1, 29–42, 1988; *The Journal of Pastoral Care*, for D. D. Schurter, 'Fowler's faith stages as a guide for ministry to the mentally retarded,' 41, 234–240, 1987, and for S. S. Ivy, 'A faith development/self-development model for pastoral assessment,' 41, 329–340, 1987; *Journal of Psychology and Christianity*, for T. A. Droege, 'Pastoral counselling and faith development,' 3, 4, 37–47, 1984; *Living Light*, for M. Ford-Grabowsky, 'The journey of a pilgrim: an alternative to Fowler,' 24, 242–254, 1988, and for C. E. Nelson, 'Does faith develop? an evaluation of Fowler's position,' 19, 162–173, 1982; *Moral Education Forum*, for J. W. Fowler, 'Religious congregations: varieties of presence in stages of faith,' 12, 1, 4–14 and 36, 1987; *New Directions for Student Services*, for M. Rutledge, 'Faith development: bridging theory and practice,' 46, 17–32, 1989; *Pastoral Psychology*, for R. M. Moseley, 'Forms of logic in faith development theory,' 39, 143–152, 1991; *Perkins Journal*, for J. W. Fowler, 'Perspectives on the family from the standpoint of faith development theory,' 33, 1–19, 1979; *Religion*, for S. Kwilecki, 'Personal religious belief development: the "articulate authoritarian" type,' 18, 231–253, 1988; *Religious Education*, for W. O. Avery, 'A Lutheran examines James W. Fowler,' 85, 69–83, 1990, for

G. L. Chamberlain, 'Faith development and campus ministry,' 74, 314–324, 1979, for R. Y. Furushima, 'Faith development in a cross cultural perspective,' 80, 414–420, 1985, for R. R. Osmer, 'James W. Fowler and the reformed tradition: an exercise in theological reflection in religious education,' 85, 51–68, 1990, and for S. Parks, 'Young adult faith development: teaching in the context of theological education,' 77, 657–672, 1982 (*Religious Education* is published by The Religious Education Association, 409 Prospect Street, New Haven, CT 06511–2177 USA, Membership, $43 US per year [full-time student, $ 23 US]); *Review of Religious Research*, for C. W. Green and C. L. Hoffman, 'Stages of faith and perceptions of similar and dissimilar others,' 30, 246–254, 1989, and for M. Barnes, D. Doyle and B. Johnson, 'The formulation of a Fowler scale; an empirical assessment among Catholics,' 30, 412–420, 1989; *Supervision and Training in Ministry*, for W. O. Avery, 'Enhancing supervision using Fowler's developmental theory,' 10, 3–18, 1988; James W. Fowler, Centre for Research in Faith and Moral Development, for the extracts from the *Manual for Faith Development Research*.

Index of subjects

Index of names